COUNTER PUNCH

FLOYD G. BROWN

FRONT
LINE

While the author has made every effort to provide accurate internet addresses at the time of publication, neither the publisher nor the author assumes any responsibility for errors or for changes that occur after publication. Further, the publisher does not have any control over and does not assume any responsibility for author or third-party websites or their content.

Visit the author's website at floydbrown.com.

Cataloging-in-Publication Data is on file with the Library of Congress.
International Standard Book Number: 978-1-63641-163-7
E-book ISBN: 978-1-63641-164-4

23 24 25 26 27 — 9 8 7 6 5 4 3 2 1
Printed in the United States of America

Most Charisma Media products are available at special quantity discounts for bulk purchase for sales promotions, premiums, fund-raising, and educational needs. For details, call us at (407) 333-0600 or visit our website at www.charismamedia.com.

To the young men in my life—Gideon, Nehemiah, Thaddeus, and Ezekiel. I pray God will bless you and keep you as you learn the important lessons God taught each of your namesakes.

CONTENTS

PREFACE

On April 16, 2021, I traveled to Tulsa, Oklahoma, at the request of local business leader Clay Clark. He asked me to speak at a conference focused on ending the COVID lockdowns. Clay is a business coach and entrepreneur who'd seen his clients' businesses devastated as the "two weeks to slow the spread" lockdowns had entered a second year.

The conference attendees were an eclectic bunch of every American race and ethnicity. Doctors who'd been publicly disgraced or even fired for advocating the use of ivermectin, hydroxychloroquine, vitamins D and C, and budesonide to treat COVID were there. Pastors of all faiths fighting to keep the doors of their churches open under a police state regime unprecedented in American history showed up. Owners of restaurants serving Mexican, Thai, Chinese, and American cuisine were there to talk about their struggles to keep their doors open. Small business owners of nearly every kind, police officers, teachers, nurses, firefighters, and military personnel—both enlisted and officers—were all there to join in fighting back against a government response to COVID that was clearly nonsensical. What happened next deeply touched the hearts and consciences of my wife, Mary Beth, and me. To this day we still talk about Tulsa.

What happened there was profound. Unity broke out. Both the love of fellow man and love of God filled what had been advertised as a business conference. We were touched by God and what the Bible calls the Holy Spirit. My desire to author this book was ignited.

In the middle of a pandemic, there we were participating in a healing and restoration experience unlike anything we'd ever witnessed. Masks came down, and we cried. We hugged and held onto each other. We reconnected with fellow human beings. We broke the back of fear together and united.

Since that day I've traveled the country with Clay Clark and others sharing a simple message: we need not fear if we trust in God and work together to restore the pre-COVID America.

As a sixty-one-year-old man, I grew up in a time when Americans still drank at the deep well of knowledge. I attended public school when we saluted the flag and learned the stories of ancient Rome, Greece, and Egypt. We learned about medieval Europe and the Renaissance. We also learned about the dark days of history when humanity failed and the guillotine ruled France, the swastika ruled Germany, the hammer and sickle ruled the USSR, the Cultural Revolution ruled China, and countless millions perished.

As Americans we have become disconnected from history. We are no longer learning from past mistakes; instead, we are making them again. This book lays out the course corrections we must make for a more commonsense and less arrogant future.

We are truly in a battle to save the American promise that has long held the world's imagination and must continue to. We know our very foundations are being attacked from within, and the America we love and wish to pass on to future generations is now on life support.

The only way America can be saved is by a thousand more local "conferences" like that one in Tulsa, where people set aside their differences and, drawing strength from unity, take the battle into the streets of our communities one after another.

America's colonists realized the importance of uniting for a common goal. They set aside their differences, and with God's help they formed the United States of America. Throughout history God often uses everyday people who are willing. History is full of examples of small groups making unbelievable contributions to their fellow humankind.

Good governance is about understanding where we are now and how we move forward together as Americans.

What is it going to take to save America? Concerned citizens working together with courage, boldness, and conviction. It is time to step up, unite—and save America.

My prayer is that you have been led to this book so you can join this special adventure to save America.

Together we march.

—FLOYD G. BROWN
SEPTEMBER 2022

HOW MIGHT YOU BRING DOWN A COUNTRY?

A GRAND PLAN LIKE this is unthinkable. This kind of destruction is just plain meaner than anything any normal, loving person is capable of. This brutal pounding down right into the dirt of an entire country is simply beyond the pale. It's as if the devil has risen from the depths, a monster unleashed upon us.

The extremes of the plan go to the depths of depravity. But if a small group of people tried to, how do you think they'd break a country as badly as America has been broken?

Well, they might build very tall towers in which all the people could live, and those towers would be given catchy names such as "vertical self-management centers" to entice the people to move there.

And every floor in these thick, concrete towers would have a center square cut out, from the top of the building to the bottom, so that at mealtimes you could lower a big concrete slab down from the top, laden with the finest cuisine and tasty treats, stopping for only a minute at each floor down its long flight to the bottom.

Residents on the top floor can eat their fill, play with the food, gorge on it without a care, whatever they want. As the slab descends, there is less and less edible food on it, until those on the bottom floors are greeted with empty platters of chicken bones. They are left to starve, or they turn on their floor mates to survive, or they just leap into the darkness of that center void.

And if any of the rules are broken, unseen authorities who are watching on hidden cameras crank up the heat or the cold until they have forced compliance.

To artificially induce both hope and hatred, every thirty days at midnight, the authorities pump anesthetic onto all the floors, then they come in and move all the knocked-out bodies to a different floor. So you might be on Floor 5 one day and Floor 95 the next—for a very different experience.

Yes, this is the kind of platform of a full-fledged prison nation.

In fact, I've just sketched the plotline of a 2019 Spanish horror film called *The Platform*,[1] which took a jab at both capitalist *and* socialist forms of government.

Yes, a horror film. A dystopian tale of a world gone utterly mad. Yet in its methods and monstrous ambitions, this world is not so different from what a small group of people are trying to shove down our throats today.

There are so many similarities that *The Platform* is practically a metaphor for the disgraceful disintegration we are witnessing in America today.

So let's go deeper into the metaphor, into what these people would do if allowed—how they might construct a soul-destroying platform aimed at taking a nation's proud, enduring ideals, including faith in God, and crushing them for their own personal gain.

And most importantly, we'll see how good people would rise up against the platform—and counterpunch.

PULLING THE LEVERS

You'd need to gain control of every lever of modern power, for starters.

That would mean coaxing all the biggest bases of power into joining you in a strategic camaraderie of sorts. You'd promise all these allies that everyday citizens were going to love what you were doing, even fall down in worship to your ingenious plan as it moved some 90 percent of the nation's wealth out of their pockets into your own.

You'd have to corral both the executive and legislative branches of government, as well as the vast, sprawling Washington bureaucracy. Having the judiciary would give you all three arms of government, which would be just awesome. But you could live without the judges, since they could become a proxy for government and useful in making citizens believe the republic was still working.

Both political parties would have to be bought off—the easiest job of all, since the core principles of each party and their commitment to actually doing anything have long since blown away in the wind. Simply showing them how they'd be able to parlay their election-night victories into plum positions in the wealth extraction machine would seal the deal. At a minimum, acting lessons would be called for, since a lot of—OK, all of—their time would be spent performing before the cameras, selling a narrative that few of them could otherwise manage.

Among the hardest tasks—in fact, surely the hardest of all—would be convincing left-wing activists to go along with the scheme. The solution— and a brilliant one, at that—would be to give them a seat at the table. Not a real seat, of course. A fake one you could call stakeholder capitalism, which they would think is peachy (unless they bothered to look up the meaning of the words; nah, not likely).

You would actively support all their delusional desires with something you'd call environmental, social, and governance (ESG) standards. Pretty much covers all bases. Anything the radical Left could dream of desiring would be instantly supplied to them in a rainbow splash of conscious caring. Now they'd be happy to go along.

Sure, this would require intense levels of deception. It would also require that all the suits on Wall Street get down with the lingo. But the cost would be far less than a single boycott that the lefty race-baiters used to use so effectively. Hard to beat it for flat-out brilliance.

People would need to be convinced that government was fully capable of spending trillions and trillions of dollars, all legit, no consequences. This would be critical, since a good chunk of those trillions in spending "for the people" would end up in your pocket. So you'd get some crazy academics from an obscure university to invent a *Modern Monetary Theory* that explained how budget deficits no longer mattered. So spend on, big government.

Silicon Valley would be a key player in this—since technology has become something of a defining ethos for the nation and its communications gatekeeper as well. So having an easy and effective way to tamp down or outright "disappear" any voice that might speak out against the wholesale plunder of the national treasury and the debasement of the culture would obviously be vital. And not at all hard, as it turns out.

All the tech bros talk a big game about caring for humanity, but they mostly want to bag unicorns—companies with billion-dollar valuations. The entire business model of Silicon Valley revolves around it. And billion-dollar companies don't just build themselves. Government antitrust regulators need to look the other way while the techies are monopolizing one industry after another with their crafty new algorithms. So if the government would like them to silence anyone on their platforms, that's really a small price to pay, right? The rewards for compliance are huge.

With the way Silicon Valley has gutted journalism, controlling the media becomes child's play. Sure, there will always be a few independent journalists striving for the truth. But the mainstream media has already divided itself into left stream and right stream and gone to war with each other, battling over ratings. Simply by feeding a steady diet of partisan sludge to each opposing camp, they can keep audiences hating on each other, completely distracted—right where you want them.

You must continually divide people. You must isolate people. You must make sure neighbors don't talk, care for, and help one another. Oh, a pandemic will make sure we keep people in families, much less on the same block, from seeing, hugging, and caring for one another.

You would throw open the southern border. This would give the Democratic Party fresh supplies of voters and entitlement program enrollees. It would give the Republican Party cheap laborers while, as a big bonus, keeping them riled up about out-of-control border crime. A marriage of convenience for both parties—check, check.

Out in Hollywood, where the manipulating is easy, you'd give all the latest stars incredible scripts and deep budgets to kick out films everyone adores. Films that with a little of that old subliminal magic steadily alter people's ideas of right and wrong until few even remember what a moral nation looks like. Villains become heroes, and traditional heroes become villains.

With all this nation-destroying going on, you'd want it to have staying power. You couldn't just beat down one generation and let another pop up. You'd have to get into the schools, colleges, and churches, teaching tomorrow's "leaders" how much they have to gain from embracing your kinder, gentler, authoritarian way. Fortunately, since you already have the thought leaders on the Left in your pocket, your work will be done for you.

Civic institutions, Rotary Clubs, Lions Clubs, Chambers of Commerce, and parade committees must all be shut down. Churches especially must be silenced. Singing banned and preaching remote and rote. No meals served, no food pantries open, no help for the helpless. Every building with a steeple and a cross standing empty with the doors chained shut.

Finally, you're going to need the nation's great military apparatus on your side, with the Pentagon, Homeland Security, the CIA, and the FBI working something of a triple play for you: keeping the world destabilized and ripe for arms sales; convincing conservatives to line up early to vote for ever-bigger defense budgets; dispatching any dissent on the home front. And for good measure, eject patriotic people from institutions if they don't go along with your new rules. Police, soldiers, nurses, doctors, firefighters, and whistleblowers who don't comply are simply fired for not going along. A perfect purge of the noncompliant from any agency.

This is pretty much describing the American smackdown we've seen.

Yes, people did this. Only a couple thousand people, to be precise. All with seats at the head table of a shapeless, shadowy, and often lethal power structure—an elite state. We'll look at this elite state, how its members pulled off a top-down swindle of unmatched scale, and how they're now running into something they were not expecting.

They're running into an unlikely alliance of Christians, old-school Democrats, Blacks, Latinos, Asians, and conservatives who are all uniting in their communities from the bottom up and hitting back—throwing the counterpunch that can save America.

This is a book about this unlikely alliance of Americans. It is neither of the Right nor the Left, but of the big heart where most of us live our lives. It begins where we are today: deeply worried about the nonstop strife in our politics; how our country seems to be *resegregating* into tribes hating on one another; how most of the nation's wealth and power has slipped into the hands of a few.

In these pages you'll see how this unlikely alliance of Davids is landing punches against the Goliath—counterpunches, really, for we've been taking a beating as well.

You'll see how good people are uniting and finding a way to fight successfully for the ideals we must cherish—having the fullest liberty and freedom in our daily lives, the fullest opportunity to prosper.

It isn't a movement with leaders living in Washington, DC. Instead,

America is being rebuilt and retaken, block by block, street by street, city by city with nothing but opposition from the power elites.

Our American experiment, as it approaches its 250th anniversary, has come to the inevitable fork in the road at which every living thing arrives. We must now find a way to extend our nation's golden years, or we will fall deeper into a death spiral.

It is no longer a decision to be put off for another day. It is ours, now.

We must make it right!

CHAPTER 1

SHAPELESS, SHADOWY, LETHAL

WE JUST LOOKED at how you'd build a platform to rain destruction down on a nation to consolidate both power and wealth into your hands. How it has actually happened has been a whole lot messier.

For starters, it's a given that the few thousand people vying for a seat at the world's most elite table all come with massive egos barely under control. There are the temperamental billionaires refusing to play nice—even after sealing the deal between ski runs down the snowy slopes of JatzPark in Davos, Switzerland. There are the constant squabbles over who gets to devour the most peasants or swim in the biggest pool full of crypto. When these elite behemoths gather around the big table, it's always awkward and tense, since each of them is accustomed to sitting at the head of the table. So there's nothing monolithic about this group.

But they've nonetheless succeeded in a plain-daylight theft of America's once widely based wealth and cultural traditions. And they did it by perverting the very workings of our republic from the top down. (This tells us that the only remedy and reversal of their perversions will come from the bottom up, as we'll see in chapters ahead.)

Like the royals in old Europe, these elite behemoths tend to be an inbred lot. Members send their kids to the same prep schools and then buy passage to the Ivy League universities. They marry one another and shuttle in their private jets between their beachfront villas and their mountain castles. They entangle in the most exclusive social networks, leveraging their privileges for all they're worth, and then much more. They hop back and forth between government and the private sector through those famous revolving doors. And the unfathomable wealth they accumulate is tidily stashed away on Caribbean islands beyond the reach of the tax collector.

They are also a self-aggrandizing lot, always telling us how heroic their actions are. This elite-state behemoth is "an unusual predator whose power comes in part from his keen ability to adopt the guise of an ally,"

7

as Peter Goodman put it so well in his excellent book *Davos Man*.[1] They operate on an entirely different level, pretending concern for the common people, positioning themselves as caretakers of the public interest, and seeking acclaim for their goodliness, arguing that their obscene wealth is good tonic for us all.

With control over Hollywood, the behemoths can elevate their lifestyle to the level of celebrity, offering glimpses behind the castle walls and into the lifestyles of the rich and outlandish. Billionaire porn, they call it. Shows like *Succession* and *Billions* arouse the simpleminded into a bit of transference, making them think, "Yeah, I could be part of this gilded world; I could fit in." Upon such delusions are a people kept drugged.

Our film tastes aside, we can all admire the builder who creates great wealth from wonderful new products, jobs for talented workers, progress for us all. That we can admire and respect, but it is not the way of these behemoths.

Over the last four decades, the wealthiest 1 percent of all Americans have ripped $47 trillion in wealth out of the hands of the rest of the country. This is not some random number, this $47 trillion. It comes from serious analysts at RAND Corporation, which we'll learn more about.[2] But summing up, if people had continued to earn the way they earned until the 1990s, then every working American would now be making $1,144 more a month, or $13,728 more a year, or a half million plus over a career span.[3]

When the pandemic hit, these elites took their wealth-stealing to nosebleed levels. While most of the country was struggling with the impossible math of managing their bills with shrinking paychecks, the elites were backing up trucks to the Feds' loading dock and shoveling up free cash.

They got interest-free loans totaling more than $1.5 trillion, then took that money and invested in depressed assets.[4] They didn't help to bail out a bankrupt government, like J. P. Morgan once did. They didn't create soup lines for millions of the unemployed, like Andrew Carnegie once did. No, our new elites took the free money and ran. Turned it into $3.9 trillion more wealth for themselves in 2021 and probably more in 2022.[5] That's right, they more than doubled their money—at zero risk of loss, because the Feds gave it to them.

And lest there be any misunderstandings about all that free money they were getting when so many others were genuinely hurting, they announced they were joining the fight for so-called social justice. That would shut up all the critics on the Left, especially if they played it smoothly. And it had the added virtue of potentially being wildly profitable. It was a brilliant gambit, in their view.

They could see how America had failed to fully deliver on the social justice ideals that were core to its founding. So they figured, why not change the definition of social justice altogether? Rewrite a few thousand years' worth of morals and ethics books overnight. Then hand the baton to progressive politicians to run with these new definitions. Give them all the seed money they need.

With a bunch of well-funded progressives running around, it wouldn't take long to further rend the culture even deeper, divide neighbors who'd long gotten along, turn communities into cauldrons of hate and animosity, and pit states against each other in a final shredding of federalism—just as the Founders had feared would happen.

No longer would Americans be united and civilized toward each other, because when they are hateful and divided, they are much easier for the puppet masters to control.

Yes, they could see this happening. Could see how very profitable generalized civil disarray would be for them. An early advocate for this social justice gambit was none other than John D. Rockefeller III. Back in 1973, he penned a booklet titled *The Second American Revolution*.[6] In it, he trashed the "old fashioned nationalism" of his father and laid out the kind of "humanistic revolution" he saw emerging from the sixties, the kind that'd be good for us.

What is humanism? Secular humanism is "a worldview based on atheism and naturalism in which 'man is the measure' of all things; man, not God, is the ultimate norm by which truth and morals are to be determined," says David Noebel, founder of Summit Ministries.[7]

Rockefeller's foundation even produced a suggested draft of a new US Constitution. That project quickly went sideways. But Rockefeller's deep pockets kept utopian idealists on staff, mapping out ideas on how we ought to live. (Side note: never trust a trust-fund baby; they play with unearned money.)

This gambit I refer to was all made "official" in June 2020 by the people who ripped that $47 trillion in wealth out of the hands of the country. I'm speaking of the World Economic Forum (WEF), which likes to convene in the beautiful mountains of Davos. There you'll find a who's who of the tyrannical and megalomaniacal. And it's important to note the timing of their announcement.

Just three months earlier, the economy had been strong and vibrant—until March, when the two-weeks-to-flatten-the-curve plan slammed on the brakes and instantly killed a thriving economy, the biggest and fastest economy crusher the United States and the world had ever experienced or witnessed. Not only was the economy throttled, but freedoms long enshrined in the US Constitution, which protected Americans, were suddenly ignored or thrown out the window entirely. Almost everything—including small businesses, schools, churches, events, organizations, clubs, athletics, and much more—was instantly closed. Multimillions of jobs were lost due to this fear-filled, rash government fiat. Children and adults alike were isolated and force-fed fear on a daily basis.

Then the WEF announced it was time for a "Great Reset."[8]

A Nice Con, If You Can Run It

I can share one conversation *nobody* in the WEF had. And that is this: If all these noble social justice goals of helping the poor and saving the planet are so very pressing, as the organization and its allies insist in speech after speech, then why not pitch in half the combined wealth of those who convene in Davos, easily a cool trillion dollars or thereabouts, and pick up the tab? It wouldn't put much of a crimp in their lifestyles to give half their net worth to such a legitimate cause.[9]

But of course, the aim of this Great Reset is not altruism. It's the other *a* word: *autocracy*. That's the goal of the reset—autocracy, where they, in their benevolence, tell us to jump, and we, in our acquiescence, ask, "How high?"

To pull off a reset on the scale they imagine, a con must be run. Now, any sharp person will tell you that it takes two to con, and it's true. So the WEF participants gave their big, flowery speeches, and then the forum published a book, aptly titled *COVID-19: The Great Reset*, roping in the marks (us).

If we will simply pledge allegiance to a central world authority of their making, all will be "reset," and life will be good.

Who can argue with that? Certainly, it works for the average bloke walking down the street following a navigation app to his destination, earbuds feeding the hits, news bits packaged in snack-sized form. "And why not?" our fellow says. "It's called the Great Reset, after all, and everyone knows, in our techie world, that things need to be reset from time to time, right?"

Plus, the goal of this reset, we are told, is the most wonderful thing you can imagine: *a common prosperity.*

Sounds promising. Again, who can argue with that? Certainly not anyone who attended an American university in the last two decades and bought the drivel they've been selling.

And who can argue with all the smart, beautiful people at Davos? I mean, look at Jennifer Morgan. In 2020, she was the head of Greenpeace International—once a bunch of crazy but impressively committed hippies floating in dinghies, now with a seat at the big behemoth table in Davos. In an interview, Morgan said COVID offers the hope of reshaping the world in a way reminiscent of the "new world order" established after World War II. "The World Economic Forum has a big responsibility…to be pushing the reset button and looking at how to create well-being for people and for the earth."[10]

Other WEF supporters added that even if the "reset" doesn't work out, it is still the right thing to do. Isn't that like saying you should keep wandering deeper into the forest if you're lost since that's the right way out?

If you haven't heard much about this Great Reset, don't blame the conspiracy theorists. They've been working nonstop to create nefarious links between the WEF and the Council on Foreign Relations, the Trilateral Commission, the United Nations, the World Bank, the International Monetary Fund, and a few of the other usual suspects. But here's the thing: these elite relationships *do* exist, now and as always, right out in the open.

Look at the letterheads and rosters of each. You'll find many of the same names spread about. Nobody is hiding anything. These are people who consider themselves the rightfully unelected overlords of the world. Their kind are far from new.

What *is* new is having Silicon Valley's unicorn handlers at the elite state table. This gives them enormous new powers, not the least of which is having the tools needed to subordinate the US government to a global government more to their liking.

That is very new. That is something to be frightened of.

In *COVID-19: The Great Reset*,[11] WEF founder Klaus Schwab argued for a new "stakeholder capitalism" to replace the old system of free enterprise. The old system, he says, no longer worked for "favouring competition over solidarity, creative destruction over government intervention, and economic growth over social welfare."[12]

And since free enterprise no longer works, he says,

> To achieve a better outcome, the world must act jointly and swiftly to revamp all aspects of our societies and economies, from education to social contracts and working conditions. Every country, from the United States to China, must participate, and every industry, from oil and gas to tech, must be transformed. In short, we need a "Great Reset" of capitalism.[13]

And accomplishing this reset "will require us to integrate all stakeholders of global society into a community of common interest, purpose and action."[14]

Note Schwab's use of the word *must*. He is a smart man who uses language precisely. He could have written that the global economy "should" change or "ought to" change. No, he chose the word *must*. And how must it? Through companies.

> The purpose of a company is to engage all its stakeholders in shared and sustained value creation. In creating such value, a company serves not only its shareholders, but all its stakeholders—employees, customers, suppliers, local communities and society at large.[15]

So going forward, every company must turn the utopian ideal of a perfectly operating business world into a strategy with metrics for measuring results. A strategy they called ESG—short for environmental, social, and governance.

With the elite state at that Davos mountaintop all in agreement, the new ESG metrics were handed down to the world from on high. ESG is now being widely used by companies, investors, and regulators around the world to determine which businesses are good and which are scoundrels—and what should be done about that.

What could possibly go wrong with this Great Reset?

If you care to dive into Schwab's book, you'll find it chock-full of capitalist buzzwords like *markets* and *investments*. It's all framed as a cracking new and improved capitalism, an inclusive capitalism called "stakeholder capitalism," and that sure sounds reasonable. Who wouldn't want that?

Well, it is also a clear rejection of free-market economics—the way it is supposed to work and did work before the people in that Davos room perverted and corrupted it. So the idea here, if we're following along, is that the very same people who led the looting of the global economy are now best situated to "restore things to rights." And the tiger can change its stripes overnight too.

Makes you wonder what's really going on.

You do have to hand it to the folks up at Davos. They know that nobody under the age of forty has seen proper market economics work in their lifetime. To a millennial generation just taking the reins of leadership across America, it sounds reasonable to go along with a reset because, to them, the markets don't work.

But how would this Great Reset actually come to pass—like, how would it be administered, enforced, funded, and so on?

Well, there is a society-ordering model in the world that fairly resembles the Great Reset. They call this the "common prosperity" model. It first appeared in communist China in the 1950s and was followed up until its emphasis by Chinese president Xi Jinping in 2021. Interestingly, the Chinese have of late chucked it overboard for reasons we can only guess at. But this pursuit of a "common prosperity'" has definitely animated the Chinese politburo.

In comparing the two models side by side, author Glenn Beck made a number of head-shaking observations in his book aptly titled *The Great Reset: Joe Biden and the Rise of Twenty-First-Century Fascism*:

...You will probably notice...the Great Reset's parallels to the Chinese "capitalist" economic model, which has for decades attempted to blend corruption, technology, despotism, and corporatism together into a soft-authoritarian smoothie that tastes a lot like the delectable poison being peddled under the Great Reset brand today.

The Great Reset is not really about helping the poor or saving the planet. It is about making the rich richer and expanding the power of the ruling class—goals that many elites have shared across cultures, historical eras, and geographies.

The Great Reset is both shocking and wildly ambitious: to transform the global economy, eliminate free markets, impose a new, more easily controllable and malleable economic system, and change the way people think about private property and corporations.

Rather than focus on profits, private property rights, supply and demand from consumers, the cornerstones of free market economies, Schwab wants to develop a system based largely on environmental, social, and governance (ESG) metrics which involves rewarding companies for working toward social justice goals such as climate change, addressing racial inequity, and removing Aunt Jemima from syrup bottles.[16]

This is the reset now rolling across the land, American-style. With President Biden's blessing, ESG is being put into action at the US Securities and Exchange Commission. SEC chairman Gary Gensler has proposed giving public businesses hundreds of pages of new forms asking how they're measuring up, including whether they are putting the climate at risk (as the SEC claims), what they are doing to remediate all the harm they inflict (you *can* buy "Get Out of Jail Free" cards), and what enforcement actions should be taken for noncompliance (lose your right to do business here).

Over at the Federal Reserve, Chairman Jay Powell is doing the same thing: building a regulatory framework that forces the banking community to adopt the climate, social, and energy policies judged most important by the Davos crowd.[17]

And lest any major corporations balk at this new stakeholder capitalism and the urgent need to reset to the Davos attendees' desires, there are enforcers. Larry Fink is the CEO of BlackRock Inc., the world's largest asset manager, with control of approximately $10 trillion in investor assets. He's now making it clear that companies that do not comply with the ESG metrics will find the capital markets drying up for them.

COVID produced a tiny, elite group of winners and a gigantic group of losers.

Over at Amazon, Jeff Bezos is publicly on board with this stakeholder capitalism, though I doubt his exhibit A for demonstrating his support is the estimated $202 billion he made during the first twenty months of the pandemic—double his previous earnings—thanks to the extreme closures of and restrictions placed on other stores and businesses.[18]

In a similar vein of hypocrisy peddling, there's the climate czar John Kerry endorsing the Great Reset, saying, "It will happen." This is the same John Kerry who gave a commencement address not long ago and proudly told the graduates, "You're about to graduate into a complex and borderless world."[19] He spoke with pride because he spoke of what he knew. And apparently he knew little of how his globalized world panacea had committed so much of America to living in moribund cities that were face-planted by those same open-border, cheap-labor policies.

Kerry was later called out on the disconnect in his political stance, and he sought to deflect criticism by insisting that "it's the corporate tax code that has killed so many US jobs." This might have sated progressives—*Look, squirrel!*—but certainly not anyone who understands how taxes truly work. Nor anyone who lost their job to the truth of globalization as it fully enriched Kerry's elite behemoth state.

WHAT'S REALLY DRIVING THIS "GREAT RESET"?

Among the Davos attendees signing the dotted line on the Great Reset, plenty are good, bighearted people just trying to make the world a better place. They've been invited to the big table, and while they are flattered and excited about it, they are totally unaware of who the mark is, for they are the mark—the useful idiots, as some would say. Useful for putting a caring face on the proceedings (ooh, Leonardo DiCaprio; ahh, Matt Damon; oh, Bono! And Angelina! And Mick J!). With marquee names like these so impressively reciting the words you give them, it's not hard to sell the world on your deep concerns for climate change, social justice, and all that other stuff.

Meanwhile, behind the curtain, the real problem you face as a paid-in member of the elite state is being hammered out. That problem is *technology*.

Because of technology's advances, our planet's once-vast resource base has been fully tamed, and the old, ever-expanding-markets business model is broken. To fix this problem, which technology created, the solution in their view is…technology.

All the finite markets around the globe need to be restructured so that everything can be efficiently managed by a handful of owners and handy artificial intelligence. This is an efficient kind of digital feudalism, one that blows right by the clumsy methods of medieval feudalism, thanks to scanning technology—every person, every resource, every asset digitally tagged and traced by the superefficient AI, managing all. Reset complete—check.

The wonderfully opinionated writer Tessa Lena put this so well in a Substack article:

> In order for the super wealthy to manage global inventory, individual governments have to act more like mid-level managers accountable to international authorities than like independent federal governments. (Remember how "mom and pop shops" were pushed off the market and replaced by chain stores? Same thing here except in this case, the mom and pop stores are countries.)[20]

So the only real obstacle the elite state still faces is an independent-minded, liberty-loving America. That is why COVID was such a convenient contagion as well. It gave license to wipe out so many of America's small businesses and family farms—especially those still wedded to yesterday's old, analog ways. Noncompliant businesses are mostly small businesses. What small business owner has time for ESG mandates?

OTHERS HAVE CALLED IT THE FOURTH INDUSTRIAL REVOLUTION

As branding goes, the fourth industrial revolution never really floated the proletariat's boat. But it had a certain undeniable logic. We know the first revolution was a mechanical one, with eighteenth-century steam power and mechanized production. The second was electrical, with Thomas Edison and Nikola Tesla's work. Then came the digital revolution, with a shift to electronics and computers taking over. This fourth revolution is meant to be an AI-driven synchronicity of big data, quantum computing, nanotechnology, genetic modification, and robotics—basically merging our physical, biological, and digital worlds into a single, controllable, android creation that may well be efficient but is lacking autonomy and a human soul.

Behind this is an elite group of greedy people who are at the height of arrogance, trying to replace God with their own "intelligent design."

Gone is the heuristic—the discovering for yourself. Gone too is free will and the moral responsibility that comes with it. In its place are massive monopoly machines controlling our every human activity from the cradle to the grave. Controlling and financializing, as we'll see in later chapters, is the real endgame.

Some have called this melding of tech and human the "new transhumanism," and again we turn to the clear-eyed Tessa Lena to put it in perspective:

> Thus, on a sensory level—as it relates to money and power—this conveyor is an attempt of the super wealthy to organize and monetize their "assets," including people—more efficiently than ever before. On a theological level, the initiative is shaped by transhumanism, a formal belief system rooted in a pathological feeling of being repelled by all things natural—and a resulting view of biological forms as defective robots, which are made perfect, serial killer perfect, by merging with machines in a way that redefines the meaning of being alive and defies death itself....
>
> What we are looking at here is a new religion—and as much as I want to believe in the general cleanliness and rationality of the system—on the higher level, we are *not* dealing with a rational,

scientific, honest, benevolent—or even misguided—attempt to make things better. When it comes to the masterminds of the Great Reset, we are dealing with a combination of standard greed—and the emotional pathology of restless, rotting madmen who are freaking out over the maintenance of their property in this new era, and who resent their biological nature as such and want to be gods.[21]

None of this is to suggest that twenty-first-century technologies have not improved our lives in fantastic ways. But when technology becomes both problem and solution for those who would rule our lives and tirelessly extract our wealth, then clearly we need a different solution—one based in the dignity of the human being before God, created by and in God's image (as it says in the Book of Genesis).

Historian, intellectual, and professor Dr. Yuval Noah Harari has spoken several times at the World Economic Forum in Davos. He describes the new paradigm this way: "This will be the greatest revolution in biology since the very beginning of life four billion years ago....Science is replacing evolution by natural selection with evolution by intelligent design, not the intelligent design of some God above the clouds, but our intelligent design and the intelligent design of our clouds; the IBM cloud, the Microsoft cloud—these are the new driving forces of evolution."[22]

CHAPTER 2

WHAT IF THEY FORMED A UNIPARTY AND DIDN'T ANNOUNCE IT?

ONE OF THE enduring conceits of our time is that, despite all the Kabuki theater, we still have a semi-functioning two-party system in American politics.

Most people still don't believe their lying eyes. They can smell the rot in Washington, DC, as far away as Sitka, Alaska. But they have been so conditioned into believing that if only we swap out the treacherous rascals in Washington, everything will turn up lilies and lavender.

They do not truly grasp that there is no longer—and has not been for several decades—any difference between the two parties, between liberals and conservatives. That all have been silently horned into a unique party.

To keep the rules alive and people believing, there are rules to the uniparty:

1. Republicans and Democrats must continue to carry out the pomp and pageantry—and vote stealing—associated with elections.

2. Republicans and Democrats must carve up different slices of the federal whale for themselves, respecting each other's cuts like sushi chefs in a crowded kitchen.

3. Republicans and Democrats must pretend to be constantly fighting to the death for their very survival.

Oh, and the rules are firm. As for any considerations of the proper role of government in a free society, checks and balances, that kind of thing? All that kind of thing is gone. By design, by very careful design.

Those few politicians who object to these firm rules and try to stand on the principles that got them elected soon find themselves occupying basement offices without windows or reliable mail services, sweating through do-nothing committee assignments, and receiving one-way tickets back to their home districts gifted to them by their party leadership. There's no place for them in Washington, DC, today.

This is a cousin of another conceit: the belief that solutions even come from Washington, or that Washington can help in reform and renewal. If I have learned anything in my forty-five years in politics, it is that no solution to a problem will ever come from Washington. Washington is the place where solutions to problems go to die.

DESTROY THE TEA PARTY!

Remember how a libertarian group of citizen-politicians who were angry at President Obama's overreach rose up from the streets, beholden to no party? These "Tea Party activists" took Washington by storm. Big headlines for all. But the moment they got the slightest traction with all the good ideas they had in tow, the uniparty swung into action. Neither Republicans nor Democrats dared allow anyone not willing to play by the new rules to win.

The Tea Party had called the two-party charade for what it is—a uniparty running errands for the elite state. And that kind of heretical thinking simply could not be tolerated inside the Washington, DC, Capital Beltway.

One by one they picked off the newly elected Tea Party members, offering whatever spices or vices it took to do so to these inconvenient interlopers, then fold them into the uniparty apparatus.[1] Yes, it was like moral castration, accomplished in just a few short years. And the Tea Party, which had landed the most effective counterpunch against Washington in modern memory, became one for the history books.

LIBERALISM FAILED; FANATICS WENT NUCLEAR

Liberalism's last great triumphs were the Civil Rights Act of 1964; the Voting Rights Act of 1965; the Food Stamp Act of 1964; the Social Security Amendments of 1965, which created Medicaid and Medicare; and the Clean Air Act of 1970 and Clean Water Act of 1972.

Since then, liberals have accomplished…what?

Perhaps the best evidence that leftists are out of ideas is that they're trading on old ideas. They used to be all about freedom of speech. Now they join forces with corporations to censor views they dislike. Now they have campus speech codes. Only it's not speech itself they oppose, of course; it's speech they happen to disagree with at the moment. They call it "speaking their truth." The irony is lost on them, apparently.

Bookstores—or rather, Amazon—are full of liberal authors shouting about the assault on democracy posed by a few hundred radical "White supremacists" since (a) it doesn't come from the Left and (b) see a. These books shed big crocodile tears over democracy's failure to silence these radical nutjobs. But there is no defense of the actual democratic principles themselves. There can't be. They'd rather resort to name-calling.

The modern American liberal no longer believes in either individual liberty or equality. They may say they do. But topping their list of priorities is a full rehearsal of America's past failures—and they are doing it all this week. (Isn't it odd that these same people who call themselves "progressives" are so stuck in the past about failures that have since been corrected and redressed? Shouldn't progressivism be about moving forward?) So affirmative action comes before equality. Political correctness comes before equality. Identity politics comes before equality. Equity creation comes before equality.

As for equality itself, it's now sealed away in the liberal locker stamped *DNR* ("Do Not Resuscitate"). I predict that it will return, like Saturn, in seven years, with liberals swearing it never left their hearts. But I digress.

I'm not trying to bad-mouth liberalism here. No help is needed. I'm simply pointing out that liberalism has morphed into something else in the last few decades.

First, there was President Carter's Department of Education. Its function has never been clear, except to spend $76.4 billion a year on a big building full of rules-flinging bureaucrats in Washington who have walked back our children from receiving anything even closely resembling a classical, liberal-arts education.[2]

President Clinton did sign a monumental welfare reform law, but the only real point of that was to steady an unruly welfare train before it hopped the tracks.

President Obama gave us the Affordable Care Act of 2010, which helped a few million people get medical care, but at a tremendous cost to the rest of us, with the net effect of a deeply flawed system becoming even more deeply flawed.

President Biden has— Well, in fairness to the man, he outlasted everyone else in Washington and fell into a job he's far too old to manage. Props for even trying. But everyone knows how little he matters to the running of things. And how little his Schedule C political appointments matter—however bright they may be.

Other people matter on the Left now—the progressives, as they are known. They are responsible for the big ideas in the party now: Medicare for All, the Green New Deal, reparations for slavery, statue removal, taxes on the wealthy, saving the planet from certain ruination. None of these is a serious policy proposition. Most flame out as fast as they creep up. But that may be fine with the progressives. They are not serious people. Their ideas are mostly "look at me" memes meant to grab fifteen minutes of political fame.

They can't be serious, on their own terms, in fact. If these people actually believed the planet was threatened by CO_2 emissions, for example, so seriously that an extinction event is imminent, then they would straightaway throw their full support behind the immediate expansion of zero-emission nuclear power. But they don't.

Climate change has one purpose for liberals: to lock in the votes of about 15 percent of the electorate who are (a) single-issue voting and (b) gullible enough to believe the scientists paid handsomely to announce the fast-approaching end of the human race, then when the deadline passes, announce the fast-approaching end of the human race, then when the— Well, you get it.

This process can go on and on because the scientists can always be changing the measuring models, achieving different results! And also because they don't want to lose their job forecasting the fast-approaching end of the human race, now do they? So the scientists can sleep at night, figuring that if the politicians run amok with their findings, at least the world's attention will be kept focused on the need for some action.

This is not to say liberals are stupid and lost—at least not any more than conservatives are.

CONSERVATISM FAILED; FANATICS WENT NUCLEAR

My friend Stan Evans used to tell a joke during the Reagan years about how conservatives rode into Washington after campaigning about it "being a cesspool," only to discover to their amazement that it really is a "hot tub." Their principles slammed headfirst into the organized crime of the growing elite state, with the principles usually being the first to go.

One of those young conservatives riding in was another friend of mine, Lee Troxler. When he played a consequential role in getting Ronald Reagan elected, he soon found himself working in the White House. But after just one term, a point at which most are just getting comfortable, he got out. He could see what was coming: how he too would soon be on a conveyor belt to some deputy assistant undersecretary position for SomethingOrOther, or maybe an office up on Capitol Hill, or a lobbyist for the American Meat Association—various faces of a beast he recognized.

Politics has always attracted actors—good and bad—because the same skills are required to succeed. Both actors and politicians must inhabit a character they are not, bringing that person to life with compelling flourishes. They must memorize scripts and deliver on the character. So there has always been "theater" in politics, and there surely always will be. But after their performances in the old days, the actors would scrub off their makeup and then go have a beer together. Those days are long gone, because now there are eyes on the politicians twenty-four hours a day.

There's no chance to change out of character, no chance to let the guard down, because someone is always watching, watching, watching, just itching to report any deviance from the script. It has created absurdist theater 24/7—an exercise in amateur dramatics, constantly having to strike an attitude to impress your public. Lines crafted for you by the smart ones in Washington, the speechwriters. The only difference between the two parties is the script itself.

Speeches given to the Left have to make persuasive cases for bigger government solving all our problems. Speeches given to the Right have to make persuasive cases for cutting back on needless bureaucracy. So the speeches are given—all sound and fury, signifying nothing, but certainly full of nightmare scenarios and emerging crises meant to keep folks watching, to keep them scared, to keep them paranoid (any strong emotion will do). As long as the audience is kept entertained, the politicians' job is done.

In turn, the media do the filtering—one set of sound bites for the Left stream, one set for the Right stream—so each side thinks they're getting great truths and their opponents are a bunch of depraved, evil child molesters.

Your average cell phone–worshipping bloke laps it up.

It's as if a nation has left reality for some "political and cultural metaverse," as Gerard Baker puts it.[3] A crackerjack commentator for the *Wall Street Journal*, Baker suspects that we fled reality for its alternative because so many of us were already there, giving hours a day over to video games and social media, the "ultimate reality-distorting platforms."

He's no doubt correct. Also correct is accepting how complex our world has become. This complexity means that any bill coming out of Congress runs to hundreds if not thousands of pages. Most of it is posturing and padding with stretches of legal skullduggery thrown in to satisfy all the interests. But there are legitimate complexities involved in legislating for a nation of 333 million with 1.3 million attorneys looking to muss things up for billable hours. So yes, complexity helps explain how our political process got so far gone.

Two good explanations, yet each falls short somehow. How about a third?

If there are no functioning political parties, the whole idea of checks and balances crumbles and falls. True power then falls into the outstretched palms of the deeply permanent elite state machinery. Just as they wish.

THE GREAT TRICK: PUNISH DISSENT WITHOUT FORCE

Though much has changed in America over the years, there has been one constant: every thinking American, it turns out, detests totalitarians in all their shades of shamefulness. We recognize their sort when we see them, and we just don't like them.

A lot of us own guns, know how to use them, and would not hesitate to use them in defense of the freedom these authoritarians threaten. An equally large number of us don't know the first thing about resisting aggression, however much we loathe it. But all of us have gotten rusty on the ABCs of freedoms and the genius-level checks and balances our Founders put into place to protect those freedoms.

It is our intellectual laziness as a nation that has allowed the elite state to undermine those checks and balances, as we'll see in the pages ahead.

KNOCKING AMERICA OFF-BALANCE WITH THE PATRIOT ACT

Boxing champ Muhammad Ali had a mean right hook, but he's remembered for his strategy to "float like a butterfly, sting like a bee." So it was on a terrible September day in 2001 that our government chose to meet localized terror with generalized terror, launching a barrage of misdirects and feints meant to neutralize a distant enemy while succeeding only in slamming the American people. Look at these headlines from just the summer of 2006 alone to see the American ideal thrown off-balance.

"CIA Worker Says Message on Torture Got Her Fired"

CIA employee Christine Axsmith posted a message on an *internal* network criticizing waterboarding, pointing out that "waterboarding is torture, and torture is wrong." It cost her both her job and top-secret clearance.[4] (Today she has a private law practice.)

"Blogger Jailed After Defying Court Orders"

Freelance video blogger Josh Wolf was jailed after refusing to hand over to the FBI a video he took of a San Francisco protest march. Although the jailing of American journalists has become more frequent, Wolf was the first *blogger* thrown in jail by federal authorities.[5] (He served 226 days in prison.)

"On Prosecuting Detainees Draft Bill Waives Due Process for Enemy Combatants"

The Bush administration's Military Commissions Act basically tossed due process—ending speedy trials, making hearsay information admissible, and holding enemy combatants in prison indefinitely.[6] Gone were the Geneva Conventions, which had long represented the highest principles of civilized nations. "Enemy combatants" can be whomever the executive branch says they are, which gives them the power to knock on any citizen's door, pull us off the street or a plane, take our phones, blindfold us, and toss us into a military prison, where we can be kept in isolation for as long as they desire, and delaying our trial for months if they like. And if in torturing us they break some confession out of us, that can be used against us in court—if the trial ever happens. Basically, we are presumed guilty.

We saw this kind of treatment of al-Qaeda combatants. We'd see it later turned on US citizens.

"Doctors Outraged at Patriot Act's Potential to Seize Medical Records"

Doctors have been forced to divulge confidential medical records without a warrant. What had long been a private doctor-patient relationship could, after the Patriot Act, be accessed by any government agency interested in a US citizen, for whatever reason.[7]

We dredged these headlines out of the archives because they show early-stage moves by the elite behemoth to consolidate its power base.

The great feminist author Naomi Wolf dug into this post-9/11 rights-shredding spree in an extraordinary book, *The End of America: Letter of Warning to a Young Patriot*. She looked at all the civil liberties violations suddenly raining down from Washington and went searching for precedents in world history.

> So I read about Mussolini's Italy in the 1920s; Stalin's Russia and Hitler's Germany in the 1930s; I read about East Germany in the 1950s and Czechoslovakia in the 1960s and Chile in 1973, as well as about other Latin American dictatorships; I read about Communist China in the late 1980s and early 1990s.
>
> The countries I looked at were very different, of course, and the violent dictators had a broad range of ideologies. Stalin imposed totalitarianism over a communist state, itself built upon the ruins of a toppled monarchy. Mussolini and Hitler both came to power legally in the context of fragile parliamentary democracies. East Germany and Czechoslovakia were communist systems, and China still is; and General Augusto Pinochet closed down Chile's young democracy in a classic Latin American military coup d'état.
>
> Violent dictators across the political spectrum all do the same

key things. Control is control. In spite of this range of ideological differences, profound similarities in tactics leap off the pages.[8]

These tactics that Wolf identified are generally employed by all dictators, each in their own way. They are being employed here in America today.

That is why we all have this vague sense of unease, of fear that a nation is dying, that our long-standing system of checks and balances has been compromised beyond the tipping point. Suddenly, we realize, we could tip into something we no longer recognize as a free country. As Ernest Hemingway famously put it, change comes "gradually and then suddenly."[9]

Yes, there is an urgency to our national condition now—no longer a hazy, easily shrugged-off fear that something's not right. There's wrong now. All around us now. We recognize that the playbook dictators have always used is now being used against us.

On that September 11, we witnessed in real time a horrific attack on our nation. An attack that told us we faced a new enemy—one we barely understood. Soon the Bush administration was defining these attackers as "evildoers" who hated our freedoms and were determined to annihilate us. Within six weeks, the USA Patriot Act rushed through Congress with 342 pages of new decrees that few, if any, legislators read in their entirety.

We were facing an "axis of evil" that posed a threat to civilization itself. Islamofascism was a cancer spreading across the globe, and so a global "war on terror" had to be fought.

Few saw it any other way. Those few—most of them either leftist hipsters still digging on Marxist ideals or emigrants from Eastern Europe wary of those same ideals—knew precisely what was happening. They knew that a government wishing to close down an open society had to first invoke the most terrifying external threat possible to stir up fear, confusion, and generalized chaos.

And so Bush administration speechwriter Michael Gerson placed an article in the then widely read *Newsweek* magazine painting a vivid picture of Islamic fascists bent on harnessing both technology and weaponry to make "radical Islam a global power, allowing new killing on an unimagined scale."[10]

All this for a sickly man hiding in a cave, living on a dialysis machine.

Oh, we did have a newish enemy. Or at least a new wrinkle on an enemy we'd had since our CIA deposed Iranian Prime Minister Mohammad Mossadegh in 1953, fueling a surge of nationalism in that country that led to revolution and a thorough poisoning of US relations in the Middle East ever since.[11] This enemy had finally struck us effectively. A military response might have been justified, but did it also require our leadership to whip up waves of terror and dread on the streets of America?

Or was the bombastic rhetoric coming out of Washington a calculated effort to scare the American people into forfeiting the freedoms they had long treasured for the security of their families?

After all, the attack on 9/11 did little to change our nation's underlying strength, or the affluence we enjoy, or the love we have for our neighbors in our communities. The attack didn't do that, but perhaps our response did.

We took a terrible hit that sunny September morning. We would have to hunt down Osama bin Laden, as well as his sympathizers, on their native soil. Our military was more than up to the task. So was it necessary to wildly distort the wherewithal of the enemy and inflame a nation, creating a kind of hysterical OCD that has worked into the national fabric like cigarette smoke, hard to wash out?

This inflaming of America served but one purpose: to scare people into a full-throated acceptance of a vast new security industrial complex. A complex driven not by the security it truly provided but by the profit it amply generated for the elite state behind it.

Within hours of the twin towers falling, hundreds of security company lobbyists were swarming the offices of friends throughout the government, making the case for investing in surveillance technologies. Soon there would be 569 companies registering Homeland Security lobbyists.[12] Not just the usual behemoths like Lockheed Martin, Acxiom, and ChoicePoint slopping away at the public trough, but an entire new generation of businesses angling for a seat at an all-new and much larger elite state table.

APPARENTLY, PEACE WAS BAD FOR BUSINESS

When the Soviet Union collapsed in the early 1990s, the US defense industry saw business dry up. They needed a new enemy. And man, did 9/11 deliver. Its baby was a vast Homeland Security apparatus that cost $36.2 billion when first ramped up, and it just kept growing to $97.3 billion in spending plans for 2023.[13]

By the time all the accounting was in, the government had doubled in size and become half as effective. There were all the new organizational charts with an indecipherable tangle of alphabet agencies, overlapping command structures, and redundant directives creating more interagency fighting than you can get from crabs stuck in a pot, trying to crawl out but certainly not letting any other crab crawl out.

Twenty years later, this new security arm of the elite state is still with us, with people showing up for work, or calling it in remotely, expected to do *something*. So if the Islamic terrorist threat has receded—and clearly it has, thanks to our military efforts and their middling competence as terrorists—what is this surveillance apparatus supposed to do all day? Swipe through photos on social media? Play with their fidget spinners? Sure, but after a while they're going to default to a handier enemy in need of constant monitoring—the American people.

THE US GOVERNMENT IS SNOOPING— JUST SAY THE MAGIC WORDS

They were stealthy about it at first, certainly aware that nobody likes their private conversations being snooped on. (Even those who barrel down the street loudly conducting their business on their cell phones don't like it, say the pollsters.) But then all manner of surveillance became so commonplace.

It's on every cop show on TV now; it's the butt of comedians' jokes. It has been normalized—accepted on a bunch of rationales such as (a) maybe my government needs me, (b) I'm innocent and have nothing to hide, (c) what harm could come from it?, or (d) there's nothing I can do about it.

All these rationales can end badly.

If you speak certain keywords on your calls, a surveillance program may be triggered, and a human is then tasked to listen in on what you're saying. There's a great disagreement on how often this is being used. Tim Cook of Apple, for one, insists this practice should not be happening at all. But there are now many examples of this happening all around us.[14]

It's a system patterned after the infamous East German Stasi listening stations, which were programmed to record conversations when a certain word came up.[15] Not just the Stasi, of course, but the Gestapo, the KGB, and their ilk practiced similar surveillance in their day.

Today, the communist government of the People's Republic of China actively tracks its citizens' computer use. The Chinese spy on their citizens for the same reasons we do: to break down the people's belief that they are free to act against those in power; to erode people's loyalties to the civil and professional groups of old; to redirect the people's focus and primary loyalty to the new state order.

It works.

Surveillance is chilling dissent in America. People seem more reluctant to sign petitions or join rallies. And forget about opening the door to a stranger. Most of us don't want to do anything that might stir up *trouble*.

Not all citizens have been stifled and suppressed or effectively deadened. Many of us still exercise our First Amendment right to peaceably assemble and petition the government for a redress of grievances. But even as we do meet in group settings, we have to ask ourselves if everyone present is really who they say they are. Incredibly, hundreds of FBI agents spend their days working to infiltrate citizens' groups. They show up after the computers have tagged keywords in the texts and emails the groups use.

Usually, these agents do little but listen; other times they actively provoke the group to illegal action to trap them. We will see how they've done it again and again and with an almost malicious glee in the pages ahead.

We'll see how they've been able to portray dissenters as bloodthirsty threats to society. So threatening, in fact, that these FBI agents have no choice but to resort to violence and subterfuge to "restore public order."

It's well known that the TSA keeps a "list." To its credit, the TV news magazine *60 Minutes* got a copy of the no-fly list and found it was more than 540 pages long in 2006, with 44,000 names on it—ultimately including hundreds of people who never should have been harassed: a journalist, a soccer coach, a US constitutional scholar and retired Marine colonel, a businessman. Some found themselves on the no-fly list and their lives turned upside down because of obviously sloppy work by the TSA. Others made the list for reasons no TSA official will publicly acknowledge.[16]

This no-fly list is years old now, as is the so-called terrorist threat, but the FBI is still adding to it, still enforcing it. (Set aside the post-9/11 airport security systems' deterrent value in the first place.) These systems are still fully operating today. Everyday citizens stuck in already tedious airport lines are being yanked out of line, detained, and strip-searched. Some even find, months later, certain job opportunities have been closed off to them, and they don't know why.

Plenty of low-level bureaucrats with plum jobs for life in Washington know, though. They know they must regularly "bust" people to keep the rest of us on edge. They know the funding for their jobs requires activity of some sort. They know that the people must be kept agitated, at each other's throats if possible—because that's what keeps the funding coming for the security arm of the elite state.

So it was that on the eve of the Iraq War, the very talented Dixie Chicks were playing in London. Lead singer Natalie Maines clued in the audience, saying, "We're ashamed that the president of the United States is from Texas."[17] It was her right, but radical-Right bloggers immediately began attacking the group, calling for a boycott of the "traitors." Cumulus Media, which then owned about 260 radio stations, shut down the band on many of them. Other artists at the time became leery of expressing views critical of the Bush administration out of fear of being "Dixie Chicked."

Later in the timeline the roles would reverse, with radical-Left bloggers shouting down conservatives just as nastily. Whether from the Left or the Right, it's all of the same origin—the absurdist theater show, with players all in their roles, dividing the nation and drawing their funding for doing so. Further weakening the bonds that unite us, that once kept us free and safely untouched by the elite state's wealth extraction and culture corrosion machinery.

So many of us now find ourselves afraid to dissent because of all that we've seen. Or we speak in soft tones, hiding our true opinions for fear of losing our jobs, our friendships, our standing in the community.

The authoritarian path.

Although we aren't at the point of Munich in 1938, we are headed in that direction. America is fractured, cut off from its birthright. Our culture, which has long relied on a trusty pendulum to right the excesses, now finds the pendulum stuck, unable to be moved except through some new force, some kind of counterpunch.

It all comes down to perspective and how you see yourself in this messy situation we're in. An old story can bring some clarity to this.

One day there was a young woman having a terrible time. Everything was a struggle. She felt like giving up, since one problem seemed only to lead to the next. She found her mom and laid on the woe.

Mom took her into the kitchen and filled three pots with water, and then she lit a flame under them. In the first she placed some carrots, in the second some eggs, and in the last some ground coffee beans. She let them boil for a while and then turned off the flame, putting the carrots, eggs, and coffee each into their own bowls.

"Tell me what you see," Mom said.

"Carrots, eggs, and coffee," the daughter replied.

Mom explained that all three foods had faced the same difficulty— boiling water—but each had reacted differently. The carrots went in strong and hard but came out soft and weak. The eggs went in with a fragile outer shell protecting a liquid interior but came out hardened. And the ground coffee beans uniquely changed the water into a delightful drink.

"Which are you?" Mom asked. "When you are facing challenges, how do you respond? Are you a carrot, an egg, or a coffee bean?"

WHAT KIND OF PERSON WILL YOU BE?

I'd like to think you're up for changing some water and joining with good people in defense of the highest values of our republic, the values we've seen pounded down. I'd also like to think you're ready to step into the ring with us—and counterpunch!

I can tell you, I've worn through my share of sixteen-ounce gloves. I met the first vestiges of today's elite state early in life. In 1983, I had just graduated from the University of Washington, and I'd loaded all my belongings into my Mustang for the long drive to the nation's capital and an even longer-lived dream to work for President Reagan.

I was soon appointed executive director of the US International Youth Year Commission, and I was ecstatic. Little did I know that I'd been hired as a fresh young face to front for the elite state. While I fully believed that I was working for America on the front lines of the Reagan Revolution, I was in fact a front man for an intelligence operation that was targeting youth in America and abroad.

Back then, the elite state was something of a fledgling operation, far less offensive and not nearly as lethal as today's fully mature organization. Since they were so well hidden behind a façade of government respectability, it would take me many years to fully understand how arrogant and greedy these new American royals had become, and how that same arrogance and greed has become their biggest vulnerability, the way we can strike back.

Doing just that—counterpunching with all our might from our communities on up to a knockout at the top—is what this book is all about.

Nobody pretends that jumping into the ring will be easy. So many of us have become disillusioned and spiritually cold. It is this robust faith that has always safeguarded our American freedoms. But the fires of that faith have almost burned out, and like a campfire that has burnt all night, there are only embers. Now we must kneel before them and, with God's help, blow on those embers. With the oxygen of a renewed spirit, our American dream can be revived.

It all starts in the hearts of good people yearning for that revival.

The first step, as in the days of our founding and the words of Patrick Henry, is an appeal to "the Majesty of Heaven, which I revere above all earthly kings."[18]

CHAPTER 3

COVID WAS THE ELITE STATE'S DARKEST VICTORY

W E MAY NEVER learn how COVID escaped to wreak its havoc. But we can look back to those early days in March 2020 and see that COVID was merely the symptom of a larger "infection of the soul," as the insightful Naomi Wolf put it.[1]

On her Substack page, Wolf tells how in the early days of COVID a large group of medical-freedom advocates would gather in a Hudson River Valley community park, coming together repeatedly throughout the lockdown in relaxed potluck dinners, children playing and touching and romping about without any suffocating zombie masks, with dogs being petted, neighbors hugging, and nobody asking any personal medical questions.

Meanwhile, back in the cities, a dark, poisonous miasma had settled into every corner, with scores of people frightened into believing—truly believing—that their neighbors were trying to kill them with each sniffle or cough. Highly educated people began repeating only the talking points from MSNBC or CNN, refusing to hear otherwise. Wolf's lifelong friends literally told her, "I don't want to see that; don't show it to me."[2] If they accidentally took in any information that contradicted the narrative, they risked losing their social status, their potential opportunities, or their jobs—they weren't sure what.

> Whole belief systems were abandoned painlessly and overnight as if these communities were in the grip of a collective hallucination, like the witch craze of the 15th to 17th centuries in Northern Europe. Intelligent...people suddenly saw things that were not there and were unable to see things that were incontrovertibly before their faces.[3]

For simply reporting what she saw, Wolf was verbally attacked and threatened. Twitter suspended her. CNN, a channel she'd appeared on for decades, blacklisted her. CNN's Matt Gertz publicly called her a "pandemic conspiracy theorist" doing "crackpottery."[4] So Wolf gave a lot of thought to what was truly happening, and in time she came to pray on it.

> I had started to pray again…to speak about God publicly because I had looked at what had descended on us from every angle, using my normal critical training and faculties; and that it was so elaborate in its construction, so comprehensive, and so cruel, with an almost superhuman, flamboyant, baroque imagination made out of the essence of cruelty itself — that I could not see that it had been accomplished by mere humans working on the bumbling human level in the dumb political space.[5]

What could possibly explain this "infection of the soul," as she called it?

> I don't think humans are smart or powerful enough to come up with this horror all alone. So I told the group in the woods, that the very impressiveness of evil all around us in all of its new majesty, was leading me to believe in a newly literal and immediate way in the presence, the possibility, the necessity of a countervailing force—that of a God. It was almost a negative proof: an evil this large must mean that there is a God at which it is aiming its malevolence.[6]

Wolf asked one of the medical-freedom activists at that Hudson Valley gathering how he found strength in the midst of it all. He replied with Ephesians 6:12, "For we wrestle not against flesh and blood, but against principalities, against powers, against the rulers of the darkness of this world, against spiritual wickedness in high places" (KJV).

So she concluded it was "time to start talking about spiritual combat… to call, as Milton did, as Shakespeare did, as Emily Dickinson did, on help from elsewhere; on what could be called angels and archangels, if you will; on higher powers, whatever they may be; on better principalities, on whatever intercessors may hear us, on Divine Providence" for we are in "a New Dark Age" and "evil abounds."[7]

Wolf was early to see what was starting to happen across our country.

PRACTICALLY A CRIMINAL BETRAYAL OF OUR CHILDREN

Stacey Lance teaches morals and ethics in an Ontario, Canada, high school, and from early on in the pandemic she saw her students thinking of themselves as "vectors of disease."[8] This was the message they were getting at home, on the street, and in the media. That there was somehow something wrong with *them*. COVID hysteria had turned every conversation into a deeply scarring one—when it never had to be.

With COVID directives coming out of government offices like drunks spilling out of a bar, schools were in then out, partially open then semi-closed, masked then not. Stacey could see it wreaking havoc on her students' mental development. She wrote:

> When we were physically in school, it felt like there was no longer life in the building. Maybe it was the masks that made it so no one wanted to engage in lessons, or even talk about how they spent their weekend. But it felt cold and soulless. My students weren't allowed to gather in the halls or chat between classes. They still aren't. Sporting events, clubs and graduation were all canceled. These may sound like small things, but these losses were a huge deal....We kept hearing, "They'll be fine. They're resilient." It's true that humans, by nature, are very resilient. But they also break. And my students are breaking.[9]

Stacey saw firsthand how deeply we betrayed our children since the risks of COVID were always, obviously, for older, vulnerable people and never, obviously, for healthy, young children. She, like all of us, wonders why our leaders handled the pandemic so capriciously, so nearly criminally. We are now learning why.

RIPPING SMALL BUSINESSES TO SHREDS

"One of our employees is pregnant; another is a nineteen-year-old kid," Mitch said of his COVID experience. Mitch has owned the Spangler Family Restaurant that has operated in Jonesville, Michigan, for thirty years. Mitch took it over from his mother, making payments to her that she needs for retirement. More than twenty employees' livelihoods are dependent on the diner.[10] But folks in Washington treated the diner's shutdown as a minor inconvenience, the price we all have to pay.

Sure, there were bailout funds aplenty for the big companies, but very little of the CARES Act relief and Paycheck Protection Program funds trickled down to the neediest businesses.

If actual "caring" was the criteria for disbursing relief funds, far less would have gone to the richest people in America (the top 1 percent got a quarter of all PPP loan funds).[11]

Few major companies were going to lose sleep over COVID. They also had an open window at the federal government where they could borrow unlimited sums at zero interest. So lockdowns sounded good to them.

Big Tech companies would see their profits predictably soar, and they did, outpacing the overall stock market's increase.[12] So lockdowns sounded good to them too.

Small businesses, on the other hand, account for just under half the economy and are the most vulnerable when struck with the sudden loss of business such as from lockdowns.

Why did the political class leave many small business owners out in the cold during the height of the pandemic? And why didn't corporate America suffer the same fate?

Because the entire response to COVID was driven by the imperatives of the elite state; forty million small businesses in America were affected by the lockdowns, considered mere "collateral damage."

Mitch Spangler saw this up close and personal at his diner. He saw the rank hypocrisy of it all. So when the Michigan governor callously ordered a second lockdown from the back seat of her limo, Mitch kept his diner open. He posted a sign on the door and on Facebook that said, "IF YOU CANNOT SUPPORT US, WE UNDERSTAND, BUT PLEASE ALLOW US TO HAVE THE FREEDOM TO DO WHAT WE HAVE TO DO."

Mitch also took all the precautions—disinfectants, distancing, scan codes, the works. But the wheels of Michigan bureaucracy began to grind. Health department officials stopped by. Licensing officials stopped by. He was fined, threatened with forcible closure. But he never backed down, and the diner stayed afloat with locals as well as folks from neighboring Indiana and Ohio driving in to show their support.

Nearby Hillsdale College offered Mitch help with legal representation.

The community mobilized for one of their own.[13] Just one diner's story, but an important one. Pounding down working Americans from the back seat of a limo is no way to run a country.

Mitch saw how a community can come together to counterpunch, and his experience would soon reverberate across a nation.

INCUBATING A MASS DELUSIONAL PSYCHOSIS

While the world struggled to understand this latest virus exported by China, first responders were soon grappling with something even more terrible. People were showing up in doctors' offices with crippling anxiety, insomnia, drug cravings, depression, new addictions, violent behavior, contemplating suicide.

Good doctors like Los Angeles–based psychiatrist Mark McDonald could see a mental health disaster rising, fueled by public health officials' erratic behavior and blown completely out of proportion by a reckless media chasing ratings points.

Dr. McDonald began to tell a story of twin pandemics: one viral and one psychological, with the latter potentially more dangerous. And he offered a diagnosis for what most of the country was suffering from:

> Mass delusional psychosis [since] adopting a worldview that rejects and attacks reality is psychotic. Although we most often see it in individuals—cult leaders, homeless drug addicts, celebrity stalkers—psychotic illness can also affect groups of people and, indeed, whole societies. This can happen when everyone becomes hyperfocused on one issue, when fear becomes the predominant emotion, and rational faculties become paralyzed en masse. That is exactly what happened to Americans in 2020.[14]

He said we saw this psychosis play out in the most awful of ways:

- An eight-year-old put his fist through a plate glass window because he couldn't tolerate being confined to a two-room apartment twenty-four hours a day for months on end.

- After being cooped up indoors for so long, a girl apparently just snapped and grabbed a kitchen knife and attacked her brother.

- A suicide prevention center in Los Angeles reported receiving eighteen hundred calls to its hotline in March 2020, up from an average of about twenty before the pandemic.

Dr. McDonald wrote, "As thousands of Los Angelenos rioted maskless in the streets and in the name of racial justice looted and burned down billions of dollars of property...those same people then joined in insisting that we lock down the city and shut down personal liberties to keep everyone safe from infection."[15] Clearly there was something else at work.

Dr. McDonald could not sit idly by, staring at his prescription pad. He knocked out a book, *United States of Fear: How America Fell Victim to a Mass Delusional Psychosis*. And he spoke to whoever would have him, such as the Orange County Board of Education:

> Why are we even having this meeting tonight? We're meeting because we adults are afraid....We must agree to make decisions in the best interest of the children. If we do not—if, paralyzed by fear, we continue to act purely out of self-interest—we will ensure an entire generation of traumatized young people, consigned to perpetual adolescence and residency in their parents' garages, unable to move through life with independence, courage, and confidence. They deserve better—we owe it to them as parents.[16]

Dr. McDonald also reached out to other medical professionals, such as Dr. Simone Gold, founder of America's Frontline Doctors. Along with several other physicians, they took their case to microphones at the steps of the Supreme Court. These weren't conservative doctors or liberal doctors. They were people with impressive credentials asking publicly whether the closing of America's schools was "the greatest mistake in the government response to the pandemic," as McDonald wrote in his book. Was their position right, wrong?

That should not have mattered. They were contributing to what should have been a healthy debate in a time when scientists all needed to be weighing in—for the situation was fluid, uncertain. The left-stream press refused to cover the event; Breitbart.com did a live internet feed reaching an estimated seventeen million people.

And to the media platforms allied with the state, that just couldn't be allowed.

Within hours, all social media postings of the event were being expunged in real time, wiped clean by the censors at Facebook, YouTube, and Twitter. Each time someone tried to forward or tweet the day's speech, that too disappeared. Lots of accounts were suspended that day as well.[17]

Keep in mind Twitter would still encourage any garden-variety axe murderer to plead his or her case on the platform, but some of the nation's most accomplished doctors were too dangerous for them.

Other deplatformed doctors include Dr. Joseph Mercola, who wrote a well-received book with more than five thousand sales in its first month of release. But based on the title he chose, *The Truth About COVID-19: Exposing the Great Reset, Lockdowns, Vaccine Passports, and the New Normal*, he just had to be silenced.

One doctor, who was found to be fabricating stories to fit the narrative the elite state needed to profit handsomely from COVID, was the government's own Anthony Fauci. You could be excused for thinking Dr. Fauci suffers from epilepsy from his jerky, seemingly uncontrolled handling of the puppet master's strings. Stay in. Go out. Mask on. Mask off. Separate six feet. No, twelve feet. No, eight feet. Get a shot. No shots available. Show your records. No records on file. Don't take drug A. Or drug B. Drug A is OK. Jab the kids. Under eighteen. Under ten. Under five. Why? Why not?

And on and on, jerkily the strings were pulled for over a year while America's small-business economy was hammered, millions were thrown into unemployment lines for the first time in their lives, thousands died needlessly beyond COVID's own toll since the system was shut down to other surgeries and psychological traumas induced by the puppet master in the white coat. And Dr. Fauci's response to all this? "It's easy to criticize, but they're really criticizing science because I represent science," he said. "That's dangerous."[18]

To say you can't write this stuff is almost cliché. Did he think he was talking to an elementary school class? Did he figure he had control of the government health apparatus and the left-stream media as well, so it really didn't matter if he stood before the cameras and drooled? Was he unconcerned that he sometimes looked like a simpleton and other times a dark monster since he knew the tech platforms would shut down anyone who dared challenge his all-abiding authority?

Maybe all of the above?

As it turned out, the dozen or so doctors and scientists who had assembled at the Supreme Court steps in July 2020 grew to tens of thousands who were so outraged by Dr. Fauci that they risked their reputations and livelihoods to get "dangerous."

In something called the Great Barrington Declaration and again in the global Rome Declaration, doctors and scientists spoke out against the "irreparable damage" the prevailing COVID policies were causing, saying they "may actually constitute crimes against humanity."[19] This is the kind of language usually reserved for despots and rogue dictators. But here it was coming from leading scientists and epidemiologists from Harvard, Stanford—the finest minds in the country—arguing for a saner approach to COVID.

They argued for an approach based on targeted protection and not general lockdowns, as had been tried successfully in other countries. But not in America, because there were people with agendas, people behind the puppet master who really liked all the wealth and brute power they were consolidating.

ALARMING UNDERREPORTING OF VACCINE SIDE EFFECTS

Not only in America, but worldwide, there was a vast underreporting of the side effects of the COVID vaccines. Words like *myocarditis, pericarditis,* and *persistent brain fog* became common conversation. Germany's largest health insurance provider reported side effects ten times more common than being reported.[20]

Our own government tamped down the reporting on the side effects of COVID as well as the true number of deaths. How? By sealing records and paying hospitals a big bounty to report a death as "COVID-related" no matter the actual cause. Money talked; truth walked.

In the last fifty years, normally new medications and such are thoroughly tested on a small group of volunteers for a reasonable time period to make sure there aren't unforeseen problems and to avoid devastating side effects, such as were seen with thalidomide in the 1950s and early 1960s. All that changed with COVID-19. Now, with COVID, before they knew whether the vaccine prevented the virus or caused serious side effects, before it ever received full approval, the government, businesses, the military, and others were encouraging and even forcing the masses to get the experimental jab.

But shouldn't the experimental jabs rushed to market and pushed on people be part of the discussion, rather than the result of heavy-handed state mandates?

ROOT OF THE CONTROVERSY OVER IVERMECTIN

Why did Dr. Fauci's government enforcers threaten to de-license any doctor who dared prescribe the long-proven drug ivermectin for COVID?

The good folks at Merck are among the behemoths in the elite state pod, and they were working around the clock to get an FDA approval for their drug molnupiravir to combat COVID. Molnupiravir may ultimately work better than ivermectin; we don't know. We do know that ivermectin costs around thirty dollars for twenty tablets while Merck is charging the government $700 for each forty-pill course of molnupiravir.[21]

Despite thousands of doctors prescribing ivermectin, backed by hundreds of studies done on it, even today they are still denouncing the medicine and smearing doctors using it in any media in which Merck can buy commercial coverage.

Big Pharma has made billions on the COVID vaccines, and it sees this pipeline stretching for as long as they can keep the charade going. The elite state is very pleased with how COVID turned out.

CAN'T LET A CRISIS GO TO WASTE

In the early days of COVID, there was great uncertainty. To not be fearful was just plain stupid. But a month into panicked lockdowns, the data was becoming clear to scientists, first at Stanford and then elsewhere. Clear that early models were off by millions of deaths; that infection rates were significantly lower; that outside the big cities, the hospitals would never be overflowing with patients.

Yet the lockdowns continued in nearly every area of every state. And why?

Some health officials were genuinely aiming for over-caution, however tunnel-visioned their thinking. But up on Capitol Hill, that gray and red virus was all green to them. A chance to spend trillions to buy voters' favor, with no wondering how that money would be paid back or whether it would trigger an inflationary spiral that would soon pound the middle class all over again (as predictably later happened).

In March 2020, before we knew the first thing about the virus, Democrats laid out a sweeping wish list of infrastructure spending, an expansion of Social Security benefits, vote-by-mail systems, and much more having little to do with containing a possibly deadly virus. They saw, as Rep. James Clyburn of South Carolina absentmindedly admitted in public, "a tremendous opportunity to restructure things to fit our vision."[22]

Establishment Republicans were no different, just slower to act, caucusing in July 2020 to decide how many "stimulus checks" they should push out the back of low-flying planes across America. Or they might as well have, for all the usefulness of their own COVID-combating strategy. After the meeting, Senator Rand Paul summed it up, saying there was "no difference" between the two parties in spending.[23]

Trying to sound halfway intelligent, Democrat politicians insisted on CNN and Republicans on Fox News that stimulus checks would also stimulate the economy. And true enough, in Vegas, there was a big uptick in people returning to the tables to gamble away their stimulus check, ultimately leaving town poorer than they arrived. And on Rodeo Drive in Beverly Hills, there were traffic jams as people came from poorer neighborhoods nearby to buy merchandise they couldn't actually afford.

Of course, most of the economy was shut down, so there were few places where people could go shopping. Few—except for the massive corporate retailers and the online behemoths. Exactly the kind of stimulus the elite state could get behind.

As a bonus, the stimulus checks and $600-per-week unemployment bonuses that Washington sent out destroyed any incentive for the unemployed to go job hunting—a case of government making a mess, then stepping in it.

And undoubtedly the first time in US history that we deliberately decimated the Main Street economy so the elite state could explode their own bank accounts.

It must become the last time.

WE ARE MOVING FORWARD IN PRAYER

We are seeing, as Naomi Wolf reminded us earlier, that we are truly engaged in a spiritual battle in a dark age, a battle to reclaim so much of what we've lost.

We have learned that a free nation can become decidedly less so.

We have watched torrents of rules and ridiculous mandates laid across the land like a wet wool blanket, suffocating the lives we once took for granted.

We know the government will keep the COVID spirit alive as long as it can use it to lord over our very ways and means, constantly announcing new variants and new strains. (On a side note to that, I can't help but wonder why medical authorities named the COVID variants Delta and Omicron and skipped over Xi. Did they get orders from Chinese president Xi Jinping not to use the Greek letter for his name, since officially the virus did not originate in China? Or was Omicron an inside joke to Dr. Fauci and company, since with a little rearranging it spells "moronic"?)

Yes, we can see the authoritarian impulse and how it can grow like a cancer if left unchecked. Certainly, we recognize that when aging rock stars who once took to the barricades are now lining up to silence opposing viewpoints, there is a cancer *somewhere*. There is top-down mind control of our culture, and we wonder how we can possibly fight back against the arbitrary self-interested dictates gushing out of Washington.

Turns out, we already are. We're already working meaningfully for the life we want our families to be living.

ARIZONA WOMEN OF ACTION TAKING ACTION

"Why don't people wake up?" Kim asked over coffee in Phoenix.[24] Before I could answer, she went flying through all the actions she's taking to do just that, to wake people up. Kim Miller founded the Arizona Women of Action (AWOA), and they're more than an overnight sensation in Arizona.

They're taking back the decision-making about their lives at the local, county, and state levels—where the decisions should be made.

Until recently, Kim Miller was principally a mother concerned about the quality of education her children were receiving. She had the usual text chain going with other moms at the school, kvetching about mask mandates and curricula changes. Next thing she knew, there were fifty women on the chain, and it was consuming them. "We quickly spun out of control," she admitted.

So the women formed AWOA with the goal of turning their frenzied text chain into genuine citizen activism. Doing it without outside funding or allegiances to any organizations. Just doing it to do right.

One day Kim got so angry she made a signboard shouting "Socialism Is Slavery" and forced passersby to engage with her, to talk about it, to think about where things are headed in America.

Another day she learned that the city was going to allow a Black Lives Matter mural to be painted on a downtown street. She looked it up, hopped on a Zoom city council meeting, and asked, "What gives? Why not a pro–law enforcement mural?" Why pretend that the BLM mural was anything more than a political statement from a corrupt organization walking point for the Democratic Party (based on an audit of BLM funds disbursement)? Through her actions, and those of others on the call that day, the mural was nixed.

What most fascinated Kim were the types of people joining AWOA. There were the conservative blondes like herself, of course, but there were even more Hispanic mothers coming, Asians concerned about their children and their businesses, Black fathers who'd been ostracized for questioning the race-baiters' tactics, all looking for a way to begin repairing a clearly broken country, repairing it from the bottom up since there is no other way that'll work.

And together this unlikely group of citizen activists began making that very same local difference.

They've been taking back the decision-making at the local, county, and state levels and learning that the closer your elected officials are to you, the more responsive they are to your needs and desires and the more impact you can have.

As Chris Evans, a Washington state attorney and Scottsdale dad, put it:

> Arizona Women of Action was one of my first follows on Twitter—right away I could see they were a serious group, an organization with substance making the case, day after day, for serious-minded reform not just in education and politics but culture as well. They "get it" that politics is downstream of culture, that no substantive reform of our politics can occur outside a change of hearts and minds, and that no heart is transformed but by the Grace of God, through prayer and humility.[25]

From the Christian hearts of these remarkable women and men across the spectrum of local activism, they are

- writing stories for the local press;

- preparing information packets on candidates and assembly bills;

- attending city council meetings and writing up notes;

- giving out phone numbers of elected officials to contact on specific issues;

- assembling internet safety tool kits and distributing them to new parents;

- hosting movie screenings of the few wholesome movies out there;

- raising funds to empower women in business and politics; and

- speaking at political gatherings across the state.

In a short time, AWOA has grown to more than three thousand members and helped hundreds of citizens become poll captains at election stations—to labor on behalf of honest voting.

They've joined with FreedomWorks[26] to fight the terrible wave of sex trafficking at the border. Programs launched along with Blexit[27] have helped Black individuals freely exit the Democratic plantation's hold.

Other programs are underway with grassroots groups like the West Valley Christian Men, the Arizona Free Enterprise Club,[28] and the Red State Coalition[29] to bring groups of people together in a big, welcoming tent at the local level, where citizens can make a genuine difference. And always prayerfully, as in Kim's closing in a recent communication with members:

> Dear heavenly Father, You sent Moses from tending sheep in the desert to confront Pharaoh and then to deal with a rebellious nation in the wilderness. Jesus was called the Lion of Judah. Like Moses, the Lord can empower us to be bold and courageous to face our wicked culture, to take on the giants in the land as David did.
>
> Lord, help us not just focus on Jesus as the Lamb of God— gentle and obedient—but also on Jesus as the Lion of Judah. We desire to be used by You in the battle to overcome darkness in America. Help us be mighty! In the name of Jesus, we pray.

CHAPTER 4

DRIVING VIOLENCE AND OPPRESSION
FROM OUR COMMUNITIES

To save the young man on her operating table, Dr. Deepika Nehra knew she'd have to slice open his belly to clear the bullet's damage. Cases like this used to be rare at Seattle's Harborview Medical Center, but now they were routine. When the trauma surgeon tried to open the man's belly, a thick knot of scar tissue made it tough. Scar tissue from another gunshot wound. She couldn't work through it fast enough to save him.[1]

Meanwhile Seattle's police chief, Adrian Diaz, was awakened again, his phone set to buzz with each new shooting called in. Even before Diaz arrived at the crime scene, his phone had buzzed with another multiple shooting at a nearby nightclub. An hour later, yet another buzzing. And an hour after that, another. Seattle used to average two homicides a month; now there are close to two shootings a night.[2]

The hardest part is the heartbroken mothers, crying over their sons' fallen corpses, calling out for the police to find the thug killers when just months earlier these same mothers had marched in the streets demanding a defunding of the police.

Shootings, domestic disputes, bar fights, road rage—everyone's stress levels were jacked up, some beyond the breaking point, by COVID and by the government's handling of it. Groups that used to help stem the violence, like Seattle's Community Passageways, were shut down during COVID, when they were needed most.

No more in-person meetings, no more effective mental health counseling, no more steering young people away from crime, no more aiding families in crisis. All these programs were put on hold. How much did that contribute to the 30 percent increase in gun violence nationwide during the pandemic?[3] Quite a bit, obviously. Because these outreach programs are so important to the communities they serve. But they were shut down without a reasonable plan or a thought to the consequences, the hair-trigger environment they were causing.

That didn't have to be.

A locked-up nation had spilled into the streets in the summer of 2020, some of them angry over police shootings, but most just angry at what their lives had been reduced to. They torched buildings and looted them bare, causing billions in damage. They beat Korean bodega owners to death while media cameras captured it all. They gunned down police officers and blocked ambulances from bringing the wounded officers to hospitals, shouting "I hope they die!"[4]

They got themselves arrested knowing they would be instantly released back into the mayhem with bail money from folks encouraged by people such as the future vice president, Kamala Harris.[5]

Reporters for CNN and MSNBC called them "mostly peaceful protests" over and over until liberal audiences believed it must be so.[6] Fox News fed a different narrative about a "form of tyranny," which, while closer to accurate, did not begin to capture the true magnitude of what was happening,[7] for even when the riots settled down, the smash-and-grab mayhem continued unchecked.

Criminals learned that states were no longer prosecuting thieves as felons unless they stole more; the magic number is $950 in California. In San Francisco alone, five theft-plagued Walgreens stores closed forever. Small businesses reported a 54 percent increase in shoplifting. Only one in four people committing a crime faced any consequences at all.[8]

A generation of elected prosecutors had decided that the solution to the nightly riots, killings, and mass theft was to go easy on the rioters, murderers, and thieves because, well, would you believe "police brutality"? Or the "circumstances of their birth"? Or "going light on them won't encourage more"? All these excuses were put up straight-faced by a new generation of elected prosecutors.

Cook County, Illinois, prosecutor Kim Foxx had been elected with 72 percent of the vote in 2016. She was highly popular. Translating her mandate into policy, she opted to bring only *misdemeanor* charges for thefts of less than $1,000 unless the perp had at least ten previous felony convictions (not a typo). Foxx dismissed charges on three in every ten people charged with felonies, including murder, attempted murder, or sex crimes. This at a time when Cook County was witnessing three murders a day on average. A message was sent to criminals: carry on, nothing to see here.

Similarly minded prosecutors in Baltimore, Boston, Milwaukee, most of New York City's boroughs, Philadelphia, San Francisco, Seattle, and St. Louis all decided that, like Foxx, they knew better than "old White men" about ensuring law and order. So they tossed out the rule book on bail, letting hardened felons out on the streets within hours of capture, practically encouraging a full-on crime spree.[9]

It was no surprise then that attacks on police escalated amid calls to defund the police. What had happened to George Floyd in Minneapolis in May 2020 was terrible. It was an aberration, clearly. And no excuse for a nationwide riot with police being ambushed across the nation, also clearly. And yet the number of police killed in ambush or unprovoked murder tripled by 2021 to thirty-two—or about one every eleven days.[10]

This betrayal of our nation's police was far from a spontaneous occurrence. It was, in fact, loosely orchestrated and involved the following:

- Thugs on the street happy enough to go bananas if there was no policing going on

- Decent-minded folks who could be manipulated into thinking a couple of terrible events truly added up to systemic injustice

- Progressive activists who doubled as university students, clean-fingered urbanites, trust-fund babies, tech bros, and others eager to fist-bump with their downtrodden brethren from the safety of their condos and ride-shares

- A well-intentioned Democratic Party that passed deeply flawed Great Society legislation in the 1960s that would only give welfare to families if there was no man in the house. A chain of unintended consequences followed. In this order, the men left behind historically faithful families, the Black culture fell apart, Democratic politicians tried to distance themselves from the mess they'd made, and race grievance hustlers moved in to trade on the guilt that a nation felt for an abject failure of policy

- An elite state far removed from it all in their shiny high-rises and chalets but profiting greatly from the nonstop strife that kept everyone in the country fighting with each other, Left versus Right versus cities versus towns versus Black versus White versus Brown versus gay versus straight versus old versus young in an unending national brawl, leaving little energy to care about the real issues that people used to care about

This kind of loose orchestration of events from the thug on the street up through the ranks of progressive politicians into the elite state suites benefited them all, at America's expense. And the mayhem would surely have continued if good people had not started hitting back. But they did. They started counterpunching.

Seattle's slide into progressive-led mayhem was reversed at the ballot box. New elections brought in a moderate Democrat who vowed to bolster the police and combat gun violence, and a no-nonsense Republican to the city attorney slot.

Around the country, people who had bought the progressive line said *no mas.*

Backpedaling faster than Wile E. Coyote over a cliff, House Speaker Nancy Pelosi loudly insisted that "public safety is our responsibility" and defunding the police is "not the position of the Democratic Party."[11] President Biden shouted to New York cops that "the answer is not to defund the police; it's to give you the tools, the training, the funding to be partners, to be protectors."[12]

The pendulum had swung because good people had had enough. But a lot of damage had been done—especially in the blue states, where the prisons were emptied and the laws were severely weakened.

BE CONSTANTLY SUPPORTING THE POLICE *AND* REFORMING THE POLICE

We were born a nation of laws, and we can only continue as a nation if we hold to those laws. We should not decrease but rather increase the funding and resources going to all our first responders. We are playing catchup, and we must work doubly hard to restore the trust we have in our law enforcement officers—and charge them with earning that trust. This should include certain police reforms as well.

It makes sense, for one, to create a national registry of officers who have been fired for cause. They shouldn't just be shuffled around from precinct to precinct, as they are now (thanks to police unions that serve little positive purpose).

We should also reduce the use of no-knock warrants. Our right to privacy in our homes is a fundamental freedom for us all, and we are a better nation if law enforcement builds cases instead of breaking down doors.

And we should ban the transfer of military equipment to the police. Having armored carriers rumbling down suburban streets, often on the flimsiest of evidence and without a warrant, is simply unacceptable in a free society.

BE SENSIBLE ABOUT GUNS, SAFE IN OUR COMMUNITIES

With the number of firearms in America now topping four hundred million, a thing that began as a simply obvious constitutional right has devolved into a *mishegas* of misplaced emotions and crazy talk. We don't have intelligent conversations about guns. We should, obviously. Here's one attempt.

Every gun owner has an overriding responsibility to make sure guns are used safely, stored securely, and don't end up in the wrong hands. We should be fully educated on the proper use and risks of guns. Gun ownership is a constitutionally protected right, but when the US Constitution was written, most able-bodied men would drill with neighbors in the town square forming a militia to protect each municipality.

We have laws about learning to drive a car safely; we should encourage laws about learning to use a gun safely. Hunters routinely take courses on the safe use of firearms. It's a small step that might result in more responsible gun ownership. It might reduce the number of minors (est. 350) who accidentally shoot themselves or someone else every year in homes (est. 4.6 million) where children live and firearms are believed to be unlocked and loaded. It might also lower the number of guns (as many as 500,000) that are stolen from private gun owners every year.[13]

All of us who believe strongly in our Second Amendment rights have an obligation to promote gun safety and responsible ownership in our communities.

Armed communities are safe communities. This can be seen in the simple fact that mass shooters often choose gun-free zones for targeting. Schools are targeted because these miscreants know bullets won't be coming back in their direction.

With each tragic gun shooting, a nationwide groundswell of very distraught, very well-meaning citizens rises up and pleads for some kind of solution to prevent future shootings. Emotions boil over. There's an urgency to stop the next taking of an innocent life. But if we just leap at solutions, without looking at what makes actual lifesaving sense, we are emotionally knee-jerking around.

We can reduce gun violence and school shootings—if we go about it the right way.

As a gun owner and a father who cares about safe communities, I can fully support firearms training as well as enforcement powers to get those guns out of mentally incompetent people's hands.

There are too many guns in sick people's hands. Citizens agree that we face a mental health crisis, and community by community we must seek to end this blight. Policy must at least try to chase problems. Let it do that. But let's also get opposing sides talking to one another, not past each other.

America fell apart during COVID, but until then the country had actually *not* been seeing more violent crime—despite the pain and impotent fury we all feel when another horrific school shooting happens.

There were 37,155 gun-related deaths in 1990, dropping to 28,663 in 2000, rising to 31,672 in 2010, and returning to 1990 levels at 39,707 in 2019. Gun violence did spike during COVID, with 45,222 deaths in 2020.[14] And the government's handling of COVID bears much of the blame for that spike.

Given that the nation has eighty million more people living here than in 1990, gun-related deaths per capita are decreasing. This sounds cold or like an excuse. But it is far from that. It is meant to guide us in fashioning sensible gun policy.

Sadly, guns are used more for suicides than homicides. So attempts to control guns when an unstable person chooses suicide are sure to be fruitless. And more people are stabbed or bludgeoned to death than are murdered with a rifle. These are hard facts that matter—should matter—especially to those who would shout from their balconies, "Just do something!"

There is, truly, unfortunately, no relationship between gun laws and shootings—especially these terrible mass shootings. "Gun freedom" states such as Idaho, New Hampshire, Oregon, and Vermont have some of the lowest homicide rates. Conversely, strong gun control states such as Illinois and Maryland suffer among the nation's highest homicide rates.[15]

The harsh truth is that more than half of all murders occur in just 2 percent of the nation's 3,142 counties, and then, narrowing in, they occur mostly in neighborhoods blighted by broken families, gangs, and drugs. And narrowing in further, they occur two out of three times when a Black man is shot in a Black neighborhood. Yes, it's a harsh truth.

Just saying this will instantly mobilize the Race Grievance Industrial Complex, boisterously spitting out their prerecorded condemnations when they should be spending that energy to deal with the true root causes of the murders in the neighborhoods they've safely escaped.[16]

Speaking of which, Barack Obama. He was a community organizer in gang-infested Chicago neighborhoods. Violent crime didn't drop a bit from his efforts, but he sure used that platform to seek higher office. This is the persistently sad and basic truth of how neighborhoods have been left behind by those purporting to care about them.

When he became President Barack Obama, he ordered a study on gun violence because he did care—despite his having helped not at all in Chicago. His CDC research team found that "self-defense can be an important crime deterrent."[17] Some would say the researchers put a fine point on the obvious. But those findings sure didn't fit the progressive running-dog narrative that eliminating guns would make the country a thousand times safer.

Having the means of self-defense not only makes the nation safer, it makes the nation more law abiding. Another study found that concealed-carry permit holders are the most law-abiding people.[18] They are often "the good guy with a gun" and get credit for saving others' lives in city after city across America. (We just don't hear about these "good guys" because outrageously overpaid cable news stars only keep their jobs by blowing up every tragedy into Armageddon at our doorsteps.)

How Can We Diffuse Folks Wired to Explode on Contact?

Just about everyone thinks that they are the ones who cannot be brainwashed, who are too smart for that. In fact, the most- and least-intelligent among us tend to be most easily manipulated, according to psychologists. And we have all been "carefully taught" by people we don't even know, people who are experts in inserting words into our heads without us knowing it, words we'll spit out if properly triggered, words meant to explode on contact.

This is not new information. Back in the 1940s, US Senate chaplain Dr. Peter Marshall spoke of this:

> Words are freighted nowadays with life or death, with simple truth or sinister falsehood. On every wavelength, words are whispered or shouted around the world in a propaganda war in which the guns are ideas, and the bullets are words.[19]

All of us are susceptible to this brainwashing, this conditioning, this programming—call it what you like. It happens because we're up against pros. And pro is pro. I've worked with some of the finest wordsmiths and "message men," as we used to call them. Very good at what they do—though the wordsmiths on the Left have always been far superior to those on the Right, owing to an idealistic impulse that bubbles up more artful language in their big brains.

And so we've been carefully taught. A liberal and a conservative will square off on an issue and spray each other with one-liners that have been crafted just for them. They may think they are speaking their mind, and to an extent they are. But most of their thoughts were formed for them by others. We know this is true. Anecdotally, we know it because they are often saying things they did not even believe and would never have said just a few years ago but now hold to be the truth, the only truth.

These "truths" are now packaged up so cleverly in the form of radical zingers, Bronx cheers, clever memes, and pious sound bites so that one side's truths fly past the other side's truths like high-speed trains on two tracks. Nobody on the passing trains has the first clue that unseen wordsmiths worked really hard to make sure both sides are kept maximally inflamed and infuriated and completely oblivious to the truth of the issue.

Oblivious, yet instinctively believing that they are doing the right and honorable thing.

This happens because of our desire to find justification and decency in our actions and cherished beliefs. So when we do challenge someone's cherished beliefs, we are often surprised when our "opponents" retreat into what psychiatrists call defensive avoidance. Rather than deal with the emotional stress of the situation, the opponent instead sidesteps or ignores the unwanted information, even if it is valid and proven so. To avoid dealing with the conflict, they leap to a flawed conclusion as protective armor.

More specifically, if you stand up to some progressive-minded person and say that all the trillions spent on welfare have clearly not helped the poor, you will hear back straightaway that "You hate the poor!" or "You want to let them starve?" or maybe even "Do you eat babies?" since that's how political conversations go these days. At no point in this harangue do they think their position is nuts. They've just been programmed to respond to certain verbal cues. And so they respond, often without knowing whom they were programmed by or why.

Or if you point out any of the shortcomings in our immigration policies, you'll be shouted down for your obvious bigoted, racist, xenophobic, patriarchal, fascist hatreds going back centuries. None of that makes sense, but making sense is not the point.

Or if you believe in the Second Amendment as the Founders did—because a well-armed citizenry is one of the reasons our republic has endured through all the faddish attempts to tear it down—you are immediately painted as a machine-gun fanatic who just wants to see our children gunned down in the schoolyards.

Or make the case for a strong national defense, and you are accused of wanting nuclear war and slaughtering innocent women and children.

We can only get beyond these fast-passing train conversations if we put things in perspective. If we remember that just twenty years ago we weren't like this. Weren't who we are now. Weren't such nonstop extremists. Weren't until we were carefully taught how by unseen people who benefit grandly from our unending national food fight. Now we can see why we must throw all the rotting garbage into the trash. That is why we must dial down the extreming. Dial down calling the other side "depraved idiots!" since they usually just have a different point of view— and there's beauty in that.

There's hope for us all if we can take a breath and think about the "us all" part of "hope for us all." A good reminder is found in the Book of James:

> The tongue is a small thing....But a tiny spark can set a great forest on fire. And...the tongue is a flame of fire. It is a whole world of wickedness....No one can tame the tongue. It is restless and evil, full of deadly poison. Sometimes it praises our Lord and Father, and sometimes it curses those who have been made in the image of God. And so blessing and cursing come pouring out of the same mouth....This is not right!
>
> —JAMES 3:5–10, NLT

WE FOLLOW IN DR. KING'S RIGHTEOUS RESISTANCE

In his famous letter from a Birmingham jail, Martin Luther King Jr. wrote:

> Injustice anywhere is a threat to justice everywhere. We are caught in an inescapable network of mutuality, tied in a single garment of destiny. What affects one directly, affects all indirectly.[20]

Dr. King issued his passionate plea in a time when the American ideal still excluded Black citizens. It was a very different time than now. But his central message of mutuality is every bit as important today in the continuing work of fighting inequality and cruelty that affects us all. Just as with official Democratic Party–sponsored racism back then, so too with elite state cruelty today, Dr. King's approach offers valuable instruction to us all.

Instruction 1: To mount a successful resistance to cruelty and repression, we have to first recognize it and name it. We must get clarity on it, which is easier said than done, because in the most unjust situations, both sides can lose moral clarity.

Exploitive elites can lose their clarity because they are the ones defining the terms of the situation, and invariably those definitions are self-interested. Their view of reality is biased since their power—always a corrupting influence—renders them blind to their ethical shortcomings.

On the other hand, those who feel exploited will often accept what the elites say about them, thinking themselves somehow "less than" for not being rich or famous, or for idly fantasizing about joining the elite ranks themselves someday. This can be very isolating, very weakening.

Dr. King understood this when in December 1955 he took to the pulpit and urged the Black citizens of Montgomery, Alabama, to join a bus boycott to protest the disgrace of segregated seating. He called for moral clarity to rise out of apathy and dejection. With that we have our next instruction.

Instruction 2: Step up and claim moral authority for causes that matter. Say it out loud: "There is righteousness in this cause!" You may be greeted by silence, especially if you're alone when saying it, but your position becomes a strong one. Your protest against cruelties will echo, and an echo cannot be silenced. Others will share your moral position and say the words out loud with you. Remember, one person has to be the first to say it out loud. Why not you?

Instruction 3: Resistance is the harder road, the more difficult task, the longer line. There are no shortcuts or workarounds when confronting the elite state. There will be some casualties. There will be a hundred opportunities to turn back, to give in, or to give up. There will be defeats—more of them than wins—and sometimes the goal will seem to be dipping further over the horizon than coming close. Don't give in and stop. Press on. Like Paul the apostle said, "But as for you, brethren, do not grow weary in doing good" (2 Thess. 3:13).

Dr. King urged resisters to also resist the anguish and misery they felt, and to march on. When facing up against malevolence—which the elite state has become—the act of standing up can be exhausting and only doable when you consider that not standing just lets them tighten the chains of oppression tighter, freedom slipping further.

Instruction 4: From resistance comes an awakening to God's role for us. Each of us must find a way to summon courage when the challenges we face are greatest. Again to Dr. King with his greatest challenge to us, now engraved on his memorial in Washington:

> The ultimate measure of a man is not where he stands in moments of comfort and convenience, but where he stands at times of challenge and controversy.[21]

CANCELING OUT THE RACE-BAITERS WITH LOVE

Like the weeds that invade even a well-tended garden or find the tiniest crack in the concrete to burst through, we will always have the grifters, the charlatans, and the profiteers among us. These "weeds" blight us the most on matters of race—because they can take us to a place of guilt, shame, and remorse over the actions of long-dead people, when we'd all rather go instead to a place of love for our neighbors. Love that's demonstrated the best we can every day.

So we have a race grievance industry that has, paradoxically, swelled in our country as racism has shrunk. They've done it by widening their remits, shifting the goalposts, whatever they can think of to keep the bogeyman of racism alive. It's a matter of survival for them. If they don't keep stepping on the few racist shards that do exist in society, and screaming bloody murder every time they do, well, they'll have to go out and find real jobs.

So today we have folks like Elie Mystal, a Black lawyer born in Haiti and a lifelong Mets fan, all good. He's also a progressive thought leader who writes for *The Nation*, which is a big-circulation magazine. Asked whether the US Constitution should be a "living document" or a "sacred document," he replied:

> The Constitution is kind of trash....It was written by slavers and colonists and white people who were willing to make deals with slavers and colonists. They didn't ask anybody that looked like me what they thought about the Constitution.[22]

With this kind of talk, what is Mystal hoping to accomplish? To elevate public debate as the progressive thought leader he is? To advance social justice for a new generation of Americans? To inspire young Blacks looking to work in the legal profession?

How do his words accomplish anything productive—for folks of any race?

They do not, of course. For his aim is *not* to elevate, advance, or inspire. His aim is to get his face on TV as the face of enlightened progressivism. Oh, and to promote his books.

On another occasion, Mystal went on MSNBC to talk about Senator Josh Hawley's questioning of Supreme Court nominee Ketanji Brown Jackson:

> What Josh Hawley is doing…is he's trying to get her killed. He is trying to get violence done against a Supreme Court nominee.[23]

This from the man who also said Justice Brett Kavanaugh was "credibly accused of trying to rape somebody."[24] With that deceit, I wonder, was Mystal trying to get Kavanaugh killed? In fact, just months later a deranged man guided by progressive coaching did try to kill Kavanaugh. Mystal had no comment.

Nonetheless, I would like to ask Mystal or any of his progressive friends a question about systemic racism: Why are Blacks *over*represented on the athletic fields and *under*represented at high school graduations? That can't be systemic racism at work. So what is it? Let's talk about it, Mystal. Let's have an honest conversation that can better everyone's lives!

Let's talk about the oppressive agenda of the elite state that progressives once naturally lambasted (before being bought off by that same elite state). Let's talk about working together to bring God's love into broken Black communities. Let's follow Paul as he wrote in Romans 8:31 of the oppression delivered by the ruling elites of his time: "What, then, are we to say about these things? If God is for us, who is against us?" (CSB). Let that guide us now.

CHAPTER 5

THE HIGHER THE BORDER WALLS, THE MORE CIVIL AMERICA BECOMES

ELITE-STATE MASTERS FEEL the pain of border policies the deepest when one of their illegal maids gets caught stealing meal leftovers to take home to hungry children. Elites know little of the devastation open-border policies inflict on border communities. Or the steps citizens' groups in these border states must take on their own, with little help from Democratic administrations, to lift their communities above the raging floodwaters of illegal immigrant problems.

One such group is the North Valley Constitutional Republicans. They meet twice a month at Amped Coffee in Anthem, Arizona, just north of Phoenix. Easily half the attendees at a recent meeting were older and retired, as expected. But the other half included people of all kinds— young liberals fed up with their party's sellout on the border, crusty old conservatives who can still remember when Republicans championed open borders and Democrats fought them, Hispanics angry at policy changes that actively tear immigrant families apart (the Great Society redux), and a smattering of people who'd been lured by flyers they saw posted around town during the lockdowns: "GET YOUR BUTT OFF THE COUCH. COME MEET SOME FELLOW HUMANS!"

At their first get-together, you could see how eager people were to get back out again, to actually talk with fellow humans. They talked about how they could impact policy from the local level on up. How it begins with education—that is, learning what got us into this mess.

Not so long ago, politicians of both parties got it. They knew the basics of nationhood. They knew that no country has ever existed for long without a strong border. Whether that border is constructed of stone-block walls and moats filled with snakes or lined with gun-toting border agents backed by militias of concerned citizens, borders have always mattered. (Except in countries no longer on Rand McNally's radar.)

Politicians knew how unchecked immigration could create massive

61

disasters by flattening wages for all workers, straining government services and the tax base, driving up criminal violence, fragmenting people into old warring tribal allegiances, fueling narrow-minded identity politics, intensifying racial divisions, and importing poverty to spread around.

This knowledge goes back before the founding of America. Even the Bible admonishes respect for borders. (Note the border descriptions in Deuteronomy 1–2.)[1]

Our ever-prescient Founders feared that if immigration were ever left unchecked, America might break into independent nation-states not unlike the Europe they had left behind with its constant internal civil, religious, and ethnic discord driving interest in a hundred separatist movements at any one time (kind of like we see in the United States now).

So the Founders gave us "checks and balances" meant to coax all newcomers to the country into a common Americanism. Immigrants would adopt English as their language and swear an oath of citizenship. For a record-setting two-hundred-plus years it worked because every adult in the room knew this was how our republic could continue to thrive.

As recently as 2006, a bipartisan majority of Congress gave us the Secure Fence Act—directing Homeland Security to take "operational control" over the borders to "prevent unlawful entry" with "at least two layers of reinforced fencing, the installation of additional physical barriers, roads, lighting, cameras, and sensors."[2]

That Act added thousands of border patrol personnel, advanced monitoring technologies, and 650 miles of new walls between 2006 and 2011. Everyone in the government supported it, because it was the right thing to do. Then-senator Barack Obama said in 2005:

> We simply cannot allow people to pour into the United States undetected, undocumented, unchecked, and circumventing the line of people who are waiting patiently, diligently, and lawfully to become immigrants in this country.[3]

Then senator Joe Biden, sounding a lot like a future president he would beat out of a second term, said in 2006:

> Let me tell you something, folks. People are driving across that border with tons, tons—hear me, tons—of everything for

byproducts from methamphetamine to cocaine to heroin, and it's all coming up through corrupt Mexico.[4]

A few years later, Senator Chuck Schumer chimed in:

> Illegal immigration is wrong, plain and simple....People who enter the United States without our permission are illegal aliens and illegal aliens should not be treated the same as people who enter the US legally.[5]

A decade later, all these Democratic leaders were slamming President Trump for carrying out the very policies they had once so stridently supported. Calling the president a racist, immoral, anti-human, and all the regular invectives for his trying to enforce immigration law.

So what happened?

And while we're at it, what happened to the voices of principled environmentalists who had complained since the 1960s that mindless population growth was befouling the land and overstretching our limited resources?

Where were the principled conservatives trying to protect what Russell Kirk called the "permanent things" in our culture, the folks who stood strong against chaos at the border and illegal immigration for decades?

Simply put, the elite state needed a source of cheap imported labor and none of the bother of union organizers. And progressive politicians needed big influxes of poor people to create a politically useful new voting bloc that might just turn a radical Left fringe ideology into the governing ideology of the country.

So the elite state and once-marginalized progressive ideologues found common cause in open borders and set about preaching for a humanitarian solution to the world's displaced poor. They really stepped it up. Threw big tony fund-raisers—such as 10Ks in Central Park—because nothing says concern like keeping fit.

They knew or cared little of immigration's darker side playing out in the back alleys, arroyos, and river basins where the "stuck betweens" huddle and scratch out a living, having given all their money to smugglers to cross the border, now resigned to taking state handouts if they dare even go down to the office to apply.

Both political parties were given roles to play to ensure that there would be zero practical enforcement of border laws going forward.

Republicans were easiest to turn, Democrats not far behind—all beholden to elite-state political contributions now. In return for the politicians not doing any, say, political work in Washington, big business would be handed platters full of more eager workers than they could possibly use, giving them leverage to suppress the wages of those they did hire.

Democratic political machines would have millions of newcomers to sign on and embrace the Left's culture of victimization, thus supporting expansions of programs to fight victimization.

Conveyor belts of attorneys out of middling law schools could go to work clogging the courts with pleadings and writs of poppycock on behalf of their fearful clients. To lend credibility to this "humanist" fight for immigration, radical racist groups like La Raza—which literally means "the race"—could be deeply funded to agitate on the streets with clever chants such as "the borders crossed us, we didn't cross the borders," as if the Spanish genocide of three centuries ago is worth embracing or the nineteenth-century presence of a few thousand Mexican castaways in a vast unpopulated region constituted sovereignty.

Add it up, and one in every seven people living in our country was not born here. Pew Research put the number of *illegal* immigrants at 10.5 million by 2017.[6] Others put it higher. Nobody knows.

Some supporters of open borders and accommodating immigration rules are no doubt animated by big hearts and open minds. They know that many arrive at our southern border seeking asylum from terrible atrocities in their home countries. These altruists seem unaware, or unconcerned, that there were three or four other countries over *thousands* of miles that the asylum-seekers had to travel through before arriving at our border patrol. So it's a rather selective asylum they seek, and relevant in the making of proper border policy.

Prior to the Trump presidency, politicians had torn down the Secure Fence Act with three policy agreements often summed up as "catch and release":

1. **Flores Settlement Agreement (1997),** which later came to mean that no immigrant families or unaccompanied minors could be detained more than twenty days (creating mass confusion at border stations that were seeing thousands crossing every night)

2. **Trafficking Victims Protection Reauthorization Act (2008),** which instructed border agents to place unaccompanied minors with the Department of Health and Human Services (so families began separating before attempting to cross—an obviously fraught situation)

3. **Deferred Action for Childhood Arrivals (2012),** again telling traffickers they could smuggle in children alone (creating fresh images of children lost and alone—ignored by the media until Donald Trump was elected, then the images were trotted out daily)

Combined, these statutes were a boon to smuggling organizations. They switched the focus from mostly single adult males to families seeking a better life.

In response, President Trump negotiated an agreement with Mexico that came to be known as the Remain in Mexico Program. Under this program, people illegally entering with a minor could no longer stay simply by requesting asylum. This ended "catch and release," and by the end of Trump's term, customs officials reported a 75 percent reduction in families attempting to enter illegally—proving that policy matters.

PRESIDENT BIDEN PROVES HE'S HIS OWN MAN (AS SCRIPTED FOR HIM)

Soon after taking office, President Biden dispatched Secretary of State Antony Blinken to go before the cameras and lay out "the president's vision" to address the "root causes" of the migrations. And what were those causes? One was poverty back home—and few would disagree. Another was climate change—and few could keep from laughing out loud at that absurd sop to a nutcase special interest group.

When the laughing died down and the new immigration policies were Biden's to own, we saw an immediate 900 percent leap in illegal immigration—more than 170,000 illegal immigrants apprehended every month at the border. Immigration and Customs Enforcement (ICE) effectively shut down.[7] It was the worst border disaster in US history.

It's not like the incoming Biden team hadn't been fully briefed. Or warned about the consequences of rewriting policy. Or shown how undermanned border patrol stations were. Or how the social workers at the border didn't have enough resources to detain all the people flowing over. Or how the smuggling organizations would surely exploit a return to catch-and-release.

They were told all that. But it mattered not, because the elite state had finally "run that troublemaker Trump out of town and their man Biden was up for business as usual." You had to feel a little sorry for the administration's public-facing spokespersons. They too could see the mess they'd made and the need for a gross lot of lipsticks for that pig. To watch Biden's people stretching for explanations was like watching *Saturday Night Live*.

First they tried outright denial, insisting that "the border is closed." But the nightly news shots of thousands pouring over forced a different response—blame shifting. It was Donald Trump's fault, they said. Somehow he had personally "torn down" the entire system that had worked so well. The Trump-haters could be expected to buy that. Next came make-believe, where they attributed the surge in migrants to seasonal trends. "Happens every year" in the winter months, Biden insisted. Either he was poorly briefed or riffing, since there had been about 170,000 illegal border crossings every month in 2021—many of them unaccompanied minors, because the smugglers were just working the new policies. Lastly, the Biden administration went for the tried-and-true cover-up. As secretly as they could, they began marching the illegals onto planes and flying them to cities all across America, dumping them there.[8]

This might have remained a half-joke if they weren't also dumping huge numbers of drug and sex traffickers all over America.

In 2021, the border patrol captured 8,000 criminal aliens—including 46 murderers, 393 sex offenders, and 880 assailants. Included were members of MS-13—one of the most violent gangs in Central America—and

Yemeni nationals in the US terrorist database. Also netted were 600,000 pounds of drugs, including 6,000 pounds of fentanyl that was headed for America's streets. And this is what they did catch, not what they actually helped distribute nationally through their relocation programs.

Plus, they were catching less than expected because Biden yanked nearly half the agents off the front lines and tasked them with humanitarian duties.[9] You know, helping the illegals to feel better about themselves before queuing them up for free-food vouchers, free medical insurance, and all the other benefits of full citizenship.

Either unwittingly or with malice of forethought, Biden had created an express lane for drug smugglers, sex traffickers, and potential terrorists. That's just what happened. My heart cries for the young boys and girls who ended up in sex slavery when they came to America in search of freedom and a better life.

Back in the 1970s, about 50 percent of the border crossings were handled by paid smugglers. Homeland Security puts that figure at 95 percent now.[10] These smugglers charge up to $15,000 per person for the voyage north.[11] Under the new rules, the cartels have made massive profits, which they use to finance other illegal activities. Much of the fentanyl entering the country comes in with migrants who are forced to carry it (serving as mules, as they're called) to pay for their trip.

Americans were told that the COVID health emergency meant we couldn't open our businesses or attend church. Yet at the same time, thousands poured across the southern border every day, testing positive for COVID and being driven to nice hotels and put up there at taxpayers' expense.

However fortunate or fraught the initial crossing into the country, life for illegals is obviously going to be tough. A lot of good people are turned bad, and bad are turned worse. So it's no surprise that 64 percent of all arrests by federal authorities are of noncitizens, even though they comprise about 7 percent of the population.[12]

US Customs keeps count of the crimes committed by noncitizens. The short version of the story is this: President Trump made it clear the border was closed, so there were fewer crossings and arrests. President Biden made it clear the border was open again, so crossings and arrests shot up again:

US BORDER PATROL CRIMINAL NONCITIZEN ARRESTS

FY16	FY17	FY18	FY19	FY20	FY21
12,842	8,531	6,698	4,269	2,438	10,763

These are arrests for assault and battery, domestic violence, burglary, robbery, larceny, theft, fraud, DUIs, homicide, manslaughter, drug possession, trafficking, illegal entry, illegal weapons possession, trafficking, sexual offenses—the gamut.

When you look at the numbers more closely, you find that homicides committed by noncitizens were fifteen times higher in President Biden's first year (sixty total) than President Trump's four-year average (four).[13] Yes, policy makes a difference.

I had a wonderful friend who was killed by an illegal alien in a local store parking lot in Kingman, Arizona, because she refused to give over her purse. She was a Christian lady who had spent countless hours volunteering to help others. She is only one of many victims of this sad policy vacuum and the chaos that has ensued.

ALLOW IN THE BEST AND BRIGHTEST

The first principles of immigration policy should be to benefit our American economic well-being. Foreigners with strong minds or strong backs should be welcomed in the numbers that our intake systems can handle.

For instance, young foreigners who graduate from American universities should have a path to citizenship. Those who serve in the military or graduate from our colleges have skills to contribute to our economy, and they should be welcomed on a swift path to citizenship. We benefit from that.

What about migrants seeking work in the fields? About half of US farmworkers are here illegally, and American agriculture could not function without them or hold prices as low as they do.[14] The problem, though, is not with the farmworkers but with a dysfunctional immigration bureaucracy that moves at a glacial pace to process and approve work permits. Here's a solution:

Every bureaucrat should go to work picking strawberries for a year, and then come back to processing papers. If they haven't improved on their performance, back into the fields. In all seriousness, our nation needs a higher fence and a usable door. Combining both honors and extends our immigrant nation's traditions.

HOW CAN WE HELP TO SECURE THE BORDER INTELLIGENTLY?

There's a political group on Substack calling themselves the YoungConservatives and confronting establishment Republicans with a fresh millennial way of thinking. On immigration, they take a strident stance, calling for a complete moratorium on "third world" immigrants, including refugees seeking asylum. The basis of their thinking: if we are honest about addressing the environmental threats that put pressure on our resources, that create more development, then we have to stop growing the nation. As they say in their manifesto:

> We support a 100-year moratorium on all third world immi-
> gration and refugees....We recognize that both legal and illegal
> immigration are a problem and are tired of the Cheap Labor
> Lobby (people like Soros, Singer, Zuckerberg, Kochs, et al) using
> third-world legal immigration to drive down wages. We also
> oppose the treasonous and corrupt Refugee Resettlement Racket
> which profits (off taxpayers) by facilitating the third-world ref-
> ugee invasion of the West. We have zero tolerance for boomer
> talking points like "I'm against illegal immigration but support
> legal immigration" or "we're a nation of immigrants." We oppose
> all amnesties, chain migration, visa lotteries, etc. We want a
> complete and total moratorium on all third-world immigration
> and refugees.[15]

This is some hard-line thinking, oh yeah. And for it, these YoungConservatives have had shovelfuls of leftist vitriol hurled at them. But they're arguing a position, and it's great to see honesty and intelligence shining upward in politics. Hopefully they continue organizing at the community level and take their case to elected officials on up the ladder.

In my own view, immigration policy requires at least some basic reforms to restore safety for Americans living near the border, and fair treatment of the immigrants themselves. At the very least

- return to the Trump-era policies that better secured our southern border;

- base qualification for immigration on merit, not on numbers; and

- simplify and accelerate visa/green card reviews for skilled applicants, such as doctors, nurses, and computer programmers in short supply.

With our borders secured, we can look to the problems in the heartland.

WIPING OUT THE AMERICAN FARMER COSTS US DEARLY

When it comes to hard work, few know it better than the American farmer. Jim and Barb Kalbach started out in cattle and hogs, corn and oats a half century ago on the Iowa plain. Like generations before them, the Kalbachs raised their children on the values of hard work, thrift, and enterprise and figured their children would carry on. Same as with the other family farmers in local communities built up to support one another in business, to care for each other as neighbors.

But today the Kalbachs are the last surviving family farm in the region, and they don't expect it to pass to the next generation. Neighboring farmhouses stand empty, their roofs falling in. Others have been bulldozed after the owners had no choice but to sell to the big operations.[16] It's a story we've all heard a hundred sad times echoing across the central plains, but it's a much bigger story than most realize.

When Big Agriculture moved into the heartland, they came with a message: they were bringing an abundance of new farming opportunities as well as lower prices at the store—so most everyone was a winner. That was the message. The truth was, farmers were being picked off by waves of collapsing commodity prices, while prices in the store kept rising even faster, and the old farmhouses became computer sheds dispatching robotic wizards to bring the harvest in perfectly, and the rural communities were hollowed out in a tremendous transfer of wealth to offshore islands, where the elite state likes to vacation.

Having debased the communities in which they operate, these massive farming outfits had only one way to keep growing: by debasing our food supply. Soon we can expect the biggest export from America's megafarms to be deadly pathogens not so different from the viruses we saw escaping China's wet markets. How could we not? These farms are run by computers. Livestock is jammed into the unhealthiest confines. Produce is encased in pesticides. Regulators have their feet up in plush Washington offices. The FBI is cued up to leap on any malcontent who seeks to gum up this state of affairs.

We see early signs of a health crisis in the food supplies that have been leached of nutrients. We see it in the dust storms across the prairies from land that's been overworked. We see how the elite state has bought up most of the land, maximized acre yield, tossed stewardship of the land into the dust storms in their wake. Surely more health problems are coming our way.

Down in Arizona the five Cs—copper, cattle, cotton, citrus, and climate—turned a deserted state into a thriving modern economy, and still with 95 percent family farms. There are stresses of water and worker shortages, volatile commodity markets, big new supply chain disruptions, and one natural calamity after another, as is nature's way. But that's not stopping farmers in the state with the motto *Ditat Deus* ("God enriches"). No, the problem is a skyrocketing population with developers paving over the land to make way for houses. Big Maricopa County has lost most of its family farms.[17]

Those still hanging on are once again facing an inheritance tax threat from Washington that will make it difficult to keep the farm in the family.

Another concern is the Section 1031 exchange, which allows farmers to invest their earnings back into their land without getting walloped by a big capital gains tax bill.

These are concerns that deserve the support of us all—out on the farmlands and in cities—because family farmers live on, however diminished, and must be able to continue stewarding the land and ensuring safe, healthy food for us all.

As a nation we must treasure the small family farms that still provide 21 percent of the food we consume.[18] That means giving them a choice beyond going big or going broke. That choice is going profitably. That's the kind of policy we need at the national level, and it begins by pushing our leaders at the local levels. Yes, as with so much that we face, it's a long way from the town square to Washington. But it is the only way we can go.

Why Let China Buy Up Our Farms and Homes?

America is one of several Western countries that allows foreign-owned companies to buy up property. And they've bought up Ohio by size—foreign agencies purchased acreage valued at $54.4 billion in 2021, and foreign persons and entities held an interest in 35.2 million acres of US agricultural land in 2019, a total area about the size of New York state.[19] Most of it is forest land, but there's plenty of crop and grazing land as well. And nobody in the state or federal government seems to care if we sell off the land, even if it is going to the Chinese.[20]

Well, a few care. Legislators in the 117th Congress sought to (a) restrict foreign ownership of US agricultural land and (b) stop paying farming subsidies to foreign companies.[21] This second bit mattered, since the world's largest meat-processing company (Brazil's JBS, with revenues of $17.7 billion) received millions in bailouts from the US government in 2018, even though the prices for their meat has increased.[22] As for actions taken by Congress on that legislation to rein in foreigners, not much has happened.

"This is about food security for [foreign investors]; it needs to be about food security for us," says Jake Davis of Family Farm Action. His group is working in Missouri, Ohio, and Oklahoma to convince lawmakers to ban foreign ownership of US farmland.

Another group in the fight is the Missouri Farm Bureau led by Blake Hurst, who makes the valuable point, "U.S. ownership provides better stewardship of the land, and it's better for rural communities."[23]

Progress is being made to bar foreign ownership of farmland in Hawaii, Iowa, Minnesota, Mississippi, North Dakota, and Oklahoma—but much more is needed.

Away from the farms, in the cities of California, one in every four homes is being purchased in an all-cash transaction. Many are being sold to foreign buyers, most from China.[24] Cash is used in the initial purchase, and when the property is resold, the proceeds become legal gains. Complex shell companies, offshore bank accounts, and the usual payoffs are required to close the deal. By making no effort to control this illicit flow of funds, America has overtaken Switzerland as the world's top money-laundering destination, according to the Tax Justice Network.[25]

Is that the Olympic event in which America should really want to overtake Switzerland? Money laundering? Of course not. Our focus should be on promoting the largest stock of affordable housing for as many citizens as possible and upholding the enduring American dream of home ownership as best we can. Driving foreign money out of the equation is a minimal contribution to that dream.

CHAPTER 6

MEET THE ENFORCEMENT AGENT
FOR THE ELITE STATE

IT STARTED GETTING ugly at the Drury Inn in Dublin, Ohio. Some rough-looking guys had been dropping in all summer in 2020 to drink, smoke dope, and rant about COVID lockdowns—both at the Drury Inn and in other similarly seedy locations across the country. Some were far from model citizens, some undercover FBI secretly recording it all. Recording guys like Barry Croft saying, "Might kill a cop...not being hypothetical...have a team standing by to grab a [expletive] governor."[1] Soon the FBI swooped in and accused thirteen men of plotting to kidnap Michigan governor Gretchen Whitmer and deploy explosives to distract any police pursuers.

When the trial date finally came, it became clear the FBI had been so desperate to prove White supremacy was running rampant that they had fabricated it.

Of course, the FBI does need to take potential terrorist threats seriously. And there are good agents at the bureau doing just that. But in the Governor Whitmer case, we saw just how vicious some people in our government have become, and what they'll do to people they don't happen to like.

Defense attorneys for the case played hundreds of hours of secret recordings making it clear that Barry Croft was "absolutely bonkers out-of-your-mind stoned" much of the time. He blathered on, for instance, about attaching a kite to Governor Whitmer and flying her across Lake Michigan.[2]

Crazy talk, as long as there was no plan of action to go along with it. There wasn't, and the FBI knew it full well. One of their informants even testified to it. Dan Chappel, whom the FBI paid $50,000 to monitor the group's activities, had grown frustrated over the months with the group's lack of direction. To keep his FBI handlers happy, Chappel told them he'd take command and make things happen. In court, defense counsel asked again and again if Chappel stood behind his testimony that "these guys don't have a plan...you said they're wasting your time." Chappel agreed that's what he said.[3]

And this was before the FBI's case fully imploded.

Next the court learned that the FBI's star informant, Steve Robeson, had turned double agent. That he had gone so far as to help these stoners flesh out their plan, when he was supposed to be only monitoring. So the government withdrew Robeson from the witness list.[4]

Another FBI informant had been planted to provide information nobody in the group had: explosives-making information. Even the proudly liberal investigative reporters from BuzzFeed couldn't withhold their scorn:

> Working in secret, they did more than just passively observe and report on the actions of the suspects. Instead, they had a hand in nearly every aspect of the alleged plot, starting with its inception. The extent of their involvement raises questions as to whether there would have even been a conspiracy without them.[5]

But the FBI was not done stinking. Lead agent Richard Trask had to be booted from the case after he was fired for assaulting his wife in a drunken rage following a swingers party at a local hotel. Other agents had to be scrubbed from the witness list for running illegal side hustles and committing perjury in a separate case. (It must have been pretty damning perjury since, as we learned from former FBI director James Comey, perjury is one thing the FBI is good at.)

Sensing that their deteriorating case could become a damaging public spectacle, the Justice Department went dirtier. They singled out one of the more vulnerable defendants, Kaleb Franks, and made him an offer before he could see what the jurors would later see: texts and recordings showing the FBI's entrapment scheme. The pressure from the Department of Justice involved the following:

- They would choose to charge him with planning to make and sell a "ghost gun" to a convicted felon.

- They would publicly discredit him for a home invasion conviction many years earlier.

- They would force a psychiatric evaluation on him, becoming part of his record.

- All this, unless he confessed to a crime that he knew and the FBI knew was very different from the facts of the case.

Within days Franks had buckled, as most people would, and pleaded guilty to conspiracy to kidnap.[6] Without this strong-arming of Franks and the false confession it yielded, the government would have lost their entire case. As it turned out, two defendants were found not guilty; the jury deadlocked on two others (they were scheduled for a retrial in August 2022).

Defense lawyers summed it up:

> The key to the government's plan was to turn general discontent with Gov. Whitmer's COVID-19 restrictions into a crime that could be prosecuted. The government picked what it knew would be a sensational charge: conspiracy to kidnap the governor. When the government was faced with evidence showing that the defendants had no interest in a kidnapping plot, it refused to accept failure and continued to push its plan.[7]

After such a humiliating public spanking for their handling of the Whitmer kidnapping case, you'd think the FBI and Justice Department would try to mend their ways. But instead, they doubled down on their vendetta against any group they could shoehorn into their right-wing terrorist category. They threw their entrapment nets even wider.

In March 2021, the FBI and Homeland Security issued a joint memo warning that a militia group (believed to be QAnon, threats mostly to themselves) were planning a second Capitol rally. Or in the words of the memo, "to take control of the US Capitol and remove democratic lawmakers on or about the 4th of March." Turned out there was little more than a flurry of joggers on the Mall on or about March 4.[8]

A month later, in his first address to Congress, President Biden uttered some of the most divisive, inaccurate, and nakedly partisan words ever from a US president: "The most lethal terrorist threat to the homeland today is from white supremacist terrorism."[9]

But nonetheless, Homeland Security went to work carrying out the president's implied threats. They warned that in June 2021 a commemoration of the terrible Tulsa Race Massacre was going to be a target of some horrific extremist action. Nothing happened at the event from either right- or left-wing radicals. We don't know if a plot was, in fact, thwarted or if a fantasy narrative was simply kept alive for rank political purposes.

April 2022 found Homeland Security secretary Alejandro Mayorkas before the cameras, once again insisting that White supremacists were the "most prominent threat" facing our country. Since nothing was happening in the news, there was speculation as to why he made such a divisive pronouncement:

1. Was it because it would soon leak to the public that the FBI's entrapment schemes we've talked about here were, in fact, manufactured in order to associate all Republicans with White supremacists ahead of the 2024 election?

2. Or was it because the nightly news would soon start filling with images of hundreds of thousands of migrants surging over the southern border in a chaotic, mad, and violent humanitarian crisis that even Vermont liberals couldn't stomach, and a diversion was needed, stat?

It did appear that Mayorkas was out in front of the cameras running damage control—more and more a staple of his days on the job under this administration.

So how does the FBI manage to identify a potential terrorist threat in every backyard gathering of nutjob stoners?

It's done now through an intelligence-gathering network that reaches into nearly every home and conversation being had. (We'll go deeper on this later.)

Aiding the FBI in identifying potential terrorists are organizations like the Anti-Defamation League. Known as the ADL, they got their start more than one hundred years ago defending American Jews from the bigotry and hate crimes they faced back then. It was noble work—truly—and today the ADL insists on their website that they call out "extremist threats from across the ideological spectrum."

Why, then, are they publishing lists of primarily radical-right terrorists, not radical-left? Surely there must be a few radical-left terrorists running loose and the ADL would want to warn about them, right? Apparently not. Scour their website and you'll find a tally of some 150 radical-right terrorist acts, near acts, conspiracies, and plots uncovered in the twenty-five years leading up to 2017.[10]

That's all you'll find, because the ADL has chosen their poison. They depend on funding coming from their elite state benefactors; it's how they keep their jobs. So they dutifully marshal some impressive Jewish talent to identify suspects for the FBI to go out and harass—under the sanctioning cover of the oh-so-venerable ADL.

And the FBI has the cover it needs to go after the people the elite state fears most. As FBI director Christopher Wray testified in February 2020 before the House Judiciary Committee:

> [We've] elevated to the top-level priority racially motivated violent extremism so it's on the same footing in terms of our national threat banding as (the Islamic State) and homegrown violent extremism.[11]

A documentary filmmaker took up the banner next, extending the narrative to a generation of more-video-literate citizens with the cleverly inclusive title *The Informant: Fear and Faith in the Heartland.*[12]

So even before watching the film, the viewer was being primed to equate White nationalism with the Christian faith, an obvious absurdity since Christianity teaches that we are all of "one blood" regardless of skin color. But the filmmakers, backed by ABC News and given a huge budget to work with, wanted to blacken and besmirch as broadly and deeply as they could, apparently.

This story shared plenty of similarities with the Whitmer kidnapping plot. Once again the FBI infiltrated a group and offered to buy explosives for them. Only in this case it was clear these guys meant the local Somali community terrible harm. They meant to follow through. The FBI had done its job properly this time.

Which is why the elite state wanted the film out there—telling the world that the FBI was not the cesspool of corruption it appeared to be, and smearing Christians as well. In their eyes, a twofer.

A three-fer, actually, for the film also drew a straight line between right-wing extremists and President Trump and the January 6 demonstrations. A clear effort to give all conservatives a guilt complex by association. At every hold-your-breath turn in the chilling storyline, you felt haunted by the subtext: America is not safe as long as these dangerous extremist-Trump-voting-conservative-ideologues are on the loose all around us.

Knowing it was a waste of time but wanting to give ABC News the benefit of the doubt, I went in search of film specials they've done on radical-left terrorism. A Google search came up with—none. Then, knowing that Google hides stories that their algorithm decides I shouldn't see, I went over to DuckDuckGo to check their search listings.

A Google search of "ABC News" plus "radical-left extremism" returned only stories on radical-right terrorism. A DuckDuckGo search returned stories mostly from thirty years ago, the last time the award-winning journalists at ABC News were able to uncover any radical-left terrorist activities, apparently.

Looking wider, I found a report on domestic terrorism from the Center for Strategic and International Studies—a fair-minded think tank in Washington. In their careful parsing of the data, they found that 66 percent of all terrorist plots in 2019 and more than 90 percent in the first four months of 2020 were radical-right plots.[13] Two years later they updated their report and found the following.

> Of the 38 white supremacist and other like-minded terrorist attacks and plots in 2021, 16 used firearms, 9 involved explosives and incendiaries, 4 were melee attacks using weapons such as knives or bludgeoning weapons, and 2 were vehicular attacks.
>
> Of the 31 anarchist, antifascist, and like-minded terrorist attacks and plots in 2021, 19 were melee attacks using weapons

such as knives or bludgeoning objects, 3 primarily used explosives or incendiaries, 2 used firearms, and 1 was a vehicular attack.[14]

So about 55 percent radical-right, 45 percent radical-left. With margins of error and testing biases, you could probably conclude from this that the terrorist threat from right-wing nuts is a little higher than from left-wing nuts. But that's not a message from which the elite state benefits. It won't transport leftist audiences away from transference thinking that every conservative is "an insane, depraved, knuckle-dragging dimwit; I knew it!" That's a leftist mindset that needs to be supported, along with other incentives to seal the deal, lest leftists go back to wondering (like they used to) why the elite state's wealth has catapulted to obscene levels at their (and everyone else's) expense.

As well, the elite state doesn't want liberals to face the music for stoking the largest terrorist onslaught in American history following the 2020 murder of George Floyd.

That season of terror began righteously as citizens poured into the streets over a terrible injustice. As many as twenty-six million people made their outrage heard in more than two thousand cities and towns—the largest protest in US history on the issue of racial injustice. Then, with left-wing politicians through their media mouthpieces egging them on, the protests escalated into riots, billions of dollars of looted and burned stores, twenty-five innocents killed, a police station burned down, city blocks abandoned to thugs, shop owners beaten and their life's work destroyed.

So intense was this national wave of terror that approximately ninety-six thousand National Guard, State Guard, 82nd Airborne, and 3rd Infantry Regiment service members were activated in the largest military operation *ever* on domestic soil. But when arrests were made, many of the terrorists were quickly released on bail provided by left-wing political groups. As for after-action measures, there were none.

This makes clear how corrupt America has become. Pulling us back from the brink is not going to be easy. It's going to require folks of all political leanings uniting in defense of our nation's highest enduring principles of individual liberty and justice for all.

Principles that brought our nation into the twenty-first century.

Principles that will always need bettering but cannot be lost.

Principles that guide our actions in our own communities, for that is where we must begin. That is how goodness radiates up from our familiar neighborhoods to the faraway marbled halls. How we begin at the lowest levels to restore the highest ideals for all to benefit.

Whenever we see these principles becoming effective policy in one community, we want to see it happen for others. Many of the best organizations working in the inner city are Christian ministries. From the drug rehab of Teen Challenge to the food programs of rescue missions and churches, Christians are providing the volunteers and help that people need.

For instance, the Dream Center in Los Angeles has a program to combat human trafficking. They run an emergency center for women who are escaping human trafficking.

> Once our program staff identify women who are victims fleeing from human trafficking, the individuals are placed in a secure and private location where they receive all their basic needs. This includes three meals a day, a bed to sleep in, clothing, and more. Furthermore, each survivor meets with our Women's Emergency Shelter Director to connect them with additional local resources.[15]

A gun violence abatement program in Poughkeepsie is called SNUG Street Outreach, and it takes mental health therapy out of the doctor's office and into the streets. Says Erika Mendelsohn of SNUG (*GUNS* spelled backwards): "There's so much trauma in these communities, and so much healing that needs to be done. This is a first step toward addressing it."[16]

A similar program is being run in New Jersey, where the Democratic governor awarded $8.2 million in state grants to twenty-five nonprofit groups who take their activism right to the streets, trying to intervene in problem situations before they escalate into deadly violence.[17]

How different these kinds of programs are from those FBI smackdowns we just looked at. The FBI has lost so much trust it cannot be made whole again without a top-to-bottom overhaul of the entire organization. Maybe it should even be abolished.

We can press our elected leaders to undertake such a wholesale reorganization, though surely the current lot will do nothing.

What can happen is a steady punching up above our weight in our communities, punching up on principles that can carry all the way to 935 Pennsylvania Avenue NW, the FBI's headquarters. It's a long route from our neighborhoods to there. But as on the road to Damascus, it is the only way to change a nation.

More immediately, you may be wondering: What else can be done tangibly in our communities to correct the FBI's corrupt culture?

Well, one thing is for certain: if someone in your group is advocating for violence, it's probably an FBI informant come to put you in jail. Kindly disinvite them and then sweep for the bugs they've left behind.

OUR COURTS MUST ENSURE INDIVIDUAL LIBERTY, NOTHING MORE

Our Pledge of Allegiance is not a legal document, but it has been a remarkable guide for the nation. It was not even written until 1892, and only then by the socialist minister Francis Bellamy, who had fond hope of it catching on worldwide.

His original words were, "I pledge allegiance to my Flag and the Republic for which it stands, one nation, indivisible, with liberty and justice for all." In 1923, "the Flag of the United States of America" was inserted. And in 1954, President Eisenhower encouraged Congress to add "under God" to create today's pledge.[18]

In fact, the core phrase in the pledge, *"with liberty and justice for all,"* is the most radical phrase ever uttered. Few thought it could last. It was also the most fragile phrase. Many have tried to break it and nearly succeeded; they are trying now. Yet the core idea endures as a guiding light because of our third branch of government—our court system.

This judiciary branch is pretty much the only one still working, and then in a haphazard way. The executive and legislative branches spend most of their time staging elaborate theatrical productions meant to convince folks they're actually doing something. So the "voice of government" has been filled, by default, by judges. They've become the ultimate and often arbitrary lawmakers on a whole range of issues—from the values we hold dear, to the quality of our society, to the very essence of human character.

This is not how it should be. A three-legged stool with only one functional leg inevitably falls over before long. But this is where we are.

The best we can do, short-term, to keep the stool holding up the weight of the country is this: support judicial appointments dedicated to protecting the liberties of every American regardless of gender, race, economic status, political ideology, or religious beliefs.

In short, everybody respects everybody else.

Yes, I know this sounds somehow trite. But it's far from it.

This is each of us simply reminding ourselves and our neighbors that we are a diverse nation of individuals and that our court system must be made to work for every one of us.

Going as far back as Old Testament prophets such as Amos, they knew that justice is about more than giving "attaboys" for good behavior or punishments for bad. It is about creating opportunities for each one of us to live our lives fully. And that is what we must stand for.

We are caught in a high-stakes moment when America's center—normal, everyday people like you and me—are being slapped about by elite state ideologies of excess, extremism, and ego. We must stand to rescue the great middle of this country, working from our own neighborhoods on up to the top. And we know how.

We know how to make things and are unbothered by those who only take things.

We know how to build things and not give in to the red-tape brigades.

We know how to create things, even amidst monopolists trying to shut us down.

Few of us have ever thought of ourselves as part of any movement, but we also know that we must become just that—and it is this new movement that I hope to chronicle here.

A movement of parents unwilling to let fringe ideologies hijack our children's education and contaminate their minds.

A movement of family people still clinging (yes, Obama, clinging) to the belief that our strength as a people originates at the family hearth and only then radiates out into our communities, our states, our nation, and our world.

A love-thy-neighbor movement concerned for the less fortunate, the hurting, and the mentally broken in our own communities.

A Main Street movement that recognizes the great importance and value of small businesses providing jobs and opportunities right near home.

A free-market movement, because when markets are truly open and competitive, they are the oxygen of opportunity for all.

A movement that's had enough of the elite state overreach and is throwing a counterpunch.

CHAPTER 7

YES, THE CHILDREN ARE OUR FUTURE; WE MUST TEACH THEM WELL

❝IT'S REALLY CHILLING," Jennifer Hough told a reporter from *The Nation*. "The message that's being sent to the teachers in this school district is that nobody's safe."

And what message was that? Well, Hough is a leader of Dignity for All Texas Students, which claims to be advocating for diversity and inclusion. And the message she was referring to was one sent by parents at the Dallas-area Southlake school when these parents learned precisely how racism was being fought in a fourth-grade class there.

It began when a fourth grader took home a book from the classroom library titled *This Book Is Anti-Racist: 20 Lessons on How to Wake Up, Take Action, and Do the Work*. When the student's parents read it along with their child, they couldn't believe their eyes. This purportedly anti-racist book was the most racist thing they'd ever read. So they filed a complaint with the school district, a complaint that fell on deaf ears. That's when they joined up with other Southlake parents to take it to the school board. Only then was action taken, though that action was nothing more than a reprimand placed in the teacher's file.

Yes, it was just a reprimand that was so "chilling" to the progressive parents (why they're not called "regressives" is beyond me). And chilled as they were, they got into the faces of other parents outside the school board meeting. It was a scene of democracy in action. Progressives shouted their outrage over parents having any say in district teaching policies. Parents had no right telling the teachers what their children should be taught, they said.[1]

So what were the contents of that textbook that progressives want every fourth grader across America to be reading? Here are some unedited excerpts from *This Book Is Anti-Racist*:

What does it mean for me to be a light biracial Black cis female? Action takes the form of being aware and noticing injustice and checking stereotypes. It's using my lens of anti-racism, figuring out what it is I'm seeing, and taking action.

Remaining silent is not okay. It is not an option. Black folx, Brown folx, Indigenous folx, and Folx of the Global Majority are being harmed, oppressed, and killed every day. If you are white, light (like me), or a non-Black Person of the Global Majority, use your privilege and your proximity (or closeness) to the center of the dominant culture box to fracture the very foundation of our racist society. If you keep doing this and continue to put more cracks and dents into the structure, you'll shake it all up so it can crumble.

In your notebook, draw a box. Inside of it write down the identities you hold that are a part of the dominant culture. On the outside of the box, write down your identities that are marginalized. Those identities of yours that are inside the box are where you hold power. This is the privilege you can spend. Use the agency that comes with those identities to work in solidarity with folx who exist outside the box. Those identities of yours that are outside the box are where you are marginalized. This is where you have been systematically oppressed.[2]

If, going in like me, you had no idea what "folx" means, other than guessing it's some crazy take on "folks," I'll save you a run to Merriam-Webster. The word is listed there, sadly. Being folx means being marginalized. So in this "anti-racism" book, the premise is made clear: all White people are oppressors; all others are oppressed. Also hard to miss was the lowercased "white race"—inferior, and the uppercased "Black race"—superior! This book and hundreds more like it are flooding our schools. Truly they are fighting racism the way they tried building houses on my favorite stop on Gulliver's travels—building them from the roof downward.

In this book there's not a whiff of judging people by the content of their character, as the Reverend Martin Luther King Jr. admonished us to do. The only thing that matters is the color of your skin, which, of course, is the precise definition of racism.

So yes, this is a blatantly racist book, and we're expected to believe it's really meant to fight racism? Fight it by turning our children into racists? One parent who reviewed the book on Amazon said this:

> It has a good overview of racism, but it was hard to find behind the author's thinly-veiled prejudice, limited historical information, logical inconsistencies, and superfluous presentation of extravagantly erudite verbiage. To top it all off, some of the advice was counterproductive.[3]

Reviews like these went on and on for pages on Amazon. But then the tenor of the reviews suddenly changed. You could sense that the author's own friends, or allies anyway, were becoming alarmed. They began weighing in with glowing reviews. One of them insisted the book is "perfect for kids and adults."[4]

If that were true, this book *would* belong on the shelf of a fourth-grade classroom.

But from just a couple of excerpts, even a fourth grader can see otherwise. Or maybe not, which is the point. Most of us were at our most impressionable around the fourth grade, open to being carefully taught. The progressive activists know this, so they begin there to shape minds. Parents at the Southlake school understood as much. Every one of those parents had no doubt busy lives, no extra time on their hands. But they took the time to matter in their children's lives, to make a difference.

LEAKED VIDEOS OF TEACHERS PREPPING ON CRITICAL RACE THEORY

We hear most often about something called critical race theory (CRT) and how progressives are trying to slip CRT into the classroom. So what is it, really?

CRT had been kicking around faculty lounges in marginal universities for decades. Little had come of it, presumably since little had gone into it. But then progressive activists picked up on it, some of them earnestly, I'm sure, to address the lingering taint of racism in America. They began making progress in slipping this new dogma into school systems that had long since failed their children and become breeder farms for radical politicians. Basically running under the radar. But then they began getting some traction in real achievement-oriented schools.

That's when CRT caught the eyes of Andrew Gutmann (founder of Speak Up for Education) and Paul Rossi (co-host of *Chalkboard Heresy*). Their early investigations brought it all into the light of day. These two men weren't just making allegations. They got their hands on one hundred hours of videos from workshops held at the National Association of Independent Schools' People of Color Conference—a group that sets policy at over sixteen hundred independent schools nationwide.[5]

Some of the workshop titles tell the story themselves:

- **Racial Trauma and the Path Toward Healing:** How to segregate students into tribal groups and process the deep trauma their ancestors suffered from "intergenerational violence."

- **Let's Talk About It! Anti-Oppressive Unit and Lesson Plan Design:** Why a teacher who neglects to link science class lessons with social justice is committing "curriculum violence."

- **Breaking the White Centered Cycle:** How to eliminate White-supremacist concepts such as perfectionism, punctuality, urgency, niceness, writing, progress, objectivity, rigor, and capitalism.

- **Small Activists, Big Impact—Cultivating Anti-Racists and Activists in Kindergarten:** Effective methods for grooming social justice warriors.

- **Feeding Yourself When You Are Fed Up:** How to "call out" faculty and students you disagree with and shut down conversations by interrupting speakers whose words are unacceptable and should not be tolerated.

Actual titles, actual course descriptions—along with video after video of similar titles laying out the agenda for grade-school teaching at over sixteen hundred schools all across America! You could wonder if this was some Monty Python riff or a *Saturday Night Live* parody. My own first thought was that these are not serious people. But I suspect they are, in their own way. They're trying new approaches to education and doing so for a reason. What could it be?

Did they grow frustrated with the old approaches, such as Martin Luther King Jr.'s nonviolent resistance, concluding that White supremacy is so deeply rooted in this country that the whole land needs plowing under?

Or maybe they've been played by an elite state that callously funded their ideas with a certain quid pro quo—that the kids be kept dumb, drugged, and compliant, and that their parents be kept angrily lunging at each other's throats over the new teachings, too distracted to notice the bigger con going on?

I believe both of these things happened together.

Education is the black eye of America today—precisely because the elite state has focused so much energy on it. They know the demographics they face. They know the country is dividing into two classes—a few fortunate rich and everyone else. They know this because they manufactured it all. They know that as much as people are hurting now, it's going to get much, much worse. You can't impoverish a nation and expect folks to take it lying down. Not for too long anyway. At some point the peasants reach for their pitchforks. They know this.

So they needed a way to fog the minds of a new generation, to befuddle and distract folks from the truth of this new impoverished existence. They could do it with disinformation campaigns run through the media they control. They could do it by legalizing drugs to keep people comfortably numb. And they could do it most effectively by turning parent against parent in the classroom.

CRT could do that perfectly. And all at little cost to the elites. With a couple billion in funding, they could create all kinds of friction and strife. Black against White, liberal against conservative, apartment dweller against country truck driver. Name any two groups with differences of opinion and toss them into the fight cage. It could completely consume them.

And so they did.

And so it has.

Once, people would work out their differences as a matter of civic duty. But that had to end, because that kept the controls over people's lives in their own hands. That wouldn't do. Instead, there needed to be some thoroughly corrupt and abusive redo of education.

Such a system would have to have all decision-making and control centralized at the federal level, as far from the students and their parents as possible.

It would have to have influence over every classroom in the land.

It would require that teachers be trained up in the new curriculum and approved orthodoxy, and that they believe this training is their own idea, their meaningful contribution to the education of their charges, so they would fully buy in.

It would require all new textbooks, with publishers told they'll have massive new orders and a captive market for their texts, so they're happy to toss all the old texts into the dumpster.

Most useful would be a general endorsement of theories of relativism. So that the teachers are primed to accept the idea that everything under the sun changes—even history, even principles, even morals.

And continuing the ruse, it would be necessary to purge all the old teachings, label them heretical. In that way, the old could sensibly be replaced with the new: CRT.

A plan like this could work like a charm, the elite state thought to themselves. And it did gain a lot of purchase until some good people caught on and said, "Enough!"

We can be thankful to Gutmann and Rossi for opening our eyes to this. Equal thanks to writer and filmmaker Christopher Rufo, who did deep research on how widespread these toxic CRT and CRT-like teachings truly are.

Rufo identified public school districts in Arkansas, California, Illinois, Indiana, Maine, Massachusetts, Montana, Ohio, Oregon, New Jersey, Pennsylvania, and Washington state that are proudly using books like *Not My Idea*, which also teaches children to judge people based on the color of their skin, something kids do not naturally do.[6] A 180-degree reversal of how we were taught just a generation ago.

I can't help but think of a song I learned as a child, and then sang with my own children and now with my grandchildren. It's a simple song, but it teaches a much healthier viewpoint about race and a more positive way to think about others that unites and equally appreciates everyone:

> Jesus loves the little children,
> All the children of the world;
> Red and yellow, black and white,
> They are precious in His sight,
> Jesus loves the little children of the world.[7]

I hope and pray other parents are approaching this just as positively. I know that many are. In more than two dozen states parents are counterpunching, hitting back in their own local school districts and taking the fight up to state legislatures with bills prohibiting these inappropriate and racist teachings in the classroom.[8]

Not just a few parent groups in these states, but hundreds of groups are getting organized and counterpunching—groups such as Arizona Women of Action in the Phoenix area. And larger support groups such as Parents Defending Ed and Moms for Liberty helping parents take stands in their communities.

A list of parent groups can be found at CounterpunchBook.com. Parents are

- meeting informally in coffee shops to learn from each other's experiences and plan strategy;

- attending school board meetings and forcing officials to listen to their concerns (which is often difficult with so many school boards trying to silence parents);

- recruiting and supporting candidates for school board positions who hold to reasonable, thoughtful, compassionate beliefs about education;

- writing letters to the local press—which can still be more powerful than many people think;

- taking the matter to court when school boards have gone off the progressive deep end and won't allow parents a say in their children's education; and

- opting to move their children to another district or home-school them when that is the only satisfactory option.

Here's a model letter one parent used recently to begin a dialogue with their school's teachers and school board:

> Respectfully,
>
> How can you as a teacher take stands against physical bullying in the schoolyard as you should, then go back into your classroom and emotionally bully White children into believing that they are either racists or chock-full of legacy racist blood and thus irredeemable?
>
> Surely you are aware of the harm this is causing?
>
> How can you defend this new curriculum on any grounds whatsoever?
>
> Violence begets violence; racism begets racism. Books like the improperly titled *This Book Is Anti-Racist* can only widen racial divisions, not narrow them. You should know this. But perhaps you don't.
>
> So I propose that we meet over coffee to talk about something I believe you care about as I do—teaching our children well.
>
> Until we speak,
>
> A Very Concerned Parent

Just a letter, just one initial counterpunch of boldness to say or do what is true, right, and just. We are called in this time to counterpunch because the progressive cause has gone so far off-kilter, so far off that they are actually appropriating the language of conservatives, oddly enough, in a bid for legitimacy.

In *The Nation*'s story above about Southlake school, the headline writers called it "The GOP's Grievance Industrial Complex Invades the Classroom" and tagged it "When parents become a posse of vigilantes, outrage is in the saddle instead of teaching or learning."

But in simple historical fact, the original progressive mantle was constructed to take the people's grievances about the system and agitate for action. Over the years that mantle grew and grew and became its own industrial complex. Now it seeks to replace traditional "teaching and learning" with clever memes about White supremacy run amok.

You can argue that old White men gave us the military industrial complex and be correct. But the grievance industrial complex is the work product of people who (a) tossed Dr. King's teachings overboard, or (b) enjoy getting grants from the elite state to keep people snarling and distracted from the larger wealth extraction going on, or (c) both.

These kinds of people cannot be deciding our children's future with their dangerous dogma. They cannot keep playing their role in the "big distraction." If they are interested, they are welcome to join with reasonable people seeking commonsense solutions to the problems in our educational system, solutions everyone of honesty and integrity can embrace.

THE MORE DIVIDED WE ARE, THE RICHER THEY GET

This "big distraction" theme fills these pages and cannot be overemphasized. Just as the British once used cheap gin to keep the peasants underfoot and opium to waylay the Chinese while extracting the tea and spice they craved, today's elite state has profited grandly from provoking a continually distracting national food fight. The insightful Glenn Beck writes on this as well in his latest book, *The Great Reset*:

> It is tempting to fall into the trap of seeing controversy…as yet another left-versus-right debate.…[They] want Main Street Americans to be divided. They want us to spend all our time yelling at each other about Dr. Seuss book bans and COVID-19 mask mandates so we do not see the bigger, much more important forces at work. The truth is, the fight against the Great Reset is not a struggle between liberals and conservatives; it is a fight between the ruling-class elites of Wall Street, Davos, and Washington, D.C., and everyone else. And if the American people lose sight of that vital point, there will be no stopping the grand alterations of society that Reset elites have long yearned for.[9]

Beck's focus in this passage was on the larger threat of the Great Reset, which we've talked about, but his message applies in our schools as well.

Schools should rightly teach about the racial difficulties our nation has faced along with everything we've done, and still must do, to advance individual liberty for all. The two belong in the same teaching assignment. This should be obvious, but sadly it is not.

We saw as much in the Maryland Montgomery County Public Schools, for example. Parents of children attending there were recently emailed a new social studies curriculum that "strengthens students' sense of racial, ethnic, and tribal identities, helps students understand and resist systems of oppression, and empowers students to see themselves as change agents."[10]

This is not a curriculum, of course; it is dogma. It's not about learning critical thinking. It takes as a given that all of White America is deeply racist, Blacks are systematically beaten down, and students should revolt. This Montgomery County story comes from David Bernstein, founder of the Jewish Institute for Liberal Values. He wrote in the *Wall Street Journal* of his son's experience under the new dogma:

> His English teacher recently asked him point-blank what he thinks the black American experience is in America today. "I wanted to say that I think black people are as different from each other as white people are, but I could never say that in class," he told me. Instead, he kept silent. Kids are expected to parrot back only one answer: To be black in America is to suffer continuous discrimination and indignation. There is nothing wrong with holding this view, but it clearly isn't shared by everyone in the black community.[11]

That there are some individuals who are racist in this country cannot be denied. There is racism in every country with every color of person.

What's also true is that America has made tremendous strides in stamping out racism. (Which by the very fact means racism is *not* systemic.)

And true as well is the fact that we must continue to fight for our fellow humanity and the rights of every American. But that is not what CRT is doing. While I'm taking some liberty with the language, these are the net arguments made by proponents of CRT:

- We have to resegregate America to save it.

- We can never end four hundred–plus years of systemic racism—nothing has changed!

- We must teach Black children that all Whites are evil racists (and that when those Black children return home to communities blighted by Black crime, it's not the Black community's fault—it's the White cops, the Asian bodega owners, etc.).

Most people can recognize a hustle when they see it—or they used to be able to anyway. But when the actions of a few reprehensible cops in the summer of 2020 sent a nation of good people into the streets in despairing protest, the hustle got a do-over. It was repackaged as "reform" needed now more than ever. And who was doing the packaging?

The elite state, of course. They had funneled hundreds of millions into the Black Lives Matter organization, turning it from a well-meaning group into a degenerate shill for extremists eager to blow a hole in the moral center of the country and separate people and their common sense.

ILLINOIS IS HOME TO A NEW MOB—THE TEACHER INDOCTRINATION MOB

If Illinois grade-school teachers wanted to hold on to their teaching licenses in 2022, they had to step up to new "Culturally Responsive Teaching and Leading" standards in their teacher-prep programs. Which means what?

In looking at the long list of new performance standards, a few stand out. Here's what Illinois teachers must do (and how a circumspect teacher might react):

Understand and value the notion that multiple lived experiences exist, that there is not one "correct" way of doing or understanding something, and that what is seen as "correct" is most often based on our lived experiences. [So I can't possibly know what is "correct" if, for instance, I grew up on the right side of the tracks?]

Engage in self-reflection about their own actions and interactions and what ideas motivated those actions. [So I'm a closet racist and not even aware of it—is that what you mean?]

Explore their own intersecting identities, how they were developed, and how they impact daily experience of the world. [So I'm super-privileged, on a teacher's pay?]

Critically think about the institutions in which they find themselves, working to reform these institutions whenever and wherever necessary. [So I find myself a teacher; how can I reform this institution when you will fire me if I don't follow your reforms?]

Assess how their biases and perceptions affect their teaching practice and how they access tools to mitigate their own behavior (racism, sexism, homophobia, unearned privilege, Eurocentrism, etc.). [Sorry, but what English writing class did you take? Please explain what you mean. Feel free to give examples.]

Be aware of the effects of power and privilege and the need for social advocacy and social action to better empower diverse students and communities. [OK, so my job title is now "Social Justice Warrior." Does that come with a raise?]

Know and understand how a system of inequity creates rules regarding student punishment that negatively impact students of color. [Got it. If a Black student misbehaves, I give 'em a lollipop.][12]

I didn't make up these standards, just the teachers' thought bubbles, in case you were wondering. These are the word-for-word teaching standards developed for a state best known for its mob violence, so I guess they're just keeping it coming.

Sadly, however, this is not just Cook County run amok.

These education mobsters shipped these very standards out under cover of COVID to any state that would take them. And with so many teachers holed up at full pay for the extended school lockdowns (that they and their unions insisted on while students fell behind), there's been plenty of time to study up on the new rules, er, standards—which is just one more case in point for parents across America joining together and counterpunching!

> My people are destroyed for lack of knowledge.
>
> —HOSEA 4:6

A few years ago, Del Tackett, former president of the Focus on the Family Institute, taught a small-group curriculum on the biblical world-view called The Truth Project. "This video-based home Bible study... takes you through 13 engaging video lessons on the relevance and importance of living the Biblical worldview in daily life."[13] I viewed the entire series as part of a small group through my church, and I highly recommend it for anyone wanting to gain deeper insights into the broad sweep of Western civilization.

One of Tackett's videos covers the importance of knowing the past because it is the key to understanding the forces at work in the present. As he explains:

> If I can change your historical context, I can change the way you view the present. This is the power of historical revisionism.[14]

Every worthy analyst, going back as far as you'd like, makes it clear that great power can come from influencing people's perspective about the past. George Orwell put it this way: "He who controls the past, controls the future." Even Karl Marx weighed in on this: "A people without a heritage are easily persuaded."[15]

In the Bible, God is frequently commanding His people to remember, to not forget how He delivered and helped them in the past. For one thing, it makes you grateful to God, and it reminds you of how mighty and amazing He is, that nothing is impossible for Him. Remembering what God has done for you in the past also helps you trust Him in your present situation, and in the future.

In one instance, God told Israel to take up stones and pile them up along the banks of the Jordan River to remind future generations of God's acts of deliverance (Joshua 4:1–9).[16]

Christian writer Brandon Clay took this to mean:

God had just saved the entire nation of Israel from being slaves in Egypt and they were finally entering the Promised Land. The first command he gave them after they crossed the Jordan River was to build a memorial to the event. So God would tell Israel to remember particular events throughout their history.

The consequences of forgetting God's activity in history can be fatal to the future of any people. When a people forget their history, then they are ripe for a takeover of other leaders who will rewrite history for the sake of the new regime.[17]

These lessons from the Bible could not have been more relevant on the day they announced something called the 1619 Project.

FROM 1619 TO 2019, SKIPPING 1776

Someday they will say about this period that people took greater pride in their hatred of "the other side" than they did in the principles they once held dear. So it was that the *New York Times* launched the 1619 Project. Its goal? To convince the world that America formally began not with the 1776 Declaration of Independence, but instead when a boatload of African slaves arrived in North America in, yes, 1619.

No serious person has ever denied the scourge of slavery. But that's not what the 1619 Project is all about. Instead, it aims to make race the central organizing myth of the nation. That is, we fought England so we could go on being slavers. Slavery, not freedom, was the defining fact of America's founding.

This is obvious twaddle, but such is the state of journalism that the author received a Pulitzer Prize for her work. And with that credential featured in the marketing, the 1619 Project has been taught in forty-five hundred classrooms and will find its way into many more.[18]

The 1619 Project began as the fever dream of Nikole Hannah-Jones, who would no doubt still be little more than someone mouthing off in the long tail of the internet had the *New York Times* not gone whole hog promoting her pulp fiction.

Though her 1619 Project was debunked by every reasonable person on the planet (and surely they're shaking their heads in distant galaxies), Hannah-Jones has managed to rebrand America in a lot of unthinking people's minds as a slave owner's paradise instead of the truth: a far-from-perfect union at its founding, but one that nonetheless has done far more than any country ever has to advance freedom and dignity for the individual.

Elevated by the adoration of the radical Left, Hannah-Jones now sees herself as some modern-day beacon of freedom. Meaning that when a reporter calls her for a quote, she gives one. Such as on the subject of the summer 2020 riots, which caused dozens of deaths and more than $2 billion in property damage. She said it'd be "an honor" for it to be called "the 1619 riots" since "non-violent protest has not been successful."[19] At least she was honest about those riots being violent and deadly—that lifts her high above the entire Democratic Party and the left-stream media.

WE NEED TO BETTER TEACH THE POLITICS OF FREEDOM

Students stuck learning about 1619 should also learn all they can about one man, Thomas Jefferson. Not the underhanded portrayal so many get—that he was a slaver who found time to write the Declaration of Independence. No, they should get the depth of scholarship that Larry Arnn, president of Hillsdale College, brings to Jefferson's apprehension with the slavery that existed worldwide at the time:

> They don't learn what Jefferson wrote in *Notes on the State of Virginia*: "I tremble for my country when I reflect that God is just," he wrote in that book regarding the contest between the master and the slave. "The Almighty has no attribute which can take side with us in such a contest."[20]

Dr. Arnn goes deeper on how little today's students learn of Jefferson:

> They don't learn that when our nation first expanded, it was into the Northwest Territory, and that slavery was forbidden in that territory. They don't learn that the land in that territory was

ceded to the federal government from Virginia, or that it was on the motion of Thomas Jefferson that the condition of the gift was that slavery in that land be eternally forbidden. If schoolchildren learned that, they would come to see Jefferson as a human being who inherited things and did things himself that were terrible, but who regretted those things and fought against them. And they would learn, by the way, that on the scale of human achievement, Jefferson ranks very high. There's just no question about that, if for no other reason than that he was a prime agent in founding the first republic dedicated to the proposition that all men are created equal.[21]

Yes, students should learn the whole of history—how brilliant Jefferson was, how imperfect, and how far he took our nation beyond history's reach. Students should also be steeped in the long timeline of chattel slavery:

- how pervasive it was for centuries in every country, and still is in some;

- how most African slaves were sold off by their own villages or rival chieftains to English slaving transports;

- how slavery didn't really end with the Republican Party's emancipation but continued in even more sinister Jim Crow and redlining practices for which the Democratic Party has never apologized; and

- how the children of slaves began to assimilate beautifully into Christian society, but then the Democratic Party's Great Society programs ripped Black men from their families, creating a mess that will take generations to overcome.

How many of today's kids know all this, or any of it?

Students should also learn about other forms of slavery that matter. That begins with required reading of totalitarian novels such as George Orwell's *1984*, Aldous Huxley's *Brave New World*, and C. S. Lewis' *That*

Hideous Strength. Reading and talking about these will focus young minds on what's at stake. And how there are always forces arrayed against the privileges of freedom—dark forces aiming to undermine or undo the privileges they take for granted.

Ronald Reagan warned Americans about this:

> Freedom is never more than one generation away from extinction. We didn't pass it on to our children in the bloodstream. The only way they can inherit the freedom we have known is if we fight for it, protect it, defend it and then hand it to them with the well-thought lessons of how they in their lifetime must do the same. And if you and I don't do this, then you and I may well spend our sunset years telling our children and our children's children what it once was like in America when men were free.[22]

Today's students would be wise to look into the eyes of those who've been fighting for social justice for nearly 250 years—fighting one battle after another. Sacrificing their time and treasure so that kids today are able to while away the hours swiping through meaningless photos on their phones, riding the dopamine hits from clickbait placed just so for them, lamenting what a terrible world they've inherited.

And then they should learn how the old slavery of chains is being replaced by a new slavery of government thought control, as well as the new slavery of sex trafficking and exploitation of young boys and girls in pornography.

Evidence of this new thought control surfaced early in the Biden presidency when they rolled out a Disinformation Governance Board (DGB). Right away it was clear, even to the administration's most loyal supporters, that such a ridiculously named agency was going to be a wholesale fiasco. And within days of its launch, the DGB was quietly deep-sixed. But look for it to resurface later in Biden's term with a name that sounds less like KGB and more like rose petals. Oh, and carrying the same mission orders:

- Keep an eye on people everywhere who might not like what the US government is doing.

- Detain any dissenters, using armored tanks if necessary to bust down doors of resistors.

- Monitor all communications, and if anyone is found watching unapproved videos, for example, bring them in for questioning.

Some will think I'm kidding with this scenario. But it closely resembles what we saw in the aftermath of January 6, when people who had only been protesting the election's integrity were grabbed out of their homes, along with innocents and children, treated as terrorists, and thrown into jail without any rights to due process.

Yes, slavery can still be brought to bear. And students should study this modern form of it, to better resist it.

PARENTS ARE RISING UP FROM SAN ANTONIO TO, YES, SAN FRANCISCO!

"This is a political earthquake," said Autumn Looijen, a parent who led a recall effort against an out-of-control school board. "San Francisco is standing up to fight for its children and for good governance."

Mayor London Breed said after the recall, "We are going to be looking for well-rounded school board members who are focused on the schools, who are focused on our children and their success, who are focused on collaboration and working together."

San Francisco parents and politicians using words like *well-rounded*! I was speechless at first. And even more amazing were the results of the recall campaign. Voters took out three darling progressives on the school board by votes of 79 percent, 75 percent, and 72 percent against. If it can be done in the heart of liberal San Francisco, it can be done anywhere.[23]

This all began when the school board shuttered classrooms for the entire school year due to COVID. Well, almost the entire year. They did order students to return for a single day in May so schools could qualify for $12 million in funds that Governor Gavin Newsom had promised them for reopening.[24]

People noticed. They also noticed that while their children were falling behind academically, the school board was still meeting. Their agenda?

Focusing on how their boarded-up schools had terribly racist, oppressive, and patriarchal names like Abraham Lincoln, Thomas Jefferson, George Washington, Francis Scott Key, and Robert Louis Stevenson. Those were simply unacceptable names, the school board decided, so they made it a top priority to go about renaming about a third of the district's 125 schools. Though their efforts didn't prevail, that is what they decided was valuable work that would truly benefit the children they were responsible for.

Then, in their own racist way, the school board shut down merit-based admissions at Lowell High School, which catered to lower-income families, many of them Asian families. The reasoning for the shutdown, as one school board member patiently tried to explain, was that these Asians were adopting "white supremacist thinking," and of course, that was unacceptable. Parents saw it differently and were furious.[25]

You could say the San Francisco school board was an easy target. Prior to the pandemic, they had tried to paint over a series of Depression-era frescoes that had graced a local high school since the 1930s. The popular frescoes were the work of a Russian communist calling out cruelties in American history—but no matter. The school board decided that these frescoes were racist and cruel, and worse, possibly secretly coded right-wing art!

San Francisco's art community was flabbergasted by this, as they should have been, and rose up to stop the painting over. But not to be outmaneuvered, the school board brought in huge barriers to mostly conceal the frescoes. It wasn't until a new school board was elected that the barriers came down.

This shows the kind of people operating, often with little citizen input, on school boards. Surely few, if any, are as clueless as San Francisco's. But many school boards are fully detached from the normal concerns of parents and families. It's as if they're operating in some abstract universe thinking that their decisions validate their anti-racist *bona fides* and should be praised for it.

And why, really, should the school board members have thought to worry about closing schools, renaming them, or destroying art? No doubt they had watched the Democratic National Convention in August 2020. No speaker there even came close to denouncing the urban protests over

George Floyd's death turning into the most destructive riot in American history.

Then there was the Loudoun County case. Parents there had loudly objected to the school board's mandating of CRT curricula. When they did, the US attorney general unleashed a phalanx of FBI enforcers on them.[26] And President Biden rarely lets slip an opportunity to shout awkwardly loud, "It's Jim Crow!" (as if he's somehow making policy).

So the San Francisco school board surely thought they could ignore any challenges to their ersatz power games. But then they took it too far. Parents might go along with an odd ideology—until their children are sacrificed to it and made the losers. That's when they fight back.

And that's what's happening all across the country—parents and grandparents are rising up and making a difference. Getting involved and taking responsibility for their children's future. This can mean standing up to hostile administrators, as Ohio mother Ashley Ryder learned recently at a Big Walnut school board meeting.

Ryder wanted the school to provide mental health services for students, and she had good reason to question the genuineness of the school board's position on the issue. Speaking up at a school board meeting, she asked, "Now that you've made a complete 180, my question for the board is this: Were you lying to your base to get elected, or are you lying now to the parents?"

She was told to "zip it" and not allowed to speak further. Left without recourse, Ryder went to court. Her lawyer showed how the school board's policy was an unconstitutional assault on free speech, correctly noting, "What's more important than a member of the public being able to state grievances about their government's performance?"

One wonders if those Ohioan school board members are even familiar with our First Amendment freedoms of religion, of speech, of the press, of the people peaceably to assemble, of the right to petition to government for a redress of grievances. Well, they know now. In April 2022, the school board settled with Ryder and agreed to walk back its restrictions on speech.[27]

Ryder's victory is one for every parent across the country who is discovering that you can counterpunch. It's a shame that sometimes it takes a lawsuit. But the outcome, for our children, is worth it.

CHAPTER 8

ALTERNATIVE EDUCATIONAL CHOICES FOR OUR CHILDREN

EDUCATION ISSUES ARE complex, and with the breakdown of the family these issues become more challenging. Teachers' hands are often tied by administrators hired by liberal politicians grafting their reelection chances. Or at least that's one view of it, roughly drawn. Whatever the explanation, it adds up to a strong argument for alternative educational choices for our children. That is, strong and accessible charter schools.

Parents who want the very best cultural experience for their children—and by very best, I mean the liberal arts education that managed over centuries to advance the greatest experiment in individual liberty ever known—should have support for moving their children into charter schools.

Parents should be given educational savings accounts to send their kids to the K–12 school they wish—whether it's public, private, or at home.

These programs have been popular for decades. Many school choice programs have proven to improve student test scores and parental satisfaction. A 2018 survey by the American Federation for Children found education savings accounts favored by 70 percent of Democrats, 78 percent of Independents, and 81 percent of Republicans.[1] Yet politicians in both parties have not acted, because the teachers' unions have shut them down.

Instead, it should be the teachers' unions that are shut down. What value do they provide teachers anyway? Maybe all those labor organizers can take their Cornell educations and instead of hounding teachers help out the underpaid workers at Amazon, Google, and Starbucks who've begun organizing. Just a thought.

Another great idea for making education work better: turn teachers into small-business people. Scott McKay has a fresh take on this:

> You want happy teachers who won't quit the profession?...Make them small businesspeople. Put that education money in the hands of the parents, remove the strings, and give them the freedom to make good choices for their kids' education.[2]

Sounds like something worth fighting for! Sounds like an effective counterpunch.

Yo, Socrates, Meet My Man, Lia

So what's a parent to do? Your little girl of five tells you she's a "rainbow kid, a boy-girl." You wonder if she has any idea what she's talking about. Did she pick this up in kindergarten? From some website she shouldn't be visiting?

One of those little girls, named Phoenix, made her way into a British medical journal study. She had apparently known since she was five that she was neither girl nor boy. At eleven, Phoenix went into puberty and freaked out that her breasts were growing and menstruation was coming. She *demanded* that she be given puberty blockers. Her parents, who'd always wanted her to soar like a mythical creature apparently, got their wish and obtained the medicines to halt puberty. So it was done.[3]

Now Phoenix will live her entire life as a prepubescent or forever in the early stages of puberty. Her brain and bones will probably never go through the transformation of puberty. She'll probably be sterile. Doctors say that statistically, there's an 84 percent chance she'll try to reverse the process in five or six years.[4] That reversal may work, it may not. Either way, this is going to be one messed-up kid.

Yes, this thing is fraught. As a medical freedom issue, how does society deny a child with consenting parents the drugs or surgery that will change their sex? Is this, uh, child abuse?

How does society wrestle with such a thorny question and deeply psychologically disturbed young people?

Lamentably, some three hundred thousand Americans between the ages of thirteen and seventeen now call themselves transgender.[5] They're swallowing hormones, or cutting up their bodies, to alter who they biologically are.

As the witty Mark Steyn writes:

Think of it. Your daughter has been training since she was a little girl to run in school sports. Now at 17, she's in the state high school track championships, and you are forbidden even to notice that she's competing against a woman who is 6'2" with thighs like tugboats, a great touch of five o'clock shadow on her face, and the most muscular bosom you've ever seen. You're not supposed to notice the craziness of this.[6]

In the spotlight here is William Thomas, who now prefers the name "Lia." He was athletic enough to make the University of Penn men's swimming team, where he competed and did OK. When he began hormone replacement therapy and went on to compete as a transgender athlete against women, he was suddenly tops in the nation. At the NCAA Division I national championship in March 2022, he won the 500-yard freestyle final, tied for fifth in the 200-yard final, and finished eighth in the 100-yard freestyle.[7]

Here is a grown man who feels entitled to enter the locker rooms of women, to share in their intimate spaces. A grown man who is emotionally unstable by definition. How many of these "Lia" types are going to be emotionally unstable testosterone-fueled narcissists or predators? Surely there will be many.

What of the women—the true women? Where are our leaders in defending their rights and dignity? Where is the courage to step into this new breach?

In June 2022, the International Swimming Federation took a position on this—if you could call it a position. They banned men who call themselves women from competitions unless they had done their "transitioning" before turning twelve.[8] Really. Somehow they considered this a responsible policy position, though it strikes me as calling yourself vegan except you eat bacon. Utter silliness.

Not to be outdone on the Mad Hatter front, President Biden made his position clear in a March 2022 speech: "To transgender Americans of all ages, I want you to know that you are so brave. You belong. I have your back."[9]

So the federal government under Biden is not only encouraging men to become women or vice versa as a matter of policy, but it seems to be ready to support and possibly provide through funding a range of medical interventions including puberty blockers, cross-sex hormones, and physical mutilation surgery.

Biden also insisted that puberty blockers can be reversed if desired later on. Follow the science, he basically said. Over in Europe they are following a different science then, since several governments there have begun withdrawing support for these brutish interventions, having seen all the damage they cause.[10]

Republicans who try to pass legislation on these gender questions often feel as naive as Robespierre thinking he could lead the French to revolution but avoid the guillotine. Florida governor Ron DeSantis tried to act responsibly with the "Parental Rights in Education" bill that was so effectively trashed by progressive cranks that few know what the bill actually says.

The key passage in DeSantis' bill reads as follows:

> Classroom instruction by school personnel or third parties on sexual orientation or gender identity may not occur in kindergarten through grade 3 or in a manner that is not age-appropriate or developmentally appropriate for students in accordance with state standards.[11]

So all the governor was saying is don't talk to preadolescents about anything sexual—it's way too early, *obviously*. Even talking about these things in the fourth or fifth grade can be creepy. Matters of sexuality used to be discussed in middle school, which is early enough. Why can't grade-school teachers just leave the indoctrination manuals at home and focus on the ABCs and 123s—which is what education should be about?

Other pieces of the Florida legislation set out what school districts must do:

> "Notify parents of healthcare services and provide parents the opportunity to consent or decline such services" and not stop "parents from accessing any of their student's education and health records created, maintained, or used by the school district."[12]

Basic parental rights, commonsense rights, how can these be controversial? They aren't and shouldn't be. But warriors in the culture wars give no quarter, and the placards above their doors read "Victory, no matter how bloody." Oh, and often pretty fancy doors, since these social justice warriors have deep-pocketed patrons in the elite state funding their poison pens and bitter tongues.

Not all these social justice warriors get paid a couple hundred grand a year to cause mayhem (like the guy in the Allstate commercial), but a lot do. For all I know, they study those Allstate ads for tips on destroying the world around them.

One of those elite state patrons slipped uncomfortably into the spotlight in early 2022 with a pledge of $5 million to support the radical activists slinging lies about DeSantis' bill. That company was Disney—once a place of magic, now more a den of iniquity.

DISNEY GOES LONG ON THE CULTURE WARS

Recently, a small handful of employees at Disney decided to get active in teaching kindergartners how Mickey would kiss Mickey. Feeling differently were most of Disney's thousands of employees who believed very clearly that this kind of education falls way outside the Magic Kingdom's remit.

Disney's CEO, Bob Chapek, initially tried to steer clear of gender politics, but it was difficult in Florida, where progressives were busy organizing Disney employees. Those employees, reportedly only a handful of them, were dead set on turning Disney parks into some kind of gaypalooza. Chapek caved and went straight to work turning Disney into a toxic place to work for most of the employees.

It was so toxic that the employees said as much in an open letter to Disney management, a letter sent anonymously for fear of retaliation. The letter was straightforward and sensible, asking Disney to stay out of politics. Here are key excerpts:

> We have watched as our leadership has expressed their condemnation for laws and policies we support. We have watched as our colleagues, convinced that no one in the company could possibly disagree with them, grow increasingly aggressive in their

demands…and openly advocate for the punishment of employees who disagree with them….

Left-leaning cast members are free to promote their agenda and organize on company time using company resources. They call their fellow employees "bigots" and pressure [Disney] to use corporate influence to further their left-wing legislative goals….

Employees who want [Disney] to make left-wing political statements are encouraged, while those of us who want the company to remain neutral can say so only in a whisper out of fear of professional retaliation…..

Disney shouldn't be a vehicle for one demographic's political activism. It's so much bigger and more important than that…. Please don't let Disney become just another thing we divide over.[13]

It was a thoughtful and beautifully written letter from employees who deeply care. A letter in which the writers had to *formally* request that Disney not retaliate against them for speaking truth to power. This story will continue to unfold. We admire these employees for standing on reasonable grounds. We support them in fighting for the true magic of Walt's vision for Disney—that it entertain kids of all ages and leave the politics at the gate.

WHAT PURPOSE DO COLLEGES EVEN SERVE ANYMORE?

I will "literally fight you, [expletive]," the woman spat as she cornered her target. A street fight? No, a Yale Law School classroom. But there she was—a next-generation attorney demonstrating her legal chops.

The occasion was a debate on civil liberties, hosted by the Yale Federalist Society. Kristen Waggoner of the conservative Alliance Defending Freedom for the affirmative, Monica Miller of the progressive American Humanist Association for the negative—though the debate opponents did generally agree on the constitutional importance of free speech.

Not so the hundred law students who flooded into the debate room, shouting down the speakers and moving in to attack—apparently intending violence before the debaters and spectators were escorted out by security for their safety. Video recordings obtained by the *Washington Free Beacon* confirmed it all in pathetic detail.[14] But it was no aberration.

Polls of college student attitudes tell us that a clear majority feel it's OK to shout down a speaker they just don't happen to like. These polls can be notoriously unreliable, of course, especially when they involve college students. But even if these polls are way off, it's still a problem because one in five of these same students say it's fine to get violent to stop a speaker who is somehow hurting them with words. And that's a big number—however far off. Basically, the personal has become institutional to this generation. They've bought into the elite state con that colleges will always shelter them from the storm, their enemies will be smitten and their consequences few. They have no idea how badly the con ends for them.[15]

All they seem to know is that progressive violence is condoned. Cool, they say. And so the melee at Yale Law that day was not an outlier but the new normal.

Nobody was physically harmed that day. Nor was any punishment meted out—despite the school having once been the vanguard of free speech with a thick rulebook to prove it. Yale has become another Poison Ivy League school. A school that would not welcome the legendary novelist Salman Rushdie with his Cambridge credentials, it would appear, since Rushdie has said:

> The university is the place where young people should be challenged every day, where everything they know should be put into question, so that they can think and learn and grow up. And the idea that they should be protected from ideas that they might not like is the opposite of what a university should be.[16]

At university, and especially at law school, an individual's mind should be opened wide, ideas should be tumbling all about, challenged, debated. Heartily debated! It needn't be pretty, nor even comfortable, but it can never be violent or silencing. For this verbal give-and-take is the beating heart of our republic. Without it, all our other freedoms shrivel and die.

This is something every law school professor surely understands. But few will stand up to the mob. And most support it. Take Professor Rory Little, for example, of UC Hastings College of the Law. A similar mob of students had gone berserk when a visiting speaker took the podium in his classroom, and the good professor twisted himself into knots trying to defend the protestors:

> Physically intimidating conduct…should not be countenanced [but after] intermittent chanting and speaking, everyone quietly and peacefully left the room….The message of the protesters has finally been heard….The protest was free speech under any definition….Let's be honest: constitutional law is murky, inconsistent, and unsettled as to what messages and techniques of expression have priority when two conflict….Refusing to hear the message of discontent from a group of neglected and undervalued members of the community is also "canceling."[17]

Fair to say, law students are a long way from "neglected and undervalued members of the community." And any song-and-dance about speaking for their brethren back in the hood doesn't change that it's privilege they're exercising. Indeed, they act like it. By insisting that it's their way or the highway, they are practically parroting the caricature of the privileged old White man they profess to hate. How will that work out for them in the courtroom, if they somehow slip in under the bar?

TODAY'S ACADEMICS ARE ANYTHING BUT

UCLA once gave us Jackie Robinson, Rafer Johnson, and Kareem Abdul-Jabbar. Today the university is sinking under the weight of race-and-equity administrators like Jonathan Perkins, who calls himself "the voice of a growing movement" and recently posted that he's wishing for the death of a Supreme Court justice:

> No one wants to openly admit [we all] hope Clarence Thomas dies….This whole rule we're not to wish ill on people is silly. Uncle Thomas is a sexist token.[18]

He's paid good money to spout this drivel. In fact, university costs are shooting through the roof, and quality is dropping through the floor precisely because of people like Perkins. They embed themselves in layers of administrative barbed wire, and then you can never pry them out.

If only Perkins were an anomaly. One analysis found that from 1987 to 2012, universities added more than half a million administrators to the payroll, doubling the number of administrators and raising the cost of higher education. Without them, student tuition would be more affordable for the very people "race and equity" directors are supposed to be helping.[19]

Yale's own director of race and equity was nowhere to be found on the day racist students *inequitably* bullied a speaker out of the room under police protection. But the event did catch the eye of the adults in the judiciary. Federal judge Laurence Silberman of the DC Court of Appeals snapped off a letter to his fellow judges:

> All federal judges—and all federal judges are presumably committed to free speech—should carefully consider whether any student so identified should be disqualified for potential clerkships.[20]

That should trigger the student, as in triggering them to grow up. They may not care about civility or the First Amendment, but they do hope to snag a clerkship after graduating and then sail on into a big-name law firm, where they can go full "I'll literally fight you" mode at $1,000 a billable hour.

So kudos to Judge Silberman, and we'll have to see what happens.

Some will say that these students just need time to "grow up." But these are not college freshmen. They're grad students at a law school that, oddly, still garners great respect. They're spot-on center of the whole "protecting the rule of law" thing, as they might call it. If their go-to strategy is shouting down people they disagree with, then God help us, because the American legal system is going into the tank.

Instead, this must become an object lesson. Their shenanigans should be packaged up into teaching material for aspiring lawyers still in middle school, still forming ideas about how freedom works. Even in writing this it feels like a desperate lost cause. But it cannot be. It must instead be the constant work we do—for freedom is always on trial.

MAJORING IN STUPID: FOR THIS, PARENTS FORK OVER $60,000 A YEAR?

Every college has its fluff courses. For some of us, it kept the GPA presentable. At UCLA, it was History of Jazz and History of the Turks. Lots of fun, easy As. But with college costs now soaring at twice the rate of inflation, you'd think they'd get serious about creating courses that run deep into the classics or into technical training to prepare their students for a harshly competitive workplace.

You'd think that. But in looking at course offerings at schools that call themselves "prestigious," you will find the following:

- Arguing With Judge Judy (UC Berkeley)

- Queering the Bible (Swarthmore)

- Feminist Critique of Christianity (University of Pennsylvania)

- GaGa for Gaga: Sex, Gender, and Identity (University of Virginia)

- How to Win a Beauty Pageant: Race, Gender, Culture (Oberlin College)

- Power of Whiteness (Providence College)

- Surviving the Coming Zombie Apocalypse (Michigan State University)

- Tattoos, Piercing, and Body Adornment (Pitzer College)

- Textual Appeal of Tupac Shakur (University of Washington)

- The Unbearable Whiteness of Barbie (Occidental College)

- Transgender Latina Immigration (Bowdoin College)

- Demystifying the Hipster (Tufts University)

- Interrogating Gender: Centuries of Dramatic Cross-Dressing (Swarthmore)

- Cyberporn and Society (SUNY Buffalo)

- Elvis as Anthology (University of Iowa)

- God, Sex, Chocolate: Desire and the Spiritual Path (UC San Diego)

- How to Watch Television (Montclair)

- Philosophy and *Star Trek* (Georgetown)

- UFOs in American Society (Temple University)

- Wasting Time on the Internet (University of Pennsylvania)

- What If Harry Potter Is Real? (Appalachian State University)

- Zombies in Popular Media (Columbia College)[21]

You can see a recurring theme in these classes: they're all about sex, race, class, gender, and finding your tribe. In the name of advancing broad-minded learning, the schools are pitting people against one another, creating divisions instead of cooperation, and insisting that individual identities matter more than the collective good. They've pitched the liberal arts education into the ditch. It's a wonder people still attend many of these schools, as they serve little useful purpose. What's more?

THESE SCHOOLS COULD BE VIOLATING THE CIVIL RIGHTS ACT

A potentially effective counterpunch has been suggested by Vivek Ramaswamy, author of *Woke, Inc.* and a superstar thinker. He makes the case that these cultish, racist new teachings, including CRT, could be considered a *"secular religion."*[22] Proving this in court would bring the First Amendment's "establishment clause" into play, prohibiting the exercise of religion in the classrooms.

Of course, all students can benefit from God's teachings in class—with faith and principles that teach respect and kindness, treating other people the way you would like to be treated, based on Matthew 7:12 and Luke 6:31. This can have a unifying, uplifting force for good. It can uphold American values that have long made America so attractive to millions around the world. It can bring Americans of all stripes together in an alliance to save America. But at the very least, it makes sense to keep a godless religion from seeping into classrooms. This idea of Ramaswamy's should run through the legal system to see where it leads!

How Did Our Colleges Get So Far Gone?

With so many college professors reverting to their hippie glory days—that is, acting like the children they were—their students are now offered little in the way of a responsible moral compass. So these students are allowed—no, they are often encouraged—to run through the quad shouting out catchy phrases like "systemic oppression" and "old White men" to register their outrage with a system they clearly don't have the first clue about. If these students have any inkling that these buzzwords have been ginned up for them by the elite state's ghostwriters, there's little evidence of it.

They think themselves proud social justice warriors, as if they invented the whole concept or that time began with them. Would it change things if they learned they are being played? If they saw the script, counted their lines in it the way actors do, and found out how they are playing the roles once reserved for Christians fed to lions in a brute spectacle meant to keep the peasants' minds off the grain shortages while the emperor's golden palace grows higher into the sky, they wouldn't believe it. Or most wouldn't, not least because they've been carefully taught from a young age to shout down the very voices of freedom that could save them. Taught to hate on people who can help them. Taught it all backward, and completely oblivious to the real roles they're playing.

So the important things are not being learned by people approaching their third decade in this world. This catastrophic failure of our educational system is a very real problem that we can no longer brush off. We must deal with it head-on.

We must teach young people outside of schools if they cannot be taught inside them. We must show them all that can be learned from disagreeing with somebody and talking or arguing or debating their way to an understanding of each other. We must do what we once took to be obvious. We must show young people that disagreements are the bumps of life, not roadblocks.

This is how we counterpunch, for we know the elite state is using colleges to turn young people into foolishly quarreling social justice warriors for one purpose—to keep the so-called educated classes distracted and too busy to even care that the bulk of the nation's wealth is being secreted into the pockets of a few thousand people.

This we can hit back on.

CHAPTER 9

THE ELITE STATE CONS PROGRESSIVES INTO SUBMISSION

A BOUT A DECADE ago members of the elite state found themselves facing the most intractable problem. Their grand plan for uniting business, government, and technology into a kind of hypersonic wealth extraction machine had hit a wall. They had succeeded in moving 90 percent of the nation's wealth into a few thousand hands, but they couldn't edge that number higher. The problem was not the Republican Party—which was totally on board already. It was those pesky progressives. Some of them wouldn't stop hammering home tropes like "income inequality." It was such a buzzkill at the Davos gatherings. So they put their minds together, so to speak, and thought about their problem.

I can imagine one of the younger, more free-spirited initiates to the elite state table asking, "If you can't beat 'em, why not join 'em?" After a little head-scratching, the wheels might have started turning.

Rather than constantly fighting with progressives, why not just latch on to their latest causes, no matter how harebrained, and become the biggest champion of those causes?

Make the support "real" by adding in mandates and edicts and sanctions, ooh!

Give it a nifty name such as "stakeholder capitalism," since that sounds like everyone now has an equity interest in a new capitalist order, right? The golden-haired idealists and greasy revolutionaries would both feel like their interests were being served. They wouldn't have the first clue how hand-tied independent stakeholders truly were. How little equity they'd really have. Why tell them?

Instead tell these progressives they no longer needed to be agitating for that whole "equal rights for all" thing—since where did that get them? They could now pivot to a new, more enlightened position, "equity for all." So, for example, they could just replace *racial equality* with *racial equity*, and Bob's your uncle, or Lia's your uncle, or something.

Maybe even some Christians could be tricked into buying this stakeholder capitalism, since didn't old Samson pass his judgments with equity in mind, not equality? There has to be some scripture that could be twisted into service. (At least this is how I imagine the conversation around that elite state table.)

Finally, to put ribbons and bows on this new "champion of the underclass" plan and at the same time disarm any progressives wary of overtures from megalomaniac billionaires, some chump change could be thrown at them. It just might work.

And in fact, in just 2021 alone, the elite state sprinkled more than $12 billion over any progressive cause capable of differentiating equality and equity in a sentence.[1] I imagine a run on dictionaries for a while. Progressives soon found that nice offices and making rent suited them. Plus, they could be kept busy managing all the newly minted victims of inequity they'd soon have, all the court cases to attend to, all the grant applications to write up—it could be exhausting!

Plus, there's a win-win for the elite state. With all the new equity-shortchanged victims being identified, one or two could be invited to their swanky, white-tie fund-raising galas to show off on the paparazzi's cue, always a good look, as long as security's beefed up.

As for the $12 billion that the elite state had to pony up, piece of cake. The Ford Foundation gave $3 billion, Jeff Bezos $2.9 billion, JPMorgan Chase $2.1 billion, the W. K. Kellogg Foundation $1.2 billion, the Bill & Melinda Gates Foundation $1.1 billion, the Silicon Valley Community Foundation $1 billion, the Walton Family Foundation $689 million, the William and Flora Hewlett Foundation $438 million, the Foundation to Promote Open Society $350.5 million.[2]

The contemptuousness of this elite-state con caught the attention of Vivek Ramaswamy, a successful health-care entrepreneur who has worked with many of today's captains of industry. In his delightful book *Woke, Inc.*, he has this to say:

> Their tactics are far more dangerous for America than those of the older robber barons: their do-good smoke screen expands not only their market power, but their power over every other facet of our lives. As a young twenty-first-century capitalist myself,

the thing I was supposed to do was shut up and play along: wear hipster clothes, lead via practiced vulnerability, applaud diversity and inclusion, and muse on how to make the world a better place at conferences in fancy ski towns. Not a bad gig.

The most important part of the trick was to stay mum about it. Now I'm violating the code by pulling back the curtain and showing you what's really going on....

Why am I defecting? I'm fed up with corporate America's game of pretending to care about justice in order to make money. It is quietly wreaking havoc on American democracy. It demands that a small group of investors and CEOs determine what's good for society rather than our democracy at large. This new trend has created a major cultural shift in America. It's not just ruining companies. It's polarizing our politics. It's dividing our country to a breaking point. Worst of all, it's concentrating the power to determine American values in the hands of a small group of capitalists, rather than in the hands of the American citizenry at large.[3]

This "do-good smoke screen" to which Ramaswamy refers has been whirling away unchecked on Wall Street for almost a decade now. Since all the old checks and balances on corporate chicanery have long since been swallowed up by the con itself, there has been nothing to stop it.

Take State Street Global Advisors, for example. They sell financial products such as exchange traded funds (ETFs). In 2017 they commissioned a statue of a young girl, called *Fearless Girl*, and positioned her on the street so she was locking eyes with the iconic statue of the Wall Street bull.

At the unveiling, there was all the right-word-saying about gender diversity. The plaque at the girl's feet said, "SHE makes a difference." Turns out SHE is the ticker symbol for State Street's ETF—what they were really promoting.[4] Also, State Street had recently been sued by female employees for underpaying them relative to the men.[5] So the statue did duty to cover them on several fronts, from State Street's view.

From the larger societal view—that is, to those of us who do genuinely care about the women and men in our communities—that statue showed how corrupt it can get when businesses get involved in social causes.

Then there was Goldman Sachs. In January 2020, CEO David Solomon announced that Goldman would no longer be taking any company public unless it had at least one "diverse" member on its board of directors. The left-stream media applauded the loudest. However, by the end of 2019, there weren't any all-male boards in the S&P 500 anymore.[6] Big companies had already met this "diversity" standard even before Goldman began trumpeting it. This scaled new heights of hypocrisy, even for Goldman. So why even bother?

Most certainly, it was a diversionary tactic. Goldman execs had helped the Malaysian outfit 1MDB steal billions from that nation. So heinous was the crime that Goldman ended up paying more than $6 billion in fines to governments around the world for enabling the scandal.[7] Once again showing how corrupt it gets when businesses steer from their lanes.

Coca-Cola makes a big deal about the good works it supports, and how its diversity training sessions include teaching employees "to be less white."[8] Meanwhile these corporate con artists fuel an epidemic of diabetes and obesity among Black Americans through their products. It's much harder to change the formula for Coke, apparently, than pander to the race-baiters.

Once again with the corruption.

Amazon's Jeff Bezos is practically the blackface champion of corporate America, recently pledging $10 million to groups actively fomenting racial divisions in their communities. In doing this, was he hoping people might overlook how Amazon had just fired a bunch of workers of all races who dared to speak out on social media about sweatshop-level working conditions in the Amazon warehouses?

No company runs the racial con more corruptly than Nike. It pledged $40 million to Black Lives Matter and other organizations "to support the Black community in the U.S."[9]

- Not caring that most of BLM's budget went straight into one party's political campaign—not into helping Black communities.[10]

- Not caring that BLM's stated goal is "disrupting the Western-prescribed nuclear family structure" even though that very disruption is the core of Black people's problems.[11]

- Not caring that BLM's founders spent their donations lavishly on themselves, including a $6 million mansion in Southern California.[12]

And for the cherry on top of their ice cream (rocky road, one imagines), Nike showcased former NFL quarterback Colin Kaepernick taking a knee for the national anthem to protest social injustice. While a nation fiercely debated that clown act, Nike was shielded from the outrage it deserved for using child labor in Asian sweatshops to produce $250 sneakers marketed directly to inner-city Black kids who couldn't afford to buy books for school.

As for Kaepernick himself, only a simpleton can loathe a country that made him rich and famous. His loathing is his right. If his conscience troubled him so, he could easily have refused his monstrous salary or refused to play. His kneeling, along with the others', was but corrupt theater.

For any thoughtful liberal, it has to be disconcerting to watch the Democratic Party flip from intense anti-business rhetoric to "Go Big Business" cheerleader. No story tells this better than the Citizens United story.

I'm familiar with it because I founded Citizens United in 1988, though I'd mostly handed over the reins by the time the Supreme Court got involved. In a nutshell, there had emerged a seriously lopsided disparity in election-financing laws. Corporations were capped in how much they could contribute, which was fine. But unions had no such limits on them. Plus, they could give their employees paid days or even weeks off late in the campaign cycles to work the polls. It was plainly unfair back then, since businesses reliably went right, and unions left, in elections.

So Citizens United sought to test the finance laws. It produced a movie about Hillary Clinton that was sure to trigger some constitutional questions. Namely, could corporations be considered people and therefore not subject to campaign contribution limits? The Supremes ruled in favor of Citizens United, and liberals went berserk—a sure sign the ruling was a correct one. And yet that Citizens United decision did pretty much exactly what the new stakeholder capitalism does. Stakeholder capitalism requires the funneling of billions of dollars into political campaigns. It also calls on corporations to pursue the progressive agenda, what they labeled the Environmental, Social, & Governance (ESG) agenda.

So what does ESG add up to?

Big corporations give progressives the policy victories they want in order to (a) shut them up primarily and (b) run interference secondarily—distracting a big swath of the nation from the con they've got going.

Ideally, there would never have been a need for the Citizens United decision. Unions shouldn't have outsized control over elections any more than businesses should. Voters should, obviously. That's why we have elections. When dollars mix with votes like oil in water, dollars rise in influence.

The only way to push out the oil, to continue this idea, is to add more water from below. That's what local organizing is all about—filling local ballots with decent candidates, good people serving at the local level. And as they rise through the political ranks, hopefully they will maintain the values that launched them, the values that can sustain the country.

FORGETTING WHO WE WERE JUST A FEW YEARS AGO

Every sector of society is afflicted. As recently as 1983, the college textbook *American Government: The Rules of the Game* was a standard read for political science students.[13] It was a portrait of how similar Americans were at the time. Ideologically, similar. In spoken language, similar. In reading and TV viewing habits, similar. Even in the clothes we wore, similar. There were plenty of differences across regions and ethnic backgrounds, of course, but culturally we were remarkably similar.

Politically we were all nineteenth-century liberals. That is, we believed in individualism, private property, capitalism, competition, limited government, free speech, the rule of law, and the freedoms of the First Amendment.

We could not be more dissimilar just four decades later.

English is not an endangered language, but soon to be a minority language. From Los Angeles to Miami and especially in the cities, the primary language is Spanish. Chinese is coming on strong in many cities.

Residents in the flats of Oakland speak a language that cannot be understood at all.

On TV there is one set of programs for each major demographic group; it's the same for print media and radio. Certainly, the internet has contributed to this fragmentation, but the changes predated the internet by years.

Old-fashioned ideals of individualism and First Amendment freedoms have no purchase with many Americans. There is little respect left for private property. Capitalism has become a four-letter word. Big corporations are bent into competition-destroying monopolies. Free speech is to younger people like an analog clock.

THE CHURCH BECOMES WOKE

Even the church is not immune. Owen Strachan, PhD, provost and research professor of theology at Grace Bible Theological Seminary, wrote an entire book on this, *Christianity and Wokeness*.[14] He said that in 2020, America was the epicenter of a renewed socialist revolution inside its churches:

> In our time…"wokeness"…is running amok. [In the summer of 2020], riots broke out all across America in the name of equity, fairness, and social justice, America was put to the torch. Shockingly few responded. The revolution…struck, you see, at the very nerve of law and order. It was…supposedly unjust law and order that precipitated the entire crisis.…
>
> A single instance of purportedly racist police conduct was emblematic of an entire system of oppression.…Our response will not merely respond to the charges, but will ultimately aim at a theology of public engagement such that we punch back against the darkness, speak the truth in love, and live as salt and light.

Strachan shared a shocking example of wokeism in the "Prayer for a Weary Black Woman" by Chanequa Walker-Barnes, PhD:

> Dear God, please help me to hate White people. Or at least to want to hate them. At least, I want to stop caring about them, individually and collectively. I want to stop caring about their

misguided, racist souls, to stop believing that they can be better, that they can stop being racist.[15]

Strachan sought to explain:

Wokeness involves becoming awake to the nature of systemic racial discrimination in a society, one like ours....Once you go woke, you resolve to fight the existing order....

In the American past, there are real racial sins...with regard to slavery and Jim Crow, and even individual, personal acts of racism....We understand that...it's because of the natural partiality of the human heart...we all, in our sin nature, come equipped, preloaded, with partiality....

[But in wokeness and in critical race theory] racism is structural...you're always going to be racist. You're all racist.... Wherever this ideology goes, it divides....It blows up communities; it blows up institutions; it definitely blows up churches.

Ibram X. Kendi is probably the leading woke academic theorist today [and wrote]: "The most threatening racist movement is not the alt-right's unlikely drive for a White ethnostate, but the regular American's drive for a 'race-neutral' one."

Wokeness...saves its strongest firepower...for ordinary men and women who lead quiet, normal, un-racist American lives, [and] in this system you're never cured of racism....

Once-strong, gospel-preaching churches where there was a great deal of Gospel-driven diversity, there were a lot of people... of a variety of backgrounds and...there was a lot of unity...and that was all a display of gospel love....And then, the pastor went woke. [Wokeness] is an ideology that will take you captive, it will hijack you, it will ruin the way you think as a Christian....

We must never stop preaching the Gospel as our plan of unity, as our means of justice, as the gateway to hope.[16]

RACISM IN THE NFL IS RAMPANT

Recently, NFL commissioner Roger Goodell told the world that the NFL is one blatantly racist organization, and therefore, the NFL is requiring every team to hire a minority offensive coach.[17] Goodell is right, of course, to look out on the field. There's a nearly complete lack of White guys playing in the defensive back positions.

"JINGLE BELLS" GETS CANCELED

Yes, the song "Jingle Bells" was wiped from the songbook at Council Rock Primary School in Brighton, New York, when the principal there discovered how deeply offensive its lyrics are. The superintendent of schools, Kevin McGowan, explained:

> The fact that "Jingle Bells" was first performed in minstrel shows where white actors performed in blackface does actually matter when it comes to questions of what we use as material in school. I'm glad that our staff paused when learning of this, reflected, and decided to use different material to accomplish the same objective in class.[18]

McGowan took pains to assure Brighton parents that he wasn't some nutjob liberal run amok, noting that "Jingle Bells" has been known to offend non-Christians, satanists, pagans, and Voldemort.

He needn't have worried. Most of Brighton's parents were with him. A year earlier, all had agreed that their school mascot name of "Barons" should be changed to "Bruins" lest anyone spot any White privilege running rampant in town. Surely that upscale city's racial makeup of 78.5 percent White and 6.6 percent Black is just happenstance.

SCIENCE IS IDEOLOGY, DON'T YOU KNOW?

Science magazine has boasted some fascinating covers over the decades, with breakthrough articles on immunology and quantum sensors among others. But in a recent week, a look at *Science*'s home page found "The Toll of White Privilege: How the Dominant Culture Has Discouraged Diversity" and "For LGBTQ Scientists, Being Out Can Mean More Publications," among other breaking science stories.[19] This is not science, of course. It is a political ideology that is hostile to intelligent scientific inquiry.

GOOD PARENTS STAND UP TO THE MIND POISON

In Southern California, a group of parents formed the Inland Empire Family PAC to support school board candidates who hold to Judeo-Christian values. As was reported in the Western Journal:

> Some main issues of concern for the PAC are the sexualization of children through school curricula, the teaching of critical race theory and parental rights over any medications children receive, such as transgender therapies and vaccinations. Parents have the ultimate responsibility for raising children, including instilling values.[20]

When the local progressive group Temecula Unity learned about this PAC, they went ballistic. They allegedly accused the parents of trying to install a theocracy in the school board and found it "extremely offensive" that a school should focus on teaching children reading, writing, and arithmetic and that's all.[21]

Progressives next went full Saul Alinsky. They released the location where the PAC was planning to meet—a car dealership. And, according to the leader of the Family PAC, they allegedly ordered their people to "flood that location with calls; tell them, you're going to picket." The car dealership's phones rang off the hook, so much so that they had to shut down business and cancel the event.

This is what good parents are up against. In this case, another venue was found, and the PAC isn't backing down because they've seen what our kids are facing.

A local teacher, Nick Pardue, spoke at the PAC meeting about the kids. About how rough it has been to see changes in their personalities from the colliding of COVID lockdowns and cancel culture:

> They really aren't the same, and they are terrified of cancel culture. They're self-conscious. I hear kids saying, "I don't want to take my mask off because I've become accustomed to being able to hide in anonymity behind this mask," and that's really sad.[22]

Pardue's concerns run deep enough that he's running for a spot on the Murrieta Valley Unified School District board—to try to make a difference. Other parents are joining him in running for local board seats, with one saying the purpose of schools "should be education, not indoctrination" and another adding, "If we're going to save America…it starts with school boards, so I'm in."[23]

These are parents and concerned citizens standing up for a generation of kids—these are the truest American heroes today. We salute them and join them in fighting to keep simple decency and righteousness as staples of our American communities. It is the very definition of a counterpunch.

FACING THE GIANTS

What is the first step in facing the giants?

Prayer: "So I prayed to the God of heaven" (Neh. 2:4).

Our nation was born in a prayer to live free of a tyrant's bounds, to face up to the giant oppressors of old and begin life anew. Through the Lord's blessings, an exceptional country came to life, offering hope and freedom in a world of great oppression and cruelty. How ironic, then, that our nation has grown more and more secular in its daily practices, leaving behind the very prayer that led to our exceptionalism.

But again, we are finding what it takes to stand up to giants.

AT THE 50-YARD LINE OF CHURCH AND STATE

Students may "feel that they have to join religious activities that they do not wish to join," Justice Elena Kagan lamented as the Supreme Court deliberated on whether Bremerton High School football coach Joe Kennedy should have been suspended for his practice of taking a knee to pray after a game.[24]

That such a thing would even require a Supreme Court ruling is shameful, and it is made even more so by Justice Kagan's sophomoric reasoning. The coach wanted to pray. He didn't ask or require his players to join him. He waited until after the game and then took a knee. In the minds of some, evidently, that action of his was putting terrible pressure on his players to join in the prayer.

What, then, of a science teacher at Bremerton High marking down a student for writing a paper questioning anthropomorphic climate change? Would that also be unacceptable to Justice Kagan? Somehow I doubt it, though I can assure the good justice that the student feels intense pressure to write what the teacher wants to hear, what the teacher is rumored to grade up. Such examples of hard pressure happen all the time and feel very different from a coach choosing to pray on his own after a game.

Justice Clarence Thomas made that point crisply by asking the Bremerton school's attorney, "If the coach, instead of taking a knee for prayer, took a knee during the National Anthem because of moral opposition to racism, how would your school district respond?"[25]

It's certainly true that people can feel pressured to act in a certain way when facing up to someone in a position of authority. But there are differences between a coach praying on his own, a teacher holding a grade over a student's head, and a coach taking a knee during the National Anthem. Differences that no court could be expected—should be expected—to referee. So the justices should rightly let constitutional principles guide them.

And they did. They upheld the "establishment clause" in the First Amendment. The coach was not preferring one religion over the other, not halting anyone from practicing his or her religion in public. In a landmark June 2022 decision, coming after an arduous seven-year battle through multiple courts, the Supreme Court ruled in favor of Coach Kennedy. In his way, Kennedy said, "The First Amendment is fine and well for everyone."[26]

In another time, it would have been a slam-dunk case. One of Coach Kennedy's lawyers, Jeremy Dys, saw it as a clear-cut constitutional case and was surprised that the ball kept getting kicked on up the court system to the top: "We thought, when we took this case on, that we'd be working on it for three weeks. And everything would move on. But the school district kept moving the goalposts."[27]

It all began for Coach Kennedy in 2008, after a twenty-year career in the Marines. "I watched the film *Facing the Giants*—and just like in the movie, I made a commitment to God that I was going to give him thanks after every football game, win or lose."[28]

Kennedy believed it was a personal act of worship, and no player or student was ever coerced to join him. He did this for eight years until someone complained and he got fired by the school district. But Kennedy persevered because he knew he had done nothing wrong:

I was optimistic every step of the way, and I was surprised that the lower courts ruled against me—some of them so harshly.... This was just me thanking God for 15 seconds, after a football game....This is about the First Amendment. It has nothing to do with infringing on anybody else's [rights]. This is somebody exercising the freedom that is in our country.[29]

MICHIGAN COACH TEACHES BALLHANDLING— AND CHARACTER BUILDING

"Thou shalt no longer shake hands" came the directive from the front office, but Michigan State basketball coach Tom Izzo was having none of it. His players were going to shake hands with their opponents after the game—win or lose. Because shaking hands is about showing character, on the court and in our culture at large.

> We've already taught these poor 18-year-olds that when you're told to go to class and you don't like it, you can leave. We've already told these kids that if you're not happy, you can do something else. We've already told these kids that it's hard to hold them accountable. And now we're going to tell them to not man up and walk down a line [to] someone who's kicked your butt and have enough class to shake their hand—[it's] utterly ridiculous.[30]

Coach Izzo is a role model we need—not only for his players, but for us all. Whereas politicians in Washington turn away from thorny problems, Coach Izzo is teaching his charges to face up to problems square-on, shake hands with opponents whether in victory or in defeat, for we are all in this together.

Two coaches—Kennedy and Izzo—offering examples of bravely "facing the giants." As Joe Kennedy was inspired by the movie *Facing the Giants*, I've shared his inspiring story of a local person having courage, sticking to his values, and winning a national battle. His story, and those of the other courageous individuals in this book, are examples of brave Americans standing up and counterpunching—and you can do the same in whatever circumstance you find yourself.

WHAT SHALL WE DO?

In the Old Testament Book of 2 Kings, I find one of my favorite stories. This story has encouraged me through forty years of public activism. It is the story of Elisha and his servant. I wish I had time to do an entire teaching on Elisha because this dude rocks, but I will just share several verses:

> When the servant of the man of God got up and went out early the next morning, an army with horses and chariots had surrounded the city. "Oh no, my lord! What shall we do?" the servant asked.
>
> "Don't be afraid," the prophet answered. "Those who are with us are more than those who are with them."
>
> And Elisha prayed, "Open his eyes, LORD, so that he may see." Then the LORD opened the servant's eyes, and he looked and saw the hills full of horses and chariots of fire all around Elisha.
>
> —2 KINGS 6:15–17, NIV

We must not get discouraged but remember that there are many more people who want to save America than destroy it. This is precisely why we have had so many victories of late. Always remember, we greatly outnumber them.

We need only the courage to stand up for what is right. There's a time for everything, and now's the time to be strong and courageous—and stand firm.

In a time when the very fabric of truth is often being manipulated, there can be great risk in standing for truth. But that is our moral obligation.

Standing for truth is also the proper response to an ideology-obsessed mob that noisily demands our children obey their nonsense and lies.

Standing for truth is the proper response to the foolish lies that long-held Judeo-Christian values are just White supremacist window coverings.

Standing for truth is the proper response to race-baiters who would rewrite our country's history without regard to all that civil rights pioneers have accomplished.

Standing for truth is the proper response to the statue-toppling of Lincoln, Douglass, and Jefferson, for those men built a great nation.

There is only one way to counterpunch courageously, and it begins with standing for truth right in our own neighborhood and working patiently on up from there. It's a long way up, yes, but each victory along the way becomes the announcement of the next.

THE TIME FOR COMPROMISING IS PAST

It comes down to a progressive agenda running our lives, or us running our lives. It's this pursuit of liberty that drives us now, just as it drove a man nearly 250 years ago to give one of the greatest speeches ever voiced. Speaking to the Second Virginia Revolutionary Convention meeting at St. John's Church so as not to be shut down, Patrick Henry made the case for resisting the British tyrants, a case that resonates clearly today as we again face elite tyrants bent on subjugating a nation:

> Mr. President, it is natural to man to indulge in the illusions of hope. We are apt to shut our eyes against a painful truth, and listen to the song of that siren till she transforms us into beasts. Is this the part of wise men, engaged in a great and arduous struggle for liberty? Are we disposed to be of the number of those who, having eyes, see not, and, having ears, hear not, the things which so nearly concern their temporal salvation? For my part, whatever anguish of spirit it may cost, I am willing to know the whole truth; to know the worst, and to provide for it....
>
> I know of no way of judging of the future but by the past. And judging by the past, I wish to know what there has been in the conduct of the British ministry for the last ten years, to justify those hopes....Ask yourselves how this gracious reception of our petition comports with these war-like preparations which cover our waters and darken our land. Are fleets and armies necessary to a work of love and reconciliation? Have we shown ourselves so unwilling to be reconciled that force must be called in to win back our love? Let us not deceive ourselves, sir. These are the implements of war and subjugation....
>
> If we wish to be free—if we mean to preserve inviolate those inestimable privileges for which we have been so long

contending—if we mean not basely to abandon the noble struggle in which we have been so long engaged, and which we have pledged ourselves never to abandon until the glorious object of our contest shall be obtained—we must fight! I repeat it, sir, we must fight! An appeal to arms and to the God of Hosts is all that is left us!...

Sir, we are not weak if we make a proper use of those means which the God of nature hath placed in our power. The millions of people, armed in the holy cause of liberty, and in such a country as that which we possess, are invincible by any force which our enemy can send against us. Besides, sir, we shall not fight our battles alone. There is a just God who presides over the destinies of nations, and who will raise up friends to fight our battles for us. The battle, sir, is not to the strong alone; it is to the vigilant, the active, the brave....

The war is actually begun! The next gale that sweeps from the north will bring to our ears the clash of resounding arms! Our brethren are already in the field! Why stand we here idle?... Is life so dear, or peace so sweet, as to be purchased at the price of chains and slavery? Forbid it, Almighty God! I know not what course others may take; but as for me, give me liberty or give me death![31]

Still to this day my eyes fill with tears at the bravery of the Founders, at the sacrifices they made, not because they wanted to, but because they had to.

Again we are called to unite a diverse nation of immigrants—each of us simply yearning to live free.

Again we are called to rise up against this new face of tyranny so that our children can inherit the promise of liberty.

This will not be an easy struggle. But it is righteous. At every turn, the mouthpieces of the elite state will be lobbing their attack missiles, taunting us, labeling us racists, deplorables, bigots, and all the blasphemies they can pull from their baskets of hate.

Some of us will be—already are being—censored in our postings, left out of local social events, even cut off from financial opportunities. It will not be an easy fight, this fight for individual liberty. It never has been. But it is the fight that has come to us, the one we must win.

We are being called, just as Patrick Henry was once called, to save America. The stakes could not be higher, and yes, we have it within us to rise to the challenge of this moment. Each of us in our communities can take a stand for liberty, each in our own way.

And if we can support you in taking a stand in your community, find us at CounterpunchBook.com.

CHAPTER 10

THE ELITES' WEALTH EXTRACTION MACHINERY MUST BE SMASHED TO BITS

W<small>E WERE ONLY</small> weeks into the COVID scare in early 2020 when five things all became clear pretty much at once.

1. The government was largely incapable of handling a genuine health crisis.

2. Our emergency response systems resembled those of third-world countries.

3. Critical supplies once stockpiled for times of need were nowhere to be found.

4. Health insurance programs were completely inadequate to the demand.

5. Vaccines were being developed at warp speeds without concern for side effects.

COVID was a legitimate national health crisis, and one to be taken seriously. But our government's performance in that crisis was so unserious, so madcap, that it twisted the national psyche as if into a rubber-band ball of collective anger. Soon those bands began snapping off in a stinging barrage of irrationality, paranoia, and terror, with people becoming the worst version of themselves. It will be many years before we collectively recover from this, and it never had to be.

Were we to face a truly serious threat today—such as having to confront Hitler's military ambitions—we'd be turned back at Normandy. If we now tried to put a man on the moon, we'd be doing studies of the moon's surface composition for decades to come. For we no longer have a functioning government. What we have is a giant stage in Washington, and all the politicians are players. From behind the proscenium arch, a few thousand people pull all the strings on their puppet players. And the performances are all a farce.

You could call this characterization cynical and overly simplistic, and I wouldn't disagree. But take this little quiz with me.

1. Hasn't our federal government always been run by a handful of rich elites?

2. In a country as big as ours, isn't it simply far-fetched to believe that a few thousand people have an iron-fist control over every lever of power?

3. Even if a few people have consolidated power, aren't they checked by other powermongers wanting to control things themselves?

4. And even if all levers of power are wielded by a few, isn't our country still a lot better off for a lot more people than at any other time in history?

Answers:

1. No

2. No

3. No

4. No

All are no because of one word: financialization.

It's quite a mouthful, I know. Not many people have any idea what it means. But we're about to see here how it's doing the kind of damage Pharaoh's slavery, the Black Plague, and climate change did—all combined. *Financialization* is best defined by what it has accomplished.

- **Financialization has ripped apart the social fabric** that once bound us together as neighbors in communities.

Even before COVID, people were turning away from their communities into more isolated existences, rarely seeing their neighbors, going bowling alone, staring longer at their cell phones than at anyone else in their lives. This didn't just happen—it was one of the side effects of the financialization project launched in the late 1980s.

- **Financialization has turned intelligent people into authority-loving fools.** And since it is much easier to turn people into fools than to convince them they've been fooled, financialization has exceeded its promoters' wildest dreams.

- **Financialization has created a new kind of slavery**—or at least it has if you accept that moving $50 trillion in earnings out of the pockets of 250 million workers into the pockets of a couple thousand masters is, in fact, slavery.

All this could only work if the people were deftly distracted. Otherwise they'd never allow it to happen. So the people behind the financialization project needed some way of stirring things up, inciting people into a frenzy of constant quarreling, keeping them lunging at each other's throats instead of discovering that their six-bit project was really a single-syllabled con—a con that played out on three levels: ideas, individuals, and institutions.

Controlling all three meant game, set, match.

Here's how it happened. That figure of $50 trillion of wealth extracted from the pockets of 250 million workers? It's not some shiny round number meant to stick in your brain. It's a rather in-depth calculation done by analysts at the RAND Corporation—which is as close to honest and nonpartisan as anything gets anymore.[1]

RAND analysts figured that if people across the board had from 1975 to 2018 continued to earn at the steadily increasing level seen in the post–World War II period, every single working American would be making, on average, $1,144 more a month, or $13,728 more a year, or a half million dollars over a career span.

This lost income has not been the same for everyone, of course. It cuts harsher on lower-income families than on higher; harsher on minority workers than White, as you'd expect. For the average middle-class American working full-time, the loss is $42,000 a year. All this is before inflation, mind you, which makes the overall losses much worse.

Had the financialization con not been run, our lives would be dramatically different.

For some, there'd be enough extra money to take genuinely relaxing and fulfilling vacations every year. For others, it would mean a chance to actually retire at the age of sixty-five instead of having to work unhealthily beyond the productive years—foregoing so much. For all of us, there'd be more time to engage in community activities and civic pursuits—helping others and enjoying the rewards of service.

Instead, that money went right into the pockets of a few thousand people. And not because that's just how it worked out. Not at all. It happened because these people figured out how to turn every bagel, bicycle, and barnside into a financial product. That's a little more of the financialization definition.

How They Snuck One By Us

As recently as the late 1980s, the financial-services sector accounted for only about 10 percent of the nation's GDP.[2] It served as an enabler—helping other companies achieve their ends. Then a series of steps were taken to double the finance, insurance, and real estate sectors to 20 percent of the economy—officially.[3] But that doubling of an industry doesn't begin to tell the story.

It doesn't tell how those financial whiz kids ran through industry after industry rolling up companies into bundles of securities that Wall Street could bet on. Just about everything in the country—from the corner bodega to funeral homes to bottled water—was turned into a security to be bought and sold on some trading exchange. No longer were these businesses providing a service; they were now financial instruments. And the financiers behind all this corporate consolidation, knowing full well that most people had no idea what was going on, slapped some really crafty and cool-sounding explanations on it. The happy patter went something like this: You're seeing creative destruction at work here, and it's the natural evolution of all organisms. Besides, just look how consumers have benefited from lower prices and convenient shopping!

"Sure, right, why not?" we all said. And the financial complexities of it all went right over our collective heads, for truly, finance can be heady stuff. And how were we supposed to know what questions to ask?

How were we supposed to understand the mechanics of corporate stock buybacks and how that once-illegal activity would enrich a few shareholders while leaving companies completely vulnerable to the next financial downturn, at which point taxpayers would be called in to bail them out?

How could we have foreseen that a wave of giant corporate mergers and acquisitions, all of which seemed to have the blessings of government antitrust overseers, would give us a new kind of monopoly capable of crushing the competitive spirit and cultural traditions of a nation?

How could we have known that when companies moved production overseas to exploit the gains of dirt-cheap labor, avert liberals' eyes from the toxins flowing into other people's rivers, and buy local politicians far more handily than could be done back home, the heartland of America would turn from proud and hardworking to jobless and opioid-addicted?

How were we even to fathom the mindset of someone who believes playing games with other people's money and their jobs is the new winners' game, and producing goods and services that create jobs is for losers?

How could we *not* be excited by the lower prices we saw on so many consumer items? So excited that we didn't think twice about those prices. But if we had, we'd see how the quality had been stripped from those products. We'd see the paint so thin the steel soon rusts out, the materials so shoddy the veneer peels off, the chip so brittle it fails and takes the entire appliance down with it.

We'd see this and do the math. Whereas once that washing machine cost $500 and lasted twenty or even thirty years and rarely needed repairs, now we got it for just $250, but it fails predictably in four years and can't be repaired. So, thanks to planned obsolescence, we're paying more. Much more.

One more question: How long could this financialization spree go on before it all came tumbling down on the backs of everyday Americans?

We got our answer in May 2022.

INFLATION IS GIVING THE LIE TO POLITICIANS' WORD-SAYING

About one hundred million people have become US citizens since the word *inflation* was last on everyone's lips. Many of them, if asked, would guess that "the CPI" is a new cop show on TV. They have no real concept of what inflation is or the kind of financial destruction it can wreak. And they have no idea how it happened so suddenly in May 2022.

President Biden knew, but he couldn't be honest about it lest he be immediately impeached by his own party. So first the president blamed it all—everything, you name it!—on Trump. The Left loved that. Then he broadened the appeal of his message, claiming it was "oil and gas companies [padding] their profits at the expense of hardworking Americans." Then it was "the cost of prescription drugs."[4] Then it was the Russian invasion of Ukraine.[5]

It's certainly true that greedy oil companies and bad old Putin contributed to the sudden spike in consumer prices. But why did a carton of eggs climb from 88 cents to $1.60 in some states since late 2020?[6] Why did food prices climb 49 percent between May 2020 and January 2022?[7] And why did rents spike as much as 30 percent in some cities, with median rent in locales such as Fresno, California, and Tulsa, Oklahoma, up nearly 40 percent for a one-bedroom apartment?[8]

And what about inflation's stealthy cousin, shrinkflation? Consumer product companies are keeping their packaging and pricing the same but shrinking the actual product: Kellogg's Corn Flakes has been reduced from 27 ounces to 21 ounces; Dove soap shrank from 4 ounces in 2020 to 3.17 ounces today; and Pringles has dropped from 7 ounces to 5.8 ounces.[9]

What about all those "I Did That" stickers at gas pumps with Biden pointing at suddenly high prices? If those stickers were more honest, they'd be much larger, to share billing with Presidents Trump, Obama, and Bush. All their administrations ran up government spending like Kardashians marooned on Rodeo Drive. And that—the presidents and not the Kardashians—is what blasted inflation out of its forty-year slumber.

Blasted is a strong word. What's stronger? The sudden forty-year increase in inflation to 9.1 percent in July and then down slightly to 8.5

140

percent in June is actually a sleight-of-hand misrepresentation—or more accurately, a lie. The real number—that is, the inflation we feel in our daily purchases—actually shot higher than the June 1980 peak of 13.6 percent. The reason you don't see it in the media is that the government has changed the things they measure so it doesn't look so bad.

Economist John Williams has calculated the inflation figure the way they used to in the 1980s before President Clinton's Bureau of Labor Standards changed it to make the boss look better. That figure is far from 9.1 percent—it's 16.8 percent in annual terms, almost double the official figure.[10]

So the federal government has created a mess they have no idea how to get out of, and no interest in either. In the last few years the government and the Fed have together pumped about $13 trillion into the economy. When you do this—no matter how you try to rationalize it—only one thing can follow: inflation.

Here's how it played out and where we're likely headed next.

When COVID first hit, Federal Reserve chairman Jerome Powell moved fast to marshal his staff, calling on them to "Get in the boats and go," as had been the call at Dunkirk. His email to staff said this: "Focus turns 100% now to liquidity, where we may have a lot to do!"[11] What did he mean by that?

Big banks had been allowed to borrow money for years at near-zero interest and then go ahead and invest or lend that *same* money often six times over. So they would borrow $100 million, for example, and invest it six times—turning $100 million in free money into $600 million in profit potential.

When you and I do this, it's called fraud and we can land in jail. When banks do this, it's called leverage and they can make obscene sums of money. And should some unforeseen event come along and spoil the profiting—a coronavirus, for example—the bankers can count on the Fed to make good on that $600 million they've floated into the markets. You can imagine how uncomfortable Wall Street financiers would feel having to pay back that $600 million themselves! But no worries. That's what the Fed is there for now: to cover any bad bets the bankers make. And by cover, I mean shift the liability for those debts over to the American people. That's just what Powell set out to do—full speed ahead.

Left unsaid in Powell's Dunkirk speech was that giant corporations were sitting on $1.8 trillion in hard cash.[12] That's cash they could have used to ride out the COVID crisis—or many of them could have anyway. But they chose to use those cash reserves to enrich their shareholders instead, or just to keep the powder dry, knowing they would be made whole. Not for nothing did the average Wall Street bonus climb above $257,500 in 2021 amidst all the market danger![13]

Also not for nothing was the true state of the stock market when COVID struck. Yes, the Dow index suddenly dropped a massive 10,000 points and traders were running around in "sheer unadulterated panic" shouting, "Hell is coming."[14] But really, was it?

Since March 2000, the long-term moving average of stock prices has been rising. So even after the massive crash in March 2020, the market was still above its long-term trajectory. Then the market went flat-out bonkers for fifteen months—doubling, which is unheard of. Then it corrected a bit but remained well above its historical average gain, leading us to three questions we should run to ground:

- Was the government's massive bailout of big business really needed, or was it just envelopes stuffed with cash for paid-in members of the elite state?

- Is it, in fact, *criminal* for the government to hand over so much cash when the price for it, predictably, is going to be a blast of inflation?

- Now that the Biden administration is stuck behind inflation's wrecking ball, what is it likely to do?

Bringing In the Cleanup Crew

Governments faced with inflating prices and enraged consumers rarely reflect on their own actions that led to those prices. Instead, they send in the political version of the old mob's cleanup crew to dispose of the bodies and scrub the floors clean again, aiming for that "nothing to see here" look.

And so in 1933, with the Great Depression leveling a nation, President

Franklin Roosevelt launched his National Recovery Administration to set price floors for products and wages across hundreds of industries.[15] The net effect, in the view of many experts, was a deepening and extending of the Depression for several more years.

Again in 1971, when the Vietnam War was winding down but inflation appeared to be winding up, President Nixon responded with "a freeze on all prices and wages throughout the United States."[16] Soon the store shelves had emptied, gas lines formed at the pumps, and inflation came anyway. Within a few years it would devastate the nation.

Now the Biden administration is trotting out the finest economists in the land to insist that inflation has not taken root and we'll not repeat the wrenching wage-price spirals of the past. They say it won't happen because (a) we now have a more activist Fed, (b) unions have lost the bargaining power they once had, (c) global trade flows are now very different, (d) the multitrillion-dollar Build Back Better spending bill will bring down the prices it jacked up in the first place, (e) that spiral you see of people demanding higher wages, and companies in turn charging higher prices, would be much worse if the Republicans were in charge!

All of these explanations may make for passable political theater— which is, of course, the entire point—but they are not likely to change the economic nightmare we're now facing for several years' worth of indiscriminate money printing. What was true in the 1770s (the Continental Congress couldn't yet tax citizens to fund the war, so they just printed money, leading to near 30 percent hyperinflation) was true again in 1917 (though taxes had begun, the United States funded a lot of World War I with printed money, driving inflation to near 20 percent) and again in the 1970s and early 1980s (when an oil embargo and spending for the Vietnam War led to more money printing, and inflation exceeded 14 percent).[17] Simply, when you print one new dollar bill without at the same time increasing the supply of goods and services by one dollar, you get inflation. That's how money works.

So when you print *trillions* of dollars in a flat economy like we just did, you're looking at very nasty inflation taking root, possibly even blowing up into hyperinflation, which levels the economy.

How this leveling takes place, and when, is anyone's guess. But when people really start to feel the pinch and they can no longer afford the basic supplies they usually count on, the politicians will have to move beyond cheap rationalizing and start delivering *something*. That's when we'll see real desperation and its economic cousin, price controls.

We saw price controls with Presidents Roosevelt and Nixon, and now with President Biden almost certainly. These controls may take the form of a national $15 minimum wage, though when tried at the state level, it has actually hurt the low-income people it was meant to help.[18]

Price controls could take the form of caps on fuel prices, actual ceilings beyond just temporary tax holidays (none of which would be necessary if liberals would simply compromise on the need to balance fossil fuels with renewable energy sources until we finally get beyond the need for fossil fuels).

Only one solution will actually work, as the libertarian Ron Paul has summed up:

> To put an end to the welfare-warfare...Congress can drastically reduce the military budget, end all corporate welfare, and shut down all unconstitutional Cabinet departments. The savings can be used to pay down debt and to support those truly dependent on government programs while responsibility for providing assistance returns to local institutions and private charities.[19]

Of course, Dr. Paul's prescription isn't going to happen anytime soon, since that would drive a stake through the heart of the elite state. But that *is* what's called for. Without it, the inflationary spiral unleashed by reckless monetary policies and financialization is almost certain to plunge our nation into a disaster not seen in many decades.

BIGGEST STOCK MARKET BUST OF OUR LIFETIME?

Nobody can accurately forecast stock market prices because at its core the market is a roulette wheel that spins on an axis of its own choosing. The house can, and regularly does, tamper with the ivory ball so it lands just right. And with the help of AI-driven computers, stock traders can game the wheel to make great fortunes. If they can keep the game running long enough, they'll create a "bubble" in the market that must inevitably burst the fortunes of everybody. When this happens, the traders can usually count on their elite-state protectors to make them whole, but not before taking the economy down all around them.

Not a pretty picture; just the truth.

As for these market bubbles, there is a fundamental rule about them: each will be *bigger* than the last. We could take pages to lay out why this is true. Suffice it to say it has to do with the exponential function of system scale. The bigger the market, the larger the collapse.

In the last half century we've seen three financial bubbles rock the markets—each bigger than the last. And a fourth is near, likely to rip away half to three-quarters of the stock market holdings of investors not prepared with a proper exit strategy.

Japan's asset bubble lopped 49 percent off the Nikkei stock market's value.[20] Then the dot-com bubble of 2000 took the Nasdaq down 78 percent before, with the help of the Fed, stabilizing things at a 50 percent loss.[21] Then the housing bubble of 2007 crashed the stock market 44 percent, with the government spending $900 billion to cover the elite state's losses, zero to cover everyone else's losses.[22] Next will be the—nobody knows, as we've said, but the betting is on a commodities bubble bursting next. The pandemic shocks to the global supply chain, the Russian invasion of Ukraine, energy resources and vital materials being held hostage by enemy nations…the list of contributions to a sudden commodities crunch is long.

Russia is a major supplier of vital raw materials—more than a third of the world's palladium and enriched uranium,[23] 17 percent of natural gas, 11 percent of platinum,[24] 10 percent of gold,[25] 10 percent of oil, and on and on. As well, Russia and Ukraine supply nearly a third of the world's wheat. Acute food shortages are already threatening developing countries. A number of scenarios could trigger margin calls that giant commodity producers could not meet—at which point all hell breaks loose.

Savvy investors are already moving into the safety of hard assets that hold their value in times of crisis. This is the time to be holding a larger portion of invested assets in gold and precious metals.

Some have moved into crypto, having bought the shameless pitches of highly paid actors that "fortune favors the bold." Anyone who foolishly thought that crypto was the new El Dorado or that it would replace gold as the new safe haven got smacked hard in May 2022, when the entire sector crashed. Saddest to me is how many young people thought themselves hip and clever to "buy in early." Some gambled away their stimulus checks; others invested heavily rather than paying off student loans. Now that money is gone.

I do believe that crypto and the blockchain will someday become a legitimate asset class and accounting tool, respectively. But for the next several years, the federal government will be figuring out how to manage and regulate this brand-new thing. And by manage and regulate, I mean co-opt. It's a time for investors to be cautious.

SOCIAL SECURITY IS STILL INSOLVENT

Two words that no politician dares combine: *social* and *security*. The last one to try in a serious way was Chris Christie in his 2016 presidential bid. Didn't work out too well. Social Security is by far the biggest slice of the federal pie, sucking down $1.12 trillion in 2021. Despite its size, not a peep is said about it. That's because it's on course to be the biggest train wreck in our nation's history—and no politician wants to be anywhere near those tracks.

Now, we know politicians go to Washington precisely to deal with such hard issues. Ha! Most go to Washington to first shed the idealism of youth, then to get rich and bask in the winds of power blowing across their faces.

Meanwhile, some sixty-five million Americans are expecting to receive a monthly payment averaging $1,537 this year. Expecting, rightfully, since they did pay it forward. Forty percent of these Americans rely on Social Security to cover almost all their living expenses.[26] This is America's most important social program.

Yet the numbers of Americans still working and contributing to the fund is fast dropping off. Many are even quitting the workforce. So the Social Security payroll tax receipts are shrinking even as the ranks of seniors expecting payments is exploding. Within the decade, some sixty-eight million of us will be drawing those checks every month. Or hoping to—meaning something's got to give. By 2028 or thereabouts the Social Security trust fund will be so depleted it will only "be sufficient to pay about three-quarters of scheduled benefits."[27] More specifically, a 22 to 25 percent cut in monthly payments is coming very soon.

It's likely that this 22 to 25 percent cut in payments will be combined with (a) higher payroll taxes, (b) a higher retirement age to qualify, and (c) a cutback in cost-of-living adjustments—even as inflation drives up the cost of living. That's a solution sure to anger everybody—from the old guys not getting what they were promised to the young bucks not keeping more of the money they earn.

There is another solution, the kind of solution that needs to be applied to all government programs. It is, simply enough, means testing.

This would involve looking at the annual income of Social Security beneficiaries to decide whether they should receive a full benefit check, a reduced check, or no check at all. For instance, someone making under $80,000 in adjusted gross income gets the full check, under $120,000 a partial check, over that no check.

This way we ensure that Social Security benefits go to people who really need them, which is how the program was meant to work when Roosevelt started it.

Yes, people who've paid into Social Security over a lifetime would be punished for their current high earnings, but all government programs discriminate against someone. And of late, just about every law tumbling out of Washington is meant to discriminate against the legacy of a productive America. A means-testing mandate would at least focus on helping the neediest without unduly overburdening younger workers.

Means testing alone would not erase Social Security's projected $13.2 trillion cash shortfall. That could only be done by stealing back all the money the elite state has stolen from working Americans. That's our bigger goal! But means-testing is a positive step we can take now to move in the right direction.

SAY HELLO TO MY LITTLE FRIEND, THE GLOB

Let's say your goal is to get the entire world using a single currency in order to (a) dethrone the US dollar as the world's reserve currency and (b) set you up to control the economic activities of people everywhere. You could take a page from Al Pacino's Tony Montana in *Scarface*: "Say hello to my little friend," the GLOB.

As eloquence in the face of opposition goes, it's hard to beat an angry Cuban aiming a fully automatic rifle outfitted with a grenade launcher at ten paces. So it is that our national economy is very close to being "blown away" by the GLOB (my term for the global looting and oppression bombshell the elite state is aiming at us).

Backing up a bit, the US dollar has reigned for almost eighty years as the world's reserve currency. This is what's known as seigniorage: foreign governments and businesses are willing to trade one dollar's worth of goods and services for a one-dollar bill that costs our US mint a fraction of a cent to produce. It works the same for our US treasury bonds. So almost all financial transactions internationally—from oil to onions—are priced out in dollars. This is a really big deal when you think about it.

It means the United States can devalue the dollar as much as we like, and the currencies of other countries are dragged down with us. It means the United States can behave badly without consequences. As President Nixon's Treasury secretary, John Connally, said, "It's our dollar, and your problem."[28] Back then, Connally was stating the obvious in his big-hat Texan style. But in the years since, that same self-interest has transformed into something of a theory about how money can work for us.

FOR OUR NEXT MAGIC ACT, BEHOLD, MODERN MONETARY THEORY!

This new idea about money has been long in coming, long enough to get the branding experts involved and inject a little gravitas into it. And so, *ta-da!* Modern Monetary Theory, or MMT. The big mind behind MMT is Stephanie Kelton of New York's Stony Brook University. In online ratings, students say the school is "boring" and "no fun," but hey, the mascot is the sea wolf, which uniquely swims like an otter and fishes like a bear— so it may well be an imaginative place. Kelton is surely an imaginative one, based on a reading of her 2020 book, *The Deficit Myth: Modern Monetary Theory and the Birth of the People's Economy.*[29]

Joining Kelton in providing the "intellectual framework" for MMT is L. Randall Wray, a professor of economics at Bard College.[30] Interestingly, another man, named George Soros, has given $500 million to Bard College to advance MMT in America.[31] Some would call this a red flag, but let's look beyond it.

The last several administrations all adopted some version of MMT, and why not? MMT says that debts and deficits don't matter. As long as our government controls the currency (which we still do), we can print as much money as we need right up until when inflation kicks in. Then, the argument goes, the government can slap some price controls and new taxes on the people to nip that inflation in the bud.

All neat and tidy, the last four presidents have agreed, and so the government spent and spent. Numbers tend to numb after a while. Millions become billions become trillions, and "What's next?" we absently wonder.

But there's no numbing away the financial facts before us.

For the hundred years leading up to 2000, all our national debts totaled about $5.6 trillion. That covered two world wars, the Korean War, the Vietnam War, a long Cold War with the Soviet Union, Franklin Roosevelt's massive New Deal, and Lyndon Johnson's even more massive Great Society.

But since 2000, the national debt has shot to more than $30.5 trillion—five times higher than a hundred years of costly government programs. Even when you adjust for all the value the dollar has lost, this is still obviously an absurd number. We've spent right into technical insolvency, and the only reason the United States hasn't toppled into the Venezuelan neighborhood of failed nation-states is the dollar's continued reign as the world reserve currency.

We've feasted on the exorbitant privilege of the reserve currency status for so long we have no idea what it would be like to lose it.

England knows. When the pound sterling lost its status as reserve currency, largely as a result of World War I, the British economy sank to the bottom of the Atlantic and "All hail Britannia" became a punch line.

CHAPTER 11

HOW TO HALT AMERICA'S FINANCIAL INSANITY

BASED ON TODAY'S stock market valuations, if the dollar were unseated as the world's reserve currency, the stock market would definitely lose half its value within a year and could still have further to fall. The larger problem would be serious inflation. Or if inflation were already ravaging—as we now expect—we could see the kind of hyperinflation that tears the economy to shreds.

This is because about 60 percent of all US dollars in circulation, or $24 trillion in all, are in the hands of people overseas.[1] If all those greenbacks suddenly have no place to be spent except in the United States, they'll come flooding back here. Bang, inflation.

The dollar's reserve status is today still fairly strong, but under pressure. In two decades the dollar's share of global reserves has dropped from above 70 percent to below 60 percent.[2] That's only 10 percent, to be sure, but further drops signal trouble.

FOUR THREATS TO THE DOLLAR

There are four headwinds threatening trouble:

1. Out-of-control national debt

2. Inflation taking off again

3. Chronic instability in Washington

4. The Treasury bond market

On the national debt, the world long believed we would never start indiscriminately printing money because that's basically grand larceny. But we've done that now.

Inflation has, after a forty-year nap, reared its ugly head, and if it continues to eat into our purchasing power, the world goes down with us. They don't like that a bit.

There are amazingly now twenty-six nations *less* corrupt than the United States,[3] and we are a long way from the portrait of "open financial systems" and "take-charge leaders" we once boasted. Bankers around the world know we cannot be trusted.

Lastly, our Treasury bond market has for decades been the safest haven for investors worldwide, boosting confidence in the dollar. Now not so much.

Taken together, these four headwinds send a message to the world that the dollar is going down and Americans don't care.

Then when intelligent overseas leaders see the US government basing decisions on modern monetary theory—which carries all the intellectual heft of the "money grows on trees" theory—these overseas leaders figure they'd better take some kind of action.

So it was reported in the *Wall Street Journal* that "Saudi Arabia is in active talks with Beijing to price some of its oil sales to China in yuan."[4] Riyadh has started the ball rolling against America and has sped up efforts since Joe Biden took over to punish the United States for (a) no longer honoring our long-standing commitment to defend their kingdom, (b) not supporting their civil war with Yemen terrorists, (c) trying to strike a nuclear weapons deal with Iran, (d) withdrawing precipitously from Afghanistan, and (e) the rest of the items on the Democratic Party platform.

China buys a quarter of all Saudi Arabia's oil exports. They would much prefer those massive sales to be priced in yuan, for it would boost the credibility of the yuan and move it closer to becoming the new global reserve currency.

For Saudi Arabia, this is a nontrivial decision. Their own currency, the riyal, has long been pegged to the dollar. Undermining the dollar thusly undermines the riyal. So their active talks with China may merely be a stalking horse in hopes of gaining more favorable treatment from America. Or they may be leaving America behind. We don't know.

We do know that it is only our overseas purchases of oil that allow us to continue printing dollars and inflating away our economy with impunity. As summarized by security analyst Gal Luft, co-author of *De-dollarization*:[5]

The oil market, and by extension the entire global commodities market, is the insurance policy of the status of the dollar as reserve currency. If that block is taken out of the wall, the wall will begin to collapse.[6]

One collapse scenario: Putin decides to make the world pay for not supporting his invasion of Ukraine, and he sets about starving the West of key commodities, creating shortages, sending prices skyrocketing. Meanwhile his silent partner, Chairman Xi, reaches out to the world with a monetary solution backed by a new and improved yuan, gaining enough traction to unseat the dollar as a global reserve currency. It is plausible.

And it is only one of many collapse scenarios. Many are plotting the demise of the dollar. Among them are people headquartered just down the street from the White House. This is the seat of the International Monetary Fund (IMF), and they've been planning the dollar's retirement party for years.

Folks at the IMF want the dollar replaced with a basket of currencies (the pound, yen, yuan, euro, and our dollar) in the hopes it'll be more stable for use in international trade. It might well be, but only America will take the hit.

This basket of currencies is the GLOB to which I referred earlier. And if it happens, yes, the damage to the US economy will be like that scene in *Scarface*.

The world will love it, though, and it has made that clear. Former IMF director Christine Lagarde is pushing for a digital currency called the IMFCoin to become the world's new reserve currency.

Mark Carney, former director of the Bank of England, has proposed a crypto reserve currency.

Foreign exchange titan Stanley Druckenmiller, who has grown rich by being right, has said some sort of crypto will emerge as the next reserve currency.[7]

Global elites could be waiting for another US liquidity crisis, when we are vulnerable, to step in with a replacement to the dollar. They know the United States has become a cartoon country, and like the road runner, one of these runs off the cliff has to land us in the canyon below.

In the next big bubble, perhaps a commodities bubble that creates a liquidity crisis the Feds can no longer backstop, that's when the replacement of the dollar could be done within the week.

WE CAN ONLY FIX AMERICA BEGINNING AT HOME

With all the problems we've been running through—financialization's impact, the threat of inflation, the potential loss of seigniorage—the only fixes we can be sure of begin on native soil.

Our elected leaders must know that step 1 in fixing this mess is bringing America's productive capacity back home. Bring home manufacturing so American workers are making things again—and doing it efficiently enough to be competitive.

Reroute the supply chain so there are Americans on each end of it and all along the way. We've seen the fragility of global supply chains, such as China's hoarding of medical equipment during COVID. We should be more self-sufficient, and we can be.

This doesn't mean we turn isolationist. In fact, we need a strong global footprint with lots of trading partners, especially in fossil fuels, if the dollar is to remain the world's reserve currency. But we can bring an end to the vulnerabilities of far-off supply chains. We can bring jobs home.

We can disengage from people who don't share our security and trading interests.

China's fast-growing economic and military power has made it clear that we cannot go on sharing all our technology with them, knowing they will simply steal it. By stepping back from nations that wish us no favor, we can embrace more of those whose values and outlook we share.

Plus, on an environmental level, those big oceangoing cargo ships are dirty beasts. They burn through some three hundred million tons of dirty fuel a year, or 3 percent of the world's carbon dioxide emissions.[8] Cutting back on them should appeal to all.

We are already making progress in reversing the globalization frenzy of the past three decades. Rising Chinese labor costs, tariffs and trade wars, and advances in automation and 3D printing technologies have helped us produce more here at home, and produce more competitively as well.

We can see from the trials of COVID that our world should not return to an elite dreamscape ideal of globalized and financialized *everything*.

We should focus on the people inside this country over those outside, on becoming more self-sufficient here at home instead of overseas, on tackling our country's problems with American solutions.

When he was President Trump's economic advisor, Larry Kudlow argued for luring US companies back to the United States by paying their relocation costs:

> Plant, equipment, intellectual property structures, renovations— in other words, if we had 100% immediate expensing, we would literally pay the moving costs of American companies from China back to the U.S [and] it would be a very good thing for American companies here at home.[9]

What a great way for our government to help rejoin American businesses with American consumers.

How to Tax Our Way Out of a Spending Problem

In all seriousness, it would not be that difficult to take the most inefficient, wasteful, and corrupt government agency of all with its seventy-thousand-plus pages of rules and $12.6 billion budget and ship it off on one of Elon Musk's next rockets to Mars. It wouldn't even take rocket science to pack up the IRS and ship it off.

This is not about eliminating taxes. We've needed them since ancient pharaohs collected 20 percent of the grain harvests on through to Julius Caesar instituting a 1 percent flat-rate tax across his empire and on to today's tortuous system of indexing, loopholing, ratcheting, and infuriating.[10]

But we really don't need the infuriating part. We don't need a system so complex that $304 billion is spent every year just to comply with it, and another $1 trillion slips into the ether from sheer inefficiency.[11] That's $700 billion that could be saved on an estimated total federal tax take of $3.86 trillion in 2021 with income taxes accounting for 50 percent; payroll taxes 36 percent; corporate taxes 7 percent; and another 7 percent from estate taxes, excise and custom duties, and interest payments.[12]

Seriously, some sharp guys have already figured out how to ship the IRS to Mars.

Maybe you've heard about the consumption tax. Neal Boortz and Congressman John Linder championed the idea in their 2005 book, *The*

Fair Tax Plan,[13] which Linder followed up with a legislative proposal. He introduced H.R. 25 FairTax Plan to great fanfare, and then, unsurprisingly, it was ignored by 434 House mates.[14] Archive mice have probably chewed up all 133 pages of the bill that could replace 70,000-plus pages of IRS rules and regulations with one super-simple solution.

A consumption tax—an idea so simple and easy to understand that your federal tax return would fit on a 5-by-7 card, or a single box on your screen. No more doing the April 15 scramble for 1099s, old brokerage records, receipts, the whole headachy mess. Instead, one workable alternative that is also, importantly, fair.

To see just how fair, let's look at two charts and consider them.

BIDEN PROPOSES TAX RATES HIGHER THAN ANY DEVELOPED COUNTRY

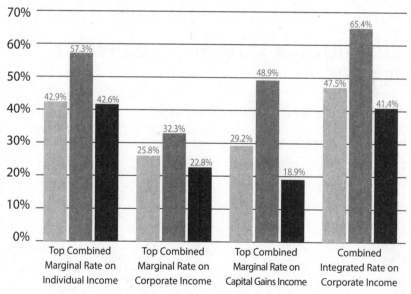

■ **Current Law**
■ **Build Back Better Act + FY 2023 Budget**
■ **OECD Average (Excluding U.S.)**

Note: Estimates include average state and local taxes.

Sources: State and local tax statutes; OECD; Tax Foundation calculations.

A quick read of this chart from the Tax Foundation shows how America's current tax structure, for all its faults, is at least on par with the rest of the developed world.[15] But President Biden's tax proposals would shoot America high above nations similar to us, effectively shooting our economy in the foot, because if these taxes become law, three things can be expected to happen:

1. A mass exodus of people and companies to locations far away from these usurious tax rates

2. Mass cheating and evasion as people gamble the IRS is no longer capable of enforcing the rules

3. Mass uprising against the Democratic Party, with voters throwing the scoundrels out and giving the other scoundrels another shot

You can view the exodus, cheating, and uprising however you like, but surely Biden should want for better. To see what that "better" could look like, here is a comparison of three different tax plans.

SIMPLIFIED LOOK AT INDIVIDUAL INCOME TAX BRACKETS

2021 Tax Brackets	Biden-Proposed Tax Brackets	Consumption Tax Brackets
10%	10%	0%
12%	12%	0%
22%	22%	0%
24%	24%	0%
32%	32%	0%
35%	35%	0%
37%	40%	0%

Whoa! In this third column you can see one very reasonable solution, a solution that has been roundly ignored by the Washington elites but could change—should change—if we begin sending the right people to Washington.

For starters, we could truly say goodbye to all kinds of taxes. Gone would be the income tax, the capital gains tax, Social Security tax, Medicare tax, corporate income tax, death tax, self-employment tax, alternative minimum tax, and gift tax.

All of them could be replaced with a simple consumption tax that's collected only when you buy something at retail. Most of our purchases are now done with credit cards and electronic funds transfers, so taxing at the point of the sale is easily done.

There would be transition issues to this new tax formula, of course. Older folks who've used retirement accounts all their lives would be impacted. There would need to be help during the transition. Sure.

But with the admin issues ironed out, working folks' paychecks would arrive whole, no longer tattered by an assortment of tax claims.

We'd all be able to save our money better, investing for our families' future and helping to build the American economy. And we'd be in control.

That's one reason Linder's bill languishes in some dusty House archive. The elite state very much wants to control the tax code. They see it as a tool for funding the legitimate operations of government, yes. But more importantly to them, it is a velvet cudgel useful for (a) controlling the behavior of various citizens and (b) strong-arming companies into contributing to political campaigns at election time.

We saw this cudgel wielded by President Obama—(you didn't think he was paid-in to the elite state? *Ha!*)—when he hinted that IRS director Lois Lerner should *illegally* harass seventy-five different conservative non-profit groups and try to shut them down.[16] Lerner later issued a formal apology, easing her without mishap into a retirement with full pension. No charges were brought against her, or the president's staff, or the president. Just business as usual in Washington.

A consumption tax is not a Republican or a Democrat thing. Or a class thing, either. It does not target one group over the other. It applies to all equally. That may be its chief shortcoming and a reason to execute on it thoughtfully.

Since a consumption tax would apply to all equally, it would appear to be regressive; that is, lower-income people spend a greater proportion of their earnings on food and hard goods at retail, so they could pay a greater proportion on taxes than they do now in lower tax brackets. This is a fair complaint.

And it could be addressed. A little complexity could be added along these lines. The tax could be means-tested. People could submit proof of income with their annual tax filing, and those coming in below $40,000 could get a 50 percent refund of taxes paid; below $80,000 a 25 percent refund; others pay full.

Retail sales in the United States were $6.6 trillion in 2021, so a 20 percent consumption tax, for example, could raise $1 trillion. That's not enough to fund the government. It should be, but it's not. So more is needed. One answer to that is to stop underwriting the wealthy by pretending that capital gains taxes today make sense. That's the biggest elite-state con of all. Everyone knows Bill Gates and Warren Buffett paid little such taxes as they amassed vast stores of wealth through their "appreciating" Microsoft and Berkshire Hathaway stock.

Conservatives have been carefully taught to insist that these lower capital gains taxes help fuel the great entrepreneurs and builders among us. They say it with such certainty they surely believe it. As in, say something long enough and you believe it. I'm wondering what J. P. Morgan and Andrew Carnegie, who built their empires before the income tax began, would say in response to that.

Theories that lower tax rates on capital gains encourage investment and in turn economic growth simply do not hold up. When the financial services sector was 10 percent of the nation's economic output in the 1980s, it might have made more sense. With that sector now officially comprising 20 percent of GDP but actually controlling almost every sector of the economy, it's a different dynamic.

In addition, studies by the Congressional Research Service (leaning left, but supposedly nonpartisan) show little correlation between economic growth and capital-gains tax rates.[17] So going forward, treat capital gains the same as income gains. These capital gains are a bit harder to calculate, but still quite doable.

Some back-of-the-napkin estimates put the recent stock market's capital value at $53 trillion and real estate's value at $43 trillion, for $96 trillion in all. There's some overlap in these figures, but let's scratch away.

Assuming long-term appreciation of stocks has been 10 percent and real estate 4 percent, capital gains for these in recent years have been about $8.2 trillion. A 20 percent consumption tax on these gains would raise $1.64 trillion.

Added to the consumption tax on purchases, you get $2.64 trillion in tax money a year. If Washington just can't make that work, here's an idea: they can pitch in the rest themselves! The more than two million people allowed to latch on to the government teat could, in a show of gratitude, clip their sweet sinecures just 10 percent and raise another couple billion to meet the goal.

Mission accomplished. Next?

Actually, there's a bigger issue in play here. Through our tax code, we've gone from subsidizing *producers* to subsidizing *financiers*. Once our tax code helped industry tame the wilderness and lift the living standards of millions coming to an immigrant nation. Now we shovel cash from Main Street to Wall Street, from everyday people to an elite state.

For a generation we've allowed the financialization of a nation, vastly enriching an elite few. We must restore a balance by hitting back on that elite state with all the power of a nation, all the power we can muster, expressed through our support of genuine American leaders.

Abraham Lincoln reforged the country in the fires of the Civil War.

Teddy Roosevelt yanked a nation from the control of the monopolists.

Ronald Reagan revived economic growth flattened out by Arab oil embargoes.

Great leaders punch above their weight and take a nation on the next step in the journey.

We are not now seeing this leadership at the federal level, but we are seeing it at the state level. Smart state leaders are using the tax code to attract the people they want. The ten states recently gaining the most *new* residents boasted a state-and-local tax burden averaging 7.7 percent while the ten states losing the most residents averaged 9.9 percent. Other factors played in, of course, but policy matters.

Everyone learned during COVID that it's no longer necessary, for many of us, to live in high-tax states. It's not like those higher taxes in mostly blue states translate into better roads, education, and other services. Most of it goes to employ a bloating bureaucracy of brothers-in-law to help get out the vote at election time—what Democrats used to call crony capitalism, until they cornered the market on it.

And so the country is dividing into three camps based on taxes.[18]

STATES WELCOMING OR WARDING OFF PRODUCTIVE CITIZENS

No Personal Income Tax	Marching to Zero Income Tax	Continuing With High Taxes	
Alaska	Arizona	California	Minnesota
Florida	Arkansas	Colorado	Missouri
Nevada	Iowa	Connecticut	Montana
South Dakota	Louisiana	Delaware	Nebraska
Tennessee	Mississippi	Georgia	New Jersey
Texas	New Hampshire	Hawaii	New Mexico
Washington	North Carolina	Idaho	New York
Wyoming	North Dakota	Illinois	Ohio
	Oklahoma	Indiana	Oregon
	South Carolina	Kansas	Pennsylvania
	West Virginia	Kentucky	Rhode Island
	Wisconsin	Maine	Utah
		Maryland	Vermont
		Massachusetts	Virginia
		Michigan	

Smart states are not just competing for productive citizens; they are enticing companies to relocate and provide good jobs for their people, doing it with a pro-business agenda. Texas has even been running provocative radio ads in high-tax California saying, "Pack up the bags and move back out." And in the last four years, 265 of California's biggest firms have done just that.[19]

Through taxing and spending policies, politicians craft behavior. So our nation will shift with people creating lives for themselves in areas that share their values.

There are worse ways to carry a nation forward.

It's a Con, and It Takes Two to Play

Looking at all that's happened in the last few years, it feels like we fell through the looking glass into some alternate world: lockdowns and bankruptcies of small businesses while major corporations get trillion-dollar bailouts, Americans handing their freedom over to global elites, powerful US businesses betraying their country and culture for pieces of silver, politicians and activist groups feeding away at the public trough.

We've seen how this "alternate world" is the work of con artists, and we know it takes two to keep a con running. If enough people separate from the con, the elite state cannot go on with it. They need the American people more than we need them, amusingly. We can paddle along just fine in our dinghies, but they can't be building bigger superyachts if they're stopped from lifting wallets at whim.

We must separate from the con and return production to American factories with American workers in American communities coming together. Some will call this "economic nationalism" and then attack it like it's a scourge, when in fact it is precisely what every country, including ours, has always done.

What is wrong with protecting and promoting American manufacturing, particularly companies that are critical to our national security? What is wrong with protecting our own? Here are three steps in the right direction.

Step 1: Help people save by expanding I-bonds.

President Biden is fond of using executive orders. He should burn one to direct Treasury Secretary Yellen to raise the ceiling on the I-bonds we can buy. Raise it from $10,000 to at least $100,000. I-bonds were set up in

1996 to link to inflation. So if inflation goes up, so does the I-bond return. In mid-2022, I-bonds were paying a healthy 7.12 percent annual return.

I-bonds are far better than Treasury securities as the inflation hedges we clearly need. Other Treasury securities meant to protect against inflation—such as TIPS—will lose value unless you hold them for thirty years. But I-bonds can be cashed out after twelve months with a modest penalty, and after five years with no redemption penalty.

It's hard to find a better "safe" investment today. People know it. Since interest rates began rising, I-bond purchases shot up from $700 million a year on average to $7.1 billion.[20] That's a ten-times increase in sales that more Americans should have access to in order to save intelligently.

Step 2: Bring the supply chain home.

We should look the Chinese in the eye and say, sorry, the world doesn't need your factory floors and your corrupt labor practices anymore. Maybe we can't produce flip-flops in Peoria economically. But we can at least make them through American-Vietnamese partnerships. And with shipping costs fast rising and production methods faster changing, we can bring home more business if we try.

Step 3: Apply the Swiss brake to debt.

We've saddled our children with unpayable debt loads, and we have to stop adding debt ourselves or else someone or something will stop us on far harsher terms, as we've talked about here. At current rates of debt run-up, the Congressional Budget Office figures the national debt will hit an unimaginable $180 trillion in our children's lifetimes, and the interest payments alone could top $4 trillion per year.[21] Clearly unsustainable. And clearly ending badly, no matter what we do.

But that doesn't mean we do nothing. It doesn't mean we tell today's children something along these lines: "Sorry, your parents sold off the family silver. I hear the lines at the soup kitchen are shorter if you go early."

Instead, we could be adults and halt the runaway debt train with a tool called the "Swiss debt brake." In Switzerland, if deficits exceed a set limit, the government is required to cut spending until the budget is balanced and debt is reduced to a sustainable level. Yes, Switzerland is a nation of only eight million, but they are not a nation of bunny rabbits. They are people like us. We can do what they have done by replacing the cowardice of politicians with the courage of true leaders.

Our Congress is supposedly bound by tax and spending limits, as well as debt ceilings, but they have never adhered to them. Their approach has been more along these lines: "Sure hope I can finish my stint in Congress and then ease into a cushy lobbying firm or a cable TV show before the debt crisis gets so ugly it triggers intergenerational fighting with bloodshed in the streets as a new generation sees the outrageous taxes they'll be forced to pay just to cover interest payments and says, 'No way!'"

So back to the Swiss debt brake. They're smart people, the Swiss. They realized that requiring the balancing of the budget every year was unworkable. It wouldn't allow any bend or flexibility to respond to economic shocks or emergencies. They solved for that problem by balancing the budget over the business cycle instead. And it worked.

Would it work in America? To answer this question, folks at the Heartland Institute modeled out a Swiss brake for our needs and estimated the impact it would have on the budget and the economy.[22]

It would be, in a word, challenging. Not at all surprising given all the debt we've piled up. But it could be done in three decades. The government's books could be brought into balance as long as politicians are forced to (a) level off spending and (b) downsize the bloated federal bureaucracy. Both good goals!

Plus this Swiss brake could boost US economic growth out of the doldrums we've fallen into as a result of the elites' financializing of America.

These are three steps we can demand of our leaders in this American revival we're undertaking. This is our chance to join with our neighbors and counterpunch with all we've got, demanding better. Unafraid, we can fight to revive America.

CHAPTER 12

HOW HARMFUL ARE THESE HOODIE HOOLIGANS?

F OR DECADES WE all gushed about an amazing new thing called the internet putting worlds of knowledge into everyone's hands, social media empowering one and all to join the civic conversation, tech innovations turning science fiction dreams into "Look, I'm George Jetson!" And then, as if overnight, something happened to the Jetsons. A recent dinner party I was negligently *not* invited to opens this story up.

This soiree was held in the Los Altos foothills overlooking Silicon Valley and boasted an A-list seating of today's top tech bros, John Galt-ish founders, massive Mensa minds, billionaire bankrollers, and the usual eye candy found at these things.

Conversation turned to bots and artificial intelligence, as it invariably does, and how soon our planet will have more AI-driven bots running around than sentient humans. How our every task in the day—from doing the housework, walking the dog, driving the car, protecting the home, monitoring all our vital signs, and taking action when needed—will be handled by the literally billions of bots coexisting among us. And out in our neighborhoods and across the states these bots and their robot cousins will be driving the trains, keeping the water and electricity flowing, policing the streets and deterring crime, ensuring desirable election outcomes.

What emerged from this conversation was a detailed rendering of a totally—or almost totally—automated future in which we'll all soon be fully immersed.

At one point an apparent newcomer asked, "What does this mean for people?"

No doubt eyes rolled. And then it was explained that for a couple more years, the coders will still be running everyone's lives, but before long the AI will be smarter than us all and begin programming itself. Humans will become, well, irrelevant.

"And when the AI decides it doesn't need humans anymore?"

That won't happen right away, everyone agreed. Could be ten years, could be one hundred before the AI deals humans out of the game. When it does happen, then *obviously* it's the next step in evolution and humans can pass into the sands of time.

Obviously is not the word all of us would choose.

The idea that we would put the fate of human beings in the hands of people who arrange 1s and 0s on a computer screen for a living is mind-boggling. These software engineers don't care about consequences. They don't think that way. They think, "If it can be done, why not do it?"

And that gets to the core of the problem with which Silicon Valley presents us, for they are changing our world in the way a cheetah changes a sloth race. Once the advances in technology simply replaced physical labor or led to greater creature comforts. Now the "advances" aim to replace our cognitive labors as well. When neither physical nor mental labors are required from us, then what or who will we be?

This is the biggest question we need to be grappling with. All of today's headline problems in tech are important, but they are only the tip of an AI-driven iceberg headed our way. Before long, a roster of smart machines will surface to rival our human thinking and reasoning capabilities. With billions in research thrown at their development, we'll see bots hired into positions from baristas to botanists, dancers to doctors, plumbers to, well, the president!

This is why decisions about tomorrow's tech, or even today's, cannot be left to the tech bros. The more decent among them would be the first to agree.

Elon Musk for one has warned that "for an A.I., there would be no death. It would live forever. And then you'd have an immortal dictator from which we can never escape."[1]

Skype founder Jaan Tallinn has cautioned that "humanity does not have anything to protect it from the potential risks of artificial intelligence."[2]

And Stephen Hawking himself warned that "the development of full artificial intelligence could spell the end of the human race."[3]

These are our brightest minds talking, but who's listening? Who in a position of authority is trying to make sense of all those 1s and 0s? Just as Washington is largely ignorant of tech ("How do I know how many likes I got?" asked the congressman at a recent hearing), the tech bros are largely ignorant of public policy ("If I can build it, then it should be built," said the coder recently). Neither lawmakers nor technologists appear suited to the task ahead.

That role falls to us.

HOW HARMFUL THESE HOODIE HOOLIGANS?

When people are asked to name the biggest problems facing the world today, they tick off income inequality, nuclear bombs, climate change, partisan deadlock, urban violence, the opioid crisis, obesity, mental health, terrorism, runaway debt—and all are very real concerns.

Less often mentioned is "tech," even though it cuts to the core of our severest problems. In that sense, tech has become something of a double-edged sword, slicing through our world in ways sometimes beautiful and brilliant, other times insidious and hidden from our understanding.

It's the insidious and hidden issues that concern us here as a matter of public policy. More precisely, how should we look through very human eyes at the social cost of advancing technologies and commit ourselves to grappling head-on with the

- personal data they are collecting on our every waking activity;

- wealth they are accumulating through surveillance capitalism;

- industries they are leveling with monopolist impunity;

- information pollution spewing from their platforms;

- addiction to technology, especially family-destroying porn; and

- automating away of millions of jobs people once held?

How do we deal with this automating, for starters, this shrinking of the human and expansion of the machine? A cold, unrelenting machine that reminds some of another machine that crushed the human spirit of tens of millions of people not so long ago. A machine not forgotten by Soviet expats like Tessa Lena.

> The establishment is deadly afraid of the spirit, because it is a machine....The wondrous, treacherous spectacle is made of all the familiar droplets: The apparatchik pundits who are eager to say anything for money and compliments; the lying and greedy statesmen; the dysfunctional and neurotic news cycle; the value system that is so arbitrary and volatile that no human being can adapt to it without forgetting how to locate their soul...nothing for the heart, nothing to hold on to....
>
> Never has the spectacle been intended to be genuine—but in the past few years, it's gotten grotesque. Perhaps the developed world almost ran out of foreign resources to abuse, and the kings got scared. Perhaps something else. But the farce became unbearable. As the economy of rich Western countries started falling into the neurotic vortex of app-induced human indignity, and the word about the disintegration of our habitat started getting out into the masses—albeit immediately commodified and castrated beyond recognition—our psychopathic feudal overlords upped both the lies and the censorship.
>
> I can barely breathe the air filled with state and corporate talking points—and as a Soviet expat, I am extra disheartened by it. I have already lived through the fall of the spectacle.[4]
>
> Today's representatives of the Machine...are flattering themselves assuming that they can control this world. They can't. They won't. A lot more people will be forced to grow spines, we'll rise, fear and pain will fall off one day, and our love will melt their scams.[5]

Over and over I've read Lena, for she gets to the core of it all: the machine is afraid of the spirit. However powerful the machine, the people behind it are afraid of us. Afraid that we put our faith in God's treasured plan and not in the algorithm. Afraid of the humanity that is granted to us from on high and celebrated in our love for one another and in the joy of progress made every day for a better world for all. It is this joyous faith that they are afraid of, and why in their fear they strike out as they have.

It is also from this joyous faith that we counterpunch.

WHEN THE INNOVATORS BECOME THE STAGNATES

Amazon founder Jeff Bezos may be the second most fascinating man of our time, up there with Elon Musk. In naming his company Amazon from the get-go, Bezos was apparently not just thinking about selling some books online; he was thinking, "Why not everything?"

His Amazonian-scale ambition was to become like the old company store, only for the whole world. He largely succeeded.

His was the third public company to top $1 trillion in value, employing more than a million US workers to sell the bulk of all that's sold online, along with offering cloud computing, grocery stores, media streaming, payment processing, freight shipping and logistics, gaming, robotics, film production, listening devices, audiobooks, prescription drugs, and advertising technology with seventy-six subsidiaries in all, at last count.[6]

Any business that aims to compete against Amazon is faced with a Faustian bargain: either they try to go it alone on the vast, unvisited expanses of the internet or toss in the towel and eke out a meager existence as a third-party seller on Amazon's website.[7]

In the fourth quarter 2021, Amazon reported $137 billion in earnings, with an operating income of $3.5 billion. At first glance that suggests far-from-greedy margins. But when you dive into those operations, you find that Amazon's cloud services unit (known as AWS) reported $5.3 billion in operating income. That means AWS made $1.8 billion more income than the total company did. How could that be? Only one way: that $1.8 billion was used to subsidize the losses in Amazon's online sales and third-party logistics operations. Essentially, AWS is subsidizing Amazon Prime.

When the price a company charges is lower than the cost of goods, that's predatory pricing and clearly illegal. Consumers may like the sometimes-lower prices, but companies trying to compete against Amazon are being all-the-time cheated. Laws are being broken, plain and simple, and action must be taken against Amazon. (More to come on this.)

Let's shift over to the media for a bit. It only appears to be a shift because while tech and media were once different worlds, tech has crushed the all-important fourth estate (news media) and blurred all distinctions.

MAINSTREAM MEDIA IS DEAD; LONG LIVE MAINSTREAM MEDIA

It's comical to me that people think we still have "mainstream media." I suppose many people think this because right-leaning news commentators keep saying it. Keep holding up the left-leaning media as some mainstream beast to beat down, as if they didn't beat down the leftist media two decades ago. Fox News attracts larger audiences than all the left-leaning cable news networks.[8] By any definition, Fox News would be the mainstream news show if such a thing still existed.

But it hasn't, not for two decades now.

Some say the internet killed the mainstream media. Others say the first shot was "friendly fire." Because television had so eroded America's thinking processes, the internet just reaped the devastation. Either way, the mainstream media was dead and buried by the time smartphones came along to stomp all over the grave.

Think about those smartphones in a big-picture way.

Suddenly there were four billion media outlets in the world. Four billion people each armed with a megaphone of sorts. Four billion people capable of broadcasting their every inane thought as broadly as they could, which in turn gave us the term *clickbait*. Now in order to get heard with four billion megaphones all stuck on transmit, few bothering with receive mode, only the most absurd, extreme, sensational, hyperventilating kook could burst through our still-limited attention spans. So all kook, all the time.

With this nonstop assault, it became harder and harder for all of us to keep perspective, to recognize fact from fake, to know what the heck was going on with any issue—much less complicated issues, which most are. So what did we do?

We retreated.

Retreated back into teams, tribes, camps—call it what you like. We divided up and picked our side much the same as we pick our favorite sports club. Then we became rabid fans, hating on the other team.

Not a pretty picture, only slightly oversimplified.

So it was natural that the media would follow suit and reshape into two fairly equal forces—the left-stream media and the right-stream media.

Each with the same agenda: to convince you that they alone are reporting the truth, and the other side are a bunch of yahoos.

This dividing up and locking into stubborn loyalties was obviously bad for the country, but it was like a summer rain to the elite state. They were ecstatic. They had an entire nation caught up in a nonstop food fight playing out on the nightly news and across the internet and even in the serious press. They had millions of viewers caught up in the drama of rotting food flying every which way over every little issue. They had the mundane fare of politics turned into a messy blood sport, winners, losers, audience handlers holding up cards to "Cheer!," "Boo!," "Hate!," "Love!" Everyone made to feel like they're in the swim, part of the big game, when in fact they've been fully distracted and mostly oblivious to the real game: extracting the wealth from America's middle class and moving it into the pockets of the elite-state few.

That is why the elite state invited the once-lowly press to the big table. To enlist them in "putting on a show." Basically paying them outrageous salaries to be dancing monkeys on the tube. Dancing, dancing, always distracting.

In the early going, more of the elite-state advertising dollars went to the right-stream media because they put on a better show. Focus groups told them the right-stream players appeared more honest, more heartfelt. But in time, the left-stream caught up and blew past the right—for the better writers have always leaned left.

Sharyl Attkisson knows of this. A TV journalist with a long career, she went on to write *Slanted*, and in it she shared the thinking of her colleagues from all the major media—ABC, CBS, NBC, CNN, FOX, MSNBC. All of them lamented the death of the news they once knew and its replacement with the absurdist theater they now host.

> Virtually every piece of information you get through the media has been massaged, shaped, curated, and manipulated before it reaches you. Some of it is censored entirely. The news can no longer be counted on to reflect all the facts. Instead of telling us what happened yesterday, the media tells us what's new in the pre-packaged soap opera they've been calling the news.[9]

We're now two decades into this packaged soap opera. Many efforts have been launched by good people to try and rescue our lost First Amendment freedom of the press. None has even come close. Perhaps that explains the desperate nature of the latest rescue effort, which comes from progressive minds and is the one thing no serious American has ever considered: censorship.

High up in the penthouse suites of New York, they see this censorship as genius. They've already divided viewers into two warring camps, already undermining all confidence in the news; now they can curate what people see—that is, they present only the "truths" that are good for you. All thinking done for you, no need to bother.

Yes, censoring the news was the final frontier for the elite state, and they nailed it.

Of course, the word *censorship* is still freighted, and it has to be handled delicately. That handling begins in our "finest" journalism schools. There the students learn how to report the news so that truth no longer matters. They are taught that their own personal truths about a story matter more than the reality on the ground. Millennials love this, oddly, since they equate it with "living their truth" despite it being the exact opposite. And with so much of TV already given over to mindless reality programming, filling the news hour with journalists' self-important personal narratives feels authentic and sure manages to insulate audiences from the hard news truths. And if any of those hard news truths do slip through the news-packaging process and get close to airing, well, then censorship is required.

This system isn't perfect. But it manages to fog things up, and that's enough to neuter the media up tight.

Again, it's no different on the Left or the Right. We could pick almost any news story and examine how the left-stream and the right-stream media treated it to see this dynamic at work. Let's look at the Hunter Biden laptop story, since it should have been central to the 2020 election.

Left Stream	Right Stream
Treatment Summary	**Treatment Summary**
Story was initially ignored, then called Russian disinformation, then laughed off as some nutjob conspiracy theory, then censored, then only years later begrudgingly confirmed to be true.	Story was initially sensationalized, suggesting dark connections and illegalities without proof that Hunter Biden was anything more than a worthless sot cashing in on his father's success.
10/19/20—Deep State Operatives Providing Cover in Politico.com Jim Clapper, former director of national intelligence; Mike Hayden, former director of the CIA; Leon Panetta, former director of the CIA; John Brennan, former director of the CIA, et al. write, "The arrival on the US political scene of emails purportedly belonging to Vice President Biden's son Hunter… has all the classic earmarks of a Russian information operation…. Our experience makes us deeply suspicious that the Russian government played a significant role in this case."[10]	**10/14/20—The *New York Post*** "Smoking-gun email reveals how Hunter Biden introduced Ukrainian businessman to VP dad….The blockbuster correspondence—which flies in the face of Joe Biden's claim that he's 'never spoken to my son about his overseas business dealings'—is contained in a massive trove of data recovered from a laptop computer."[11]

Left Stream	Right Stream
10/25/20—CBS News ***60 Minutes*** Norah O'Donnell tosses a softball to candidate Joe Biden: "Do you believe the recent leak of material allegedly from Hunter's computer is part of a Russian disinformation campaign?"[12]	**10/12/21—The *New York Post*** "One year ago, The Post revealed that Hunter Biden's abandoned laptop carried proof he sold influence while his father served as vice president—and his dad, now president, knew it. Yet most other media treated the story itself as the scandal, reporting only on vague claims that sought to undermine it rather than rushing (as they would've under the last president) to advance it themselves. And Twitter and Facebook rushed to block it, squelching vital information even as America voted."[13]

Left Stream	Right Stream
9/22/21—CNN	**12/5/21—Fox News**
Wolf Blitzer asks Democratic congressman Adam Schiff about Hunter's laptop: "Does it surprise you at all that this information Rudy Giuliani is peddling very well could be connected to some sort of Russian government disinformation campaign?"[14]	Fox News gives Newt Gingrich's analysis: "We simply do not know how much the Biden administration's weakness toward Communist China is influenced by the Chinese corruption of the Biden family and its allies. We do not know how much Vladimir Putin has been emboldened by his knowledge of the corruption of Hunter Biden—and through him the governing family of the United States. There has been a complete absence of honesty and inquiry from the FBI and the Justice Department. It is amazing that the Hunter Biden laptop has not already led to an indictment of President Biden's son for a series of amazing influence-peddling schemes.... If Joe Biden knew, he is clearly implicated in corruption involving foreign powers."[15]

Left Stream	Right Stream
3/18/22—The *New York Times*	**3/17/22—The *American Spectator***
Casually linking back to its October 2020 story casting doubt on the laptop, the newspaper wrote, "emails were obtained by The *New York Times* from a cache of files that appears to have come from a laptop abandoned by Biden in a Delaware repair shop. The email and others in the cache were authenticated by people familiar with them and with the investigation."[16]	"The Hunter Biden laptop was legit and the data and emails therein were therefore true. This obvious truth had to be destroyed because if it got out—as in on the news networks and in places like the *New York Times*, Biden's campaign likely would have been over. That had to be prevented at all costs because Trump, the designated villain, must lose."[17]

AFTERWORD ON THIS HUNTER BIDEN STORY

We'll surely never learn the whole truth of Hunter Biden's shenanigans in the lead-up to the 2020 election, but the right-stream narrative did come closer to proving correct. Not that either side cared. Each was carrying water for their respective parties, intent on confirming the prejudices of their respective audiences, giving it their all with over-the-top sensationalism.

To the elite state, the truth of the story was incidental as well. Sure, they were happy that the Hunter Biden story didn't derail his dad's always-iffy chances of winning. Joe Biden is one of them—someone they could work with, unlike the previous president.

WHO NEEDS GULAGS WHEN YOU HAVE GOOGLE?

It's a stretch to juxtapose Google and gulags in a title, I'll agree. But hold the judgment for a bit while we visit with people who lived in Eastern Europe in the 1950s under the iron fist of the Soviet Union.

In his book *Live Not by Lies*, Rob Dreher tells the story of Kamila Bendová and her late husband, Václav Benda. When Soviet tanks rolled into Czechoslovakia, the couple went underground and organized a dissident movement against Soviet occupiers. They experienced firsthand how an occupying force can take root and, like a cancer, overgrow the healthy organism that had been.

When Kamila sees what is happening in America today, she is frightened by how gullible we are, how naïve. She knows many Americans are quick to say, "It could never happen here." She recalls saying that very thing.

Kamila and Václav founded Charter 77, the main Czech dissident community.[18] More than two hundred artists and intellectuals joined them in signing the charter, demanding that the communist occupiers respect human rights. Some of the signatories landed in prison for their advocacy, just as we are seeing today in America when someone speaks out too successfully against the ruling elite state.

Kamila sees how our elite institutions abandoned old-fashioned liberalism (based on defending the rights of the individual), replacing it with a new progressive creed (based on attaining justice for all groups). She knows that siren song; she's heard it before. She knows the creed can be quite compelling, especially when so many have been regularly denied justice, or equal justice, because of their sex or skin color. But she also knows how that story plays out.

When the state gets to decide what is true and false—which she sees in America today as she saw it then—it perverts freedom at every level down into our communities and into our homes. The more absolute the control over information flow, the more absolute its use. As Kamila says:

> We know from our life under the totalitarian regime that if you know something about someone, you can manipulate him or her. You can use it against them. The secret police have evidence of everything like that. They could use it all against you. Anything![19]

Kamila's apartment still bears the scars where, after the fall of communism, her husband ripped out the wires the secret police had used to bug their home.[20]

After the fall of the Soviets, people got access to the records that had been kept on them—detailed records of the snitching culture that had been created by the state. People were shocked to learn how many of their own neighbors had given in and agreed to turn over sensitive information to the state for fear of becoming victims themselves.

People's core values had been corroded or rotted away by the Soviets' aim to make everyone equal through their progressive authoritarian creed—which bears soft similarities to today's progressive authoritarian creed in America.

It was this sacrificing of personal space, this loss of privacy, that caused a kind of mental anguish, a torment that looked very different from, but could be just as devastating as, the slugs of hot metal fired from the tanks in the streets. Milan Kundera in his novel *The Unbearable Lightness of Being* captured these torments as well as anyone has. My notes in reading his book:

> This is what happens when you lose so much of your personal privacy that you no longer feel authentic, no longer feel whole. Neighbors still gather in the bars but no longer talking to one another, just stare off absently. Everyone moves in a deliberate manner—performing the role of a good citizen who's going along with the program. People no longer get attached to anything—not to material objects, not to places, not to people. The good doctor, "Tomas," writes an anti-Communist article and refuses to renounce it, so he is stripped of his career and becomes a window washer. "Tereza" is a photographer for the newspaper, handing in her shots of civilians getting trampled by Soviet invaders only to have her editor tell her, "Have you gone mad? Don't you know that we love you? We've always loved you, want to save you to protect you." Her photos are turned over to the police to help crack down on dissidents. Finally, Tomas and Tereza flee the country. They know that one day they will be asked, "What did you do against the Communist regime?" They will live with their shame for having fled. Out in a country restaurant they hear music again playing and observe, "The only way we can find beauty is if our persecutors have overlooked it."[21]

Theirs was a different story than ours today, sure. Yet the soft similarities grow by the day as a progressive authoritarianism creeps over the country, law by law, signal by signal, censure by censure.

How could this progressive totalitarianism take hold of a nation like ours, when few would publicly admit to admiring the ideal?

Perhaps it is like the hairworm, which makes it his business to get sipped up by a grasshopper and then expands to fill the grasshopper's belly, take over its mind, and convince it to jump into the water to drown. A rather brutal business, but how far is it from what's happening in America today?

We have an unfair economy with people driven to anger. We have long-festering animosities stoked by unseen actors. We have political fighting careening toward ideological extremes. We have a nation that appears near to jumping off the cliff. How is that different?

The Bendas' story and Kundera's novel are warnings. Far from the only ones. The clearest-eyed among us have been forewarning for a long time. As far back as the 1950s, Hannah Arendt was the first to comment on how this soft totalitarianism was putting down roots in the West:

> What prepares men for totalitarian domination in the non-totalitarian world, is the fact that loneliness, once a borderline experience usually suffered in certain marginal social conditions like old age, has become an everyday experience of the ever-growing masses of our century.[22]

We see the markers of this national loneliness and alienation all around us. We see it in the senseless mass shootings that come so regularly now. In the streets of our neighborhoods, where kids no longer go out to play. In the empty faces staring into their cell phones and scrolling mindlessly. And mostly, we see it in the willingness of so many to believe in the foolish ideas of a new faith—a faith that encourages people to identify not with e pluribus unum but instead with a resegregating of the nation along racial, sexual, and social lines.

Instead with all new canons of thought, lyrics, clothing, and behaviors that are constantly varying so outsiders don't get how this new faith works.

Instead with a rejiggering of language that layers a patina of majesty and respect onto all-new approaches to social justice.

Instead with a complete forgetting that social justice ideals have long been in place and are, in fact, central to our Judeo-Christian heritage.

Instead with an enforcement mechanism that makes outsiders fear they'll become pariahs to the new faith and there will be consequences for violating the new taboos; that the "rules" of today may no longer hold tomorrow, and not knowing that could cost you your livelihood and reputation; that even expressing an unapproved opinion could provoke the mob to turn against you and rain violence down on you.

If there are ten commandments for this new faith, these are them. And all presented with an exterior face of kindness, of concern for the less fortunate among us, so how could anyone deny them?

Those who've gone through this before, in its more virulent form of communism rolling across Europe, recognize how it goes. Recognize the new social justice warriors with their faith and their righteousness and unbreakable belief that no justice had preceded their arrival on the street, their urgent abandonment of true liberalism, their embrace of the vindictive politics of Bolshevism, which ultimately gave rise to the Soviet state.

The old totalitarianism had a vision of eradicating Christianity.

This soft totalitarianism aims to silence Christians, old-school Democrats, conservatives, Blacks, Latinos, Asians, and anybody who dares question the new faith. For years it was common to dismiss this new faith as the overexcited rantings of youth not so different from the left-wing radicals of the 1960s. Back then, the common grown-up response was all Archie Bunker: "Wait 'til those bums see da real world and gotta find a job."

As it turned out, Norman Lear's fantastic "Archie" got it wrong. Because those kids did find jobs, and they took their cultural revolution into classrooms, boardrooms, courthouses, and broadcast booths, where they trained their children to be the new authoritarians.

And behind it all was an elite state pulling the strings.

This brings us to the present and the feeling that history is again repeating itself, or at least crudely rhyming. And so it falls to us to stand against these soft authoritarians, to counterpunch. To embrace genuine ideals of individual liberty and diversity, and to begin this work in our own communities.

When we see people building fake walls in our communities to resegregate people into groups, we can go to these walls and push them down—not allowing them to wall off good people. That is us taking our faith to the wall.

We can go block by block in our communities, as the Benda family did, bringing in the lone individuals in need of rescue, offering a support structure based on our Judeo-Christian values. Just as the Arizona Women for Action in Phoenix are doing and the North Valley Constitutional Republicans in Anthem are doing—carrying on the human fight for freedom because, as the Bendas tell us:

> A single generation always stands between us and tyranny. Many people can look back and see the lessons of history, but they are totally blind to the danger that the same things are happening now.[23]

So in taking a stand now, we are ripping off the blinders.

We are starting small, each of us in our own communities. We don't need many to begin. As in Genesis 18 when God said He would not destroy Sodom and Gomorrah if ten righteous people could be found there, we need only a small group to make a difference—only ten in a community to begin.

CHAPTER 13

SURVEILLING AMERICANS CHINESE-STYLE—ARE WE NUTS?

I T'S NO SECRET that the elite state has long been intrigued by, and even helped build, the Chinese government's surveillance panopticon.

From the Greek *all* and *seeing*, the panopticon traces to the late 1700s, when Englishman Jeremy Bentham learned of a Russian invention for training unskilled workers in big groups at once to become craftsmen. Bentham re-architected the idea as a more efficient prison with an outside circular ring where all the prisoners' cells could be situated, and a central courtyard with an inspection tower where the guards could see all. Because prisoners knew someone was always watching, they would modify their behavior and follow the rules to steer clear of punishment.

You can see the attraction to the Chinese a couple centuries later.

While architecting a panopticon large enough to "watch" over a billion citizens would be a mean feat, doing it with cameras—not so much. They've placed some 540 million cameras all about,[1] and images of every bit of activity within those cameras' range can be instantly stitched together by a central AI-driven computer when needed.

It's basically a computer with a gong attached to it. Do the right thing and get a prize; do the wrong thing and get gonged.

Less obvious, at first blush, is the interest that US companies tied to the elite state would have with this panopticon. Isn't our country always warning about the Chinese, and passing laws forbidding trade with China? Aren't our companies constantly having their intellectual property ripped off by China's state-supported hackers?

Answers to both questions are yes.

Yet companies as well known and respected as Apple, Cisco, Facebook, LinkedIn, Oracle, Thermo, Fisher Scientific, and Yahoo, along with the academics at MIT have provided technology and consulting services to build this Chinese panopticon.[2]

And big Wall Street firms such as Vanguard, JPMorgan, and Fidelity have invested in the Chinese companies constructing it all.[3]

Officially, US firms are quick to deny or nuance their involvement. Just read their press releases; their innocence is spelled out. But their role in aiding the mass genocide going on in China has been too much for even cynical old capitalists to bear. Stories have made their way into the press, especially the independent press that refuses to buckle under pressure to zip it.

You may have heard of the Uyghurs, the Muslim minority living in Northwest China. At least one million of them have been locked away in secret "political education" camps for the offense of practicing their own religion in their own language.[4] Here's how the freedom scholars at War on the Rocks and the University of Texas at Austin described it:

> Wrists and ankles strapped into a restraining "tiger chair," a man is used as a subject with which to "train" artificial intelligence-assisted facial recognition technology to detect states of emotion. Minute changes in facial expression are analyzed by the facial recognition technology to determine whether the test subject possesses a "negative mindset" or a heightened state of anxiety, allegedly indicating a potential for anti-social behavior....
>
> Xu Guixiang, a spokesman for the Xinjiang Uyghur Autonomous Region government, asserted on May 25, 2021, that the re-education system was required in order to "remove extremist thoughts" from Uyghur minds and "transform" them from "ghosts" into "humans."[5]

All twelve million of the Uyghurs must constantly pass through checkpoints with facial recognition cameras and Wi-Fi sniffers hoovering up the data on their devices. Every Uyghur between the ages of twelve and sixty-five has a full suite of biometric data gathered up—including fingerprints, iris scans, blood types, voice samples, and DNA samples.[6]

This is the model for the modern panopticon, the model our elite state helped build, the model they're just itching to see employed here.

But It Could Never Happen Here, Right?

We can't imagine this Chinese model being used here, just as they couldn't imagine similar crackdowns in Eastern Europe or years earlier in imperial Russia. Folks on the streets rarely believe it can happen in their "advanced" societies. But of course it did happen in China, Eastern Europe, and Russia. Can it happen here?

It already has, as we've begun to see, in a softer form. It's happening differently because our cultures are quite different. Americans are more individualistic than the Chinese, who are more likely to conform. There are many more malcontents here, people not hip to being constantly watched, tracked from moment to moment throughout their day, with the most intimate details of their lives pieced together by algorithms that dusty bureaucrats nestled in the bowels of an Orwellian gray building in Washington can diddle around with, secure in their jobs no matter how they might abuse other people's private information.

But it is happening here.

With the automated collection of every click, the voice recognition services, the facial recognition tools that scan all our photos of friends and family to analyze our faces, the biometric fingerprinting that eases us through airport lines, the location tracking in our smartphones, the digital card swipe that traces and tracks our entry to places of work and homes, the video doorbells, the fitness trackers, and on and on and all recorded, everything is observed and privacy forfeited, undermining our most basic right to be free individuals.

We see the cameras all around—rather good evidence that we are being watched even though we haven't given our consent to allow all the data about our lives to be collected.

We read about it in books and see it in cop shows. We may think some of that is just good fiction, but a lot of it is not.

We don't see the software working behind the scenes, but we know it is gathering up data that might be used to help us—or to hurt us, depending on whose hands it falls into.

We also know this software is usually released long before it is fully functioning—since that's how software is typically released. In the case of facial recognition software, the outcomes can be damning. Algorithmic biases in these software products have resulted in misrecognition of dark-skinned individuals. Still, it is being deployed.

Cities across America are looking at these systems—usually with the best of intentions, to deter crime. Baltimore ran a six-month trial with a private company, Persistent Surveillance Systems. They flew planes equipped with powerful, wide-angle cameras over the entire city, capturing a constant stream of images and stitching them together for a real-time portrait of activity on the ground.

City police insisted they needed some kind of help to combat crime in a city stuck with the nation's second-highest murder rate. Sadly, true. But a group of activists with the support of the ACLU sued to stop the program, arguing that government agencies have a history of secretly using these technologies for other purposes—such as surveilling Black Lives Matter protests and January 6 Capitol Hill protests.[7] Both true.

More than one hundred US cities are using surveillance technologies, including facial recognition, on their residents—much of it "Made in China." Some 750,000 Chinese cameras made by Hikvision watch over condos in Manhattan, hotels in Los Angeles, recreation centers in Philadelphia, etc. Major cities such as Detroit, Memphis, and Portland allow limited use of facial recognition technologies. Some, including San Francisco, San Diego, and Oakland, have banned it—but they are in the minority.[8]

In 2019, Congress ordered federal agencies to remove all Chinese cameras—but thousands of banned cameras still remain at military and government sites.[9]

In 2020, Senator Jeff Merkley of Oregon introduced S.3284, the Ethical Use of Facial Recognition Act. Bill status: nothing's happening.[10]

In the absence of any meaningful national directives, US companies are hot on this tech. Clearview AI, for one, has scraped billions of images from the internet, allowing them to identify virtually anyone in real time. Trying it out, an investor used the app to identify a man he happened to see dating his adult daughter. Our government used it after January 6 to identify protestors at the US Capitol that day and later track them down, sending armored personnel carriers into their neighborhoods.

Our financial firms are using Chinese-style social scoring. Cybersecurity experts at Kaspersky tell us a third of adults between the ages of twenty-five and thirty-four have had difficulties getting a mortgage or a loan due to their social media activity.[11] The social scoring software has deemed them untrustworthy.

This social scoring took deeper root during COVID.

Biden administration officials threatened people who chose to reject vaccines, try certain therapies, or refuse masking. With thousands of facial recognition cameras scanning our faces wherever we go, it's just one more step for the government to identify citizens "not following the rules" and deduct points from our social credit scores as well as broadcast our photos to our neighbors, identifying us as "anti-science, anti-mask idiots."

To help in this effort, Google and Apple formed a partnership to create an app to alert people coming into contact with people with COVID. Suddenly we went from every town having a snitch to a government of snitches with social credit scoring capabilities at their fingertips.

This software is out there now, and we even have a name for it—surveillance capitalism. Say it enough times and it is normalized, right? Or instead we hit the pause button—really hit it! And we step back and ask the hard questions about privacy:

- How do we keep control of any data collected about us to ensure our own personal safety and well-being as individuals?

- When are we OK with letting unknown actors comb through our personal data?

- Should our government even have access to all of our secure data like they do now?

- Should private companies working with the government be able to create social scores for rating what we can and can't do based on our "scores"?

These questions about privacy are truly questions about how we lead our lives. Having privacy has value, we all know. It protects our most intimate experiences as well as our most public—such as protesting without fear of government retribution. It enables us to share information with our doctors, for instance, but not our employers. It is both simple and layered in complexity.

The Founders, in all their wisdom, couldn't have anticipated the threats posed by today's surveillance technologies. So we must argue for clear and unambiguous use of these technologies with legislation that protects our individual liberties.

In the tech world, there are a few companies aiming in the right direction on this.

Apple, for one, is mostly committed to privacy. CEO Tim Cook has made it a hallmark of his leadership, calling it "privacy by design."[12] Apple's algorithms work to ensure that others can't see your information, you control how it is used, it is encrypted from prying eyes, and your personal identifiers are also guarded.

This is why I personally traded my Android phone for an iPhone. All our data should be treated with this kind of respect.

At the federal and state levels, we should support privacy legislation that backs out Patriot Act overreach that now allows any government official with a passcode and a grudge to listen in on any phone call or read any email or text being sent by any American.

We need to move aggressively to treat privacy as a fundamental right, not just a preference in a "Terms and Conditions" box we tick.

This can bring an end to the Wild West use of our personal information by tech behemoths and their friends in the elite state.

This can shift power back into citizens' hands.

We also need more meaningful forms of consent in the applications we sign up for online. Companies should not be able to take advantage of our laziness or ignorance in this regard and harvest all the data they wish on us. Citizens should know exactly what information is being collected and how it is being used.

For example, any device's or program's default settings should allow us to opt out of data sharing. Choosing to opt in should be a choice we make.

These rules should be enforced by a government agency such as the FTC. We know that government agencies are rarely capable of enforcing strongly *and* properly. Yet we must ask for responsible regulators to do their job.

"IT'S SO EASY TO STEAL ELECTIONS NOW" (OVERHEARD IN COFFEE SHOPS ACROSS SILICON VALLEY)

As far back as 2008, the Obama campaign was bragging about how Facebook got their candidate elected. They bragged even louder after repeating it in 2012. You could walk into any of Silicon Valley's trendy coffee shops—Red Rock, Philz, Joanie's—as I did back then and overhear twentysomethings, dressed all in black, vainly carrying on about how they'd singlehandedly skewered the giant vampire squid that had wrapped its tentacles around America.

Never mind that they were misappropriating Matt Taibbi's brilliant takedown of Goldman Sachs—more Democrat than Republican and foremost the brains of the elite state. These tech bros were so proud of themselves. And they remained so until 2016, when Donald Trump's campaign did the same manipulations of voters on Facebook. That's when this practice was all wrong, they screamed.

They even made a documentary about Trump's underhanded use of Facebook. It was called *The Social Dilemma*, and some choice lines emerged from it: "If you want to control the population of a country, there has never been a tool as effective as Facebook."[13]

Did that agitprop talk about Google's attempt to steal the election for Hillary Clinton in 2016 (though obviously falling short of their goal)? Or about the Obama campaign's prior manipulations of public behavior on Facebook? Did they even mention the pioneer of the art form who worked for successive Democratic politicians and wrote in his book *The Revolution Will Not Be Televised* that the internet would be the "overthrow of everything"?[14]

Silly questions.

In that 2016 election the psychologist Robert Epstein, PhD, had taken an interest. He monitored Google's search engine results and was so horrified by what he found, he agreed to testify before the Senate Judiciary Committee—despite being an avowed Democrat. Epstein figured out that Google shifted some 2.6 million undecided voters to Hillary Clinton—completely unbeknown to them. Manipulated them by dialing down the number of negative stories these undecided voters saw about Mrs. Clinton and dialing up the negative stories on Trump. This subliminally shifted people's perception of the candidates—without their knowing better.[15]

Epstein astutely took screenshots of his search engine results. This put a crimp in Google's four-point damage control plan to (a) deny the whole thing, (b) smear the good doctor's reputation, (c) brand the Jewish man a closet White supremacist, and (d) destroy his practice.

After failing in 2016, Google went to work writing what can only be characterized as a hate manifesto, though they chose to call it "The Good Censor." It was an eighty-five-page playbook on how the world should be, whose voices should be eliminated from it, and how those ends should be accomplished.[16]

Of course, President Trump moved to the head of the list of people to be silenced. As in the time of the Spanish Inquisition, the goal was less about punishing and more about tamping down dissent. A message was sent in the hounding of Trump: look what we have done to the most powerful man in the world; imagine what we could do to you.

So now anyone in public life has to wonder if it can be done to them. Those in private life as well. We have to wonder, as we are meant to, how badly we could be damaged from speaking our opinions out loud.

Here we had private media companies, entrusted through federal legislation to ensure open and free communications, doing the exact opposite. This was such an assault on the principles of every democracy that a global backlash arose.

Leaders around the world—few of them fans of Trump—raised their voices against the imperious folly of Google as well as Facebook and Twitter, who had by then joined in the silencings.

Heads of state of Germany, France, Mexico, Australia, the European Parliament, and even Russia declared that these rogue platforms had to be reined in.[17] They understood that if Silicon Valley was allowed to continue developing censoring technologies in cahoots with the permanent state, then America would never again have fair elections. That would not only take America down, but it would also threaten the governments of every country, allowing Google, Facebook, and Twitter to operate within their cyber borders.

So these leaders began taking action, and our US leaders must follow.

Backtracking a little, it is still really hard for some people to believe that these Big Tech platforms could be this bad. That they can effectively silence any voice they don't like. It's just beyond the pale and so very hard to believe. That's why those of us who publish online initially had to prove that we were being silenced.

At the Western Journal, the online publication I founded, we studied the impact of censorship on our business.[18] We've been completely open about it, sharing what we experienced transparently in hopes that thoughtful liberals will not have a knee-jerk reaction to anything not originating in their own echo chamber.

In one such study of Facebook and the algorithm change they slipped into place in February 2018, in time for the upcoming midterm elections, we found that liberal publishers *gained* 2 percent more web traffic while conservative publishers *lost* an average of 14 percent of their traffic. Just from a pre-election tweak of the algorithm.

Over at Breitbart News in the 2020 election, they found that almost no search results were showing up in Google for their thousands of stories. They calculated that 99 percent of their stories were "disappeared" compared to their experience in the election four years prior.[19]

Meanwhile over at *Time* magazine, they celebrated record responses to their articles featured prominently in Google's search engine listings and in Facebook and Twitter news feeds. Their bragging was full-throated—after the election results came in, anyway—about their "Shadow Campaign That Saved the 2020 Election." Saved it by rigging the news stories about it.[20]

To help tilt the 2020 election, Facebook's Mark Zuckerberg gave more than $400 million to nonprofit groups to get out the vote and secure a win.[21] He's entitled to his personal opinion. But it is immoral and illegal to use a publicly sanctioned tech platform to squelch public content he didn't happen to like. When he did that, he ran afoul of ethical considerations—and legal ones as well. That is also what can be used to break up his company, as we'll see.

PLATFORMS ARE ACCELERATING THE
SILENCINGS, NOT BACKING OFF

When you think of how many times the tech bros have jetted from the valley to the swamp in recent years to testify before Congress, with all the fines and hand-slappings and promises to "do better," you'd think they'd clean up their act at least a little. If anything, the opposite has happened.

The Western Journal has found that the platforms are getting more sophisticated in their silencings by targeting storylines, not just people. In this way, they can shut down entire conversations they don't like—even more powerfully.

Here's how this played out between January and April 2022. During that time, Western Journal's editors had to yank 183 stories out of the Facebook feed, or 6 percent of all the stories. Of course, 6 percent doesn't sound like much—but it's misleading. Those 6 percent were the most popular stories that Western Journal readers wanted to see. Stories about COVID, gender dysmorphia, vaccines, climate change, elections—the topics people care about!

But these stories had to be yanked.

That 6 percent also doesn't take into account self-censure. Because the editors know the stories won't run on Facebook, or that they'll get slapped with an "Offensive Content" label, the editors don't even try to post the stories. In this way, Facebook shuts down all but approved messaging.

Facebook becomes the arbiter of truth.

Over at Google News, they completely blacklisted the Western Journal.

And Google's Gmail can be utterly ruthless in filtering out messaging they don't like. Their bots sweep conservative emails into spam, letting liberal emails go through.

Though the Western Journal was a founding partner of Apple News in 2017, meaning it was one of the major publications invited onto the new Apple News consolidation platform, the Western Journal has since been completely "deplatformed," as they call it. Repeated attempts by editors to talk with longtime colleagues at Apple have gone unanswered. And why? Because Apple may be a leader in privacy, as we've discussed, but they're also a leader in censoring views they don't like.

I said these platforms are getting more sophisticated. They are now scaling their surveillance to identify entire networks of people they can lump together on hit lists. Allum Bokhari, the technology writer at Breitbart News, dug into this and laid out the threat to each of us:

> A field of computer science called "network analysis" is dedicated to identifying groups of people with shared interests, who read similar websites, who talk about similar things, who have similar habits, who follow similar people on social media, and who share similar political viewpoints. Big Tech companies are able to detect when particular information is flowing through a particular network—if there's a news story or a post or a video, for instance, that's going viral among conservatives or among voters as a whole....
>
> [T]hese companies will eventually have the power not only to suppress existing political movements, but to anticipate and prevent the emergence of new ones. This would mean the end of democracy as we know it, because it would place us forever under the thumb of an unaccountable oligarchy.[22]

We are well under that thumb already. We saw as much in the January 6 Capitol protests. Not so much what the out-of-control protestors did, but how the elite-state media organs responded to it. The breach of the Capitol cannot be condoned, and those who resorted to violence should be prosecuted. The bulk of the people there that day were merely protesting, and they should not be getting harassed every day of their lives since—though that's exactly what's been happening. Every day the elite state expresses some new outrage over the protests that day—for a reason. John Daniel Davidson explained why in The Federalist:

> [E]lite outrage is not really about what happened at the Capitol—about the "sacred citadel of our democracy being defiled" and so on. The outrage...is performative. It is in service of a larger purpose that has nothing to do with the peaceful transfer of power and everything to do with the wielding of power.
>
> Specifically, it's about punishing supporters of President Trump. If the pro-Trump mob can be depicted as "terrorists" and "traitors," then there's almost nothing we shouldn't do to silence them. Right? Rick Klein, the political director at ABC News...

mused (in a now-deleted tweet) that getting rid of Trump is "the easy part" and the more difficult task will be "cleansing the movement he commands."

That's not the kind of language you use when you're in the business of reporting the news. It's the kind of language you use when you're in the business of social control.[23]

Yes, social *control*. Because if the left-stream media arm of the elite state was genuinely concerned about the dangerous mobs run amok, they surely would've been deeply outraged at the far larger and more dangerous mobs ransacking America's cities all summer long in 2020. But zero outrage over that. In fact, only praise and artless justifications for that, because radical left protestors aren't a threat to the elite state; in their view, conservatives are.

The flip side of that message is this: conservatives must be censored or the elite state loses control.

And censoring conservative politicians is not enough. Ideas cannot be allowed because ideas can be dangerous—ideas such as varying COVID treatments, problems with the government's vaccinations, studies linking vaccines to the rising numbers of children born with autism, vitamin supplements that are used daily all around the world but cannot even be discussed in America. All these ideas have been added to the platform's censor list.

If anyone dares talk about them in other than the approved way, poof—*gone!* Instantly downranked, disappeared, or defamed on the platform.

Fair to conclude, then, that the First Amendment rights and ideals, which carried America to the top of nations, no longer apply.

We're now four presidential elections down this slippery slope with freedom falling into the abyss. Facing such grim prospects, what can any of us even hope to do?

The answer is easier than you may think. We've been on this slippery slope before and managed to step back in time. We can do it again. We're getting closer.

Tech Didn't Set Out to Injure Children, But Then They Wouldn't Stop

There's a sign that pops up on the internet and in yards in upscale neighborhoods that cuts to the quick of the dysfunction in society. It says: "We believe love is love; science is real; black lives matter; water is life; no human being is illegal; feminism is for everyone; kindness is everything."

If you've seen it, what have you thought about it? The talented observer Ted Bauer asked this question in an October 2021 post of his blog, *The Context of Things*.[24] In answering he goes straight to the performative nature of it, the weird virtue-signaling meant to tell the world, "I'm a good person, and look, I'm showing it!"

These signs are posted by good-hearted people, so what's the harm, right?

No harm. Interesting, though, that when these tony liberal neighborhoods find too many minority families moving in, many times new signs go up. "For Sale" signs. This is the harsh truth of the liberal mindset. Minorities want the same things everyone wants—to raise their families and be safe. Liberals don't really want to share their special spaces.

We see it in the neighborhoods; we see a generation lost to it on the internet.

Social media platforms most certainly did not create this weird performative virtue-signaling, as Bauer calls it. A more likely culprit is German chemist Justus von Liebig, who in 1835 invented the mirror. But today's platforms have sure hastened this vanity trip.

Social media has made everyone a performer of varying quality. Folks under thirty know this in their bones and without questioning it go about constantly putting on a show, trying to outdo others with an even better post, deflecting attention from the deficiencies in their lives, cherry-picking the moments that reveal them covered in their own awesomesauce.

Lost is that great old advice, "Be yourself; everyone else is taken."

To say this is unhealthy is too obvious. It is more than unhealthy and mentally retarding; it has created a tension in society that sometimes explodes in "culture wars" and other times simply degrades the values we once held dear.

Gone is the enjoyment of, say, an astounding spring sunrise. Instead of stopping to revel in the beauty of it, the first instinct now is to take a picture and post to Instagram, add filters, shoot it over to Twitter with a slew of attention-grabbing hashtags and emojis, then wait for the likes, comments, and favorites to roll in, constantly checking to see if the post has been properly appreciated, waiting for that dopamine hit of approval, that curtain call for such a wonderful performance!

Ask the performer what the sunrise actually looked like, or the feelings it elicited, and stop them before they reach for their phone; you're apt to get a blank stare.

We hear a lot about fake news; this is fake life.

A generation has grown up knowing less about being human than about playing the role of one. Children are no longer being children, developing true identities and a sense of who they are. That time for many is spent broadcasting the filtered, hashtagged version of the future writers, artists, or changemakers they want to be. No wonder today's young writers, artists, and changemakers often appear half baked. They often are.

And the platforms have been doing the baking.

Our society's breakthrough understanding of this came with the whistleblower testimony of Frances Haugen in October 2021. Haugen was a longtime Facebook employee who became sickened by the tactics she saw Facebook and Instagram engineers employing to damage the mental health of children and teenagers. She showed Congress the proof—the internal studies done on increases in suicidal thoughts and eating disorders among young girls using the site.[25]

Strangest to me about Haugen's testimony: everyone acted surprised by it. It was well-known that the tech platforms were addictive, injurious beasts. That was a feature, not a bug, as they say. It was the actual business model.

So how much did Facebook and the others contribute to the mental health crisis we're seeing among young people today?

This isn't something that can be easily measured. But if you were to say that 80 percent of the problems we're seeing in young people are the result of the tech platforms, I wouldn't disagree. And the remaining 20 percent would come from the reality-shredding virus known as COVID and, more specifically, from the government's handling of the crisis, which added all kinds of emotional, psychological, and social stressors on children.

It's hard to imagine that Zuckerberg wasn't aware of the terrible damage he was causing. Surely he could see that the vulgar, misogynistic app he'd thrown together at Harvard was injuring teen women, teen men, adolescents, and adults, in that order. He'd long been given a pass on his chauvinist aggression platform (Facebook) and his soft-porn platform (Instagram). But in 2021 it was clear his seventeen-year joyride was ending, so he decided to bail. He renamed his company Meta to literally flee the real-world mess he'd created and escape into an all-new virtual world known as the metaverse.

Coun

t on things to get even uglier there.

In the metaverse, the distinctions between reality and fantasy fade away. How will this play out for kids? Granted, we are still years away from your average seven-year-old being fooled by the imagery of the metaverse—especially since they'll have a headset or heavy glasses strapped on. Kids are quite adept at discerning reality from cyberreality. But psychologists are already deep into debate about how much harm could come from spending hours a day secreted away in a virtual world. Here are two views:

> Dr. [Jessica] Stone: "The answer is, ultimately: It depends....A young person can go into a virtual world and try out different roles. And isn't that what adolescence is? Figuring out your self-identification, what you believe in, how you want to represent and present yourself, how people respond. What an amazing gift it is to be able to do that in an environment that doesn't have direct, immediate, real-world consequences!"
>
> Dr. [Rachel] Kowert: "We absolutely have to discuss the toxicity that will occur in these spaces with our kids. If you let your children in there untethered, without monitoring, without teaching them about digital citizenship, it's going to have a negative impact on their mental health."[26]

So there are positive and negative potentials with the coming metaverse experience. And if it is treated in the same manipulative way social media was, we'll likely see a repeat of the harassment, the hating, the scarring of young people.

If the metaverse becomes the new digital babysitter for overworked or uncaring parents, we'll have an even worse epidemic of mental health problems.

The platforms won't change. Half-baking people is a business model they don't know how to improve upon and still make money.

There's only one fix for all this. Read on to discover what it is.

CHAPTER 14

TRANSFORM TECH INTO A THOUSAND WONDERS

W<small>E CANNOT HOPE</small> to reverse the innovation flowing out of Silicon Valley, nor should we. It is our nature to continue inventing and nudging the future closer. And who knows what amazing wonders lie ahead?

At the same time, we cannot sit back helplessly as new technologies are rolled out by coders oblivious to their social consequences. We can all agree that society at large should be making the ethical decisions about technology, not the tech bros.

As individuals, we can do little. But as a nation of caring parents, we can support all that is wonderful about technology, while dialing back the harmful. It's certainly not an easy task, but our understanding of it is. We simply aim to control technology instead of letting it control us. Controlling it for the welfare of all and not the profit of a few.

How better than by turning young Mark Zuckerberg's famous line about moving fast and breaking things on its face. His meaning was, it's natural to make mistakes when innovating in complex new sciences. So there is natural poetic and policy justice in moving fast to break today's tech behemoths like Zuckerberg's into a thousand little wonders.

Or at least a couple dozen.

I'm not saying to be reckless—though Silicon Valley deserves some measure of that. I'm saying very simply that the greatness of Silicon Valley is not aided by size and scale. Smaller platforms will do less damage by definition. Even though the valley's big minds built these platforms without consideration for the impact on people, they should be taken down with full consideration for the society in which they exist, and the values that are important to us:

- **Free expression**: Platforms should let individuals speak out without censorship unless endangering others.

- **Individual dignity**: Platforms should protect the basic rights of every individual and protect our children from dark experiences.

- **Strengthened competition**: Platforms should compete without using scale or monopoly positioning to restrain trade.

Delivering on these values is far from easy. But it is nonetheless the responsibility of the platforms to deliver on them. If they can't, then they can't continue—it can be and must be made that simple. Washington can't look the other way any longer.

WITH THE COUNTRY INFLAMED, WASHINGTON FEIGNED CONCERN

After years of ignoring the Big Tech tyrants' abusive drive to dominion, or more often abetting it out of self-interest, by the summer of 2020 politicians could no longer diddle around. Too many constituents had seen the dark side of these tech giants exposed (such as through my own book, *Big Tech Tyrants*) and were demanding that real action be taken.

Up on Capitol Hill, in Judiciary Committee hearings, Rep. David Cicilline of Rhode Island set the stage for a wholesale overhaul of antitrust law:

> When these laws were written, the monopolists were men named Rockefeller and Carnegie. Today the men are named Zuckerberg, Cook, Pichai, and Bezos. Once again, their control of the marketplace allows them to do whatever it takes to crush independent business and expand their own power. This must end.[1]

Unlike in earlier hearings, members of Congress arrived prepared and on the ball. They put on a show of brandishing whistleblower testimony, damning internal documents, and producing evidence of serial lawbreaking. They grilled the CEOs of the Big Four—Apple, Google, Amazon, and Facebook. They spoke in earnest about throwing open Apple's notoriously closed app stores, controlling the ad business of Google, slapping

Amazon for its mean-spirited abuse of retailers, and dealing with privacy run amok on Facebook.

These were fine performances all around, and genuine. Conservatives like Ted Cruz and progressives like Alexandria Ocasio-Cortez both find Big Tech offensive; they both also rely on the big campaign contributions that come from tech bundlers. They rely also on social media channels to get their messages out. By going after Big Tech too forcefully, they were jeopardizing their seats at the elite state's high table. Since those 2020 hearings, though, the loudest sounds coming from Capitol Hill have been from all the foot-dragging going on.

The House Energy and Commerce Committee has been preparing privacy legislation, which could take them years and years to finalize.

Over at the FTC, they are moving to (a) ban the collection of some personal data and (b) require an opt-in button for data collection. But given how long it takes the FTC to finalize a rule and wade through the tsunami of legal challenges certain to follow, it's barely a start.

Lobbyists for Big Tech are using this time to execute on a novel strategy: retreat! This strategy involves whispering in all the right congressional ears that Silicon Valley dearly wants the antitrust laws vigorously enforced. Bring it on, they're saying, because you know what's best for us.

This is known to magicians as the misdirect.

Big Tech's strategists know that antitrust law was long meant to curb monopoly power that limits consumer choices and leads to higher prices. But tech is known for lowering prices. So lawyers for the tech firms will go to trial and let the government present its case, then methodically show that consumers haven't been gouged, ipso facto, no antitrust violation.

This is how tech is likely to play its get-out-of-jail card. If Congress allows it, they are the true criminals. Because the antitrust laws were also meant to protect competition. Big Tech is in clear violation here. Government lawyers should argue that this violation is best remedied by busting the behemoths into as many competitive wonders as possible, so that each can set about delighting our collective imagination again, and in succeeding, be rewarded for it.

SIMPLE, *IMMEDIATE* REFORMS FOR SOCIAL MEDIA

On the road to breaking them up, there are fixes for social media that can make a big difference. The biggest problem with social media is not the posting of toxic content, it's how that content gets blown out of proportion and is seen by everybody. Facebook whistleblower Frances Haugen told Congress that a few tweaks to the platforms could yield big results.

For one, the Facebook share function can be modified so that content cannot be shared by a simple mouse click, but instead must be copied-and-pasted into a new post. Sure, this means the user has to get involved in the sharing—but isn't that the point of being social?

For two, deal with user honesty. Don't give anybody an account on the platforms until their identity is verified. No more posting under fake names, which brings out the worst in people. If folks want to post, they should own it. And no more bot farms and fake accounts souring the online experience.

Those are two simple reforms that can happen now.

CHILDREN'S ONLINE PRIVACY PROTECTION ACT

Congress should take additional action to protect children on the platforms. The Children's Online Privacy Protection Act currently forbids any online service from collecting personal information on children under thirteen.[2] The age should be raised to eighteen, the legal age of adulthood. Nothing is gained from compiling data for the aim of manipulating kids. Nothing.

Along with raising the age, tech companies should also be held responsible for enforcing the age requirements. Not an easy task, but they're up to it. To ensure as much, when they fail, they should be slapped with an automatic uncontestable $10 million fine per occurrence. That gives them an incentive to treat other people's children like their own.

WHITHER SECTION 230?

Social media's entire success can be linked to laws passed during the Clinton administration, most relevantly Section 230 of the 1996 Communications Decency Act. Two key things came from this.

1. Platforms are not publishers. If someone shares something disparaging about you on Facebook, for example, you can sue that person but not Facebook.

2. Platforms are excused from any liability for actions taken in good faith. So they can censor whomever they like if they maintain it was done in "good faith."

Section 230 originally made sense. It was intended mainly to prevent children from accessing porn on the internet. So yes, to be praised. But it also allowed for the censoring abuses we've seen.

Social media companies contend these abuses never would have happened were it not for Section 230. (Maybe not such a bad thing?!) However true, we know a handful of tech execs shouldn't have so much power over our communications. President Trump called for repealing Section 230. But simply repealing the law could do more harm than good. The network effects already enjoyed by these tech behemoths would only be further locked in.

There is an easier solution that sounds workable.

SEPARATE THE PLATFORMS FROM THE CONTENT FILTERS

We do not question Mark Zuckerberg's sincerity in acknowledging the shortcomings of the Facebook platform he architected: "One of the most painful lessons I've learned is that when you connect two billion people, you will see all the beauty and ugliness of humanity."[3]

But as Facebook's two billion subscribers have become three billion, the job of trying to manage the steroidal tsunami of content pushed onto the platform has become a task no human or AI could be expected to handle well. That is a strong argument for breaking up Facebook into many little interest-based platforms so people can still share and discover with friends in potentially less-polluted waters.

But the problem of content is truly a problem of filters. Filters are the source of Big Tech's power and its problems. In setting a filter to decide what is hate speech or what is misinformation, as examples, some difficult and subjective decisions have to be made by fallible humans.

How can humans working under impossible real-time deadlines do a good job of classifying one article authoritative and another one fraudulent? And what happens when human bias or prejudices creep into this real-time filtering process?

We know what happens—we've seen the impact of it. But there is another way to handle the filtering issue. This idea comes from Allum Bokhari, technology writer at Breitbart News:

> The most important demand we can make of lawmakers and regulators is that Big Tech be forbidden from activating these filters without our knowledge and consent. They should be prohibited from doing this—and even from nudging us to turn on a filter—under penalty of losing their Section 230 immunity as publishers of third party content. This policy should be strictly enforced, and it should extend even to seemingly non-political filters like relevance and popularity. Anything less opens the door to manipulation.[4]

To make this work even better, there could be two types of companies—content hosts and content filters. This way people could keep control over their online experiences and those of their children. This step could help restore the original promise of the technology platforms—enabling, not censoring; innovating, not manipulating.

LAWSUITS ARE THE WORST UNTIL THEY'RE THE BEST

In 2021 Donald Trump brought First Amendment lawsuits against Facebook, Twitter, and YouTube. Wags called it "as stupid as you'd think," but it's far from.[5] While Trump's legal papers were apparently sloppy (no surprise there!), he aims to prove that social media censorship violates the US Constitution. His central claim is indisputable: Big Tech has restricted speech and silenced elected officials in coordination with government leaders of one political party. As Vivek Ramaswamy explained in the *Wall Street Journal*:

> The central claim in Mr. Trump's class-action lawsuit—that the defendants should be treated as state actors and are bound by the First Amendment when they engage in selective political censorship—has precedent to back it up. Their censorship constitutes

state action because the government granted them immunity from legal liability, threatened to punish them if they allow disfavored speech, and colluded with them in choosing targets for censorship.[6]

By predisposition, I loathe lawsuits for they are mostly attorney full-employment measures, and value rarely comes from them. But a lawsuit against Big Tech is also a lawsuit against the brains of the elite state, and it could potentially deliver a blow we can all support.

Specific Breakup Recommendations

Break up Meta/Facebook.

Separate Meta/Facebook and the companies it has acquired to concentrate monopoly power, open Facebook's data stores to competing businesses, and mandate stronger privacy rules to protect Facebook subscribers.

Facebook could become six separately owned companies: Meta, Facebook, Messenger, WhatsApp, Instagram, and Horizon Worlds (their new metaverse). This should help accomplish three aims:

1. Reignite competitive innovation in the sector—with entrepreneurs given a realistic opportunity to challenge the behemoth platform.

2. Diffuse the concentrated control of online conversation.

3. Leave each new firm with sufficient market share so they can compete and thrive, if well-managed.

Break up Alphabet/Google.

It is sadly ironic that a company that once unleashed human creativity and learning is now concentrating monopoly power and squashing competition while advancing a narrow political agenda. But it has been proven true, and there are several ways to break up Alphabet/Google:

- Separate Google search to open search advertising to competition.

- Divide Google's and YouTube's advertising units into stand-alone companies.

- Spin off the advertising units as stand-alone companies.

- Create stand-alone companies out of YouTube, Android phone, Google's cloud services, and Google Search.

- Regulate Alphabet like a public utility, forcing it to license out its algorithms to help spur competition (as was done with AT&T in 1956).

- Forbid Alphabet from acquiring additional tech companies.

If the goal is to recognize Google's many achievements while also restoring innovation and free-flowing ideas to the marketplace, then ideally Alphabet becomes five different companies: Google Search, Google Cloud Platform, Android, YouTube, other units.

Break up Amazon.

Amazon has become such an overbearing monopoly that it should be made to choose: either sell goods as a stand-alone retail platform, or run a digital platform other merchants use to reach customers.

Amazon could ideally operate as five separately owned companies: Amazon Web Services (AWS), Amazon Logistics, Amazon Retail, Amazon Entertainment, Amazon Health & Life Sciences.

Regulate Twitter.

There is no easy way to break up Twitter, and little to be gained from doing so. Society might benefit more if Twitter were legally transformed into the common carriage entity that, in practice, it is. In short, treat Twitter like a utility.

Regulate Apple.

Apple earned its distinction as the first trillion-dollar company. It is not without its faults, but none that merits the heavy hand of government. Instead, Apple should be subjected to rigorous oversight to ensure it does not use its privileged position as a chokepoint to free and open political discourse.

It's important that we not forget how much we truly loved these platforms and hardware companies in the early going. At the same time, we must acknowledge that their wonder years have given way to monopolistic behavior that must end.

We don't relish asking the government to intervene in the market economy. But these platforms have subverted the democratic capitalist principles we treasure. If they are not turned back, our nation cannot move forward in healthy respect for the individual liberties of all.

CHAPTER 15

ON THE MONOPOLY BOARD, THERE'S A REASON FOR THE GO-TO-JAIL SQUARE

"A LOT OF my decisions are based on what is needed in my community," says Nathan Schlecht, who is something of a rarity in America. He's the local pharmacist in Forman, North Dakota. And yes, Nathan knows everyone who comes through his doors. He's the one the nursing home calls about medication issues. He gives health talks at the local school. He has time to talk through treatment approaches for patients' chronic diseases. He even opened a telepharmacy up the road and delivers prescriptions to those who can't get in.

Nathan is the very model of an old-fashioned community pharmacist, a model that's taken a beating in recent years but still survives—and can tell us a lot about how much better business could be working in America if we took some of that "old-fashioned" into the new.

North Dakota has 171 independent pharmacies, primarily because the state kept to its roots. Back in 1963 they passed a law requiring drugstores to be owned and operated by an actual pharmacist. They are the only state to do this, though it's a common practice around the world.[1]

The goal is an obvious one: to ensure that pharmacies are run by people more interested in the health of their neighbors than a bottom-line growth metric.

This kind of local human caring can make a big difference in each of our lives.

A seventeen-year-old Connecticut girl learned as much recently when her head began pounding and nausea and dizziness overtook her. Turns out one of CVS's ten thousand pharmacies had—whoops!—given her blood pressure meds instead of asthma meds. Her story is a common one when you go looking for them—but to find them you have to turn over stones seemingly glued down.

There are no real reporting requirements on pharmacy errors, so it's hard to know how often the underpaid and overworked folks behind the window mess up. But the Institute of Medicine estimates that prescription-error mistakes harm about a million and a half Americans each year.[2] That's not even surprising when you look at how the big-box owners squeeze their pharmacies to "increase throughput." Our safety is the price to pay for saving a few bucks.

But do we really save? It's just accepted that big-box stores drive down prices. So you might assume that North Dakota's 1963 law means higher prices for meds. In fact, the state ranks twenty-fifth in pricing—so right in the middle of the national range.[3]

And *Consumer Reports* surveys going back to 2014 ranked the independents higher on shorter wait times, more drugs in stock, and better quality one-on-one time with the pharmacist. Overall the independents earned "top marks for speed and accuracy, courtesy and helpfulness, and pharmacists' knowledge."[4]

So if the independents can be so competitive in North Dakota, why have they been wiped out in so many other places? If they can match or even beat the chains on price and service, shouldn't they be able to do it in more populous states? They would be able to, except for something consumers never see. It's called a Pharmacy Benefit Management company, PBM for short. These PBMs had the good sense initially of trying to manage prescription drug costs/benefits for the insurance companies. But as they built up market power, they began locking independents out of competitive contracts. The result?

Just three PBMs—CVS/Caremark, Express Scripts, and OptumRx—account for 80 percent of the entire prescription market.[5]

And with such tight control over this massive $534 billion industry,[6] they've been able to steadily ratchet up prices, slash service, and cleave the caring providers from the communities they once served so well.

This is what monopoly looks like in America. It's no mystery, no secret; it's all out in the open. Stacy Mitchell of the Institute for Local Self-Reliance dove deep into it in 2016 and shared her findings widely, but little has changed since her admirable reporting back then.[7]

Every time lawmakers call for federal legislation to bust the pharmacy monopoly, the Federal Trade Commission says *nah*. The FTC has even opposed legislation at the state level to lessen these PBMs' conflicts of interest. The FTC bureaucrats have argued that legislation "likely will raise the cost of prescription drug coverage" by limiting the PBMs' power to negotiate with insurance companies.[8] There is some logic to that. The PBMs' buying power could help them lower prices. But they chose to do the opposite of that. Why, then, does the FTC make this "cost" argument? Probably because "liar, liar, pants on fire" was already taken.

There are good tidings, then, in the announcements coming from President's Biden's FTC appointments. There are preliminary signs that the government is finally forsaking the long-standing orders of its elite-state masters and doing its job. Baby steps have been taken, as we will see here.

IN A MONOPOLY GAME, HALF THE ECONOMY WOULD BE IN JAIL

Since 1997, we've lost 108,000 local retail shops, 70,000 small manufacturers, 15,000 construction firms, and 13,000 community banks and credit unions.[9] Small businesses, once the backbone of America, now account for only 25 percent of all jobs and wealth. And all because of the following:

- One company—Luxottica—accounts for 60 percent of all sunglasses sold in the United States.[10]

- One company—Alphabet/Google—decides what we'll see in 92 percent of the internet searches we do.[11]

- One company—Microsoft—controls over 75 percent of our computer operating systems.[12]

- One company—Amazon—takes in 57 cents of every dollar we spend online.[13]

- One company—Walmart—captures half our spending on groceries in metro areas and a quarter of all grocery revenue nationally, and is angling to control home grocery delivery as well.[14]

- Just two companies—AB InBev, Molson Coors—make 61 percent of the beer we drink.[15]

- Just two companies—Charter, Comcast—service 80 percent of cable/broadband internet subscribers.[16]

- Just two labs—LabCorp, Quest Diagnostics—administer 54 percent of all the medical tests we take.[17]

- Just four companies—Cargill, Tyson Foods, JBS, National Beef Packing—slaughter and process over 80 percent of the beef we eat.[18]

- Just four banks—JPMorgan Chase, Bank of America, Wells Fargo, Citigroup—control half of our banking assets.[19]

- Just four companies—American, Delta, Southwest, United—control two-thirds of all the flights we take.[20]

- Just three companies—AT&T, Verizon, T-Mobile—provide 98 percent of all cell service.[21]

Among these monopolies there are six companies—Alphabet/Google, Amazon, Apple, Facebook, Microsoft, and Tesla—that make up 51 percent of the entire Nasdaq 100 marketplace.[22]

These are the players on the new Black Hole Monopoly Board. Through their game-playing almost every industry has consolidated and concentrated like black holes, swallowing up all the stars of commerce, all the light of innovation that once graced our nation. In another time, these monopolists would've been sent straight to the Jail square. Today they own the board.

There are ten major industry categories (agriculture; forestry and fishing; mining; construction; manufacturing; transportation, communication, and public utilities; wholesale trade; retail trade; finance, insurance, and real estate; and services), and three-quarters of these industries grew more concentrated in the past two decades, dominated by a few bigs.[23]

Of course there are plenty of benefits gained from big, well-run companies. Large firms can drive economies of scale, reaping cost savings from doing commerce in bulk, passing the savings on to consumers in the form of lower prices. This can happen and usually does at first, and then with competition wiped out, they steadily raise prices higher than before.

There's a simple way to measure what has happened. That is by looking at "markups"—the amount a company adds in to cover overhead and generate a profit. Historically in competitive markets that figure averaged 20 percent or so. Since 2016 it has been running at 60 percent, or three times higher.[24] This is the black-hole effect in action. It means one thing for consumers—higher prices paid for lower-quality products. It means another thing for the monopolists—*M*s becoming *B*s, that is, millionaire-pay packages becoming billionaire-pay packages. Net:

- The top 1 percent got $21 trillion richer.
- The bottom 50 percent got $900 billion poorer.[25]
- The middle class went sideways.

These are the aftereffects of three decades of uncontrolled monopoly building and why that story of *The Platform* we talked about at the outset feels so close to what's happened in America, with the rich growing grotesquely richer while the rest of us fight over the scraps.

SUBSIDIES "R" US

The top 1 percent did not get $21 trillion richer simply by grabbing people by the ankles and shaking them down. In fact, that's a slow road to wealth (as the mob learned early on). Better that the government give you free money. Some well-known names are getting suitcases full of cash from the government ATM:

Nike	$2.03 billion
Royal Dutch Shell	$2.04 billion

Fiat Chrysler	$2.06 billion
Ford	$2.52 billion
General Motors	$3.58 billion
Intel	$3.87 billion
Alcoa	$5.64 billion
Boeing	$13.18 billion[26]

Even the largest federal contractors who are well paid for their work on the taxpayer dime also regularly receive additional loan guarantees and bailouts.

Government subsidies once made sense. Helping farmers through poor growing seasons, for example. Now the subsidies regularly go to a handful of Big Ag companies no matter the crop yield, resulting in waste and overproduction, yes. But also meaning that fifty of the Forbes 400 wealthiest people in America received farm subsidies from recent farm bills.[27]

In the oil, gas, and coal industries, Big Energy doesn't need it, but it continues to get billions in special tax breaks. As do electric vehicle makers, of course.

Big Pharma gets most of their subsidies indirectly. That is, the government does not use the bargaining power of Medicare to negotiate the lower drug prices they could easily get, and in a free market would.

Big Finance gets to treat their income as capital gains, at a lower tax rate than ordinary income.

Big You-Name-It gets these subsidies not because they need them but because they've earned their way into the elite-state protection racket. Sure, they had to either grease the right palms or gum up the works, depending on the need, to earn their seat at the elite-state table. But if a company can't afford a couple hundred million to pay off politicians, keep lobbying firms busy, and bribe the key regulation writers spread throughout the massive federal bureaucracy, then they are surely not elite-state material.

In the past these companies had to drive up profits through innovations, product cost cutting, productivity improvements—that kind of thing. But now, as Boston University researcher James Bessen worked out, the greatest ROI comes from hiring big lobbyists to sit down with regulators to write the rules that lock their monopoly positions in place.[28] Analysts call this "regulatory capture." A Harvard study found that every $1 million spent lobbying returned an average of $220 million to the company[29] (which is how business has become like the mob).

From the regulators' perspective, it is no doubt easier to work with big business than with all the little guys when it comes to writing regulations. Big business brings lawyers and writers to the task, getting it done more easily. They also bring the swag—the gifts that can help out a poor bureaucrat who might only be scraping by on a guaranteed annual $160,000 salary.

So these bureaucrats tip the scales in favor of monopoly business rather than competitive markets. They sometimes don't even know they're doing it. After all, what would they know about free markets and competition? They didn't learn about any of that stuff in their sociology classes in college, and they surely don't see it in their drab twelfth-floor offices in the Washington Wealth Consolidation Complex. Some call this "crony capitalism" and lament how it's an unfortunate *side effect* of big government. In fact, it's the *natural result* of big government.

Here's another example of this regulatory capture.

PRICING LOWER-INCOME PEOPLE OUT OF AFFORDABLE HOUSING

Home prices have busted through the ceiling in recent years, pricing middle-class buyers out of the neighborhoods in which many of them grew up. There are solutions out there to try to help home buyers. For one, there are low-cost alternatives to traditional on-site construction: factory-built homes. They begin at $60,000, whereas a single-family home built on-site averages $300,000.[30]

But the National Association of Home Builders, working with bureaucrats at the Department of Housing and Urban Development, has blocked these factory homes in most areas.[31] So instead of having a home of their own, millions of Americans have no choice but to rent.

Making matters worse, private equity firms have been buying up homes, turning them into monopoly blocks of rental properties, and then jacking up monthly rates, squeezing middle- and lower-income families, many of them beyond their breaking point.

Once, the Democratic Party championed affordable housing programs, but no more. After decades of executing terribly on these programs and wanting to join with Republicans in enjoying the perks of elite-state membership, nobody is left to care for the millions of Americans facing the housing monopolists.

Small businesses are doing no better.

Burying the Little Guy With COVID's Help

COVID has been, and may well continue to be, a small-business steamroller. At the peak of the rolling lockdowns and supply-chain disruptions, America's small businesses found out just how vulnerable they were.

For ten years Ethel's Baking Company had operated in the Detroit area and placed its regular weekly or monthly orders with suppliers for chocolate, butter, and the like. But suddenly the supply chain choked closed for the little guys, and big food manufacturers with their annual contracts got all the supply.[32]

Similarly, Superfit Hero, which makes plus-size activewear in Southern California, couldn't secure the specialty fabric it needed during the pandemic. Big brands jumped the line on all fabric coming out of Taiwan. With delivery times stretching out six to eight weeks, Superfit wisely moved to diversify their fabrics and product line—but as a small company, the going was tough.[33]

These are just two stories illustrating what an estimated two out of three small companies went through during the pandemic: Their material and raw-goods supplies were redirected to the bigs.[34] The little guy was cut loose, not for the inability to pay but for trying to do business in a monopolist's world.

A different kind of monopoly problem arose in California.

TECH ELITE PREACHES MYSTICAL BEAUTY AND PRACTICES RITUAL SUFFOCATION

In the boom decades after World War II, most cities of any size could boast a big company headquarters. Executives in those companies often got involved in local civic affairs, sat on charity arts and sports councils, and sent their kids to the same schools as everyone else. When times turned hard, they resisted laying off workers, no matter what some MBA consultant penciled out as "balance sheet optimal." Companies were tied to their communities and felt a responsibility to the people there.

A social contract was playing out—often unspoken, but generally understood.

This all changed when a new organizing principle took root in America, a principle pioneered by the Japanese and known as *zaibatsu*. In this, a few favored companies would merge and acquire their way into conglomerate positions with government help, then extend their interests into practically every economic activity, leaving behind the tired, old ideas of free-market economics.

In Silicon Valley, this came to mean moving fast and breaking things, or at least that was the libertine ethos they were peddling. More accurately, they were moving fast and breaking *capitalism*, wiping out companies that had cared about their employees and their communities, replacing them with something more reminiscent of a distant time gone by—toll collectors at the king's bridge; barons exacting a fee from all who passed; gatekeepers accountable to no one, having killed off the competition.

Funny thing about this new ethos: these tech bros in hoodies very much wanted to be liked. They saw themselves as different, smarter, better. So they began taking their tolls with a smile, giving inspired talks to screaming fans, spending heavily to convince us that we're all pals here.

That might have made them feel good about themselves, but it was not enough. These tech bros also wanted us to believe they were leading us into a mystical new age of enlightenment. If only we would follow, they said, all our cares would be whisked away. And so follow we did, by the billions of us. Soon two of the tech behemoths (Google and Facebook) had more users than any religion has members. In time, the tech bros no longer even cared whether or not we liked them or watched their speeches online, for they had it all. As Scott Galloway has quipped about the moral status claimed by the newly wealthy, "Privilege looks in the mirror and sees nobility."

The idea that these tech elites might care about the American community as other than a big market to exploit is laughable now. Unlike generations of business captains before, these elites stand only for the good squares on the monopoly board. If that means cooperating with the US government to illegally surveil its citizens, for example, fine. And so Google has on numerous occasions opened up its non-public search logs to government officials without a warrant, repeatedly and questionably legally (as we'll talk about in the tech chapter).

Or if holding on to a monopoly means selling sensitive technology to China, where it will be turned against US national security interests, also fine. And so Apple's secret 2021 deal with China guaranteed Tim Cook's company a $275 billion pipeline of sales in the Middle Kingdom in exchange for undisclosed promises to hand over citizen-control technologies to their authoritarian-minded government.[35]

KNEECAPPING ANY WOULD-BE COMPETITORS

Everyone loves the Steve Jobs Apple story—it is amazing! But as time evolved and all the adoring films and books about the black turtleneck legend had been written, Apple continued on and basically became two companies: one that makes phones so cool that people line up for days to get the newest models; and the other, which takes tolls higher than medieval kings once took for the privilege of selling in the *only* marketplace that exists for apps on Apple devices, the App Store.

Any software developer that wants to sell an app on an Apple device—which is basically half the entire marketplace[36]—has to comply with Apple's terms and conditions. Whereas the Google Play equivalent for Android phones charges developers $25, Apple takes 15 percent of all sales under $1 million, and a whopping 30 percent of all sales over $1 million.[37] Apple has been able to charge such high tolls, arguably circumventing restraint-of-trade statutes, simply by being too cool for school. Who'd want to point out the worm in Apple anyway?

Well, finally, a company named Epic Games did. They're the maker of the wildly popular Fortnite game. Frustrated at giving up 30 percent of their sales to Apple, Epic Games started selling virtual currency to make some money on their Fortnite game, and not running it through Apple. At once, Apple locked them out of the store. Epic was forced to sue. Surprisingly, Epic won.

In the court's ruling, the judge said Apple could not stop developers from selling their own products on their own websites. Not a hard decision, legally. But the judge stopped short of calling Apple a monopolist, saying, "Success is not illegal."[38] Certainly that's true, and nobody would disagree—if that were the whole story.

Apple is more than successful. They control the massive platform upon which an entire ecosystem of apps lives. That is like controlling, well, the road. Letting private companies control the road is a throwback to medieval times. There are good reasons for the government to be involved in the "roads" of this country. Apple is one of those reasons.

MONOPOLIES STRIP PEOPLE OF LIBERTY, AND PEOPLE WITHOUT LIBERTY CANNOT FLOURISH

Decentralized economies—that is, lots of little companies spread all over the country—have long been responsible for a whole flourishing of economic opportunity. It was a formula for local success that translated into national success. We just didn't fully appreciate how successful it was until it was taken away.

Looking at thirty years of data across fifteen countries, economists have found that as smaller-sized businesses have given way to larger-sized businesses, the gap between rich and poor has expanded.[39] Larger-sized companies pay their employees more, generally, but most of that pay goes to a handful of executives at the top levels. On down the corporate ladder the salaries drop way off. Mostly because the workforce has been offshored.

Many American cities, such as St. Louis and Cleveland, were once flourishing economic centers. They were home to thousands of locally owned companies that nurtured homegrown talent, that fostered thriving regional networks of trade, where clusters of businesses could source goods and services from one another and give them the edge to also compete nationally.

But when the government first failed to recognize the monopolizing capability of the new tech-dominated economy, then embraced the emerging monopolies to get in on the action, market clout shifted to a handful of dominant cities, leaving far too many cities behind. Over time a great yawning gap in wealth opened between cities like New York and San Francisco, on the winning end, and places like St. Louis and Cleveland, on the losing end.

A researcher at the Atlanta Federal Reserve Bank studied this.[40] He found that cities not broken by the monopolists and able to keep larger shares of their economic output in the hands of smaller local businesses have turned out to be more prosperous, with faster income growth and lower poverty rates, becoming all-around better places to live.

This is much more than a big-is-bad versus small-is-beautiful debate. This is the key insight that can lead to a bottom-up restoration of America. It must lead to it. Community businesses must become the spotlight of our collective attention again. Entrepreneurs must be set free at the local level to try and fail and try again, and hopefully succeed. Buyers must be brought back to Main Street, with neighbors doing business as neighbors, enriching communities by reviving individual liberty closest to home.

Of course this is not an easy ask.

Just as it was not an easy ask at the founding. Early Americans knew the Boston Tea Party was about pushing back on the fearsome power of the East India Company just as much as it was against tyrant King George's latest demands.

And again, it was not an easy ask in 1938, when President Roosevelt declared:

> [T]he liberty of a democracy is not safe if the people tolerate the growth of private power to a point where it becomes stronger than their democratic state itself.[41]

And it is not an easy task now, as we face the behemoth monopolists who sure didn't get that way winning tiddlywinks games. They got there through cruel ambition and an absence of morality. Busting them up will be hard. But we welcome that fight, for it is a fight to save the America we treasure.

How Public Policy Stumbled, Inadvertently

Monopolies are nothing new, of course. Adam Smith wrote extensively about their lurking character in *The Wealth of Nations*: "People of the same trade seldom meet together, even for merriment and diversion, but the conversation ends in a conspiracy against the public, or in some contrivance to raise prices."[42]

So as America marked her first century and fantastic new railroads crossed the nation and oil lit the homes, the protean businessmen behind those breakthroughs became enormously wealthy. Robber barons, they were called, and they were seldom kindly.

Nonetheless, President Teddy Roosevelt had the courage to take them on—regulating the big investment trusts, cracking down on banking houses, preventing price gouging in defense contracts in the years leading up to war, stopping the patent law shenanigans that killed so many inventions at birth, and generally restoring the competitive spirit of the American markets.

Even though the breakups were needed, it was a different time. Those turn-of-the-century legends, with names like Andrew Carnegie and Jay Gould, were market entrepreneurs who built things that mattered. They created new products, new markets, and an abundance of jobs. Those old elites mostly uplifted the country, often at their own families' expense. Our current elites uplift their families, often at the country's expense. They are political entrepreneurs intent on gaming the system tip to toe. But theirs was not an entirely premeditated murder of the capitalist order.

It happened in gradual steps. In the years after World War II, the United States began playing such a central role in the global economy that new thinking was needed about antitrust law. Experts sought a way to wrench more efficiencies out of a fast-expanding global trading system.

Scholars at the University of Chicago in the 1980s made the case that if US companies could get more efficient and consolidate their resources better, all Americans could benefit.

Prominent conservative economists led by Milton Friedman, and liberal economists led by John Kenneth Galbraith, were in near full-throated support of this new thinking. President Reagan's Justice Department and the FTC moved to step back the Robinson-Patman Act, which had long worked to keep national retail chains like A&P from swallowing up the little guys.

This new "big is beautiful" approach to antitrust spurred a decade of unprecedented growth, or it tore business away from any concerns for everyday people, depending on which party's press releases you read. Actually, there were truths and fictions in both, and the timing of it was everything, for this all happened when Walmart was still a handful of dry-goods stores. Most computers were still the size of a truck. The newly invented cell phone filled a briefcase, and China had yet to enter the global economy.

But the world was about to shift dramatically, and the best thinkers in both political parties had little idea what kind of monster they were unleashing. Soon a deregulation train was gathering steam, and Wall Street was given license to roll right over a century of market-guiding, free enterprise–promoting regulations.

With banking executives whispering in one ear and conservative senators in the other, President Clinton signed the Financial Services Modernization Act of 1999, which in turn repealed much of the Glass-Steagall Act. Since the Great Depression, that act had forbidden banks, brokerages, and insurance companies from intertwining their businesses.[43]

But now, suddenly, big-money financiers were set free to take daring financial risks that could benefit them on an unprecedented scale. And should anything go wrong, the taxpayers could be counted on to foot the bill. "Profits to Wall Street, Losses to America" did not become a bumper sticker for some reason, but it became policy.

A new age of monopoly behemoths was born with near-unstoppable powers, capable of demolishing any potential rival by using offshore banking to minimize the taxes they paid, leveraging global supply chains and cheap overseas labor pools to lower their operating costs, waging effective influence campaigns to buy the legislation and regulations they needed to own their markets, harnessing larger data sets to optimize their profit extraction—all coming together to create iron control over one industry after another.

During this time, the regulators at the Securities and Exchange Commission hung out a "Gone Fishing" sign. Wall Street knew that, save for an occasional show trial from a New York attorney general eyeing higher office, it was Cole Porter song time, "Anything goes!"

Among that "anything" were changes in telecom policy that put a mallet into the hands of Silicon Valley. Their target: America's legacy media. In fairness, the media had it coming. They had turned as yellow as Old Man Hearst's papers a century before.

They deserved a pounding.

But when they couldn't get back up from the canvas, something else in America was knocked out too.

No doubt unknown to most if not all of the tech bros at the time, the algorithms they were writing in their fevered late-night jams would not only obliterate the all-important fourth estate, but it would also deal a death blow to one of America's most enduring dreams, one that most of us still held—the dream that we could become a "soup bowl" of people assimilating for the common good instead of a "salad bowl" of people retreating from the world into our own tribal hatreds, jealousies, and animosities.

And so as Y2K came, the computers didn't crash as predicted, but the American experiment did. And nobody seemed to care.

A decade would pass before anyone even pretended to care.

WALL STREET REGULATIONS NEED A FACELIFT (NOT A DODD-FRANK POWDER)

Recently some researchers at Princeton and Northwestern sifted through nearly eighteen hundred federal policy decisions made from 1981 to 2002 and came to the same conclusion that millions of Americans already had: the elite state drives practically every important decision made in Washington.[44]

These elites even supervise the scripts for the storytelling—the elaborate theater productions Washington puts on to convince us all that America is still on track. Elections do matter, and your vote counts. Democracy is a messy business, but you're seeing it play out as it must.

But the people aren't buying it anymore. Instead, a lot of us are recalling another script from not so long ago about men and women building up communities from the soil, seeding locally owned businesses that provided for everyone's needs. And when local problems popped up, everyone in town pitched in to fix them, participating in civic affairs from a sense of belonging and connection with one another.

However idealized, this was always a much more compelling story.

If there is a thread from the first story to the second, it is the failure of the US government to enforce antitrust policy for three decades, and to allow an amoral usurpation of our national character and values.

We saw just how corrupt our government was in the wake of the 2008 financial meltdown. Everyone knew what had happened—knew the banks had gone deeply criminal—and yet nothing was done about it. Check that. Washington put on a big show of caring about those awful rascals on Wall Street, and to show their concern, they threw 8,843 pages of new regulations to the rescue. They called these regulations the Dodd–Frank Act and loudly insisted that it was kind of like deposit insurance— to protect the little guy.

But all that these new regulations did was (a) ensure that big banks would keep getting bigger and small banks keep getting smaller and fewer in number, (b) lock in a new kind of corporate socialism in America, and (c) make it policy to socialize costs to taxpayers and privatize gains to shareholders.

When the next big banking crisis comes, the big institutions will not be too big to fail; they'll be too big to save. But we'll go ahead and save them anyway. The elite state will see to that. If another trillion or two or three in free money handouts is what's needed to restore the health of our vital banking sector, shouldn't the good people of the nation be grateful?

Or at least that's what the theater producers will try to sell us.

CHAPTER 16

CRACKS IN THE ELITE STATE LEAD TO A RARE BIPARTISAN CAUSE

WHEN ELIZABETH WARREN and Donald Trump as candidates for president were both saying the system was rigged, invoking Robin Williams' line about how politicians ought to wear sponsor jackets like NASCAR drivers so you know who owns them, you knew that all kinds of populist insurgencies were rising up across America.[1]

If there was any question these insurgencies were being taken seriously, the proof came in the shock-and-awe counteroffensive the elite state organized against the surprise victor of the 2016 presidential election. This counteroffensive would go on unrelenting for Trump's entire term and beyond.

But undaunted, President Trump railed against the global elites and their use of NAFTA and the Trans-Pacific Partnership to loot American wealth for themselves. He denounced the AT&T–Time Warner merger as a dangerous concentration of power. He labeled Amazon's business methods for what they were—antitrust violations. He waded into the thick of it, but because of his off-balanced style, he failed to wrestle any real decision-making away from the elite state. He didn't fail, though, in bringing the entire country around to seeing that the Washington swamp is not only wide, it is deep.

And so in April 2021, Senator Josh Hawley of Missouri picked up the attack again on the Republican side with S.1204—the Bust Up Big Tech Act:

> Woke Big Tech companies like Google and Amazon have been coddled by Washington politicians for years. This treatment has allowed them to amass colossal amounts of power that they use to censor political opinions they don't agree with and shut out competitors who offer consumers an alternative to the status quo. It's past time to bust up Big Tech companies, restore competition, and give the power back to the American consumers.[2]

Senator Hawley's bill would ban tech platforms that offer online search, markets, or exchanges from competing with third-party vendors on their platforms. And it would ban platforms from providing online hosting and cloud services to third parties, again to keep them from squashing competition. The FTC would monitor and enforce the law. State attorneys general and private citizens would be able to bring civil actions against the platforms if they fell out of compliance.[3]

The bill was referred to committee with no other senators co-sponsoring it. As if it never existed.

A few months later, across town, President Biden went on the offensive as well, giving the first substantive presidential speech in decades on the need for antitrust action:

> "Capitalism without competition isn't capitalism; it's exploitation," he said. Biden then recalled President Franklin Roosevelt calling for "an economic bill of rights, including, quote, 'the right of every businessman, large and small, to trade in an atmosphere of freedom from unfair competition and domination by monopolies.'"[4]

Good sentiments every one. And right after the speech, the president's head of the FTC, Lina Khan, started hammering on Amazon for their latest acquisition of the once-mighty MGM studios.[5] The optics on this monopoly overreach were good, as they say, especially if the president and his team had truly been sincere in breaking up the very companies that had swept them into office.

They appeared to be.

In follow-up orders, Biden dedicated his government to fighting corporate concentration. He warned the sprawling federal bureaucracy about stonewalling his directives. And he laid out seventy-two action steps to be taken at once. All good starts.

One action was the FTC's ending of the monopoly on hearing aids that had been blocking the sale of those devices without a prescription.[6] Good.

Another action was aimed at making business non-compete agreements less onerous. The action sought to better balance a departing worker's need to find new employment with an employer's need to protect trade secrets and customer relationships. Also good. (Unfortunate that government needs to get involved in matters like this, but it's a complex world, so it does.)

That list of seventy-two actions also included the writing of new rules on data and surveillance, making hospital billing and records more transparent, curbing the abuses of defense contractors, and making the food supply chain work better for smaller grocers.

Biden also took aim at the meatpacking monopoly where four firms control the supply chain and ranchers are squeezed to the bone marrow. The "Big Four" import billions of pounds of beef from South America and label it "Produce of USA" because, they say, it is processed here. These cheaper beef imports drive down the prices of cattle raised on US ranches. It's a crooked game the Big Four have been running, and hopefully US ranchers will fare better going forward.

It's hard to know.

A raft of new regulations spewing out of the Agriculture Department may help, but a breakup plan would better restore fair competition, helping US ranchers without unduly costing consumers.

Until then and rightly, conservative groups united in applauding Biden's efforts. Folks at the American Farm Bureau, the Grange, US Cattlemen's Association, National Corn Growers Association, and Montana Farmers Union offered up big praise for the Democratic president.[7] That's a very hopeful sign, not only for farming but for other issues as well.

And so Biden next set about restoring the Robinson-Patman Act to help small companies compete against the Bigs. Again, good.

But only good if the president's "actions" don't devolve into a waft of new regulations watered down by lobbyists or left to gather dust by a permanent bureaucracy more concerned about how uncomfortable their chairs are for the four to five hours they actually show up to work. These government staff members know presidents come and go, as do their policy edicts. Waiting them out is an art form in which the staff members are well practiced.

The Big Tech liberal elites—specifically Amazon, Google, and Facebook—didn't like the first thing about Biden's actions on the Robinson-Patman Act. They made their dissatisfaction known through their lobbyist, NetChoice, which went knocking on the doors of anti-government Republicans making the tired old argument that the president was only trying to make big government bigger.[8]

And the US Chamber of Commerce dashed off a prewritten press release calling the president's executive order another "government knows best" overreach.[9]

Clearly the elite state was not happy. That suggested President Biden was on the right track.

HOW TO REATTACH THE ANTI TO THE TRUST

One reasonable-sounding line of thought is making the rounds:

It was a mistake to bail out the "too big to fail" financial firms in 2008 and equally foolish to break up today's "too big to succeed" tech companies. Anne Rathbone Bradley, PhD, a professor at the Institute for World Politics, is one who calls it a foolish crusade:

> "Too big to fail" was a mistake because it bailed out incompetent firms during the global financial crisis. Breaking up big firms today would also be a mistake and would lead to higher prices, less innovation, and more cronyism.[10]

Bradley may well be right, as far as she goes. Any breakup plan orchestrated from the federal level, which means the elite state is involved in its crafting, will surely create new distortions in the marketplace.

How could you not have a flurry of unexpected outcomes in *any* breakup plan when you consider how complex the issues are?

Just as central economic planning rarely works in any nation, bureaucrats can't guess at the optimal size and shape a tech firm should be to reestablish fair competition, economic growth, and individual liberty for all (which should be the guide in any breakup plan).

What Bradley's insightful critique does not primarily address is the debilitating effect Big Tech has had on our culture. So much wonderful has come out of Silicon Valley. But like the box Pandora opened in mythology, tech's black boxes have hurtled dark injuries far and wide. Dealing with this "cultural curse" they've unleashed may, in fact, be the biggest challenge of all.

Other economists trying to justify tech's domination (known as the "superstar effect") insist that their "bigness" is necessary. The accomplished economist Jay Ritter argues that a global tech-driven economy requires giant footprint companies to compete and win. If we clamp down on these large companies, he argues, it won't change the global economy or help small firms, but it may well put all American firms at a severe disadvantage in a global market.[11]

Ritter has written impressively, and he may be right. US firms may find it harder to compete globally if they are reduced in size.

To which I say, "Oh, well," for my own biases are revealing themselves here.

Throughout this book we talk about the competition-crushing impact of the elite state on small businesses. Dealing with this is the proper domain of antitrust law. But here the focus is also on the cultural corrosion Big Tech has wrought—first unwittingly, I believe, and then near pathologically.

Antitrust law is not so well suited to dealing with this cultural aspect.

But as times change, so must the law. For at the end of the day, there is little difference between crushing companies and crushing culture. Great harms come from both, harms that must be addressed.

And frankly, given the power these behemoth companies already wield, if we were to arbitrarily cut them all in half just for kicks and giggles, they'd still dwarf all but a few multinational companies.

Plus, many countries from Sweden to China are looking to rein in their own behemoth companies, so we'll try not to worry about Google's or even Goldman Sachs' ability to compete in global markets with a somewhat-reduced footprint.

It's worth remembering that we've been here before.

As the twentieth century broke, the US economy had grown highly concentrated, with monopolies controlling oil, railroads, and more. Standing up to those monopolies, especially after their owners had personally helped the country weather the roughest financial patch it had ever faced, was hard. And bold.

It took a Rough Rider president to do it. Under Teddy Roosevelt's lead they broke up concentrated power, leveled the playing field for entrepreneurs, and returned individual liberty to a priority. However limited that thinking at the time—women and Blacks were still denied basic rights—the country was hastened forward on the principles of our founding. Laws and enforcement powers enacted back then are as relevant today if properly updated to our time. That is what must happen.

In particular, we need to do the following.

Ensure open markets. Bring back the proven guideposts of antitrust to balance efficient commerce with open markets so all-sized businesses can compete fairly. Take apart vertically controlled markets so that dominant companies cannot manipulate the supply chain to exclude competitors.

Enforce the laws vigorously. Take swift and punitive action against any company choosing to unilaterally harm competition.

Revisit common carriage rules. Determine if any tech platform enjoying common carriage protections (for which they must, without discrimination, carry all passengers, or in current practice all "users") is in noncompliance, and if so, slap them with damages.

Restore the Robinson-Patman Act. Use the Robinson-Patman Act as originally intended—to prevent companies from using price discrimination to hurt smaller companies that lack market power.

WHY JOB NUMBER ONE IS BUSTING UP BIG TECH

When you're up against a domineering power, as the elite state has become, you pick your battles. You're entering a long war, so you want to focus your first efforts on campaigns that can deliver real results. Therein lies the reason we target Big Tech as job number one.

Tech is one head of the four-headed behemoth (along with Wall Street, the Permanent State, and the Uniparty). Its superpower addition is its brainpower and thought-control machinery. It is also, by the very nature of the people in tech, the easiest to bring around to sensibly contributing positively to society, as they did until very recently.

Some nimble minds have mapped a strategy for forcing accountability on Big Tech, showing them the way that many could support even without coercion. NYU professor Scott Galloway laid it out best in a magisterial book, *The Four: The Hidden DNA of Amazon, Apple, Facebook, and Google*, as well as in a weekly email newsletter, *No Mercy/No Malice*. Galloway says:

[T]hese firms are part of what I would call "the menace economy," and that is they will say or do anything to further enrich themselves, even if it's damaging for the commonwealth [and so] the most oxygenating thing we could do for the economy is to go into a firm that is killing innovation and break them up. If you think about all the stakeholders in a break-up—there's job creation, that goes up. There's shareholder value—that goes up.

Employees do well because all of a sudden there's several bidders for their human capital. The tax base does well, the economy does well—job growth. The only stakeholder that loses over the medium and long term in a break-up is the CEO.[12]

These tech behemoths are not inherently evil, in Galloway's view. He simply believes that sometimes the best way to ensure free and open markets is to "cut the tops off trees, just as we did with railroads and Ma Bell."[13]

Big Tech has "grown so tall" because it is not a monopoly by any strict traditional definition. They have not used their concentration to increase prices on their products. Quite the opposite: owing to their use of child labor in Asian countries and the deflationary forces described by Moore's Law, they have been able to drive prices downward in the consumers' view of things. But that is only one view.

Big Tech has inflicted great pain in the B2B sector, mostly invisible to customers.

In this sector are the people who are forced to advertise on the tech platforms—because those platforms effectively wiped out the print media. Also in this sector are entrepreneurs who want to bring their inventions to market but cannot find a toehold.

The platforms have erected barriers to entry so that only the craziest and luckiest entrepreneurs can attain a scale and survive. Or the entrepreneurs have to sell out to the Bigs (many consider it an exit strategy, in fact). But it *should not* be the only exit strategy in a nation that treasures free and open markets.

Busting up these platforms will be a Rubik's Cube undertaking worthy of a superbright Google engineer. Difficult enough to do poorly; impossible to do well. But there are ways to bring about greater overall innovation in the industry, more opportunities for smaller businesses to compete, a lowering of data-privacy concerns, and price stability across the sector.

Specifically, we must do the following.

Reward strength, not dominance. Prevent dominant incumbents from entering adjacent markets or buying up newcomers.

Enforce nondiscrimination statutes. Prevent platform owners from using their control to favor their own offerings when competitors are on the platform.

Open up source code. Any platform with "public users" should have transparent source code so folks know how their personal data is being used and their privacy is protected. What's more, consumers should have the keys to their data so they can remove it from a platform or switch to another easily.

Protect data privacy. Currently, the private data streams of consumers can be accessed by any one of thousands of government employees without a warrant. This invasion of privacy is not merited on grounds of national security and must be discontinued.

Fast on the heels of tech breakups should be the banks.

Job Number Two: Big Banks

The goal in breaking up the big banks is twofold:

1. Reduce their overall size so (a) they present less of a moral hazard and (b) the next financial disaster they engineer will not require our bailing them out.

2. Help community banks thrive again as local financial hubs that strengthen the financial and shared culture values of their communities.

And so, first, community banks can help communities thrive.

One study put the most efficient size for a bank at $10 billion or less in assets.[14] This should not be a rule, of course, but helpful in fixing public policy. Today 86 percent of US bank assets are held in banks larger than this target. JPMorgan Chase is 370 times larger, for example. So the inefficiencies run deep.

Community banks are usually less expensive, with fees as much as 42 percent lower than big banks.[15] This is mostly because small banks are not saddled with the top-heavy bureaucracy of large banks.

Community banks also do a better job of managing risks. They have far lower default rates and foreclosure rates, even though they are more likely to fund borrowers who fall outside of set lending standards.[16]

Community banks take in only about 12 percent of the industry's assets, but they supply an estimated 40 to 60 percent of the loans to startups and small businesses, building their communities and providing jobs for locals.[17] Meanwhile the Bigs focus most of their energies on the speculative trading that enriches their shareholders but not the larger economy.

Community banks have performed remarkably well in recent years, despite

- federal regulators systematically preempting the state laws that had ensured fair and open markets;

- big banks building up infrastructure to impose onerous fees and other barriers on local banks;

- waves of mergers and consolidations of financial institutions that destroyed any vestiges of competition in banking; and

- government bailing out any troubled bank with taxpayer funds, which means the Bigs can raise capital at far lower costs than local banks.

It's no secret that policy has been rigged for the Bigs. Unrigging it will be difficult, but this must happen to reestablish fair, open, and financially stable markets once again. This is the hardest fix, and it begins in our communities, with our community banks.

FOUR ARGUMENTS FOR BREAKING UP THE BANKS

1. Five banks comprise more than half the US financial system and are a systemic risk.

2. Perceived as too big to fail, banks have been allowed to engage in risky behavior, knowing they'll be backstopped.

3. Big banks are too complex to manage, and attempts to govern them are ineffective.

4. Big banks wield too much control over public policy due to their size and lobbying power.

FOUR ARGUMENTS FOR KEEPING THE BANKS STRUCTURED AS-IS

1. Any restructuring of the big banks would disrupt the overall economy and surely result in unintended consequences.

2. Consumers benefit from the economies of scale that big banks offer.

3. Size does not necessarily equate with systemic importance, so mere size restrictions would be arbitrary.

4. In the last crisis, the big banks were not the main cause— other financial institutions failed.

Looking at both sets of arguments, one fact trumps all: the too-big-to-fail problem has not been solved, and the failure of any one major bank would have enormous economic costs.

Fixing this problem can be done one of three ways:

1. Break up the big banks.

2. Turn the big banks into public utilities.

3. Tax big banks' leverage to reduce systemic risk.

Options 2 and 3 feel un-American, and they would be difficult to execute in a positive, productive way. That leaves option 1 to be applied to the five major banks. Here's how a big bank like JPMorgan Chase could be split into three parts:

1. An investment bank spun off and regulated like a hedge fund with no access to government financing. The bankers would be happy, as they could form a limited partnership with the freedom to pay themselves whatever they pleased.

2. A wholesale bank providing basic banking products, foreign exchange, and interest-rate hedges for large corporate clients. It would be insulated from making high-risk leveraged investments.

3. A retail bank limited to insured consumer banking and small-business lending. It would, like its wholesale counterpart, be insulated from all risky investments.

There would be tough transition issues in all this reform, but it does address all the straw-man arguments big-bank advocates now throw out. People would, in nearly all cases, be able to keep their current bank if they chose to do so. There would be no loss of commonly enjoyed consumer programs or services. Consumers would feel little. Banking executives would feel a lot—as intended.

This approach includes reinstituting the Glass-Steagall Act, updated and modified if necessary to our current time.

With tech and banks reined in, next is health care.

JOB NUMBER THREE: BIG HEALTH

Just as the financial behemoths hijacked the economy's productive capacity, the health behemoths captured the institutions (hospitals, clinics, insurance) on which we rely for our health and well-being. Though it would be inaccurate to differentiate health from financial, both have been swept into the wholesale financialization of our economy, where nearly every product or service is turned into a security to be packaged up and sold off for the financial gain of a few.

Only in recent decades have non-doctors even been allowed to own medical practices. Most states forbade it, recognizing that a corporation's fiduciary duty to shareholders over patients created a moral hazard to society. But even with the laws still on the books in most states, they're not enforced.

Instead, private equity firms such as Blackstone, Apollo Global Management, The Carlyle Group, KKR & Co., and Warburg Pincus have spent an estimated $340 billion to snap up medical practices. The scale tipped in 2018, which was the first year more physicians were employees and not owners of their practices.[18]

While COVID was raging and hospitals were in trouble, private equity swooped in to acquire 20,900 physicians' practices and fold them into their health-care maw. By January 2021, nearly 70 percent of all US physicians—423,800 in all—were employed by a hospital or corporate entity.[19]

Not just physicians. Hospitals, nursing homes, hospice centers, air ambulances, billing management, and debt collection systems were also snapped up. About 95 percent of metro areas now have highly consolidated hospital markets; 80 percent have the same concentration in specialist physician markets.[20]

If you've ever wondered how these private equity firms got so much money to spend, you've wondered about how the elite state really works. In the case of private equity, their MO has always been to borrow enough money to buy a company, transfer all that debt of theirs onto the company, slash the company's costs, beat down the quality of its products, raise the prices on those inferior products, then offload the entire thing in the capital markets for handsome returns.

It wasn't always a foolproof strategy, however well it usually worked. But it did become foolproof after the 2008 housing meltdown. That's when the government went and (a) bailed out every financial institution dialed in to the elite state and then (b) took interest rates all the way to zero. So these failed financiers were made whole again at taxpayer expense and then invited to walk up to the discount window at the Fed, borrow all the billions they might want, and go out and buy more companies to gut and flip.

And if they failed at it, they knew the government would be there to backstop them, to make them whole again, all at taxpayers' expense. Arguably the biggest con run by anyone since our country's beginning.

A con, because a con takes two to play.

There is the guy running the con—in this case, the elite state. And there are the conned, who want to believe the story being told—in this case, us. That is, enough of us still want to believe in the goodness and might of our elite leaders, in the trickling down of the riches and wealth into our own hands. Enough of us believed, mostly because the story was told one way to conservatives, another to liberals. Same storyteller, just with different tellings aimed at the hot buttons of different audiences.

One of those elite state storytellers is named Timothy Geithner. He now heads up Warburg Pincus, the big private equity firm that owns IT company Modernizing Medicine.[21] If you guessed that this company uses AI to game the insurance system and optimize medical billing, bingo. You may also recall that Geithner was President Obama's Treasury secretary, and he helped set up Obamacare to his company's liking. Also, as former president of the New York Fed, Geithner helped bail out the elite state bankers after the 2008 financial crisis they themselves had caused. All were made whole, unlike millions of conned Americans, the butts of the elite-state joke.

Private equity is the high-octane fuel of the elite state, but not always the bad guy in the story. There are good people in every line of work. Sometimes these good people take extraordinary risks investing in troubled companies or uncertain new industries and in turn create wonderful new technologies or all-new markets. But since private equity took over health care, two things have happened:

- Costs have headed skyward.

- Quality has headed downward.

During the peak of the nationwide COVID scare in May 2020, NBC News ran an investigation of TeamHealth, which is owned by the private equity firm Blackstone. TeamHealth, along with Envision Healthcare, owned by KKR, provides staffing for about a third of all emergency rooms. If you went to a TeamHealth emergency room with a broken arm, for example, you would pay $2,947, when the going rate at a non-monopolized hospital was $665. If you were experiencing chest pains, TeamHealth would bill $976 to look at you, or you could pay $340 elsewhere. If you needed stitches at TeamHealth, fork over an unconscionable $888, or just $200 at a non-monopolized hospital if there were any left in your area.[22]

Even before New York Governor Andrew Cuomo criminally stuffed nursing homes full of vulnerable seniors with COVID patients, killing 4,100 and trying to conceal it, nursing homes had become a national embarrassment.[23] A study of 18,000 nursing homes, of which nearly 2,000 were taken over by private equity firms, found that "[private equity] ownership increases the short-term mortality of Medicare patients by 10%, implying 20,150 lives lost due to PE ownership over our twelve-year sample period."[24]

During COVID, the shortages of vital hospital equipment such as ventilators and masks was largely the result of cost cutting by private equity overseers.[25] No need, in their eyes, to have extra equipment just sitting on shelves for emergencies. That costs. So they cut it, and lives were lost.

These private equity firms also staffed up medical practices with inadequately trained doctors. This from the American College of Emergency Physicians, which has a pony in this race. But we know that cost cutting ran the gamut from sutures to surgeons, since they're all widgets in the financialization of health care.

Recently, a patient arrived at the Calais Regional Hospital in northern Maine. He needed a breathing tube, known as intubation. Basic stuff, but the attending doctor didn't know how to do it! He had to call in a nearby paramedic. The patient survived, though others would not have been so lucky. Does it matter that the doctor worked for a services firm owned by a private equity company, KKR?

Yes, it does.

No surprise, then, that an NIH study showed that "hospital competition…can lead to an increase in the quality of hospital services."[26]

With the financialization of our massively complex health care system, it's often difficult to determine whether the source of a particular problem is the hospital company, the pharmaceutical company, or the insurance company.

It's typically all three, and by design. But insurance companies get the biggest rap—probably because their business is the easiest for most of us to understand. And clearly, the insurance companies are running some of the most brutalizing monopolies in America.

In many parts of the country there is simply no competition. In Oklahoma, Health Care Service Corporation covers 96 percent of patients. In Alabama, Blue Cross Blue Shield owns 97 percent of the market. In Alaska, the Blue Cross Blue Shield licensee Premera has a 100 percent market share.[27]

With so much consolidation in the industry, the few remaining giants can dictate the prices they charge, the reimbursements they offer, and the procedures they will—and will not—cover.

Again, in fairness, health insurance is not easy to do well. They are the backbone supporting one-fifth of the US economy. They must balance the interests of shareholders, Big Pharma, hospitals, and other health-care providers, all within a patchwork of federal mandates and state laws that are often at odds with one another. Nonetheless, there's little to commend in their handling of all this complexity. The net cost of health insurance has tripled since 2000, a rise that's 40 percent higher than the actual dollars we've spent on health care.[28] This 40 percent is what's being extracted from uncompetitive markets and moved into elite-state pockets.

Indeed, the CEOs of the eight largest public insurance companies pocketed $143.5 million in total compensation in a recent year.[29] You do the math.

A few people in Washington *have* done the math. Again, to his credit, President Biden has tried to raise the bar of scrutiny of monopoly hospitals. His July 2021 executive order noted that hospital mergers can be harmful to patients and asked the FTC to look over the merger guidelines.[30]

He asked, though nothing has yet happened.

Senator Amy Klobuchar of Minnesota has been the strongest champion of antitrust reform on Capitol Hill—whether for the theatrics helpful in her run for president, or for her strongly held beliefs, or both (which is my sense). Her Competition and Antitrust Law Enforcement Reform Act targets anticompetitive mergers. But while it was introduced in February 2021, her bill had not been put to a vote by the summer of 2022.

Congress did try to deal with "surprise billing" in 2019. That's the practice of you entering the hospital with an estimate of $2,000 and leaving with a bill for $64,000. Happens thousands of times a day. It was the kind of bill politicians love to put up—it looks good back home. But as the bill gained traction, the elite state put together a grassroots organization called Doctor Patient Unity, and after a $28 million media blitz, the bill failed.[31]

Reforming health care is wickedly difficult because it is a legitimately complex and vital system that touches each of our lives in dozens of ways every day. But there are little things that can be done, as well as big fixes that can make a difference.

Little asks:

- Give the Justice Department and FTC sufficient funds to chase after the monopolists (as good a use of federal government dollars as any).

- Expand price transparency—hospitals should show people what they're charging; doing so will almost certainly lower costs to consumers.

- Cut price controls and subsidies set up through Medicare that end up costing everyone more.

- Fix tax laws so that families who purchase their own health insurance can enjoy the same tax relief as employees purchasing through their employers.

- Restore health savings accounts so that contributions are not taxed, incentivizing us all to save for our health needs in years ahead.

Big asks:

- Break up any hospital chain that has eliminated competition in any community of size.

- Target pharmacy benefit managers (PBMs) to break up the stranglehold they have on prescription drug pricing.

- Continue to unravel Obamacare, keeping in place the worthy assistance it gave to the uninsured, but straightening out the many problems it created—such as exchanges that don't function, doctors not wanting any part of them, people getting stuck in no-choice risk pools heavily subsidized by taxpayers.

- Encourage states to waive statutes in Obamacare (using Section 1332) to expand their health care options and promote competition among doctors, hospitals, and medical professionals in their states.[32]

- Move policy making in health care to the state level to promote personal choices in the health and medicine we receive, expand competition, and slash through as many burdensome regulations as possible.

Challenging the health care behemoths is obviously hard and fraught, yet allowing the behemoths to grow even larger and siphon off bigger and bigger slices of our personal income with poorer and poorer performance is unacceptable.

Our only tool is to show our discontent at the local level, taking meetings with our elected leaders, giving them a single message to take to Washington: *If you can't do the right thing, then you're in the wrong place and you have to go!*

CHAPTER 17

BREAK THE EXTREMISTS' CHOKE HOLD WITH SENSIBLE ENERGY STEWARDSHIP

W HEN YOU LOOK at America's environmental policy making, you could begin to think that OPEC has been secretly funding America's environmental activists, right? America has billions of barrels of oil and trillions of cubic feet of natural gas sitting in the ground, mostly in the Bakken Formation. People argue over the quantity of fossil fuels down there. Some say there are 4.3 *trillion* barrels of oil; others say 4.3 *billion* barrels.[1] Clearly a lot of folks are working hard to make a case, and a lot of folks can't say with any certainty, but a lot of oil and natural gas does exist. Possibly more than the rest of the world's fossil resources combined.

We could drill for it, extract it, refine it, and distribute it to every customer in need today—far cleaner and better for the environment than any of the oil we import from the nations environmentalists profess to detest.

Far cleaner and better for the global environment because US gas companies are heavily regulated, unlike the wildcatters messily yanking oil and gas from the ground in distant lands.

But we don't do it. A small group of environmentalists control key levers in Washington, and they want what they want. Which is 1) to leave domestic fossil fuels in the ground, and 2) to lead the world in leaving fossil fuels behind for good.

To these environmentalists, taking the lead means putting cities at risk of frequent power shortages when renewables like wind power and solar power can't deliver because the wind isn't blowing and the sun isn't shining.

Taking the lead for them also means propping up foreign despots with blood oil that's used to routinely run genocide campaigns, murder political opponents and stone women who are raped for having sex, brutally invade neighboring countries, and on and on the horror show goes.

How can a decent person stand for this?

How can we not all say that we need to drill for our own oil and gas while at the same time and with intense focus try to replace carbon fuels with cleaner fuels?

Is it because OPEC *is* secretly funding just enough environmentalists to break the Democratic Party's ruling coalition if it doesn't kowtow to one seemingly even more imaginative demand after another?

It *is* a more logical explanation.

Nobody will disagree that the more secure our energy resources, the more prosperous the nation. Achieving this energy security requires that we find a way to the balancing point between what we need and what we want—between the *need* for abundant energy and the *want* of a cleaner environment.

It's a balance we must find a way to strike.

Of all the problems we face, this should be the easiest to tackle because the elite state cares little for this issue. They are rather equally invested in fossils and renewables and win either way.

The only issue here is Brad, whom you may have heard of.

Brad lives in California, and as the story goes, he got so fed up with everything—with COVID, Trump, Russian belligerence, China, global warming, racial conflict, and all the other distressing news piped into his designer earbuds. So Brad went to his garage, sealed the doors and windows as best he could, got into his car, lowered the windows, and started the car, letting it idle as his mind drifted off. Two days later, a worried neighbor peered through his garage window and saw him. She valiantly broke in and pulled Brad from the car. Surprisingly, after a little sip of water, he was in perfect condition, but his Tesla had a dead battery.

WHY IS THE ENVIRONMENT SUCH A GREASED POTATO?

As we've seen, Americans have been carefully taught to pick their side in any debate, smack-talk their opponent with clever words supplied for the moment by unseen ghostwriters, and never, ever give an inch for fear the other side will take a mile. It's the new binary theater. And nowhere is this more self-sabotaging than in environmental game playing.

Why can't the drill-baby-drillers just admit that, yes, we're now recording the highest greenhouse gas emissions from humans since we've been recording, and that can end poorly for humans and other living creatures?

And why not acknowledge that our disposable lifestyle is filling our ocean waters with toxic particles of plastics and our soil and food with disease-causing glyphosate, and the number of chronic diseases is rising along with the earth's temperature?

Why play "Climategate" games when we see extreme wildfires hitting Alaska of all places? Severe hailstorms pummeling Texas like nobody can remember? Deadly heat waves laying waste to the Pacific Northwest rain forest? Droughts in Australia triggering months-long brush fires? New mega-flash lightning in North and South America so intense the flashes are nearly five hundred miles long and last for seventeen seconds?[2]

In the same breath, why can't environment-first activists admit that the science on climate change can never be "indisputable," as President Obama so foolishly said? That in fact the very function of science is to keep on testing yesterday's findings?

And why go on funding researchers to devise intricate models to predict climate futures they can't possibly understand, so they build in a wide range of best-case and worst-case scenarios and then hold their tongues (and their jobs) when only the apocalyptically worst-case scenarios are flogged in the media, scaring kids and gullible adults into believing the world will be ending any day now?

And why not admit these Green New Deal programs are themselves unsustainable? The cost of hitting a carbon-zero future is estimated at $50 trillion on up to $131 trillion over just the coming decade.[3] That's the rough price tag for zero-carbon renewables, electric vehicles, carbon capture and storage, hydrogen fuels, and biofuels. And that means asking every adult in the United States to write a check for, oh, $524,000 to cover the costs![4]

Neither side of the environmental debate comes even close to a reasoned position.

At least on the Left it's explainable. For years, the Democratic Party had a problem. They didn't have a good rallying cause with lots of red meat and frothing at the mouth to incite their partisans to come out and vote.

Democrats had only dusty old issues at hand. They had civil

rights—which John Kennedy cleverly stole from the Republicans (who had always championed it). And yes, the battles for civil rights were an effective organizing tool for the Democratic elites for a long time. But issues age and need to be kept current, reignited constantly, and rebranded, which was difficult since the civil rights battles of the 1960s and 1970s had accomplished many of their just goals.

When making his run for president, Al Gore understood this. He knew he needed a fresh kill, still-bloody meat, and he found it in environmentalism.

It was a natural for the Left—combining the virtue of being a marginally genuine issue with all the Gaia emotions easily triggered. The gullible would jump right on, a sympathetic press would run with it, and all kinds of scary doomsday scenarios could be manufactured with the help of scientists eager for funding so voters could be whipped into a frenzy just in time to bus them to the polls and tell them how to vote.

Gore worked it like a pro, though he fell short of his goal. He then went on to work with Silicon Valley venture capitalists to make an elite state–worthy fortune from green-related investments and other ventures. So it worked out for him. And the Democratic Party now had a new cause to rally a segment of their ruling coalition.

Of course we should care for our environment—for the air we breathe, the water we drink, the soil in which we grow our food. Equally important is preserving the beauty and natural resources of our country's diverse ecosystems—which means protecting our keystone species. We've known since the 1960s that certain species are vital to maintaining the habitats in which they live.

We saw this when wolves were reintroduced to Yellowstone in 1995 after a long absence. The elk population had doubled in the wolves' absence and grazed down the shrubs and trees. But now willows returned to the riverbanks, giving beavers material for their dams, in turn re-erecting habitats for fish as well as reptiles and mammals.[5] A natural order was restored to Yellowstone and serves as a model for conserving our great natural heritage for generations to come.

Understanding and caring for our natural heritage is vital to balanced energy stewardship going forward.

It is undeniably true that fossil fuel is one of only two energy sources that can sustain our way of life until we finally manage to replace it. Jet fuel from oil is all that powers those Gulfstreams taking the liberal elite to distant resorts to give impassioned speeches about freeing the planet from the carbon monster. And therein lies the fraud of the environmental movement—and the remedy as well.

UNDER THE HOOD OF BIG GREEN

On April 22 every year I attend a nearby Earth Day celebration and force down some tasteless food, pick up the latest slicks on environmental consumerism, and ask a few questions of the misty-eyed festivalgoers: "Did you know that solar panels degrade quickly and turn into toxic heaps? Or that wind farms are destroying the natural ecology while creating even worse toxic waste dumps soon to be the size of Rhode Island?"[6]

Empty and angry stares are launched back at me.

Ask the festivalgoers if they've seen Michael Moore's documentaries, and they say, "Of course!" Then ask about the filmmaker's latest production, *Planet of the Humans,* and it's back to the empty and angry stares, as if wondering how Moore could turn on them so. How he could portray the environmental movement as irredeemably corrupt. "Maybe they got to him" is one answer that finally erupts from a boy cross-dressing as a tree and a lemur, living his truth.

Well, someone did get to Moore, that is true.

The left-stream media lambasted him, and most of the social platforms removed his film from the public eye. The gall of that man to stand on principles in this day and age!

Moving beyond the annual festival of Mother Earth, the activists are hard at work saving the planet.

- In Nevada's Black Rock Desert, environmentalists have long been blocking a geothermal energy plant because it might harsh the mellow of the annual Burning Man festival.[7]

- In the Mojave Desert, the Sierra Club and the Natural Resources Defense Council sued to block a massive solar-farm project because it threatened desert tortoises[8] (only marginally a keystone species).

- Offshore wind farms in the Atlantic are hindered by a 1920 maritime law that's totally irrelevant today, but nobody is taking it off the books.[9]

- California's Diablo Canyon nuclear power plant was threatened with a shutdown using a law designed to protect fish eggs.[10]

We could go on for pages with examples of environmentalists undermining their own environmental goals. So then how is the Biden administration supposed to spend $1 trillion on low-carbon infrastructure if those projects will be constantly blocked by protesting activists or bogged down in a tangle of bureaucratic and regulatory requirements?

As it is, the Department of Energy says we'll need to triple the number of electrical power lines to transmit wind- and solar-farm power to where it's needed.[11] How is that going to happen? It's been a decade since the United States constructed a transmission line of note. How do environmentalists expect this transition to renewable energy to happen? Is Tinker Bell involved?

Not only are solar and wind measly energy contributors, not only are they a blight on the land, not only are they killing untold animals, not only are they short-lived projects that soon degrade into tons of toxic waste, but they actually contribute to a dirtier environment. And how? Toby Rice, who runs America's largest natural gas company, EQT Corp., explains:

> One thing I think that people don't understand is how much energy demand there is in this world. And when solar and wind aren't capable of meeting that energy demand, people will turn to their next option, which is coal.[12]

Dirty coal. Half of it being burnt in China. But everywhere around the world they're burning it. Dirty coal emissions have increased by five hundred million tons over pre-pandemic 2019 levels.[13] That completely erases all the emissions reductions gained from solar and wind power in the United States over the last fifteen years. Completely erases.

If environmentalists were truly interested in curbing greenhouse gases—and not just finding fun jobs in ecotourism or whatever—they would be out there marching and chanting, "*LNG! LNG!*" They'd be on the front lines of turning America into the world's largest exporter of liquified natural gas (LNG). Yes, because as they say, we're all in this together, and dirty coal burned overseas impacts America.[14]

For a brief time the United States had become the world's largest exporter of LNG and was on track to increase our exports 400 percent in the coming decade. Rice has measured the impact that we'd see from replacing coal power overseas with LNG, and he figured it would have the same environmental impact as "electrifying every vehicle in the United States, putting solar on every household in America, and adding 54,000 industrial-scale windmills."[15]

That's the direction President Trump was taking America. President Biden was hours into his new job when he caved to the small group of environmentalists.

What's more, if America had still been actively exporting relatively clean LNG when Vladimir Putin's armies invaded Ukraine, we could have come to the aid of Europe, which had to go on buying Russian oil. Sure, the Europeans had been foolish in turning too radically to renewable energy sources, so they were stuck. It was lights-out if they said no to Putin. But the United States could have sent shiploads of LNG to Europe to save them. That would also have shut down Putin's $1 billion daily profit from oil export and, in turn, his ability to wage war.

Dealing smartly with LNG is just one piece of responsible energy stewardship.

Current regulatory *roadblocks* (such as the National Environmental Policy Act, Antiquities Act, Endangered Species Act, Clean Water Act, Clean Air Act, and Jones Act) need to be more like *guardrails*. They need to open a clear path to energy sufficiency at a sensible pace rather than laying traffic spikes in the road to deflate any chance of real progress.

Another early move of Biden's was to suspend the issuance of new drilling leases on federal lands. Then, when prices predictably began rising at the gas pump, the president blamed US oil and gas companies for not producing more. In defending this apparent contradiction, Biden pointed out there are nine thousand *unused* drilling permits available to oil companies. In actuality, only 10 percent of those permits are on federal land.[16] And companies must run a gauntlet of hostile permitting authorities to access the drilling leases, then raise capital to build the pipelines, then fight all the lawsuits that come, then actually drill into the earth. It's a process that drags out across months into years and even decades. So oil and gas production is severely crimped, as intended.

Even these roadblocks aren't enough for environmentalists. So Democratic administrations play semantic games with something they call the "social cost" of carbon. The idea is to put a dollar value on the harm caused by greenhouse gas emissions. Calculators in hand, they add up all the effects these emissions are thought to have on farming, on human health, property damage from natural disasters—the list is lengthy.

Under President Trump, this "social cost" was determined to be $7 per metric ton of emissions. President Biden jacked the value to $51 per metric ton. A federal judge in Louisiana then blocked this proposed increase, throwing everything in limbo. Perhaps that's what the administration was counting on, for the net effect was to put further holds on oil lease sales. Folks at the Western Energy Alliance called it:

> The Department of the Interior refuses to hold lease sales until the dust settles. Officials are hoping to stall long enough to use the (social cost of carbon) to justify not leasing.[17]

In the year since Biden's leasing "pause," there was not a single successful lease sale.

ARE CLIMATE CHANGE MODELS EVEN CLOSE TO ACCURATE?

Back in June 2007, *National Geographic* published a story about "The Big Thaw" and how great swaths of the world's land mass would with 100 percent certainty be swamped by rising oceans by 2023, with both animals and humankind tossed into an irreversible extinction event.[18] I remember reading it and thinking, "I'd better start building me an ark."

Actually, I remember wondering if all these scientists truly believed what they were saying. Because if they did, why spend their few remaining hours on the planet studying it? Why not get cracking on their own arks?

Again and again these kinds of articles appeared over the years, soon to be joined by documentary movies with the latest stars hawking the end of times, summoning the tears and fears appropriate to the moment.

Yet we're still here.

How could so many people, many of them super sincere, be so completely wrong about our earth's falling off the proverbial edge, and then be wrong about it over and over, not put two and two together? We've talked about why.

There was a political party in need of a new faith to rally the troops. And what better way than to latch on to the insanely worst-case scenarios from otherwise reputable studies and go to town with them?

But now we're finally beginning to see some commonsense refusals from those in the scientific community to keep the charade going any longer. A handful of scientists have stepped forward with a different view from the "established science" being peddled.

OK, not a handful. A lot. Five hundred, to be precise. All of them distinguished in their fields of study. All of them speaking out at great professional cost to themselves, for surely there are retributions being planned by feverish minds. But good on these scientists for writing to the United Nations secretary-general and trying to share some truths. Their letter is worth reading in its entirety:

There is no climate emergency

A global network of 500 scientists and professionals has prepared this urgent message. Climate science should be less political, while climate policies should be more scientific. Scientists should openly address the uncertainties and exaggerations in their predictions of global warming, while politicians should dispassionately count the real benefits as well as the imagined costs of adaptation to global warming, and the real costs as well as the imagined benefits of mitigation.

Natural as well as anthropogenic factors cause warming

The geological archive reveals that Earth's climate has varied as long as the planet has existed, with natural cold and warm phases. The Little Ice Age ended as recently as 1850. Therefore, it is no surprise that we now are experiencing a period of warming.

Warming is far slower than predicted

The world has warmed at less than half the originally predicted rate, and at less than half the rate to be expected on the basis of net anthropogenic forcing and radiative imbalance. It tells us that we are far from understanding climate change.

Climate policy relies on inadequate models

Climate models have many shortcomings and are not remotely plausible as policy tools. Moreover, they most likely exaggerate the effect of greenhouse gases such as CO_2. In addition, they ignore the fact that enriching the atmosphere with CO_2 is beneficial.

CO2 is plant food, the basis of all life on Earth

CO_2 is not a pollutant. It is essential to all life on Earth. Photosynthesis is a blessing. More CO_2 is beneficial for nature, greening the Earth: additional CO_2 in the air has promoted growth in global plant biomass. It is also good for agriculture, increasing the yields of crops worldwide.

Global warming has not increased natural disasters

There is no statistical evidence that global warming is intensifying hurricanes, floods, droughts and suchlike natural disasters, or making them more frequent. However, CO_2 mitigation measures are as damaging as they are costly. For instance, wind turbines kill birds and bats, and palm-oil plantations destroy the biodiversity of the rainforests.

Climate policy must respect scientific and economic realities

There is no climate emergency. Therefore, there is no cause for panic and alarm. We strongly oppose the harmful and unrealistic net-zero CO_2 policy proposed for 2050. If better approaches emerge, we will have ample time to reflect and adapt. The aim of international policy should be to provide reliable and affordable energy at all times, and throughout the world.[19]

Whoa! Worth the read, right?

Here we have top-notch scientists who are, as progressives like to say, "following the science." They are adult enough to be honest about this issue. They are the kinds of scientists who should be getting the funding so that we approach environmental issues with intelligence and not with political expediency.

They are the kind of scientists who would have read an interesting paper in the journal *Science* in May 2022 and said to themselves, "Huh?"

That paper was about global warming. And you know how we are constantly being told the earth is precipitously heating up based on the precise scientific modeling of the melting Antarctic ice shelf?

Well, in this paper, some rather impressive scientists reported that they "used a special electromagnetic field-measuring technique to detect a vast layer of water-saturated sediment underneath western Antarctica." Water nobody has known about. Water that directly impacts how that Antarctic ice shelf sloughs off. Water the researchers said could mean the models scientists have been using are…incomplete. Said Chloe Gustafson, a postdoc at UC San Diego's Scripps Institution of Oceanography, "I don't know if you could say we're underestimating ice loss, but we are missing a process in trying to understand how ice moves off the continent."[20]

So maybe, just maybe, the models that prove that all life on this planet is doomed within decades are—how can I put this delicately—wrong.

This is no argument for full pollution ahead, of course. We don't want to return to the pre–Clean Air Act days when Los Angeles looked like Beijing today. What we want is to dial back on the sanctimonious environmental extreming and aim instead for open-minded energy stewardship going forward.

CLIMATE CHANGE TECH THAT COULD MAKE A DIFFERENCE

Our federal government's record of funding pure science and explorative ventures has had its ups and downs. But then, it's not easy. For most venture capitalists in Silicon Valley, only one out of one hundred investments becomes a big winner. And that's the precise investing strategy of some big-name houses.

So just because the Obama administration extended a $535 million loan guarantee to the solar panel startup Solyndra shortly before it went bankrupt,[21] and just because that loan guarantee was clearly a payback to one of Obama's big money fundraisers, it doesn't mean there isn't a role for government seed money in the development of renewable alternatives to fossil fuels.

It's the direction we all want to go—and we need to go. So we can only hope that future partnerships with government and energy entrepreneurs are executed with more integrity or luck than Obama managed.

Here are some of the climate-tech projects now under way that we should be watching in hopes they can deliver on clean energy mandates in the near future.

- **Enhanced geothermal**—There are more than sixty geo-thermal plants in the United States, mostly in the hot spots in the West. Cornell professors with federal funding are trying to simulate the geothermal process by firing high-pressure water at rock and cracking it to release heat, which is then captured.[22]

- **Satellite energy**—We know satellites can be used to wire-lessly beam down solar energy from orbit. Doing it safely is the rub. While in an early stage, these experiments could yield a tremendous source of never-ending energy.[23]

- **Underwater turbines**—Stacks of turbines arrayed in tall towers out at sea can capture wind from any direction and shoot electricity underwater back to shore. Units being tested could conceivably produce the energy of offshore wind farms without all their problems.[24]

- **Kite power**—Tapping into high-altitude wind a quarter mile up, these kites the size of a house are tethered to a winch and generator, which converts to electricity.[25] Pilot sites are generating a little under 100 kilowatts of clean power, and they hope to roll out commercially soon.

- Another company hoping to decarbonize the shipping industry is testing a giant "air sail" that's five times larger than a house and capable of towing a big tanker through the seas (when the wind is blowing).[26]

- **Flow reactors**—Running seawater through electrically charged meshes turns the water alkaline, which then reacts with dissolved CO_2, calcium, and magnesium in the water. The output is limestone and magnesite, as in how seashells are made. If this process can scale against the thirty-seven billion metric tons of CO_2 the world produces annually, it can make a major contribution.[27]

- **Nanocrystal electricity**—Still in its early stages and based on Nikola Tesla's lost inventions, this is basically a wireless charging station. Using a series of transmitters and receivers, it can hurtle electricity through the air to where it is needed. This could replace much of the power grid with clean energy (unless the elite-state owners of the power grid manage to subvert it).[28]

Along with these innovations in the works, there are also improved ground heat pumps, climate-friendly air conditioners, CO_2 capture machines, solar microgrids, and enhanced battery storage. All are important to pursue, and with government funding help. At the same time, the most important move we could make to draw down fossil fuels and secure our energy future is to commit our country all over again to the finest energy source of all.

SENSIBLE REPLACEMENT FOR BURNING FOSSIL FUELS

Compared with other green energy sources, principally wind and solar, nuclear energy is much more reliable and cost efficient, and it produces almost no carbon dioxide emissions.

Nuclear is talked about so little now that most people don't realize what kind of clean energy workhorse it has been. According to the US Office of Nuclear Energy, nuclear still provides 50 percent of America's clean energy—kicking out 778 billion kilowatt hours of electricity a year. And it provides 20 percent of our total energy—with ninety-two commercial reactors helping to power homes and businesses in twenty-eight states.

Nuclear is also the most *reliable* energy source, generating its power at full capacity 92 percent of the time in 2021 versus 54 percent for natural gas, 49 percent for coal, 34 percent for wind, and 25 percent for solar-driven plants.

And all the fuel rods the US nuclear energy industry has used up since it began sixty years ago could fit into a football field–sized plot only ten yards deep.[29] That's including the concrete encasements the fuel rods go into, encasements that have not failed even once.[30]

And unlike wind and solar farms that are lucky to last two decades before rusting out, nuclear reactors are good for the first forty years in their initial license and able to keep kicking out clean energy for another forty years after that.[31]

Yes, nuclear power is a marvel. And yet three locations on the map have scared so many people into believing that millions have died from nuclear power: Three Mile Island in 1979, Chernobyl in 1986, and Fukushima in 2011.

Each was a genuine nuclear disaster, but perspective, please! The World Health Organization reports that these three disasters resulted in *zero deaths* from radiation on US soil, 4,000 deaths on then-Russian soil, and 573 deaths on Japanese soil.[32]

In a raw but important contrast, more than 250,000 died from 1998 to 2017 because of tidal waves.[33] And more people were electrocuted to death in the United States in a dozen years than have been killed by all nuclear disasters going back to nuclear power's inception.[34]

Nuclear power is something to be treated with respect but not feared. The fear has come from good-hearted people watching too many horror shows and imagining nuclear mushroom clouds appearing on the near horizon. They've been taken advantage of by corrupt officials attached to the old world of coke and coal, and by the foot soldiers of the environmental movement.

It has been shameful all around.

But with all that has been corrupted, there is always hope of redemption. And we are seeing the first signs of it.

California Senator Dianne Feinstein, long a nuclear energy critic, switched her thinking when gas prices hit $7 a gallon in her state. She said that closing Diablo Canyon nuclear power plant makes little sense "under these circumstances."

Europe is doing its own about-face. Poland, the Czech Republic, France, and the Netherlands are ramping up new nuclear power plants. Even in Japan post-Fukushima they are bringing nine new nuclear reactors online in 2022. Other Asian countries are doing the same.[35]

Everywhere, countries are waking up to the realization that they cannot achieve their climate, energy, and national security goals without reviving nuclear power.

What's more, nuclear power is evolving. There are next-generation reactors that could dramatically change everything we think about nuclear power.

Leading this next-gen development is, of all countries, China. They could evolve from the dirtiest country in the world to the cleanest in just twenty years. Their test case, located in eastern China on Shidao Bay, went live in December 2021. Unlike conventional reactors, which produce steam to run the turbines at 570 degrees Fahrenheit, these next-gen reactors are smaller and modular. They use fuel pebbles coated with graphite as an energy source that can generate steam at 1,040 degrees Fahrenheit. This allows them to power many more industrial installations. They could even replace coal-burning power plants. A big decarbonization win.[36]

Other countries, the United States included, are also working on these small modular reactors in the sensible drive to a carbon energy–free future. With their simpler designs, standardized components, and newer safety features, these modular reactors come in at half the cost of the old and can lead the way forward.

Britain's Rolls-Royce is working with Chicago-based Exelon Generation to build a unit with a 2031 delivery date. Oregon-based NuScale has approval for its design and aims to have it completed in Romania by 2027. Russia is building these smaller reactors on ships in the Arctic. And for all the US foot-dragging, Biden's infrastructure bill did set aside $8.5 billion for nuclear energy projects.[37]

A big goal of these next-gen projects is to convert aging coal power plants into small nuclear reactors. It sounds very promising, though the engineering is still in its early stages and uncertain. Nonetheless, with the leap to small modular reactors, we have an opportunity for a new nuclear compact. We should take it.

A sensible energy future depends ultimately on centering our energy needs on the three-legged stool of domestic fossil fuels, renewable energy, and nuclear power as we also work toward the worthy goal of net zero carbon energy as swiftly as possible.

CHAPTER 18

HOW THE ELITE STATE METASTASIZED

VARIOUS SCHOLARS HAVE traced the origins of today's elite state back to the Burr Conspiracy of 1804, when Aaron Burr tried to enlist support from England "to detach the Western states and the Louisiana Territory from the Union."[1]

Others pin it to the Progressive Era that began in the 1890s, when reformists argued that the Founders' limited government was unequal to a new century's problems. These progressives suggested that the freedoms under God that the Founders had delivered into this world for the first time in history were, in fact, not of God at all. Instead, they were a product of the state, which they, in their wisdom, should run...into the ground, some would say, though many of their intentions were good and great progress was made in addressing the shortcomings of a cowboy nation that was then galloping from crisis to crisis. There was a logical flow, as well, to many of their arguments.

These turn-of-the-century progressives believed that a limited Constitution made perfect sense if human rights were fixed and unchanging. But that is not the case. All rights may be on loan from God, but their application has evolved over time, and our Constitution should evolve with them. Thus, our Constitution should be a living thing in tune with the times, they argued, in tune with the rights to which we are entitled. Entitlements, they should be called. No longer would it be necessary to keep a jealous eye on government tyrants as our Founders had insisted. For now, in giving power to the government, it would in return give us back more rights and benefits—Social Security, Medicare, unemployment insurance, and on and on.

This was the argument, and a bureaucracy was built up to manage all this. Then came the 1960s, and new forces began to rend the fabric of our country. In his book *The Age of Entitlement: America Since the Sixties*, Christopher Caldwell did as good a job as any of identifying three "ruptures" that cracked the culture and opened up war fronts on domestic soil.

1. **The Vietnam War.** Like most else in that war, the draft
   was handled badly. The rich and college-bound got defer-
   ments and spent the war going to Woodstock and making
   love. The poor and less educated were sent to Khe Sanh
   and were making war. From this came a new class division: those fortunate enough to sit out an ill-considered
   war—many believing themselves more moral and decent
   for it—and those less fortunate who returned home
   broken, facing a judgmental country, resentful. This division would only widen as time passed.[2]

2. **Women's rights**. The long-overdue acceptance of female
   equality and the invention of effective contraception
   divided people into two rigid views on the sanctity and
   very definition of life—each firm in the righteousness of
   their beliefs.[3]

3. **Civil rights laws.** Our nation's stubborn unwillingness to
   achieve the ideals of our founding forced a set of laws to
   fight discrimination in the courts. Though needed, the
   unintended consequence was to begin moving power away
   from the executive and legislative branches into the judiciary, eroding the separation of powers that had been the
   Founders' true genius.[4]

These ruptures radically changed the American cultural landscape.
The largest of them, though it gets little attention for it, was likely the
Civil Rights Act of 1964. For all the good it did, it basically rewired
how the government worked. In outlawing discrimination, it created
a new catalog of crimes. It altered the protections afforded by the First
Amendment. It established new agencies, new enforcement powers. It
gave the government new powers to run investigations. And it moved
governance more into the hands of bureaucrats and judges.

There is no arguing with the goals of the civil rights laws. They
were meant to force Southern bigots into some conformity with human
decency and the ideals of the Constitution. But that came at a price. For

it created a permanent victim class, which would soon tear apart families, inflame communities, and trigger moral hazards that remain with us today. Extending this thought would add a fourth item to Caldwell's list of 1960s ruptures. That would be President Kennedy's decision to create the modern public defender system.[5] This was a noble extension of the Sixth Amendment, making no-cost counsel available to anyone in need. But in turn, hundreds of law schools were opened to train thousands of new public defenders.

After a short while in the business, tired of the low pay, most of these public defenders jumped into private practice. A nation of a few hundred thousand attorneys suddenly was on track to a million-plus attorneys, each making wage fighting over every insignificant issue, transforming the "golden rules" into a complexity of arguments and counterarguments that soon turned America into the most litigious society in the world, with all those complexities breeding on themselves and everything becoming harder to agree on. The impact on government was monstrous.

Two line items in the federal budget say it all. Today Washington spends $250 billion a year on bureaucrats' wages and even more on subcontractors.[6] Yes, the federal government spends $350 million conservatively on a vast network of private contractors, state and local government grantees, and electronic partners. Every major policy initiative—from Medicare and Medicaid to environmental cleanup, anti-poverty programs, interstate highways, sewage treatment plants, cybersecurity, and so much more—is now managed through these public-private partnerships.

These private contractors have become so deeply entrenched in the government's working that they've become something of a shadow government in some people's view, a deep state in others'. They are the core of the new elite state, and nobody in government has the first clue about how to make them more effective or even accountable.

Nobody in government is even trying.

"Bigger the beast, messier it eats," I imagine Jeff Goldblum's gimlet-eyed character in the *Jurassic Park* movies observing as he looks up at those massive predators of old. Easily a third of their kills were left to the scavengers lurking nearby. So it is with our federal government today. By some estimates, fifty-one cents of every dollar of discretionary spending are squandered on wasteful projects, outright bid rigging, old-fashioned crony capitalism, and other euphemisms for grand-theft government.[7]

It is the nature of the beast—the larger it gets, the messier. Even the government's own accountants admit that 20 percent of the money taxpayers send to Washington for procurement programs is wasted, abused, or fraudulently conveyed.[8] On top of that is the vast federal bureaucracy of two million people drawing their over $90,000 average annual paychecks no matter how little they actually do.[9] And sadly, for so many of those employees "little" is the operative word. No business could survive with 20 to 30 percent shrinkage taken for granted, but the vast federal bureaucracy thrives on it.

This is not to condemn *all* that government does. At least half of everything they do is valuable—we just don't know which half! Seriously, it's a messy and wasteful business in the best of times, and it has become a larcenous business in our time. All of Washington has become the poster child for the "power corrupts absolutely" theme.

They rule now just as our Founders feared—with the blunt avarice of the monarchs of old Europe. This elite state has surrounded and swallowed up the government, and no words capture it quite like this photo of elite state offices sprawling out in all three directions from 1600 Pennsylvania Avenue, effectively capturing the president, whomever that may be.

As this metastasis in Washington has spread, it has required more offices within government proper to serve it. So the number of cabinet-level positions reporting to the president has expanded dramatically—more than most of us realize.

How many cabinet-level positions do you think George Washington had? Only four: secretaries of state, of war, and of the Treasury, as well as an attorney general.[10] Abraham Lincoln, who famously brought all his rivals into his cabinet so he could keep an eye on them, had seven.

By the time President Trump organized his cabinet, he had twenty-three cabinet positions to fill sitting atop a federal bureaucracy that included 137 executive "agencies" and 268 "units," with two million people insisting they are doing something useful for the country. Gone from one nation under God to one nation unmanageable.[11]

How much bigger might this federal beast grow if nobody can rein it in? Here's a chart of the cabinet positions we could see within a decade. This is not wild guessing. Each of the positions noted in italics has been seriously proposed by people in power today.[12]

EVER-GROWING LIST OF CABINET POSITIONS

- Administrator of the Environmental Protection Agency
- Attorney General
- Chair of the Council of Economic Advisors
- Director of Central Intelligence
- Representative to the United Nations
- *Representative to the World Economic Forum*
- Secretary of Agriculture
- Secretary of Commerce
- *Secretary of Consumer Financial Protection*
- Secretary of Defense
- *Secretary of Diversity Training*
- Secretary of Education
- Secretary of Energy
- *Secretary of Environmental, Social, and Governance Compliance*
- Secretary of Health and Human Services
- Secretary of Homeland Security
- Secretary of Housing and Urban Development
- Secretary of the Interior
- Secretary of Labor
- *Secretary of Racial Grievances and Reparations*
- Secretary of State
- *Secretary of Technology Development*
- Secretary of Transportation
- Secretary of Treasury
- Secretary of Veterans Affairs
- Small Business Administrator
- US Trade Representative
- Vice President
- White House Chief of Staff

Is this expanding government in turn expanding in service of the American people, working for individual liberty grounded in our Christian traditions, ensuring free markets that lift the general prosperity of all, safeguarding every citizen?

Of course it is not.

Simply put, government should be smart, fair, and above all, limited. It can be summarized in a simple word problem:

LIMITED GOVERNMENT ≠ SMALL GOVERNMENT

Liberals and conservatives alike long ago gave up the pretense of caring about the size of the federal government. They just grew the heck out of it—because that's what the American people rewarded at election time. Sure, people in the cities often wanted different things than people in the country. But they all had wants. If anything, liberals were more honest about wanting to tax and spend. Conservatives kept invoking the rugged individualist while whistling Dixie as one industry after another lined up at the public trough for their subsidy, their handout, their slice of pig.

So there is no call for small government anymore, but we must call for limiting government going forward. So that government can run the nation without totally running our lives—which is the current situation.

Congress gavels about three hundred or so new acts into being each year. That then kicks off the regulatory phase of lawmaking, in which lawyers turn these acts into the thousands of pages of rules, regulations, and mandates we must now obey.[13]

In 2020 the Federal Register page count was 86,356, down 10 percent from President Obama's record number.[14] President Biden and the Democratic Congress will soon take it past 100,000 pages in the regularly stated effort to regulate every human activity they can imagine. Some 100,000 pages that citizens must comply with or meet the enforcement arm of the agency in charge of how you live.

Folks at the Competitive Enterprise Institute figure that the cost of complying with all these regulations sucks $1.9 trillion out of the productive economy every year.[15] That's almost 10 percent of our country's total GDP lost to regulatory compliance. Some of that is money well spent—to keep our air clean and our water pure. But most of it is trying to regulate our way to some utopian outcome.

Even if that were possible, we naturally know better.

God gave us ten simple commandments that govern all; no human regulation can improve on the wisdom of the ten. Those 100,000 pages of regulations do have some value, but mostly they are blueprints for building more marbled offices in Washington full of even more lobbyists trying to extend the state's favor upon their vested interest.

As for all these lobbyists, here's a policy idea compliments of the tech commentator Andy Kessler. He has called, only half-jokingly, for a Lobbyist Control Act:

> Legislators and lobbyists can meet only in an arena, maybe on Washington's Capital One Arena ice after a hockey game, armed only with 5-by-7 cards. Record every meeting, capped at 30 seconds a congressman—yes, like speed dating. No more food bribes at fancy-schmancy restaurants.[16]

And in a *New Yorker* cartoon by Maddie Dai, two little aliens stand before a bigwig at his desk. After a beat, one says, "Well, then, take me to your lobbyists."[17]

Limiting government means limiting lobbyists currying favor.

There are times when we want our government to shine competently, when we want "aggressive." We want it in the energetic pursuit of true terrorists and the forceful prosecution of criminals. We want a health threat like COVID to be met with a smart, coordinated national response. We expect our government to handle air traffic control, to care for our veterans, to provide weather satellite data, to challenge cyber thieves, to keep our roads paved and bridges safe, to ensure safe food and drinking water, to protect investors from unscrupulous operators. These are all things we want done.

We should add mental health security to this list, for clearly this is a growing concern that requires a coordinated national response and resources to help those in need.

After the 2012 Sandy Hook school shooting that left twenty-six children dead, Congress got serious and output the 21st Century Cures Act, signed by President Obama in 2016. It built out useful bureaucracy and funding to help the states expand outpatient treatment for the mentally ill at the community level.

Reauthorization bills now in Congress should boost Medicaid payments for psychiatric care and weaken HIPAA rules that now forbid families from seeing their loved ones' health information. Both steps can increase the quality of treatment for the mentally ill as well as the outcomes.

So here we see the value of well-designed government programs.

I can still recall Ronald Reagan half-joking that "the nine most terrifying words in the English language are—I'm from the government, and I'm here to help." But actually, Reagan's campaign trail quips and his Oval Office directives were very different. He actually told his staff, as Don Devine recalls, "one of the best reasons to cut government was to give it less to do so it can do the rest right."[18]

This idea of doing what needs doing right—it's at the core of the good government we must fight for from our communities on up. We know that as individuals we cannot make much impact at the highest levels of government. But we can do what needs doing right at the lowest levels, then patiently work our way up. That is how we counterpunch and make it count.

MAKING OUR ELECTIONS MATTER

One of the fondest illusions of a "democracy" is that a simple majority of votes wins each elected office. There's a little truth in that, just as there's a little truth in the labels on our food products. But mostly, organized minorities elect our leaders and do so at every level.

We're not talking here about Electoral College tinkering or vote rigging, though both sides engage in these practices—always have and probably always will, since politics ain't beanbag.

We're talking about how most Americans don't give a hoot about what their local, state, and federal legislators do. Or they do care but don't think their vote matters for much. Either way, same outcome. We can curse the civic darkness that prevails, but what's gained from that? Nothing productive, of course.

But what happens when we learn to punch above our weight and strike at the vulnerabilities of the elite state? Making little marks, one at a time, with those marks adding up. That is something each of us can do, and it requires getting clear on how things work and where those vulnerabilities lie.

What we see today is the culmination of years of hard work by those with selfish ambition. You could call them fascists at heart. Or corporate socialists. We like to label things. But labels matter less than the product of their activities.

> Selfishness.
> Simply me, me, me.
> I want to be a trillionaire.
> So off I go, pillaging and plundering.

Attila the Hun went down in history for similar activities. Putin will get a name in history now, Vlad the Annihilator or some such. All the oligarchs of Russia and China and America have one thing in common: selfishness. At best they think, "What's good for me is good for you."

Yes, even as they've foisted on us the most alien of ideas, pummeling us with their self-interest, with their ham-fisted control of the political process, their siphoning off of our money, their indoctrination of our children, their hijacking of journalism, their use of technology to subjugate us—they have insisted that we love them for it, adore them.

They want us to feel so very fortunate that their largesse and sweet nature has made our lives so very meaningful. And when their programs fail, they tell us it's because we haven't given them enough tax dollars and we should surely give more, more, more.

And for all our giving, what do we receive?

In the name of liberty, they deny liberty.

In the name of freedom, they slam fists full of regulations down on us.

In the name of equality, they divide us into camps hating on one another.

They hold their power because of the elective process. If they lose it, it must be by the same method. That will occur only when good people organize in the right way.

When we recognize that most of our bruises have come from years of being punched and slammed against the wall with a knife slitting open our wallets but always, always, a smile on their faces, saying, "We care for you; we'll take care of you."

When we've finally had enough.

An old friend of mine, a California politician named Bill Richardson, played the game back when there was a simple Left-Right feud, when the elite state was still taking its first baby steps. Bill liked to say it's a waste of time fighting head-on against any agency of the government, because

> fighting bureaucracy is like pummeling a large balloon. One can sink one's arm into the balloon up to the shoulder and then watch it puff back to its original shape once the fist is removed. No matter how hard you punch and no matter how long you keep it up, once you stop striking it resumes its original shape and seems to grow larger.
>
> Is anyone naïve enough to think that once an agency swells and becomes a large bureaucracy that it remains a servant of the people and not primarily an agent for its own self-interest?[19]

Try to fight head-on against a bureaucrat at any level and you'll just punch yourself out, flailing away to no end. But fight cleverly and defeats turn into victories. Continuing my friend Bill's idea, every balloon has an air valve, and air for bureaucrats is money. Controlling the supply of air are those elected to office. And doing the electing is us. From the lowest sheriff's races through to the presidential race, we can still control the air valve. So we can still control the government's reach into our lives. This we can do!

When we talk about politics, we tend to talk about the presidential race first. For obvious reasons—it's a big deal! But for me, anyway, not much of my daily attention goes there. I know I have little influence over what the president does. My phone calls won't be returned, my advice not taken. However, at the bottom rungs of politics, at the local level, with the local officials and state legislators and even a few governors' races—now, that's a different situation.

Local candidates have an interest in me because I can make an impact on their elections, just as you can. Sure, I've spent time in Washington, DC, and like to think I made a mark there. But a much bigger mark is made when we begin in our own communities.

That's where people begin in politics, where we learn the skills it takes to rise up into the big leagues. Most of us spend our lives as fans sitting in the bleachers, leaving someone else to put on the gloves and step into the ring. But the time has come to make a choice: either watch the show or get in the ring! This means

- attending local gatherings and evening coffee shop sessions;

- meeting your neighbors and finding like-minded thinkers among them;

- choosing to volunteer at a phone bank;

- calling up voters in your neighborhood and talking about hot issues;

- registering folks to vote if they're not already registered;

- holding backyard fundraisers for neighbors who've put their hats in for local offices; and

- building up from the lowest levels a government that is smart, fair, and above all, limited.

Working from this ground floor on up is how we ultimately ensure a national government committed to our individual liberties.

This is far from easy work. But it is good work because it puts us side by side with our neighbors instead of quarreling with them, or not even knowing them. It puts us in the room with people whose opinions may be different from ours on this or that, but we know we are truly fighting a common enemy—the wealth-extraction machinery of the elite state.

We know this is not easy work because just as dogs bark, jackasses bray, and snakes hiss, elites lie. People in power lie. They lie often for no better reason than it's the easiest way to muddle through a difficult job. Politics at every level is the art of balancing competing interests. It's never easy, and somebody is always going to be upset. It's much easier to lie than to upset them. Upset voters tend not to repeat their choices.

But we must call them on their lies. We must confront them.

In so doing, you can be sure they will first deny it, then try to change the subject, then attack your character. That's the standard escalation protocol for an accomplished liar. And the more vigorously you pursue the truth, the louder they'll scream. For often they are unaccustomed to being on the defensive, not expecting it. For many years they've faced opponents who are soft. They tend to think of us as small-minded buffoons, deplorables, religious simpletons stuck in our old ways.

They see us as incapable of stopping their sophisticated strategies, their brilliant tactical maneuvers. They look at our civility and see weakness. They've been hitting us so hard for so long with so little opposition, they are often unprepared when we launch an effective counterpunch against them. It can surprise the heck out of them when we actually whip them in the political arena. (Recall Hillary Clinton's face on November 8, 2016!)

This fight does not require the use of dirty tactics. As St. Paul advised in Romans 12:17, *"Repay no one evil for evil."* We don't have to mimic the opposition in order to win. The more honest and ethical we are in this fight, the better our chances of winning.

CHAPTER 19

THE ONLY WAY TO SLAY THE ELITE STATE BEHEMOTH

C ONSIDER THE FOLLOWING statement:

> They have sent small armies to protestor's (sic) houses, often in the middle of the night or very early in the morning. They surround their houses, breaking windows and doors. They fix their weapons on women and children, handcuffing the entire families, sometimes shoeless and in their pajamas.
>
> Conveniently, there is usually some sort of media presence, and the videos of the raids are made public. They want us to see what happens if you dare oppose their tyranny. The lives of the protestors are systematically destroyed. They lose their jobs, their homes, their bank accounts, and end up sitting in jail, some of them for over a year now with no trial. It is scary.[1]

Are those words from some luckless peasants during Augusto Pinochet's iron-fisted rule of Chile in the 1970s? From Aleksandr Solzhenitsyn's tales of the gulag during communism's cruel reign of orchestrated mass starvation? Or from an honorably discharged United States Marine who, having sworn an oath to protect the Constitution, went to Capitol Hill on January 6, made no aggressive moves toward the Capitol Police, and destroyed no property but ended the day in jail?

Yes, these words are from Nathaniel Matthews' book *January 6: A Patriot's Story.*

It is the story of a man galvanized by 9/11 to become a Marine and defend a nation under attack. Putting his own life on the line between good and evil. But he found that line growing illusory, clouded by politics, perverted into a whip to be used on the homeland by a dark organization that had infiltrated every level of society—from both political parties in Washington through an endless array of bureaucracies on down through our schools and universities to our news and entertainment providers, reducing a nation once thought to be a beacon of liberty to some neo-feudal castle-building apparatus that simultaneously cracked capitalism and secreted in a new authoritarianism—something only possible when all the levers of power have been consolidated into a few hands and the media co-opted to turn their storytelling skills into narratives of division and self-loathing, the better to keep people distracted and constantly fighting with one another, oblivious to the costs of the castle building and the emergence of a new *rentier* economy notable for the surprisingly few scraps left over for the people outside the castle walls.

A story with roots in the summer of 2020, when millions of Americans poured into the streets, angered by the racial injustices they saw on TV, and rightly so. But few were even aware that their anger was being appropriated by the elite state. For a spectacle was needed by this elite state. Not just needed, but welcomed.

So they welcomed that summer of rioting and wanton destruction of property, the gunning down of both Black and White police officers, the blocking of ambulances bringing wounded police to hospitals, the beating to death of Korean American bodega owners in full view of rolling cameras.[2] They welcomed it all—encouraged it, orchestrated pieces of it in a manner so similar to the ruling elites of another time.

Back in time it was the feeding of Christians to the lions, the hooking of peasants on gin, the tossing of dwarfs at the pub. All meant to create a spectacle. Elites know the value of these spectacles. Know that throughout history when rulers have gotten too carried away with the fleecings and the repressions, the people have needed outlets for their anger. Spectacles to take their minds off things. Otherwise, they might wise up to their shrinking lives and turn up at the castle gates.

Which is what about two thousand Americans did on January 6.

Nathaniel was one of them. He'd been planning his trip to Washington even before President Trump called for a rally to dispute the election. Nathaniel had seen the violence in the streets. He'd seen how pandemic lockdowns had been used—by both political parties—to tamper with the elections. He'd seen how most of Washington joined in promoting some wacky Russian collusion hoax to bring down a president who threatened their grift. Nathaniel was there to protest it all.

He knew it was his First Amendment right to seek redress of grievances without fear of reprisal. He clung to the hope that America was still a nation of laws.

Instead he was physically beaten, humiliated, thrown in jail, and labeled a domestic terrorist as his government spun a narrative with a playwright's precision about the "bloody insurrection" in which he had been involved. Having been there, he knew what really happened.

One terrible death—that of Ashli Babbitt, an air force veteran who was shot and killed by a nervous Capitol Police officer after she was forcibly shoved by other police and undercover FBI informants into locked glass doors.

Another terrible death—that of Rosanne Boyland, who, according to the *New York Times*, was "killed in a crush of fellow rioters during their attempt to fight through a police line" while video of the day clearly showed police pushing protesters on top of Boyland and not allowing other protesters to pull her out.[3]

Another terrible death—that of Capitol Police officer Brian Sicknick. The *New York Times* again got it wrong, insisting that the officer was bludgeoned to death by a raging Trump supporter wielding a fire extinguisher, when in fact he went home just fine that day and died of a stroke the following day.[4]

An all-around terrible day for everyone involved. Apologists for the government pleaded their case in the left-stream media, since their job is to hate on the Right. Had this happened on a leftist president's watch, the right-stream media would be erupting with outrage and vitriol. All have their role—most of them fully aware they're shameless shills, a few no doubt blithely unaware of their complicity.

It was a day that began with President Trump acting out some Greek tragedy, reaching out for saviors who would not come. Entirely absurdist theater, and with President Biden joining in for his cue: "It was a dire threat to the very fabric of our nation and 'the worst attack on our democracy since the Civil War!'"[5] By "our democracy" he meant the elite state he serves.

If it was such a dire threat and the government's actions honorable ones, why are there fourteen thousand hours of video footage of January 6 events that the government refuses to release publicly?[6]

Why not provide actual pictures of these blood-raged domestic terrorists at work?

Might we also see security guards holding open doors to welcome protesters instead of those doors being beaten down?

Might we see FBI provocateurs who can be identified, provoking and clubbing the crowd and causing panic, which we suspect is not in their job description?

A year later, many of those arrested that day—seven hundred in all—were still awaiting trial. Their Sixth Amendment rights suspended. A justice system not caring.

Nathaniel is one who has seen up close what it means for us all when nothing in government works right.

All of us got another look when the inevitable House hearings followed, and the curtain was pulled back for another performance by political actors. They called it the Select Committee on the January 6 Attack, putting their prejudgments in the title. A TV producer was even hired in hopes of a ratings bonanza. Scripts were knocked out to advance the central tension in the drama.

Could the Democrats besmirch the entire Republican Party by branding January 6 a "coup attempt" and thus distract audiences from 9.1 percent inflation and six-dollar-per-gallon gasoline and an impending recession all mostly caused by a nonfunctioning government?

In their dressing rooms afterward the actors, one and all, wondered if they would come out with Watergate hearing–style boosts to their personal reputations, hastening groundswells for their own presidential ambitions.

The worst show on Netflix got better ratings, deservedly.

America is broken because we no longer have a functioning political system, or a functioning justice system, or a functioning media system. Without these trusses of liberty, the whole edifice descends into chaos. Just as the elite state likes it. For in chaos, there is opportunity with fewer obstacles to their ambitions.

This is where we've come to, and where we'll be for a while. But it will change. It will change because a new generation of heroes will step up onto the first rungs of civic leadership. Changing the narrative in our own communities and states right to the top. Guided by their faith in a greater power that is good and provident.

This is the prayerful action we are called to—and it is prayerful action most urgent.

NOW MORE CORRUPT THAN SOME BANANA REPUBLICS

Most Americans still believe that for all our nation's faults, we're still a lot better off than most of the world. But how true is that?

Transparency International is one of those rare gems doing honest work. They simply ask that governments, businesses, and civil societies renounce corruption. They publish an annual index of the most corrupt countries, based on the following:

- Prevalence of bribery

- Diversion of public funds

- Officials using public office for private gain

- Governments not containing public sector corruption

- Quantities of red tape generated by government

- Nepotistic appointments in the civil service

- Laws for public official disclosure of conflicts of interest

- Legal protection for people who report cases of bribery and corruption

- State capture by narrow vested interests

- Access to information on public affairs and government activities

A pretty thorough list of bad doing, right? And where is America in the index?

We should at least be among the top-ten *least* corrupt, right? Sadly, no. Surely, then, among the top-twenty *least* corrupt? Again, no. We are twenty-seventh out of 180, down below countries like Uruguay, Estonia, and United Arab Emirates with all the problems they have.[7]

A particularly repugnant illustration of America's now endemic corruption surfaced in the events leading up to the 2016 presidential election, which we're only now getting to the bottom of.

THE OLD RUSSIAN DOUBLE SUCKER PUNCH

When a permanent bureaucracy becomes beholden solely to its continued existence, it has a vital imperative every four years: make sure the people elect a president who supports them.

So in 2015 an email was sent by presidential candidate Hillary Clinton—wait, no. She shredded years' worth of emails minutes before investigators arrived at her doorstep. Only Mrs. Clinton knows how this story began, and she ain't talking.

The tl;dr (too long; didn't read) version of what happened next is straight out of a Robert Ludlum novel: the FBI and Justice Department used some unverified allegations made by one candidate to obtain a court order to wiretap that candidate's opponent and then leak it all to the media to maximize the damage done.

The long version goes on for thousands of pages, and it's a twisted odyssey that few of us would even try to follow. That is why in a vacuum of understanding, the initial allegations almost succeeded in toppling a duly elected president.

Over the course of a crazy plotline there would be appearances by the following people, in alphabetical order:

- James Baker, FBI general counsel

- John Brennan, CIA director

- Kevin Clinesmith, FBI lawyer

- Hillary Clinton, former secretary of state, candidate for president

- James Comey, FBI director

- Rodney Joffe, senior vice president of Neustar, a cybertech company

- Loretta Lynch, US attorney general

- Andrew McCabe, FBI deputy director

- Barack Obama, president

- Bruce Ohr, DOJ senior official

- Adam Schiff, congressman

- Christopher Steele, British spy

- Peter Strzok, FBI deputy assistant director for counterintelligence

- Michael Sussman, Democratic National Committee counsel

With a quick read of the cast, you can see that the highest levels of government were mobilizing around a single goal: to clear a path for Hillary Clinton to become president, and failing that, disgrace Donald Trump so he could more easily be impeached and removed from office.

Their motive? For some, it was love for Mrs. Clinton, but there's a limit to that. For most, it was a genuine fear that Trump would try to dismantle the deep behemoth state and their own exalted roles in it. A fear driven by campaign promises to do just that.

Reading the accounts of the whole crazy story line can lead you down the rabbit hole for weeks. Factcheck.org's *summary* of it runs forty-five pages.[8] Right-stream media have drawn one version, the left-stream media another—each serving their masters and neither quite complete nor correct. Though one takeaway emerged from both tellings: folks in Washington can mess with anyone they want to.

This time they messed with Donald Trump, and in wicked ways.

Back in 2015, when Trump's presidential ambitions became known, the permanent bureaucracy began getting nervous. Peter Strzok and FBI lawyer Lisa Page began hatching a plan to frame up Trump. This text message between them was the tell:

> I want to believe the path you threw out for consideration in [Andrew McCabe's] office—that there's no way [Trump] gets elected—but I'm afraid we can't take that risk. It's like an insurance policy in the unlikely event you die before you're 40.[9]

Certainly FBI officials are allowed to have political opinions, but what did they mean by an anti-Trump "insurance policy"?

We would soon find out. Within months the FBI launched a probe into any connections Trump might have had with high-level Russians. And conveniently, right then, the FBI found in their possession a now-famous "dossier." Cue the sinister music. This dossier was written by a British spy named Christopher Steele and paid for by the Democratic National Committee and Mrs. Clinton's campaign.[10] It was chock-full of scandalous allegations about Trump's activities in Russia.

Folks inside the Beltway were well aware the dossier was garbage. Basically standard "oppo research" rife with rumors and fabrications meant to tarnish a political opponent if any of it stuck. But nothing too real, as oppo research goes. And true enough, almost every claim made about Trump in that dossier was confirmed as truthful by the FBI.

Yet the FBI needed to find *something* to use against Trump. So FBI director Comey and CIA director Brennan teamed up to launder the Steele dossier through the US intelligence community, lending it an aura of credibility before leaking it to left-stream media outlets that could be counted on to spin Steele's fabrications into a web of misdeeds of biblical proportion. The left-stream media delivered as requested.

That dossier was used by the FBI and senior Justice officials to secure wiretap warrants to spy on the Trump campaign, to frame associates of Trump's, and to launch one of the most expensive criminal investigations in the nation's history.

They did so much snooping they had to make the most of it, right? So they took all these intercepts, laid them out in nice rows on spreadsheets, and presented them to still-sitting President Obama for his approval of retaliatory action. Though all the damage they could do to Trump was already done.

Later investigators would ask Comey, Brennan, and Rep. Adam Schiff about public comments they made that Trump clearly colluded with Russia.[11] Turns out that in private, under oath, they had testified to having no such evidence of collusion. They'd just been telling bald-faced lies in public because, well, that's their game.

By this point, most Americans had had enough of this scandal. Viewers were turning away from CNN and Fox News in droves because clearly both sides were spinning tales, and it was exhausting trying to keep up with all the plot twists. Yet the biggest—or rather, the most dangerous— plot twist was still unfolding.

PRIVACY DIES IN A PUBLIC-PRIVATE PARTNERSHIP

The first round of investigations of Trump turned up little—except that the president was a mean and often obscene bull in a china shop, by then no secret. So another round of investigations had to be launched, this one by special counsel John Durham to investigate the previous investigation. (Your taxpayer money at work!)

This investigation would prove even harder to follow than the last. But it would matter because it confirmed just how frighteningly much government snoops know about each and every one of us.

This begins with a crackerjack cybersecurity guy, Rodney Joffe. He was an unknown on the political stage, but he came to matter greatly because in the 2016 presidential election, one set of totally fabricated allegations against Trump was simply not enough to sate the elite state. They were eager for more. And Joffe supplied them. Supplied new "evidence" that Trump, a hotelier with business interests in Russia, had ties with Russian banks. Imagine! But these were nefarious back-channel ties with the apparently notorious Alpha Bank. The plot thickens.

How did Joffe discover these "ties"?

In Durham's indictments we learned that Joffe and his team had "exploited his access to non-public data at multiple Internet companies to conduct opposition research concerning Trump [and] had assembled purported DNS data reflecting apparent DNS lookups between Russian Bank-1 and an email domain, 'mail1.trump-email.com.'"[12]

Meaning? That Joffe enlisted researchers at Georgia Tech to scour the internet for any information about potential Trump entanglements in Russia. To help these researchers, Joffe gave them access to data his company Neustar had obtained as a "sub-contractor in a sensitive relationship between the U.S. government and another company."[13]

Basically, he gave them eyes on every bit of data that flows over the internet for the purpose of trying to entrap a private citizen based on his internet searches.

Joffe and his team swept up all internet traffic in and around the Trump Tower, Trump's Manhattan apartment building, and the White House Executive Office Building as well. Swept it all up and went data mining for dirt. What he found alarmed him (or so he would later testify), so he dutifully took his findings to Michael Sussmann—a high-powered attorney at the time representing Hillary Clinton and the Democratic National Committee. Interesting choices.[14]

If Joffe, as a federal contractor or even as a private citizen, was so concerned about the fate of the republic, even saying that he was alarmed by the security implications of his data, why take his findings to the Democrats? As the *Wall Street Journal* opined, "We doubt government contracts include: 'In case of threats, first call Democrats.'"[15]

Moving along, Sussmann turned the findings over to the CIA in February 2017, telling the agency that this data "demonstrated that Trump and/or his associates were using supposedly rare, Russian-made wireless phones in the vicinity of the White House and other locations."[16]

And based on that "bombshell," our entire government was thrown on high alert, and the attacks on Trump's credibility mounted. Because he used burner phones like, well, quite a few people.

A lot of heads were hanging low in Washington about that time—or would have been, if there was a decent soul about.

Joffe's credentials as a surveillance wizard owe to his involvement in a little-known group called Operations Security Trust.[17] Their members come from all corners of tech, financial institutions, law enforcement, and security. In their own words, they are "a highly vetted community of security professionals focused on the operational robustness, integrity, and security of the Internet. The community promotes responsible action against malicious behavior beyond just observation, analysis and research."[18]

At face value, this sounds valuable. We need firepower thrown against the millions of malicious threats that strike the internet daily. But this private organization is also in the position of deciding what a malicious threat is and then taking "responsible action."

In this case, they decided among themselves that a candidate for president was a malicious threat. This despite having zero evidence of any illegal or even threatening activity on his part.

Theirs was the "responsible action" of snooping on all Trump's internet traffic along with the thousands of people, no doubt, in his wide orbit. Simply because they didn't like the man.

That Trump had become a disruptive force in politics, all can agree. But only in the feverish minds of rank partisans was he a threat to the republic. Yet Trump's internet traffic was being sifted through by people who are still allowed to turn on their computers every day, log in, and surveil whomever they don't happen to like.

As Durham's investigation wound down, Joffe's legal team kept insisting that their client was "apolitical," with no idea his lawyer, Sussmann, was also working for Mrs. Clinton and the Democratic National Committee. Which is like saying Jonah had no idea he was stuck inside the whale. Nonetheless, the Durham investigation wound down, having accomplished its goal. Both Joffe and Sussmann walked with only a hand-slap, leaving only the stench of the Beltway swamp in their wake.

Peering into that stench, America could see that nothing had changed. Still active was an incestuous elite who actively enabled Hillary Clinton to pull off a dirty campaign of deceit—the chummy network of political go-betweens who used their access and influence to sabotage an election. And the message sent down from on high was that your government can lie to you, steal from you, and snoop on you, and like in some South American banana republic, there's nothing you can do about it.

It's a message we cannot let go unanswered.

For we continue to believe, as we must, that the laws of a good nation can prevail if we rededicate ourselves once more to holding officials accountable. This idea of accountability is a fascinating one to me, for what does it truly mean?

Does it mean that at the highest levels, when our president takes an unjust action or makes an immoral law, it is the responsibility of our governors to stand in defiance? I believe it does. Or if a state legislator acts unjustly or immorally, our county commissioners should stand in opposition? Again, I believe it does. Or if a city council takes an unfair or prejudiced position, as members of the community we must stand in dissent? Yes, I believe it is our duty, our obligation.

This is not a new or even a modern obligation of ours.

Back in Roman times, the emperor Trajan ruled from AD 98 until 117. One day, when he was appointing lieutenants, Trajan handed one man a sword and instructed, "Use this sword against my enemies, if I give righteous commands; but if I give unrighteous commands, use it against me."[19]

Again, on a warm June day in 1215 on the fields of Runnymede, England, Christian noblemen took up this obligation. Their king, John, had been your run-of-the-mill tyrant ruling at whim. But the noblemen stood up to the king and insisted that he sign a parchment agreeing to certain rights for men. This became the Magna Carta—one of the most important documents in the long march to set down laws liberating every individual from arbitrary state power.[20]

Once again today, our leaders must be reminded that there is an ultimate authority and that their powers can be checked. With all authority on loan from a loving God, all those in positions of authority are first accountable to God.

Should leaders issue laws that God forbids, we should not obey and should actively resist. Our government is not God; its authority is not limitless. Giving over obedience to a government, even when it claims to hold our best interests, is never required. Indeed just the opposite, as the great Christian author C. S. Lewis reminds us:

> Of all tyrannies, a tyranny sincerely exercised for the good of its victims may be the most oppressive. It would be better to live under robber barons than under omnipotent moral busybodies. The robber baron's cruelty may sometimes sleep, his cupidity

may at some point be satiated; but those who torment us for our own good will torment us without end for they do so with the approval of their own conscience.[21]

There comes a time to resist, to dissent, and to fully understand why.

CHAPTER 20

ENDING AMERICA'S LONG-CORRUPT FOREIGN ADVENTURISM

U NTIL QUITE RECENTLY, most Americans believed in the Almighty as revealed in Scripture. This belief in an all-powerful God had a defining impact on how citizens behaved and, in turn, how such an extraordinary nation as ours was formed.

Divine law has guided the conscience of America from the outset, informing our every discourse. In every early political speech laying out the laws and privileges of citizenship there was a biblical thread woven start to finish—whether the speaker was from the earlier Federalist Party or the Democratic-Republican Party, or the later Democratic Party or Republican Party.

There's no better example of this than Benjamin Franklin at the Constitutional Convention, telling his fellow delegates:

> I have lived, Sir, a long time, and the longer I live, the more convincing proofs I see of this truth—that God governs in the affairs of men. And if a sparrow cannot fall to the ground without [H]is notice, is it probable that an empire can rise without [H]is aid? We have been assured, Sir, in the sacred writings, that "except the Lord build the House they labour in vain that build it."[1]

Could there be a more convincing comment on the intent of the Founders?

Certainly everyone thought so until the 1960s, when a new view took shape. In this view, our rich Christian traditions had fallen short of a faithful presence, and the whole Christian edifice had to be torn down.

It didn't matter to these reformers that they wrapped themselves in the same "God is dead" garments of the failed intellectual movements of old Russia and Germany. It didn't matter that they were shouting the same slogans Karl Marx gave Vladimir Lenin to control and eventually extinguish the lives of tens of millions in Russia. It didn't matter that their new heroes, such as Friedrich Nietzsche, had a few years earlier inspired Adolf Hitler to march his storm troopers across Europe. No, what mattered to them was what they saw before their very eyes: their elected officials were engaged in a clearly immoral war in Southeast Asia, and they were being asked to be cannon fodder. It was hard to blame them for seeking some alternative spiritual inspiration.

They went by names such as the Students for a Democratic Society and Weather Underground, and the establishment quickly branded them "un-American." That chafed because they believed they had the right to advocate for their point of view. And legally, they did. As long as they were (a) citizens of the United States and (b) not agents of a foreign government, they could openly advocate away.

And through this advocacy, this bottom-up movement faced off against their betters and got us out of Vietnam. Citizens making a difference from the streets on up to the Oval—as it should be!

Getting much less attention at the time, though equally important, were other rights struggles. Specifically, the fair and equal treatment of women and men, as well as whom you could love in a truly free country. So truth was again spoken from the streets on up to the marbled towers by talents such as Gloria Steinem. And one admittedly deranged but riotous woman, Valerie Solanas, wrote the *SCUM Manifesto* (referring to the Society for Cutting Up Men).[2] You could only find the book in boho bookstores, but the message would soon ripple across a nation.

A lot of these kids were crazy. A lot were just high as kites. But they were right to take to the streets and then to the barricades in defiance of a government. Right to question why a nation had tossed overboard its Christian ideals on the flimsy pretext that communism was somehow taking over the world and had to be halted on a tiny strip of land that had resisted every foreign invader for centuries. Right to recognize that the people in government cared little for democratic liberties but quite a lot about feeding bodies into a war machine.

It was a war machine President Dwight Eisenhower had famously warned against to no avail:

> This conjunction of an immense military establishment and a large arms industry is new in the American experience....We

recognize the imperative need for this development. Yet we must not fail to comprehend its grave implications.…[W]e must guard against the acquisition of unwarranted influence, whether sought or unsought, by the military–industrial complex. The potential for the disastrous rise of misplaced power exists and will persist. We must never let the weight of this combination endanger our liberties or democratic processes.[3]

Ike's message was lost, though. Lost on the McNamaras and Bundys and Kennedys who became the recognizable face of an emerging American Warfare State. A face that would only grow more grotesque as it became the modern elite state of today.

An elite state now as dismissive to our founding principles as those 1960s reformers had been. There is the strangest juxtaposition, then, in those non-Christian reformers challenging the non-Christians who'd gained powerful control over a predominantly Christian country. In the end, though, those young reformers didn't actually succeed in bringing the elite state down, did they?

They sidetracked it at best, while everyone regrouped. Some—heck, *many*—of those reformers were soon signing on with the elite state machinery, lured by the expectation of sweet lucre. And the elite state was soon back to breeding like rabbits in a Miracle-Gro bramble of agencies, commissions, and endless bureaus fully insulated from the electorate, but wielding intense power.

Now this elite state behemoth has grown so powerful that absent a dunk tank filled with weed killer, they will continue to swallow up our precious individual liberties and all vestiges of our proud Christian heritage, leaving us in a limbo of uncivilization.

I found this term "uncivilization" in Peter Savodnik's March 2022 treatise on Substack titled "The Dawn of Uncivilization" and felt it crisply captured the cresting and collapsing of the American dream in the post-1960s, over three periods.

- **Period of Ascendance:** This included the nineties, the American hyperpower, NATO expansion, EU expansion, China and India embracing the market, the American economic boom, globalization, and the rise of the internet. It ended September 11, 2001.

- **Period of Hard Truths:** This was marked by a cavalcade of failures. Abroad there were missing weapons of mass destruction, the endlessness of Afghanistan, the pointlessness of Iraq. At home we had Hurricane Katrina, the housing crisis, the fall of Lehman Brothers, and the bailing out by our elites not of the little guys but of the giants, those deemed too big to fail. This period also saw the election of Barack Obama, which was historic and exciting, but he took for granted that there was nothing to do but manage the decline.

- **Period of Resignation:** Now came a growing realization that all these disasters were symptomatic of a deeper rot, and there didn't appear to be any way out. The malaise Jimmy Carter had prematurely diagnosed was now very real. A cynical resignation set in.[4]

Donald Trump saw what was happening—more clearly than any of the career politicians. He ran for office calling out the elite state, calling the operators what they were—grifters, con artists, and deeply corrupt parasites sucking the life from a country. By 2016 they were already decades into a long campaign to take a country down and enrich themselves in doing it. And they were not about to let anyone—especially not a flamboyant playboy from New York—spoil all their fun. They instantly mobilized against him. They threw every bunker-buster bomb in their mighty arsenal at him. He took hit after hit. And though he had been spot-on in his diagnosis of the elite state problem, his follow-through skills were sketchy at best. And soon the swamp he'd come to drain looked even swampier than before he'd come. After four years of Trump's histrionics and special brand of crazy, the nation was ready to elect anyone with a pulse who was not named Trump. They got just barely that.

Now we wonder what will come next, what the period ahead will be.

I believe it can be a Period of Communities Rising—and by that I mean diverse local communities working together to raise up individual liberties in neighborhoods we know, then taking this Christian presence into nearby communities and raising them with people there to fix local problems in a local way. Then they'd raise them again through the state and fix the problems there in consonance with the values of the state and ultimately go all the way to the national level by rising up like Davids punching above our weight at the mighty behemoth, counterpunching with Christian compassion and fortitude.

Yes, taking us from our own neighborhoods on out to the big American avenue in direct repudiation of the elite state and their war machine.

CRANKING UP THE WAR MACHINE FOR PRINCIPLE AND PROFIT

It would be a bit simpleminded to call the elite state a monolith war machine. While it is that to a degree, it is also populated by idealistic crusaders who want to turn as many countries as they can into liberal democracies (as they somehow still imagine America to be). They seek to spread these values far and wide:

- Protecting human rights from being violated by authoritarian states

- Building McDonald's everywhere so the world is one big Happy Meal

- Fostering international peace at any price

It sure sounds good, and a form of these values reigned as the official "conventional wisdom" in Washington for decades. So two weeks before invading Iraq in 2003, President Bush announced:

> The current Iraqi regime has shown the power of tyranny to spread discord and violence in the Middle East. A liberated Iraq can show the power of freedom to transform that vital region, by bringing hope and progress into the lives of millions. America's interests in security, and America's belief in liberty, both lead in the same direction: to a free and peaceful Iraq.[5]

But almost predictably, Iraq turned into a fiasco. Any sophomore political science major could have explained why.

Global powers can only remain that way if they keep a watchful eye on the balance of power. It has always been so. These powers, however strong, as the Romans learned when they met the Huns, need to keep it real. That is, they need to act within the dictates of realism on the ground. Throwing around a big, shiny, airbrushed vision of liberal hegemony is more of an idealist's dream and seldom appreciated in the destinations it's thrown to. And it inevitably leads to longer wars that increase the levels of conflict, aggravating authoritarians to the point of them exporting more terrorism, rarely producing the peace that was initially sought.

Understanding why this happens is key. It can be neatly summarized in a formula that the great diplomats of old, back when talent was attracted to government, truly understood: *nationalism and realism usually eclipse liberalism and idealism.*

Nonetheless, our current foreign policy community was set in their thinking. They felt certain that a global sprinkling of liberal values would (a) keep the United States secure, (b) be easily accomplished, and (c) have the added virtue of being personally lucrative. So there was a virtuous circle of self-validation going on, at least in their own minds.

To convince everyday Americans to support this ambitious agenda, they trumped up the global dangers we faced, they overstated the benefits their "global sprinkling" could achieve, and they camouflaged the actual costs of their programs.

Not all the elite-state insiders were consciously seeking to build up their own bank accounts at the nation's expense. Many of them were dedicated public servants who believed that a dominant America is good for the world. But the impact of their actions was the same either way.

To wit, on the watch of Presidents Bush and Obama the elite state sowed death and destruction across three continents. The United States was at war for three out of every four years since 1989 across eight different costly conflicts. If the goal was an *idealistic* spreading of *liberalism's* goodness, then it mostly lost out to the *realistic* drive of other countries to hang on to their own *nationalist* pride and circumstance.

Idealism is wonderful. And hats off to the many big-hearted people swathing their Apple laptops with stickers screaming "End the Wars and

Tax the Rich." They're dreamers, not such a bad thing. But I'd phrase it differently: "End the Rich, and Tax the Wars." Because that kind of realism just might work.

WHY HAS THE WAR MACHINE CONTINUED TO CHURN ON?

With so many setbacks since World War II—that is, with nearly every extended war since then ending badly—how does the Pentagon manage to soldier on?

Partly by masking the deadliness of its actions. Since 1991, active-duty troops in the US Army drew down to 487,000 from 711,000. But the army actually grew in size. Some 1,000 private companies stepped in to handle everything from comms systems and base maintenance to soldier trainings, vehicle transport, war-games simulations, and yes, pulling the trigger.[6]

By hiring these private militaries, many of them off the books, the elite state has been able to mask the true cost of all the wars they're waging. They couldn't forever hide the instability and destruction they left around the globe, though.

Donald Trump understood that liberal hegemony was an abject failure, and he sought to reverse its course. He had plans for it. But then, not far into his presidency, the global balance of power began shifting precipitously for the first time since the 1990s. A newly militant China and an expansionist Russia put "Great Powers" politics back in play.

We'll circle back around to this. But first, for all this talk about our exporting US values globally, the harsh truth is we've been mostly exporting the exact opposite.

HOW DOES A MORAL NATION "DISAPPEAR" PEOPLE?

After 9/11, Vice President Dick Cheney told us the nation went to a "war footing."[7] Historian Naomi Wolf was listening to this and recalled that in 1933, when the German parliament building was attacked and set ablaze just weeks after Hitler was sworn in, Germany went into a *kriegsfusz*, or "war footing."[8] Then, when Attorney General John Ashcroft suspected "sleeper cells" of enemies plotting against Americans,[9] Wolf noticed that the term *sleeper cells* dates to Stalin's Russia, where propagandists labeled them agents of America out to infiltrate Soviet society. Of these echoes, Wolf concluded:

> These echoes are worth noticing—but are not ultimately that important. What *is* important are the structural echoes you will see: the way dictators take over democracies or crush prodemocracy uprisings by invoking emergency decrees to close down civil liberties, creating military tribunals, and criminalizing dissent.
>
> Those echoes are important.[10]

They are important because since 9/11, our US Constitution has been torn up again and again. In the name of fighting terror, the Fifth Amendment was torn up, with hundreds of people deprived of life, liberty, and property without due process of law.

The Sixth Amendment has also been torn up, with hundreds of people not allowed a speedy trial by an impartial jury, not informed of the nature and cause of the accusations against them, not allowed to confront the witnesses against them, not assigned legal counsel.

In place of these habeas corpus protections the United States has built secret prisons reminiscent of those run by wicked dictators. And the thing about these secret prisons—there is always mission creep. First a government fills them with evil terrorists and the people say, "They had it coming." Then with dangerous radicals, and the people say, "There must be a reason." Then with those considered criminals, and the people say, "That could be me."

Being secret, these prisons get a zero on the accountability scale. Poor treatment of prisoners gives way to torture—on the belief that it's more effective. Sometimes it is, sometimes not, but a line is crossed either way—a big red line separating the good guys from the bad guys.

In time, the secret prison system expands. The party in power decides to disappear the malcontents causing them headaches, from alien terrorists at first to domestic political opponents, peace activists, journalists about to expose classified information, and clergy speaking up out of conscience to whistleblowing civil servants. And when the people see this happening, they think twice about speaking out for fear of the consequences.

These "disappearings" become the face of the nation, one of our chief exports in the eyes of the world. A shameful business.

At one point the Guantanamo Bay prison held eight hundred detainees. As best we know, after twenty years, forty-one are still there—waiting to be charged, waiting for trial, waiting to be transferred somewhere, but waiting, indefinitely.[11]

The impulse after 9/11 to make somebody pay was understandable. We all felt it. But when enemy combatants were captured, we should have put them on trial in an orderly way. Our president should not have issued a military order granting his office unilateral authority to arrest any non-US citizen deemed to be an enemy combatant.[12]

If we have enemy combatants in prison and can't show just cause for holding them, then we shouldn't hold them. Due process matters. When we toss that process out the window, we are not making our nation stronger but weaker. We are not sending signals of strength to our adversaries but signals of hate to their families, who do not forget.

We were born a principled nation, and when we stop being a principled nation, we will be a nation no more. We will be something very different.

New leadership must wipe clean this legacy of disappearing people—from aliens netted after 9/11 to citizens in our neighborhoods now being netted.

New leadership can enhance our national security by rededicating to America's core values—making them more attractive to people around the world, yes, but also to people here at home.

LEFT OUT OF THE UKRAINE NARRATIVE— EVERYTHING THAT MATTERS

Yellow-and-blue flags going up on bridges; the media filled with images of a brutal invasion of a sovereign nation; a Formula 1 racing team firing their Russian driver; the Paralympic Games banning Russians from participating; bombast turning to fury and then heartache as the civilian death toll mounts; a Russian restaurant in Washington bashed in; a former US ambassador to Russia tweeting, "There are no more 'innocent' 'neutral' Russians anymore";[13] St. Sophia's Orthodox Church having red paint splattered on its front doors; President Biden saying Putin "could not remain in power"[14]—it was a narrative a scriptwriter could have ginned up for a made-for-TV movie. But there was a lot being left out of the popular response.

Left unsaid was how Ukrainian troops had attacked their own population in Donbas prior to the Russian invasion. These attacks were not widely reported but were confirmed by multiple sources, including the Organization for Security and Cooperation in Europe—a neutral watchdog.[15] Some fourteen thousand deaths were counted as the Ukrainian government shelled the pro-Russian people in the Donbas provinces—shelled their own people with weapons provided by the US military.[16]

Left unsaid was Ukrainian president Volodymyr Zelensky's trip to Munich in February 2022 to ask world leaders for nuclear weapons to protect Ukraine from Russia.[17] Why was Zelensky asking for the keys to a nuclear war, putting his people in such peril? Because he'd rather that than honor the agreement his country had signed to end Kyiv's shelling of citizens in the country's Donbas region.[18]

Left unsaid was how the United States had once promised Ukraine that we'd come to their aid if needed. Back in 1994, President Clinton, along with the Ukrainian and Russian presidents, signed the Budapest Memorandum, which stated that the United States would seek UN Security action to aid Ukraine if they agreed to give up their nuclear weapons, which they did.[19]

Then again in 2009, the nations confirmed their commitment to the agreement.

But from Clinton on through Biden, the US commitment to that agreement was always squiggly (bringing to mind Henry Kissinger's old quip—the only thing worse than being an enemy of the United States is being a friend).[20]

For three decades we've been expanding NATO eastward from Germany and eventually, it was always assumed, to Ukraine itself. Democrats and Republicans both insisted that Ukrainian vital interests were also American vital interests, meaning Ukraine would soon be entering NATO.

Putin may well be an egomaniac and a first-rate tyrant, but he is nobody's fool. He could see NATO's forces encircling him, and he decided to free Russia, starting with a region of Ukraine that wanted to break away and repair to Russia anyway.

Left unsaid was how by 2014, Ukraine had become a cesspool of corruption with its own oligarchs ripping off the nation so thoroughly that its GDP shrank a full 33 percent, or about *$600 billion*. But Washington didn't care—they weren't about to let Ukraine swing toward Russia, no matter what the Ukrainian people wanted.[21]

So the Obama administration orchestrated a violent coup in Ukraine in February 2014, overthrowing Ukraine's democratically elected president Yanukovych for the sole reason that he had pro-Russia sympathies. Then the United States and the West handed over $15 billion to Ukraine's corrupt leaders, effectively turning Ukraine into a ward of Washington. This too was not lost on Moscow.[22]

Left unsaid was then vice president Biden's role in fomenting the conflict in Ukraine. As summarized by former National Security Advisor Michael T. Flynn:

> This "invasion" was totally avoidable....There were gross violations of previous agreements due to incompetence, arrogance and ignorance that got us to this point....[W]e continue to demonize Russia—reminiscent of the fake Russia-collusion hysteria we now know was perpetrated against the Trump administration by elements of the Clinton campaign and the Obama administration.... Putin calculated this strategic, historic and geographic play and made the decision to move....[T]here will never be justification for this invasion or any other form of invasion. However, never forget that war results when diplomacy fails.[23]

Left unsaid was how even before the Russian invasion, then vice president Biden had been meddling in Ukraine on behalf of his son—meddling in still-unknown ways in the kleptocracy known as Ukraine.

Then after the invasion, President Biden ordered over one hundred thousand US troops to NATO countries and sent package after package of economic and military assistance.[24] That aid, however heartfelt in view of the horrific images coming out of Ukraine, could only prod Putin into escalating. Potentially seriously escalating.

Sounding the right note was Congressman Mike McCaul of Texas, ranking member on the House Foreign Affairs Committee, who visited the Poland-Ukraine frontier. He emphasized the need to help Ukraine but also to recognize the risks considering all the weapons Putin has at his disposal—nuclear, chemical, biological, new-generation bombs.

> We don't want a miscalculation or an escalation that will put us into a world war….I would say also these short-range tactical nukes that Putin—Russia has many more of them than we do. If he gets pushed into a corner like a scorpion, and he's in a desperate situation, he could very well sting with a short-range tactical nuke, which would really wake up the eyes of the world. I can't see the world just standing back and allowing that to happen without further involvement.[25]

Left unsaid was how the Biden administration's energy policies drove oil over $100 a barrel, not only hurting US consumers but also directly funding Putin's war machine. Higher oil prices mean about $800 million a day in income to Russia—that will support a lot of weaponry.

Not only is the West funding Putin's invasion, but we've made it clear through our policies that we don't care about energy independence. Drilling? Don't need it. Pipelines? Don't need them. Our progressive faith in clean energy will save the planet, just you wait and see! Right. When Putin stops laughing at this, he knows that idiot Western leaders have handed him a blackmail weapon (his flow of oil), and he'll use that to keep waging war until the United States stops trying to encroach on his country.

As for seeing that idiocy in action, how's this: the United States has loads of liquified natural gas (LNG) exports it could send to needy countries in Europe, offsetting their shortages and helping them decouple from Russian oil. Biden says he wants to help Europe with these energy shortages, but he's also made it nearly impossible for US producers to build a pipeline or LNG port.

This could be a big win for US energy producers and for Europeans who've also been foolish about energy independence. But it is all held up by the biggest blackmailer of all—the environmental extremists.

If Russia's oil exports were truly shut off, that would shut down their war-making in a Moscow minute. But Biden's interests lie elsewhere. Specifically, they lie in actively self-flagellating himself at the altar of environmental extremism with its first maxim: as long as we're still using oil, it cannot be US oil.

How do we know this is true? Here's a test:

Did the Biden administration spend weeks in 2022 (a) helping US oil companies drill, (b) trying to buy oil from the mad mullahs of Iran, or (c) trying to buy oil from the tyrant crushing Venezuela?

I think you know it was b and c.[26]

With so much left unsaid in the breathless media accounts of the invasion, some things were definitely *not* left unsaid.

Definitely not left unsaid was President Biden's insistence that Putin "cannot remain in power."[27] This from the leader of a nation that has invaded more countries and deposed more "opponents" than any other in the last three decades. Was this a threat of global nuclear war, or just the cymbal-banging monkey let loose from clown car number three?

World observers mostly went with the clown car explanation, since so little policy coherence had come from the Oval in a while, much less a presidential sentence containing both a subject and predicate.

None of this "left unsaid, not left unsaid" business is meant to somehow equate decades of US foreign policy adventurism with the brutal Russian regime. The American war machine has never bombed maternity hospitals or killed journalists as a matter of strategy. Anyone saying we are no different from them has lost the plot.

At the same time, US foreign policy no longer makes the world a safer place. If anything, just the opposite. Our nation-building has failed in principle and execution from Iraq to Afghanistan. The world sure looks more despotic now, and there is also greater cooperation among those despots to counter the drumbeat of "regime change" heard across Chesapeake Bay.

With America's continued warlike posture, with our active efforts to encroach toward Russian territory with NATO-based weapons of war, how is Russia supposed to feel? Reversing the equation, how would we feel if Russia formed a military alliance with Canada? If they built Russian military bases stocked with their Kh-101 cruise missiles just across the way from Niagara Falls, New York, or Kettle Falls, Washington?

We know how we would feel, how we'd react. President Kennedy took us within minutes of nuclear war in 1962 when Russia formed the exact same military alliance with Cuba. Fewer among us know that Soviet leader Nikita Khrushchev was responding in kind to the offensive missiles the United States had placed in Turkey, on the Soviet border. Fewer of us know this part of the story because Kennedy never owned up to this US aggression. He didn't want to look weak.

At his worst, Kennedy will never be compared to Biden at his best. But in fairness, Biden could have listened to his elite-state advisers just itching to send US troops and material into Kyiv, some even salivating over the chance to "whip the Soviet bear" in its weakened state. Instead, Biden has exercised restraint (at least through the summer of 2022). It could not be easy for him. Even with the backstory that puts the Russian invasion into perspective, it is hard to sit on your hands witnessing Putin do evil. That decision will surely be the hardest this president makes. For all his missteps in the march to war, Biden has exercised proper restraint when it mattered most.

AMERICA CAN ONLY WIN THE "GREAT POWERS" STRUGGLE ONE WAY

For all our shortcomings as a fortress of liberty in an often brutal world, for all the damage done to America's global standing by an elite state who would be our masters, for all the sleaze and corruption that has seeped up through every crack in the cement foundations of Washington, our American ideal remains the high ground in a world of unending territorial struggles, and we must continue to stand for the first principles of liberty—what my friend Stan Evans called our just interests: "American foreign policy must be judged by this criterion: does it serve the just interests of the United States?"[28]

So what are those just interests? What are those things worth fighting for?

Surely our liberty here at home is worth fighting for—wherever the threats to it originate. But *liberty* is today defined in more ways than a good wine. "Individual liberty" ought to be the thing, then. The idea that a just nation must treat each individual with respect. Not as members of a group or based on the zip code they live in or their skin color, for that is not respect; that becomes identity politics faster than wine goes sour. That leads to the suppression of one group over another. That cannot advance liberty but instead return us to a tribal past where war fighting was taught in schools because it was a survival skill.

America's great achievement has been to move beyond old tribal rivalries to the individual's just needs—*however imperfect our execution.* Americans are less constrained by the circumstances of our birth or the sins of our fathers than any nation before us—*and we still have far to go.* That is why this new progressive impulse to resegregate America (not the words they use, just the outcome) along with any elite state's nation-building ideologies must both be rejected in full.

We need to continue to strive toward liberty's high ground, not only for ourselves but also for the world. When we execute on this faithfully at home, our goodness naturally spreads to the world.

For ultimately there is only one way America wins the "Great Powers" struggle and retains the high ground. That is by rededicating ourselves to the once-radical precepts of our founding—that all men and women be treated as equals because we are all created in the image of God.

ONLY LIBERTY AT HOME CAN BRING LIBERTY ABROAD

Because the invasion of Ukraine grabbed the world's attention, it's easy to forget that a couple of weeks earlier, the worst winter Olympics ever opened. Not only was it held in foul-aired Beijing with COVID thinning the rosters of talented athletes, but that is when Xi Jinping and Vladimir Putin chose to declare war on the West. The two men issued a joint statement that (a) criticized America in bitter terms and (b) laid out plans to build geopolitical bulwarks against the West.

Some called this the opening salvo in a new Cold War. It was certainly a throwback to Cold War levels of insecurity. In the view of Matt Pottinger, who architected President Trump's national security strategy:

> "[I]t's really hard to avoid the conclusion that these developments reflect a new cold war that Xi Jinping and Vladimir Putin have initiated against the West" with Ukraine being the "hot opening salvo in a cold war pitting Washington and its allies against a

fragile but increasingly powerful bloc of dictatorships" and that "[w]e would be remiss not to learn lessons from the original Cold War, not least because we won."[29]

Though Pottinger may disagree, the lessons that are most valuable to learn involve the kinds of alliances we have with other nations. Strengthening NATO was seen as a good thing for ensuring peace. But in building NATO up to thirty nations, we also provoked Russia and China, since the West's alliances grew far stronger than the East's. How, then, to find a balance with which global powers can live?

We can continue to strengthen our ties through talks such as the Quadrilateral Security Dialogue, involving Australia, India, and Japan.[30] These talks begin the morning with security covenants, sure enough. But they carry into the afternoon with a focus on commercial supply chains, making them more resilient, bringing them home when possible, protecting them from Chinese or Russian meddling. These kinds of talks with our allies matter.

There's also the new Indo-Pacific Economic Framework—an opportunity to hammer out technology standards for e-commerce, protect cross-border data flows, and expand 5G and artificial intelligence in smart, mutually beneficial ways.[31]

Ensuring the usefulness of alliances like these is a good use of Pentagon dollars—because the stronger our alliances, the safer the whole world.

With these alliances forming a centerpiece of US foreign policy dedicated to our just interests, how big does the Pentagon's budget need to be?

Not big at all, if this were the Pentagon's sole remit. But of course it is not. The great bulk of the Pentagon's budget should truly be money that, in retrospect, we never needed to spend. That is, money spent on deterrence and being ready should a nation try to attack us—as inevitably one will someday.

During the Cold War, America spent about 7 percent of our GDP on defense. That figure fell to 2.9 percent thanks to the "peace dividend" of the Soviet Union's collapse. The war on terror took the cost back above 4 percent by 2008 and has since settled down to 3 percent of the GDP. Now the Pentagon's number crunchers are arguing for bumping that defense spending back up to 4 percent—adding another $200 billion a year to the budget to address China's and Russia's military ambitions beyond their own borders.[32]

The Pentagon argues that we need to spend all this because as a nation we have since World War II *wanted* to play only away games. That is, we would rather fight wars on foreign soil than fight them here. We would rather project American firepower into distant seas than witness attacks on our own shores. We would rather rely on a "third offset" strategy that minimizes US soldiers' casualties and maximizes new war-fighting technologies. All goals Americans have long supported—but expensive goals.

How expensive these goals need to add up to—that's the tough question. When you start adding it all up in an honest accounting, you begin to have questions.

First there is the Defense Department's budget, which in 2022 was $728 billion.[33] Let's hold the thought that this figure is larger than the combined defense spending of China, Saudi Arabia, India, France, Russia, the UK, and Germany, for it is only the first number in a long tally.

There's also the Department of Veterans Affairs. Chronically poorly managed, the VA is nonetheless important, and it adds another $301 billion.[34]

America's nuclear weapons are maintained by the Department of Energy, adding another $20 billion.[35]

Then there's the intelligence community. Nobody has any idea how much the eighteen organizations under the aegis of the director of national intelligence actually spend. So much of that spending is classified, off the books, dark. But they claim it's $62 billion, so let's go with that for our purposes here.

It would be inaccurate to leave out the Department of Homeland Security and the FBI, especially since they keep expanding their job descriptions, so that adds $62 billion and $10 billion respectively.[36]

Adding it all up, America's true total spending on national security in 2022 came in at a cool $1.2 trillion. So is this money well spent?

In a time when the government seems to throw a trillion dollars at every financial problem it first created, that $1.2 trillion for our national security may not look out of line. But only because we've lost all perspective.

Let's reset it with a trip down memory lane.

I can still remember liberals going ballistic when, in the middle of a

Cold War military buildup, President Reagan proposed a defense budget of $177 billion.[37]

Now that budget is almost 1,000 percent larger, even though inflation has only risen 300 percent in the same period. And this spending is justified, we're told, for the support of our treaty obligations with fifty-one nations; our troop deployments at some eight hundred military bases in seventy countries; our black operations in unexpected places like in Kosovo and Libya; our humanitarian operations in places like Fukushima, Haiti, and Nigeria; our ensuring the shipping lanes in the Straits of Hormuz and Malacca; as well as our readiness to respond to a Russian attack on a NATO ally, a Chinese invasion of Taiwan, a North Korean attack on its southern neighbor, or Iranian mischief in the Middle East.

All of this has been justified, but not all of it is in our "just interest" going forward.

America has never been good at fashioning a national strategy and keeping to it—that's one of the downsides of political parties designed to fight, not lead. But a true leader would make a persuasive argument for cutting the defense budget *without* creating a security vacuum that Russia, China, or Iran could fill.

That argument would begin by lightening our global footprint now that boots on the ground have been shown to matter little to modern warfare. We could pull back from overseas bases, taking our bases down to four hundred bases in thirty-five countries for starters. This "cutting in half" would not by design pave the way for Chinese or Russian aggression. Instead, it would endear many countries now happy to have fewer foreign boots on their soil.

That argument would continue by turning everything we can from a military to an economic footing; that is, to R&D, which we will consider next.

CHAPTER 21

WINNING THE GLOBAL POWER STRUGGLE WITH RESEARCH AND DEVELOPMENT

AMERICA AND OUR Western allies hold most of the cards against China, Russia, Iran, and their ring of failed states. If we came to an economic Cold War, the West's dominance in critical technologies would give us a full house, to China's three of a kind with their vast factory floors and budding tech prowess, and Russia's pair of threes with their oil and wheat, each replaceable.

Chinese president Xi Jinping is fond of boasting "the East is rising; the West is declining."[1] Sure enough, China could surpass the United States as the world's largest economy by 2033.[2] They're trying to. But their own elite-state authoritarianism is anathema to so many, and they are regularly spurned by free countries, so China's rise to predominance may be that thing that's always coming but never arriving.

And it's mostly because of research and development (R&D).

The West spends much more on R&D than the East. China and Russia spent $570 billion on R&D in 2019, while the United States and our allies spent $1.5 trillion—three times as much.[3] Take a look at this International Monetary Fund analysis.

In the following graph, you can see that the East's GDP is about $20 trillion while the West's approaches $55 trillion. Spending on R&D is just as lopsided. The East is thought to have 2.5 million people engaged in pure research; the West has 5.2 million.[4] The resulting breakthroughs in finance, technology, and knowledge give us the economic advantage— an advantage that can do more of the heavy lifting in ensuring global security, with our military doing less. It is a better formula for a world at peace.

WESTERN ADVANTAGE IN R&D SPENDING

The U.S. and its democratic, market-based allies in Europe and Asia together generate far more economic output and spend much more on research and development than China, Russia and countries aligned with them.

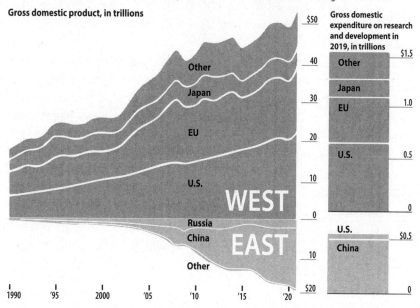

Gross domestic product, in trillions

Gross domestic expenditure on research and development in 2019, in trillions

Note: GDP converted from local currency to dollars at market exchange rates. Research and development spending is for 2019, converted from local currency to dollars at purchasing power parity.
Sources: IMF (GDP); OECD (expenditure on R&D)

"BUY AMERICAN" IS NOT A CHEAP SLOGAN

President Trump made the effort. He challenged thirty years of foreign policy that put the world's interests before our own. He called it "America First," and people across the country recognized that Trump was onto something. Our foreign policy bureaucracy saw it as well, saw how their cushy sinecures were in jeopardy—which is why they set out immediately to subterfuge his every move.

Trump openly questioned the value of NATO when most of its member nations are free-riding on America's protection. He called the Iran nuclear deal a farce, and we soon saw as much. He called the North American Free Trade Agreement a disaster that had led to "*the theft of American jobs*," which many economists believe is true.[5] He condemned our nation-building efforts in Iraq, Afghanistan, and beyond. Why be "rebuilding other countries while weakening our own?" he asked.[6]

America is best served by strong alliances that help us win economically so we are positioned to win militarily if our just interests are ever threatened. So Trump's attacks on America's treaties and security commitments were a step too far.

That's what made them just right. Because in seeking to undo thirty years of damage caused by an overly ambitious belief in liberal hegemony, Trump couldn't just tiptoe up the problem. He needed to proceed full bludgeon ahead. If things got overheated, they could always be set aside to cool off.

Meantime, a point was made.

America would no longer be the linchpin of a liberal world order, the global sheriff. Instead, every new crisis that popped up would be assessed on a transactional basis to get the "best deal" for America and force our allies to share the burdens.

This, Trump believed, would make Americans stronger and more prosperous at home and less committed to overseas adventurism that can sour so easily.

American power would no longer be used to advance the elite state's interests around the world but instead focus on the just interests of the American people.

In stepping too far, Trump left his finest mark on the government. It is up to those who follow to continue this tough-minded protection of America's just interests.

CHAPTER 22

FAITH AND FREEDOM RISE TOGETHER IN OUR COMMUNITIES

THE ANCIENT PROPHET Isaiah wrote, "Those from among you shall rebuild the old waste places; you shall raise up the foundations of many generations; and you shall be called, the Repairer of the Breach, the Restorer of Paths in which to Dwell" (Isa. 58:12, MEV). But what if the people do not rise up? What could America soon be like if we go on letting the elite state wreak their corroding havoc? Here is what I fully expect to see.

Most noticeable is how little people talk to each other. Family gatherings, going out to restaurants, the drive out to the lake—they're different now. There's a sense that you're always being watched, listened in on. And forget interacting with people unknown to you for fear of accidentally saying or doing something that might lower your social credit score (which officially does not exist, mind you). Loose lips could cost you dearly. Trust is for fools.

The FBI's Disturbance Settling Protocols have turned the January 6 aftermath into regular occurrences in neighborhoods across the country. Jackbooted storm troopers leaping out of massive black tanks that roll in at sunrise, blowing through front doors with battering rams in their search for troublemakers. Neighbors just shuttering their windows to it, since little can be done.

There's also the FBI's Informant Network, thought to number in the low millions. It grew so large with the help of a simple app known as Disinfo. Don't like your neighbor? Suspect that he's engaging in unapproved activity? Just turn him in with a tap on the app.

Polling shows that only one in twenty people know what the Fourth Amendment is about. Unlawful searches and seizures are commonplace—especially for White people. Police carefully steer clear of apprehending anyone who might escalate a complaint to the White House Office of Racial Grievances and Reparations.

In related news, nightly murders in the Chicago area have tripled and now total nearly two thousand a year, with most of them in the very community Barack Obama had once so effectively organized.

A new statue just went up in Denver, inexplicably, honoring the fallen middle class, which enjoyed such a brief run. Economists figure 96 percent of the nation's wealth has been fairly evenly divvied up between elite-state financiers, tech bros, politicians, media and sports stars, and celebrity hangers-on.

After all the energy shocks of the 2020s (the Eastern Seaboard powerless for six weeks, twelve-dollars-a-gallon gas, and millions of electric cars stranded, to name a few), there was hope the government might try their hand at more sensible energy stewardship. They might reopen domestic drilling for oil until cleaner renewable energy sources can be found. But it hasn't happened.

There is a new lottery named the Mandatory Blackout Order (they're working on a better title), but the electricity shutdowns being experienced all across the country are now all the more exciting since folks never know when their neighborhood blackout order will come up.

Both the left-stream and right-stream media still exist, despite their cumulative audiences and ad revenues dropping to sub-basement levels. Still the nightly news farceurs get their sweetheart salaries, suggesting they're being secretly funded by *someone*.

After China brutally clear-cut all Southeast Asian competition to their factory floors, America began to bring some of that manufacturing back home, and jobs along with it. But the elite state didn't like how the numbers penciled out. All that renewable energy hardware, for instance, could still be sourced cheaper from "those terrible people in China," as they called it. Sure, the solar panels and wind turbines were junk quality, and their lifespan was only a few years. But the government kept paying full premiums for them, along with deep subsidies—so the profits couldn't be topped.

The term *uniparty* is now commonly used to describe the Republicans and Democrats who have actually begun to produce good theater—with the help of Hollywood's best. No tickets are yet being sold to their performances, but there are plans. With all the time spent fighting onstage, it's truly amazing these politicians find the time to ensure that the vast administrative state they watch over keeps humming along.

Of course, the bureaucracy needs little help. And not a day passes without thousands of new regulations spewing like toxic sludge into the Potomac River and beyond. Forget trying to get a steak at the Outback; cows have been fully exposed for the foul methane polluters they are. But entire menus of *perfectly healthy food* come steaming in from Wuhan and thereabouts. Curiously, the no-GMO-in-my-body crowd has been conspicuously silent.

The world has stopped believing in America. Entirely stopped believing. Nobody will lend another dime to "Rump Uncle Sam," as they call us. When the national debt passed $100 trillion, some experts tried to explain how much money this is ("place dollar bills end to end and they will reach Alpha Centauri" is a favorite). No amount of cranking the old printing presses can stop the devaluing of the dollar, and so inflation just keeps rising and stealing away more of every worker's paycheck.

It surprised no one when the US dollar was dethroned as the world's reserve currency, swapped out for a basket of currencies including the yuan, euro, dollar, yen, and riyal. Pundits called it a big win that the dollar was even included, it being the weakest of the five. But the world's capital markets weren't impressed.

The day the new "basket" was announced, commodity prices all shot up two to three times for those paying in dollars. Many thought the US government would default. Others knew that, technically, it had been in default for decades. The president declared a "state of emergency until otherwise lifted." A state of emergency clock kept popping up in different cities, counting the days until the lifting, only to be taken down before the FBI vans stormed in.

Nobody talks about small business anymore. Not so much from fear, but regarding relevance. Chances of succeeding in a home business or going solo in something you love are about the same as "a flea becoming a butterfly," as one CEO wisecracked. Small businesses simply don't stand a chance in the monopolist haven, as the United States is sometimes called. More people now work for the Small Business Administration in Washington than own small businesses.

The perpetual crisis at the southern border recently turned catawampus.

First the Feds said they would no longer control the border, since it was simply not doable. Counts from drones put the number of illegal border crossings at about thirty thousand a day during that period. Then, in a shock to local residents, the president issued an emergency order banning sales of firearms in Arizona, California, and Texas. What happened next caught everyone by surprise.

Apparently, some Americans began working with the smugglers to bring firearms up from Mexico. These Americans then, according to reports, "found secret locations from which they fired indiscriminately into swarms of border crossers." Local sheriffs tried, they said, but couldn't find these "desperados." The FBI sent armored tanks out on patrol, so far without success. Nobody knows how this border crisis twist will turn out.

Most people rent now. They rent everything from the movies they watch to the homes in which they live. Trillion-dollar private-equity firms have financialized just about everything in the dictionary. Everyone now knows the fancy word *financialization* and how it enabled a handful of people to turn the entire economy into a security to be traded, leveraged, rented, spoiled, and ultimately discarded.

For decades Americans had been warned about the coming rentier economy (which was common in the dark Middle Ages in Europe). But few seemed to truly understand the impact of letting a small group of people take complete ownership of the economy.

They didn't understand, anyway, until it cost $5,000 a month to rent a home in most areas, $12,000 average in pricier climes. Many have no choice but to move into newly built living platforms called vertical self-management centers. (Some say these "platforms" are modeled on those found in an old Spanish horror film by the same name, but for some reason, copies of the film can no longer be found.)

Folks are still having an average of 1.7 children, with seven in ten born out of wedlock. These kids know more about the Netflix lineup than their parents, whom they don't see much. Most go to public schools since charter schools have been de-chartered and defunded.

Parents have no say in their kids' curricula. If they dare to speak up at school board meetings, they are forcibly removed by private security forces (thought to be funded from the FBI's dark budget).

Parents don't ask what children are learning anymore because nobody really understands what it is. Math and science, everyone understood. But the new desegregation protocols that took over after critical race theory was laughed out of the classroom? Are they good or bad? Nobody knows; but they know the price of speaking out.

Oh, they did break up the Big Tech companies a few years back. They did it with the blessing of the tech industry, which helped craft the breakup plan. So not much has changed. The same few people now own more companies and have the same power over all our communications as before.

And so hate speech against freedom-loving Americans is algorithmically boosted for all to see. And political speech that disagrees with the powerful elite or might be interpreted as a Christian message is algorithmically silenced with brutal precision now. The banning has gotten so effective, the words disappear the moment they hit the screen. It's remarkable. The list of topics considered offensive or triggering or just plain unacceptable has grown so large, nobody really knows the true size of the unsayable words list.

Along with the censoring of religious speech, the only churches, synagogues, and places of worship that are allowed are those with government approval—similar to the Chinese model. And just as in China, Christians have gone underground and are meeting in homes, although there is constant worry that a neighbor will snitch on them and they will be "picked up." Rumors abound of Christians being sent to offshore work prisons and even tortured for their beliefs. But there's no confirmation of it in the media.

People are now voluntarily embedding computer chips beneath their skin to hold medical and financial records. But a number of federal agencies are suggesting that this practice should become law and that the records embedded also include social credit scores, criminal records, tax records, and identification papers.

There is a silver lining in all this.

Tens of millions no longer care. They realize that social media is an alternate reality where crazy people live. So they've just logged off. Especially the new generation—the so-called Gen Alpha. They've begun experimenting with face-to-face conversations with friends. They say it is "amazing."

Yes, this is how America could turn out on its current trajectory. A bit of this has been oversimplified, of course. And surely it's off-base here and there. But it could become all too real—if nothing is done.

AMERICA'S HISTORY OF FAITH AND FREEDOM

We've seen in these pages how you and I stand at a fulcrum in America's history, where the balance can easily be tipped and powerful elites could take us to a point of no return—unless we join in our communities and set about truly saving the nation that we still deeply treasure.

We've seen how a tiny group of selfish, egotistical tyrants were able to—for the first time in history—gain control over the government, business, and technology sectors and combine those power centers in a giant wrecking ball aimed at the individual liberties we had long cherished. And how "We, the people" cannot, must not, shrink back, cower, and allow them to further demolish our once "shining city on the hill."

This description of America dates all the way back to 1630, when the pilgrim John Winthrop spoke of a new land "as a city on a hill—the eyes of all people are upon us."[1] Winthrop was referring to Jesus speaking in Matthew 5:14–16:

> You are the light of the world. A city that is set on a hill cannot be hidden. Nor do they light a lamp and put it under a basket, but on a lampstand, and it gives light to all who are in the house. Let your light so shine before men, that they may see your good works and glorify your Father in heaven.

We know that even before the earlier Puritan pilgrims set foot in Plymouth seeking religious freedom, they authored the Mayflower Compact. In it they made clear their mission was "for the glory of God and the advancement of the Christian faith."[2]

In a prayer General George Washington wrote at the end of the Revolutionary War and sent out to all the governors of the newly freed states, he said:

I now make it my earnest prayer that God would have you...in His holy protection...would incline the hearts of the citizens to...a brotherly affection and love for one another, for their fellow citizens of the United States at large, and particularly for brethren who have served in the field.[3]

More than two hundred years after the arrival of the first Pilgrims, this American outpost of Christianity had become a true emblem to the world. So much so that the French statesman Alexis de Tocqueville, touring the country in 1831, wrote extensively on it in *Democracy in America*. You could call this America's first truly distinguished foreign review:

Upon my arrival in the United States, the religious aspect of the country was the first thing that struck my attention....In France I had almost always seen the spirit of religion and the spirit of freedom pursuing courses diametrically opposed to each other; but in America I found that they were intimately united, and that they reigned in common over the same country....

[T]hey brought with them into the New World a form of Christianity which I cannot better describe than by styling it a democratic and republican religion. This sect contributed pow-erfully to the establishment of a democracy and a republic, and from the earliest settlement of the emigrants politics and religion contracted an alliance which has never been dissolved....

[T]here is no country in the whole world in which the Christian religion retains a greater influence over the souls of men than in America; and there can be no greater proof of its utility...than that its influence is most powerfully felt over the most enlightened and free nation of the earth....

I am certain that they hold it to be indispensable to the main-tenance of republican institutions. This opinion is not peculiar to a class of citizens or to a party, but it belongs to the whole nation, and to every rank of society....The Americans com-bine the notions of Christianity and of liberty so intimately in their minds that it is impossible to make them conceive the one without the other.[4]

Even as America blossomed as a Christian nation welcoming the world to its shores, there were always subcurrents of subversion that needed to be resisted. President Woodrow Wilson would say this:

> The history of Liberty is a history of limitations of governmental power, not the increase of it. When we resist, therefore, the concentration of power, we are resisting the powers of death, because concentration of power is what always precedes the destruction of human liberties.
>
> A nation which does not remember what it was yesterday, does not know what it is today, nor what it is trying to do. We are trying to do a futile thing if we do not know where we came from or what we have been about.
>
> The Bible…is the one supreme source of revelation of the meaning of life, the nature of God and spiritual nature and needs of men. It is the only guide of life which really leads the spirit in the way of peace and salvation. America was born a Christian nation. America was born to exemplify that devotion to the elements of righteousness which are derived from the revelations of Holy Scripture.[5]

With the Bible in the nation's hand, the righteousness that President Wilson spoke of carried forward. This was accepted not only by Christians but by all who could appreciate America's heritage. Author and talk show host Rabbi Daniel Lapin explains it this way:

> I understand that I live…in a Christian nation, albeit one where I can follow my faith as long as it doesn't conflict with that nation's principles. The same option is open to all Americans, and will be available only as long as this nation's Christian roots are acknowledged and honored.…Without a vibrant and vital Christianity, America is doomed, and without America, the west is doomed. Which is why I, an Orthodox Jewish Rabbi, devoted to Jewish survival, the Torah, and Israel am so terrified of American Christianity caving in.…God help Jews if America ever becomes a post-Christian society! Just think of Europe![6]

Having fought in World War II against despotic threats to our Christian liberty, President John F. Kennedy recognized what the good rabbi would later talk about. In a speech that was written, but fatefully never delivered, Kennedy would have proclaimed to the world: "We in this country...are—by destiny rather than by choice—the watchmen on the walls of world freedom."[7]

Kennedy was echoing a Bible passage, that of Isaiah 62:6: "I have set watchmen upon your walls, O Jerusalem; they shall never hold their peace day or night. You who make mention of the LORD, do not keep silent."

For his part, and it was a great part, Martin Luther King Jr. added: "If you will protest courageously, and yet with dignity and Christian love, when the history books are written in future generations, the historians will have to pause and say, 'There lived a great people.'"[8]

From Winthrop through the Founders into our modern times, our greatest leaders have all turned to biblical passages for inspiration and guidance in moving the nation forward. Through to Ronald Reagan himself, who gallantly reminded us that we remained a shining city on a hill. But since the days of Reagan, America's uniquely Christian culture has been laid waste.

Perhaps no one has better summarized the current crisis we face than Christian historian David Barton:

> This modern hostility toward Christianity in America is unprecedented, but the general conflict is not new. Throughout history, those who hate God have joined forces with one another to oppose God, His son, and His people. The worldview conflict between the two sides is ancient, but the question of which side will succeed at any given time here on earth is determined by the people; if they preserve a love for God and His things, the secular anti-God forces will not prevail; but if those who love God become apathetic, lethargic, and uninvolved, the opposing forces will triumph—which is what is occurring in America today.[9]

So yes, we stand at the fulcrum in a time when so much has been lost. When you are lost, what is the best action you take? You retrace your steps. You look back to America's foundations and founding principles to help move the nation back to solid ground. You find words of encouragement and warning from those in the past to help us join together now to save our America.

God has placed each one of us in this time of history for a reason. Our vigilance in the fight to save freedom in America is going to define this generation in history. The battle is ours to win or lose.

You and I were born in God's timing, not our own, and His challenge to us now in this time is to save this land for freedom—or else witness a new dark age.

SEVERAL THINGS NEED TO HAPPEN IF WE ARE TO SUCCEED

First, we must stand firm for the principles that made America the remarkable country it has long been. No better exemplar of this was Frederick Douglass. Born a slave, he would become America's most famous abolitionist as well as an orator, publisher, and author. How much firmer could any of us stand than this man in his 1852 speech, "What to the Slave Is the Fourth of July?"

> [T]he Declaration of Independence is the ring-bolt to the chain of your nation's destiny; so, indeed, I regard it. The principles contained in that instrument are saving principles. Stand by those principles, be true to them on all occasions, in all places, against all foes, and at whatever cost.[10]

A century later, in his inaugural address as governor of California, Ronald Reagan would echo this idea:

> Perhaps [we] have lived too long with this miracle to properly be appreciative. Freedom is a fragile thing and it's never more than one generation away from extinction. It is not ours by way of inheritance; it must be fought for and defended constantly by each generation, for it comes only once to a people. And those in world history who have known freedom and then lost it have never known it again.

Reagan added a warning that is fitting for us today: "The deterioration of every government begins with the decay of the principle upon which it was founded."[11]

How important then that we as parents and grandparents and those concerned for our children's future stand as teachers—telling a new generation these histories and truths about God, America, and liberty. How important that we follow in the steps of Deuteronomy, also known as the *Shema* in Jewish culture:

> Hear, O Israel: the LORD our God, the LORD is one! You shall love the LORD your God with all your heart, with all your soul, and with all your strength. And these words which I command you today shall be in your heart. You shall teach them diligently to your children, and shall talk of them when you sit in your house, when you walk by the way, when you lie down, and when you rise up.
>
> —DEUTERONOMY 6:4–7

It is our responsibility to teach the next generation. We can't outsource this job to schools, churches, television, or even books. We must do it ourselves.

It's Time to Speak Truth and Stop Compromising

Oh yes, it is so much easier to ignore the lies and deceits swirling through our culture. After forty years of fighting these battles and living these battles, I sometimes want to roll over and clamp a pillow over my head to block it all out. It can be hard to stay engaged—so very, very hard. But we cannot give an inch if we want to win. We cannot give in to the lies or the elite-state con or any of the malefactors or false idols. As the Bible teaches:

> But this is what you must do: tell the truth to each other.
> —ZECHARIAH 8:16, NLT

Rod Dreher's book *Live Not by Lies* encourages us to emulate Russian Aleksandr Solzhenitsyn, who refused to publicly say things he knew to be untrue. Solzhenitsyn paid a horrific price for his courage, spending much of his life in Soviet gulags, or prison camps. Dreher says this: "Too many of us are sleeping through the erosion of our freedoms, assuming that totalitarianism can't happen in America."[12]

There can be no more compromising, as Owen Strachan, PhD, says:

> Christians have spent too much time in the last ten to twenty years trying to appease the world and show them we are not "that" type of Christian. We should always be seeking to bear the fruits of the spirit (Galatians 5:22–23). We should always be seeking to speak truth in love, but we must also differentiate truth from lies. We must destroy woke ideological speculations by operating through intellectual, theological, and spiritual missions....
>
> We need to recognize that wokeness is a system of intellectual exploitation and we need an effective response to this exploitation....We must show wokeness for what it is and we cannot try to execute a peace treaty with the world.[13]

In this time, we must boldly raise the Christian banner with its imprint of faith and freedom that can return a modern country to its ever-guiding founding principles.

UNITY BASED ON COMMON GROUND AND MISSION

This is all about getting back to basics—to America's core beliefs and principles. And that begins simply enough by *not* sweating the small stuff, such as disagreements we have between friends. After forty years in public advocacy, my greatest frustration has often been with the internecine warfare I've experienced among alleged allies. Secular conservatives often don't like Christian conservatives. Libertarians the same.

I remember in the 1980s how Republicans looked down on the new activists flooding into politics because of the Moral Majority. A few decades later, the social conservatives that flooded in during the 1980s were uncomfortable with the Tea Party activists, whom they felt only cared about taxes. Another decade later, we hear disparaging comments about MAGA activists now flooding in.

None of us has it all right. I'm sure you'll find ideas in this book you don't personally like. But if you leave with only one idea, let it be this: *in order to succeed, we have to all work together and stop sweating the small differences.*

America is a multitude of people, cultures, races, and backgrounds. And we all need to lock arms if we are going to stop the progressive elite mob at the top that's eager to sacrifice America's sustaining values on the altar of moneygrubbing.

Our freedoms as we know them have always been a threat to powerful people with evil intent. Best-selling author of *Change Your World* John Maxwell speaks about the importance of being mission conscious:

> As Americans, we admire the people who founded our nation. We respect their courage, commitment, and sacrifice. We also admire their sense of vision and mission. They knew they were fighting for freedom and the future of a country that had the potential to give its people great opportunities. There is immense power in a sense of mission. Author W. Clement Stone stated, "When you discover your mission, you will feel its demand. It will fill you with enthusiasm and a burning desire to get to work on it." That sense of desire—and direction—is as indispensable for a team to be successful as it is for any individual.[14]

As we discussed in the first chapter, the globalists and progressives have sought to cause division among Americans in order to weaken and destroy America and then have it to themselves and their frankly evil plan. We saw how they used COVID as a cover story for dismantling what little community we still had left.

Yet we know we must gather.

One place we could always gather before COVID was church. Christians need to gather for communal worship, and COVID had devastating effects on the church. Researcher George Barna has predicted that approximately one-fifth of churches will never reopen after COVID.[15] One of the first steps, then, if you haven't already, is to return to church and worship in person with other believers.

This uniting is so important. Why do you think the elites dislike it so much?

In unity we have power. That is why the elite-controlled government came down so much harder on churches in some states (while allowing liquor stores, marijuana dispensaries, and casinos to remain open). They wanted to steal from us the hope and encouragement we'd gain when the country was most vulnerable.

When people are divided one from another and made to hate, made to be afraid and feel fear at their doorstep, they are easily controlled. That's why when Christians and freedom-loving Americans unite in a common cause, we can stand the strongest against these evil tyrants.

The words of Jesus are a sobering reminder in this regard: "And if a house is divided (split into factions and rebelling) against itself, that house will not be able to last" (Mark 3:25, AMPC).

America's early colonists realized the importance of uniting for a common goal and purpose. They set aside their differences—that's why they formed, with God's help, the United States of America. People from a variety of backgrounds all united to form something unique, where all citizens are seen as equals and given rights from their Creator—not from the government.

There is strength, the exchange of ideas, encouragement, and prayer for each other when we are united. But when we are separated, we are weakened and easily become fearful. In John 17:11, Jesus asked the Father to let unity be a defining mark of the church when He said, "Protect them…so that they may be one as we are one" (NIV).

THE BIGGEST HOLE IN THE ELITE STATE'S SCRIPT—HISPANIC AMERICANS

We've seen that the elite state's success is dependent on being able to divide and conquer, keeping Whites fighting Blacks, Browns fighting blues. Colors don't matter as long as enough people are kept angry and distracted and feeling deeply victimized at the end of the day. Then the elite state can hand these poor, victimized people over to the Democratic Party to be nursed back to health. It's what that party does best. But quite apparently, not every minority sees themselves as victims to be handled— especially Hispanic Americans.

This runs much deeper than Republican activists piling onto Jill Biden for calling Hispanics as unique as tacos.[16] Jill Biden clearly meant well, and the rest was cheap theater. This runs deeper. Hispanics are fleeing the Democratic Party for far bigger reasons.

Partly because today's Democratic Party is becoming such a White elitist assembly. As I write, a *New York Times*/Siena poll just came out giving Democrats an unheard of 21-point lead over Republicans among White college-educated voters.[17] But a *Wall Street Journal* poll found Hispanics favoring Republican candidates for Congress by 9 points.[18]

This after Obama won 71 percent of the Hispanic vote in 2012[19] and Biden won 59 percent in 2020.[20]

What accounts for this truly seismic shift among voting groups? There is no one reason, of course, and candidates matter greatly in these polling assessments. But some keen insights have come from David French, senior editor of *The Dispatch*:

> The Democratic Party has a huge "God gap," and that God gap is driving a wedge between its white and nonwhite voters....The most important religious divide isn't between right and left, but between left and left.[21]

The Left has become so scornful of Christianity that Hispanics and many others are saying, "*No, thank you; I do believe in God!*"

When you look deeper into this shift, as the Pew Research Center has, you find that 95 percent of White Republicans believe in God, but only 78 percent of White Democrats do. A substantial difference. Then look at non-White groups. They're the same in both parties—about 95 percent believe in God.[22] That's where the gap opens up.

Hispanic voters are inclined to attend church, pray frequently, and read the Bible. They believe their faith offers answers to questions about right and wrong, and that the Bible is the literal Word of God. When Democratic Party leaders heap scorn on traditional Christian values, they are dumping on these Hispanic voters. When leftist elites try to mobilize Hispanic voters by pushing the racial and ethnic hot buttons of identity politics, they run into individuals who are basically staring back and saying, "I believe in God first and foremost, I am an American second, and I care about my family and neighborhood far more than your attempts to tear apart our finest cultural traditions."

Nobody better exemplifies this shift than Mayra Flores. She entered a 2022 special election in Texas' 34th Congressional District and won as a Republican, becoming the first Mexican-born woman in Congress. Flores had voted for Barack Obama in 2008, but she grew disillusioned with Democrats and got behind Donald Trump.

Immediately following Flores' victory, the *New York Times* tried to explain how a Hispanic woman could win as a Republican, for surely their readers were shocked by such a thing. The writer painted a picture of life in her South Texas district:

> It's a place where law enforcement is revered....Churches are crowded on Sundays. A lot of small evangelical churches have opened up and are growing. You see American flags on the backs of cars or in front of houses and businesses.
>
> People are connected to their families. They get together often. Many residents see those ideals reflected more in the Republican Party than in the Democratic Party. Flores's slogan— "God, family, country"—spoke to a lot of voters.[23]

It's a world far removed from today's Democratic Party regulars, so the *Times* writer felt compelled to label Flores a "far-right Latina" who embraces the extremes.[24] Flores explains exactly which extremes:

> I was born in Burgos, Tamaulipas, Mexico, and raised with strong Conservative values to always put God and Family first. I have received only hate from the liberal media and constantly [been] told by the left to go back to Mexico. They don't support us immigrants, they only use us for political power and don't care about our well-being. I am here now and I won't allow them to continue taking advantage of my people. The NYT knows nothing about me or our culture. *Somos gente de Dios, Familia y Travajo* [We are people of God, Family and Work], *Si Señor!*[25]

If Flores is the face of a seismic shift, then both political parties, and especially the Democrats, should take note. Values matter. Flores faces an uphill battle in the November election since a newly redrawn electoral map favors her opponent. We're off to press before knowing the election outcome, but we're supporting her all the way. She's here to stay and standing for God, family, and work. *Si, Señor!*

One man who understands what's happening very clearly is George Soros. Seeing Hispanics fleeing the Democratic Party through which he runs his mischief, Soros has leapt into action. He's buying up dozens of conservative radio stations.[26] Soros insists that the stations will continue operating independently, but even he can't keep a straight face saying that. Since he can't stop Hispanic Americans from thinking on their own, he can at least change the format of the Spanish-language radio stations so that only one voice is heard: the progressive voice. But he's wasting his money if he thinks a Hispanic population can be so easily manipulated.

WHEN FACING GIANTS, START LOCALLY

One of my own biggest lessons of politics came from managing the Bob Dole campaign in the Midwest in 1988. In that race, George H. W. Bush was the presumptive GOP nominee because he was the vice president. Bush controlled the money and the Republican Party elites, and he had Air Force Two for his campaign plane. Yet Bob Dole came out on top in the crucial Iowa contest.

How did we do it? We went hyperlocal. Bob Dole campaigned in all ninety-nine counties of the state. He met with anyone who would show up at our hundreds of campaign events. At each event, we took the names of everyone who agreed to support him. When the caucuses rolled around, we turned these people out in a very methodical and planned way. We knew we were going to win several months before the caucus because of hard work and a hyperlocal effort.

Bob Dole in 1988 took out the political giant in Iowa, even if he eventually lost elsewhere. And I learned the key to victory.

I sincerely believe that when we take America back, it will be street by street, block by block, neighborhood by neighborhood, city by city, county by county, state by state, and then on to Washington.

There are no solutions to our problems coming out of Washington now. The solutions to our problems come from neighbors working arm in arm to solve them and essentially ignoring the elite-state behemoth that is so distant and absurd.

When facing these giants, I like how the Amplified version puts John 14:27, when Jesus told His disciples, "Do not let your hearts be troubled, neither let them be afraid. [Stop allowing yourselves to be agitated and disturbed; and do not permit yourselves to be fearful and intimidated and cowardly and unsettled.]" (AMPC).

> Live as people who are free, not using your freedom as a cover-up
> for evil, but living as servants of God.
>
> —1 Peter 2:16, ESV

I cannot accept that nothing can be done about our country's massive problems because I continue to believe the good people of this country will stand up and get in the way. We'll put on the sixteen-ounce gloves and start throwing counterpunches. We've seen multiple examples of people doing it in their communities throughout this book.

These community groups are often self-forming things. No national organization leading them, no politicians pulling the strings, no hidden sources of money with suspect agendas. These are carpenters and baristas and real estate agents and firemen doing it on their own dime, their own time. These are everyday Americans joining with friends and neighbors in their communities and counterpunching.

We are helping these groups simply by sharpening the tools needed to get going. Here at Counterpunch, we're pushing for citizens to get going in their own areas. That's what we're doing!

When you join a local Counterpunch group, you're going to find yourself arm in arm with your own neighbors. And you're going to find they have all kinds of ideas about fixing our broken nation.

You'll find Second Amendment conservatives and military veterans, strict constitutionalists, and parents intent on sacking the school board. Some are Democrats; some are Republicans; many are Independents or not affiliated with any political party.

You'll find all flavors because these groups are not affiliated with either political party, not in the pocket of any promoter. These are just neighbors getting together, trying to dial down the "messy" and dial up the "magnificent." All keying in at the local level, where the fixing must begin.

NEIGHBORHOOD GATHERINGS ARE THE BEGINNING OF TRANSFORMATION

Leadership author John Maxwell, whom we heard from earlier, is a big believer that any kind of transformation must begin small. He writes about the impact of "transformation tables" that can help us work with others in order to save America:

> Big things come from small beginnings. A movement can begin with a single person: you. One of the fantastic things about transformation tables is that anyone, anywhere can start using them to create transformation. You don't need an organization or an education or even formal training. You don't need to launch a bunch of groups....
>
> Everything good in human interaction starts with common ground. It's where connections are made, relationships are built, trust is formed around shared values, and progress begins. Transformation tables provide the fertile soil where growth happens because they offer a place and time for people to gather for a common purpose.[27]

The beauty of America is that there are people of all walks of life, colors of skin, and young to old who are united by the principles on which America was founded.

A healing, knitting, and uniting needs to take place in order for Americans to fight back against our common enemy. This new alliance of millions of Americans is what it's going to take to save America—and we can't do it on our own; it is only with God's help that America will survive.

COUNTERPUNCH GROUPS OFTEN HAVE NO ONE IN CHARGE

You may find it interesting that these Counterpunch groups often have no one in charge. There's no real hierarchy or what we would think of as traditional leadership. Instead of making these groups disorderly or chaotic, however, it can make them stronger and more resilient.

This is an approach learned from the White Mountain Apache of Arizona.

The Apache were famous for a decentralized culture, unlike the Sioux, who were quite centralized. If a Sioux leader was lost, the nation faltered. But if an Apache leader was lost, little changed, since Apache decisions were distributed to every level. The famous Geronimo never commanded an army. Rather, he stood to fight, and others joined him.

That is how good Americans are banding together now at the local level to again save a nation that faces a kind of extinction. In local groups, good people are gathering around shared goals—not sweating the small stuff or the differences they have but focusing on projects that must be taken on, local campaigns that must be launched, with everyone involved knowing what must be accomplished. Everyone is a leader in these organizations; everyone knows what must be done.

Here's one of these Counterpunch groups in action today.

NORTH VALLEY CONSTITUTIONAL REPUBLICANS

It began when he was physically confronted in an airport by a mob of baggage-toting vigilantes who considered themselves deputized by the government to correct anyone not wearing a mask. And Basil Fernimos was noncompliant. He recalls thinking, "These are the worst impulses in people coming out. They have no idea they are being manipulated by others who also have no idea what they are doing."[28]

Soon Joe Biden was president, and Basil kept hearing, "We're gonna be in a civil war now." He was beside himself with worry. He has a network of about fifty people, and on a lark he texted them and asked, "What can we do now? Let's talk!"

Enough of them said "Sure," so he reserved the local Amped Coffee shop for an evening get-together.

Fifty had been invited; 250 showed up. Within minutes the place was a madhouse. Nobody knew what they were doing. These people were from all walks of life. They'd never organized, never read Saul Alinsky. But by evening's end, they had agreed to meet again in two weeks, and they just kept it going.

Soon the Patriot Party of Arizona was trying to secretly infiltrate the group. Basil had to strenuously disinvite them; he didn't want extremists upsetting the work they were just starting. Others showed up in masks, goggles, and beanies with cameras secreted in their hands trying to provoke a problem, trying to get punched while shouting blasphemies at the group. But Basil kept the order. And people kept coming.

In the months that followed, the most fascinatingly mundane thing happened: people were getting off the couches they had lived on during the lockdowns, coming out, and making friends—real friends—something they'd almost forgotten how to do. Soon the members were going into the community without masks, and when confronted, detailing their constitutional rights rule by rule and sharing how the government was lying to them.

With the group finally coalescing around action steps to take, they got to it: signing up to be election monitors to work for fair elections, attending Second Amendment rallies and arriving with leaflets, telling folks how they could help, ringing doorbells to make sure folks were registered to vote, and working the transformation tables. Basil told me, "It's not about the wins, but about always being on the offensive so we don't backslide. About going to school board meetings—you can't speak, but just go, be there, show the concern you truly have. No shuffling off responsibilities to elected leaders. Being there in the arena when decisions are being made."

How did Basil go from being a handyman—yes, a handyman—to organizing so many people to effectively work together for their shared community interests?

Basil traces it to a spiritual awakening when, at the same time his daughter overdosed on fentanyl, he landed in the hospital with COVID. He had to help his daughter get well again. He had to get himself out to do that.

His daughter had been rescued by a friend, Dwight, who suggested Basil join his Bible study group. He did and has felt awakened since that day—awakened to do more than politics, to bring people together in Christian compassion and good works.

Basil figures his organization can keep growing in Maricopa County and then across Arizona. He's finding that state legislators increasingly want to engage with the group—because they're active. They're making their presence known and making a difference because of how they're organized. That is, there's really no leader in the group. Sure, Basil sends out meeting texts, but people can come and do what they want to do individually. They can learn from others in the room, get involved in projects that interest them, and see what everyone else is doing. It's completely decentralized, so that if Basil goes away tomorrow, everyone else in the group can carry on the work they're doing.

You Can Watch or Get in the Ring

We have seen a truth come to light here—that each of us has a responsibility to save America, from our own neighborhoods on up. And that is the great beauty of our salvation—that we can begin close to home, first getting involved in the places we know best, our own communities, and then working on up from there.

This is all about the decision we make: to just sit back and watch the beating that America has taken, or to get in the ring and start counterpunching.

There are so many ways you can put on the gloves and help to make things right.

Connect with neighbors.

Go out and meet your neighbors over coffee. Talk about what's happening. Make your meetings regular events, and invite other friends to join in, with everyone meeting to get clarity on what's happening, to help one another and protect each other, to love your neighbors by extending the Christian ideals of individual liberty to everyone.

Distribute literature.

Passing out leaflets is how Thomas Paine got the American ball rolling, and it's just as important today. Whether you stand at the courthouse pushing flyers into the hands of reluctant strangers or use email and text messages, you are wielding the most powerful weapon a free nation has—*ideas*. Put them out there!

Obtain signatures.

Running petition drives, standing at the corner with a billboard and convincing people to sign their names in support of an issue—this is the hard work of democracy, and it's just as important as ever. When people sign on in support, the petition becomes the lever that moves elected leaders in the right direction.

Write local blogs.

With blogging tools, it can be easy and enjoyable to be a citizen reporter, tracking on local events, fact-checking the statements made by politicians, and exposing the abuses you uncover in your own blog. By publishing online and using sharing tools, your reporting can reach many people in your area, making an impact on politics closest to home.

Support local candidates.

Learn about the people seeking political office, and actively support those worthy of your respect. Volunteer to be a foot soldier in the campaigns you admire. Encourage talented leaders in your community to run for a local office or position. Only by working from the bottom up can America be saved.

Attend board meetings.

Begin attending board meetings—not just meetings of the school board but also town councils, election meetings, and anywhere that decisions are being made at the local level. Be there! Listen, speak up if you can, and take notes to share.

Secure elections.

Elections are hard-fought contests, and cheating is baked in—despite any official pretense otherwise. The best way to ensure fair voting is to work the polls and take honor in ensuring one person, one vote. Become a poll captain and stand on integrity.

Demonstrate and protest.

We are fighting a long war for the heart and soul of our country, to save the individual liberties we treasure. And there comes a time when we must actively resist the elite state's attempts to beat us down, when we must pour into the streets in protest. Nobody necessarily wants to do this, but neither can we shrink from it when crises become intolerable, when a moral nation must stand to counterpunch.

It is time! Join a local group that's counterpunching. Form your own group, and we can help. Get involved in your community. Join with unlikely allies restoring faith and freedom to America. Join us now!

God bless you,

Floyd Brown, August 2022

NOTES

INTRODUCTION

1. Amy Nicholson, "Film Review: 'The Platform,'" *Variety*, September 10, 2019, https://variety.com/2019/film/reviews/the-platform-review-1203330373.

CHAPTER 1

1. Peter S. Goodman, *Davos Man: How the Billionaires Devoured the World* (New York: Custom House, 2022), 4.

2. Carter C. Price and Kathryn A. Edwards, "Trends in Income From 1975 to 2018," RAND Corporation, accessed September 14, 2022, https://www.rand.org/pubs/working_papers/WRA516-1.html.

3. Nick Hanauer and David M. Rolf, "The Top 1% of Americans Have Taken $50 Trillion From the Bottom 90%—and That's Made the U.S. Less Secure," *Time*, September 14, 2020, https://time.com/5888024/50-trillion-income-inequality-america.

4. David J. Lynch, "With Fed's Encouragement, Corporations Accelerate Debt Binge in Hopes of Riding Out Pandemic," *Washington Post*, May 13, 2020, https://www.washingtonpost.com/business/2020/05/13/with-feds-encouragement-corporations-accelerate-debt-binge-hopes-riding-out-pandemic; Jef Stein and Peter Whoriskey, "The U.S. Plans to Lend $500 Billion to Large Companies. It Won't Require Them to Preserve Jobs or Limit Executive Pay," *Washington Post*, April 28, 2020, https://www.washingtonpost.com/business/2020/04/28/federal-reserve-bond-corporations.

5. Juliana Kaplan, "Billionaires Made $3.9 Trillion During the Pandemic—Enough to Pay for Everyone's Vaccine," Insider, January 26, 2021, https://www.businessinsider.com/billionaires-made-39-trillion-during-the-pandemic-coronavirus-vaccines-2021-1.

6. John D. Rockefeller III, *The Second American Revolution: Some Personal Observations* (New York: Harper & Row, 1973), 7, 47.

7. David A. Noebel and Summit Ministries Staff, *Understanding the Times: The Collision of Today's Competing Worldviews*, 2nd abridged and rev. ed. (Chelsea, MA: Summit Press, 2006), 503.

8. Klaus Schwab, "Now Is the Time for a 'Great Reset,'" World Economic Forum, June 3, 2020, https://www.weforum.org/agenda/2020/06/now-is-the-time-for-a-great-reset/.

9. Taylor Nicole Rogers, "119 Billionaires, 53 Heads of State, and an $8.3 Million Security Bill: A Look at Davos by the Numbers," Insider, January 21, 2020, https://www.businessinsider.com/davos-by-the-numbers-billionaires-private-jets-security-bill-2020-1.

10. Anna Bruce-Lockhart, "'Vested Interests Want Their Health to Come First'—Greenpeace Chief Jennifer Morgan on Whether Climate Action Can Survive COVID-19," World Economic Forum, April 22, 2020, https://www.weforum.org/agenda/2020/04/covid19-climate-change-greenpeace-jennifer-morgan.

11. Klaus Schwab and Thierry Malleret, *COVID-19: The Great Reset* (Zurich: Agentur Schweiz, 2020), 78.

12. Schwab and Malleret, *COVID-19: The Great Reset*, 78.

13. Klaus Schwab, "Now Is the Time for a 'Great Reset.'"

14. Adrian Monck, "The Great Reset: A Unique Twin Summit to Begin 2021," World Economic Forum, June 3, 2020, https://www.weforum.org/press/2020/06/the-great-reset-a-unique-twin-summit-to-begin-2021.

15. Klaus Schwab, "Davos Manifesto 2020: The Universal Purpose of a Company in the Fourth Industrial Revolution," World Economic Forum, December 2, 2019, https://www.weforum.org/agenda/2019/12/davos-manifesto-2020-the-universal-purpose-of-a-company-in-the-fourth-industrial-revolution.

16. Glenn Beck with Justin Haskins, *The Great Reset: Joe Biden and the Rise of 21st Century Fascism* (Brentwood, TN: Forefront Books, 2022), 22, 31–32, 158.

17. "Statement of Chair Jerome H. Powell on the Financial Stability Oversight Council's (FSOC) Report on Climate-Related Financial Risk," Board of Governors of the Federal Reserve, October 21, 2021, https://www.federalreserve.gov/newsevents/pressreleases/other20211021c.htm.

18. Larry Elliott, "World's 10 Richest Men See Their Wealth Double During COVID Pandemic," *The Guardian*, January 16, 2022, https://www.theguardian.com/business/2022/jan/17/world-10-richest-men-see-their-wealth-double-during-covid-pandemic.

19. Katie Reilly, "Read John Kerry's Northeastern University Commencement Address," *Time*, May 6, 2016, https://time.com/4321733/john-kerry-commencement-address-transcript-speech.

20. Tessa Lena, "The Great Reset for Dummies," *Tessa Fights Robots* (blog), October 28, 2020, https://tessa.substack.com/p/great-reset-dummies.

21. Lena, "The Great Reset for Dummies."

22. Yuval Noah Harari, "Will the Future Be Human?," World Economic Forum, January 24, 2018, https://www.weforum.org/events/world-economic-forum-annual-meeting-2018/sessions/will-the-future-be-human.

CHAPTER 2

1. Lisa Mascaro, "End of an Era? Tea Party Class of House Republicans Fades," Associated Press, June 3, 2018, https://apnews.com/article/64b634a91a2d4933b8bca4c95baa1309.

2. "Education Appropriations," US Department of Education, March 18, 2022, https://content.govdelievery.com/accounts/USED/bulletins/30f7581.

3. Gerard Baker, "Politics Are Already Leading Us Into the Metaverse," *Wall Street Journal*, January 24, 2022, https://www.wsj.com/articles/politics-already-leading-us-into-metaverse-schumer-biden-jan-6-insurrection-woke-crt-big-lie-11643040890.

4. Mark Mazzetti, "C.I.A. Worker Says Message on Torture Got Her Fired," *New York Times*, July 22, 2006, https://www.nytimes.com/2006/07/22/washington/22intel.html.

5. Jesse McKinley, "Blogger Jailed After Defying Court Orders," *New York Times*, August 2, 2006, https://www.nytimes.com/2006/08/02/us/02protest.html.

6. R. Jeffrey Smith, "On Prosecuting Detainees Draft Bill Waives Due Process for Enemy Combatants," *Washington Post*, July 28, 2006, https://www.washingtonpost.com/archive/politics/2006/07/28/on-prosecuting-detainees-span-classbankheaddraft-bill-waives-due-process-for-enemy-combatants-span/a40c4470-deef-47ea-9fcc-e66169ad3b27.

7. Jeanne Lenzer, "Doctors Outraged at Patriot Act's Potential to Seize Medical Records," *The BMJ*, vol. 332 (January 14, 2006): 69, https://www.ncbi.nlm.nih.gov/pmc/articles/PMC1326922/.

8. Naomi Wolf, *The End of America: Letter of Warning to a Young Patriot* (Chelsea, VT: Chelsea Green Publishing, 2007), 10–11.

9. Ernest Hemingway, *The Sun Also Rises* (New York: Scribner, 2003), 141.

10. Michael Gerson, "The View From the Top," *Newsweek*, August 20, 2006, https://www.newsweek.com/view-top-108711.

11. Bethany Allen-Ebrahimian, "64 Years Later, CIA Finally Releases Details of Iranian Coup," *Foreign Policy*, June 20, 2017, https://foreignpolicy.com/2017/06/20/64-years-later-cia-finally-releases-details-of-iranian-coup-iran-tehran-oil.

12. Julie Hanson, "Lobbying for Homeland Security Funding," *CSO*, July 1, 2003, https://www.csoonline.com/article/2115979/lobbying-for-homeland-security-funding.html.

13. "Budget in Brief," US Department of Homeland Security, accessed September 2, 2022, https://www.dhs.gov/sites/default/files/publications/FY_2004_BUDGET_IN_BRIEF.pdf; "FY 2023 Budget in Brief," US Department of Homeland Security, accessed September 2, 2022, https://www.dhs.gov/sites/default/files/2022-03/22-%201835%20-%20FY%202023%20Budget%20in%20Brief%20FINAL%20with%20Cover_Remediated.pdf.

14. Sam Thielman, "Surveillance Reform Explainer: Can the FBI Still Listen to My Phone Calls?," *The Guardian*, June 3, 2015, https://www.theguardian.com/world/2015/jun/03/

surveillance-reform-freedom-act-explainer-fbi-phone-calls-privacy; Sharon Tibken, "Tim Cook Says Apple's Dispute With FBI Is Best Handled This Way," CNET, February 22, 2016, https://www.cnet.com/news/privacy/tim-cook-apple-fbi-employee-email-iphone-san-bernardino.

15. Wolf, *The End of America*, 81.

16. "Unlikely Terrorists On No Fly List," *60 Minutes*, CBS News, originally broadcast October 8, 2006, updated June 7, 2007, https://www.cbsnews.com/news/unlikely-terrorists-on-no-fly-list; "Is Princeton Professor and Retired Marine on Government No-Fly List for Criticizing the White House?," *Democracy Now!* April 12, 2007, https://www.globalissues.org/article/713/is-princeton-professor-and-retired-marine-on-government-no-fly-list-for-criticizing-the-white-house; David Lindorff, "Are Terrorism Watch Lists Expanding Under Trump?," *The Nation*, August 22, 2019, https://www.thenation.com/article/archive/trump-terrorism-travel-watchlist.

17. Andrew Leahey, "Flashback: The Dixie Chicks Are Ashamed of the President…Again," *Rolling Stone*, August 7, 2014, https://www.rollingstone.com/music/music-country/flashback-the-dixie-chicks-are-ashamed-of-the-president-again-80036.

18. Patrick Henry, "Give Me Liberty or Give Me Death," March 23, 1775, https://www.historicstjohnschurch.org/the-speech.

CHAPTER 3

1. Naomi Wolf, "Is It Time for Intellectuals to Talk About God?," *Outspoken With Dr. Naomi Wolf* (blog), January 9, 2022, https://naomiwolf.substack.com/p/is-it-time-for-intellectuals-to-talk.

2. Wolf, "Is It Time for Intellectuals to Talk About God?"

3. Wolf, "Is It Time for Intellectuals to Talk About God?"

4. Matt Gertz, "Fox Keeps Hosting Pandemic Conspiracy Theorist Naomi Wolf," MediaMatters for America, April 20, 2021, https://www.mediamatters.org/fox-news/fox-keeps-hosting-pandemic-conspiracy-theorist-naomi-wolf; Gertz (@MattGertz), "Tucker Carlson in 2019: Naomi Wolf '…You and I were raised to believe that she was really impressive, but she's really not.' But now her crackpottery is anti-vax, so…," Twitter, June 3, 2022, 6:47 a.m., https://twitter.com/MattGertz/status/1532705576240783362.

5. Wolf, "Is It Time for Intellectuals to Talk About God?"

6. Wolf, "Is It Time for Intellectuals to Talk About God?"

7. Wolf, "Is It Time for Intellectuals to Talk About God?"

8. Stacey Lance, "I'm a Public School Teacher. The Kids Aren't Alright," *Common Sense* (blog), January 20, 2022, https://www.commonsense.news/p/im-a-public-school-teacher-the-kids.

9. Lance, "I'm a Public School Teacher."

10. Larry P. Arnn, "The Way Out," *The Highland County Press*, January 29, 2022, https://highlandcountypress.com/Content/Opinions/Opinion/Article/The-way-out/4/22/75571.

11. Stacy Cowley and Ella Koeze, "1 Percent of P.P.P. Borrowers Got Over One-Quarter of the Loan Money," *New York Times*, December 3, 2020, https://www.nytimes.com/2020/12/02/business/paycheck-protection-program-coronavirus.html.

12. Ann Borrett, "Why Big Tech Stocks Boomed in the Pandemic," Tech Monitor, December 16, 2020, https://techmonitor.ai/technology/cloud/why-big-tech-stocks-boomed-covid-19.

13. Arnn, "The Way Out."

14. Mark McDonald, MD, *United States of Fear* (New York: Post Hill Press, 2021), 1957.

15. McDonald, *United States of Fear.*

16. "Notable & Quotable: Fear for Our Children?," *Wall Street Journal*, July 15, 2020, https://www.wsj.com/articles/notable-quotable-fear-for-our-children-11594854726.

17. Bob Frantz, "CFFS Condemns Big Tech Censorship of Medical Experts," *Citizens for Free Speech* (blog), July 30, 2020, https://www.citizensforfreespeech.org/cffs_condemns_big_tech_censorship_of_medical_experts.

18. Allie Bice, "Fauci: 'I'm Going to Be Saving Lives and They're Going to Be Lying,'" *Politico*, November 28, 2021, https://www.politico.com/news/2021/11/28/fauci-lying-covid-research-cruz-523412.

19. "The Great Barrington Declaration," October 4, 2002, http://gbdeclaration.org; "Declaration IV—Restore Scientific Integrity," Global COVID Summit, May 11, 2022, https://globalcovidsummit.org/news/declaration-iv-restore-scientific-integrity.

20. Tyler Durden [pseud.], "German Health Insurer Reveals 'Alarming' Underreporting of Vaccine Side-Effects," *ZeroHedge* (blog), February 24, 2022, https://www.zerohedge.com/covid-19/german-insurance-giant-reveals-alarming-underreporting-vaccine-side-effects.

21. "Merck and Ridgeback's Molnupiravir Receives U.S. FDA Emergency Use Authorization for the Treatment of High-Risk Adults With Mild to Moderate COVID-19," Merck, December 23, 2021, http://www.merck.com/news/merck-and-ridgebacks-molnupiravir-receives-u-s-fda-emergency-use-authorization-for-the-treatment-of-high-risk-adults-with-mild-to-moderate-covid-19; Deena Beasley, "Price of COVID Treatments From Pfizer, Merck, GSK Align With Patient Benefits—Report," Reuters, February 3, 2022, https://www.reuters.com/business/healthcare-pharmaceuticals/price-covid-treatments-pfizer-merck-gsk-align-with-patient-benefits-report-2022-02-03.

22. Mike Lillis and Scott Wong, "House Democrats Eyeing Much Broader Phase 3 Stimulus," *The Hill*, March 19, 2020, https://thehill.com/homenews/house/488543-house-democrats-eyeing-much-broader-phase-3-stimulus.

23. Brooke Singman, "Rand Paul Says GOP Lunch Was Like Meeting With 'Bernie Bros,' Blasts Party on Spending," Fox News, July 21, 2020, https://www.foxnews.com/politics/rand-paul-gop-lunch-meeting-bernie-bros.

24. Kim Miller, in communication with the author, April 18, 2022.

25. Chris Evans, email message to AWOA members, May 3, 2022.

26. FreedomWorks, www.freedomworks.org.

27. BLEXIT Foundation, www.blexitfoundation.org.

28. Arizona Free Enterprise Club, www.azfree.org.

29. Red State Coalition, https://www.facebook.com/people/Red-State-Coalition/100068802836638.

CHAPTER 4

1. Dan Frosch and Zusha Elinson, "U.S. Cities' Surge in Shootings Rattles Once-Safe Seattle," *Wall Street Journal*, March 6, 2022, https://www.wsj.com/articles/u-s-cities-surge-in-shootings-rattles-once-safe-seattle-11646589942.

2. Frosch and Elinson, "U.S. Cities' Surge in Shootings."

3. Alan Mozes, "U.S. Gun Violence Rates Jumped 30% During Pandemic," *US News & World Report*, October 22, 2021, https://www.usnews.com/news/health-news/articles/2021-10-22/us-gun-violence-rates-jumped-30-during-pandemic.

4. Jordan Boyd, "As Two 'Ambushed' L.A. Police Officers Fight for Their Lives, Protesters Scream 'We Hope They Die,'" The Federalist, September 13, 2020, https://thefederalist.com/2020/09/13/as-two-l-a-police-officers-fight-for-their-lives-protesters-scream-we-hope-they-die.

5. Tristan Justice, "28 Times Media and Democrats Excused or Endorsed Violence Committed by Left-Wing Activists," The Federalist, January 7, 2021, https://thefederalist.com/2021/01/07/28-times-media-and-democrats-excused-or-endorsed-violence-committed-by-left-wing-activists.

6. "Police Officers Injured Across the U.S. as Protests Continue; Peaceful Protesters Tear Gassed for Trump Church Photo Op.," *New Day*, June 2, 2020, http://edition.cnn.com/TRANSCRIPTS/2006/02/nday.01.html; "Floyd Killing," MSNBC, May 29, 2020, https://www.msnbc.com/transcripts/all-in/2020-05-29-msna1363831.

7. "Tucker: Political Class Using COVID Crisis to Gain Power," Fox News, December 2, 2020, https://www.foxnews.com/transcript/tucker-political-class-using-covid-crisis-to-gain-power.

8. "America's Shoplifting Epidemic," *Wall Street Journal,* April 8, 2022, https://www.wsj.com/articles/americas-shoplifting-epidemic-cities-theft-retail-cvs-national-retail-federation-small-business-crime-11649455129.

9. Daniel Henninger, "Blame Voters for the Rising Crime Rate," *Wall Street Journal,* December 15, 2021, https://www.wsj.com/articles/blame-voters-for-crime-wave-shoplifting-smash-grab-prosecutors-shooting-murder-stabbing-11639604421.

10. Justin Haskins and Christopher Talgo, "Policy Brief: Felonious Killings of Law Enforcement Officers in 2021," The Heartland Institute, January 26, 2022, https://www.heartland.org/publications-resources/publications/policy-brief-felonious-killings-of-law-enforcement-officers-in-2021.

11. David Cohen, "'Defund the Police' Is Not the Policy of the Democratic Party, Pelosi Says," Politico, February 13, 2022, https://www.politico.com/news/2022/02/13/pelosi-defund-police-democrats-00008449.

12. William A. Galston, "Joe Biden Is in a Bind on Crime and Police Reform," *Wall Street Journal,* February 15, 2022, https://www.wsj.com/articles/joe-biden-eric-adams-crime-law-enforcement-police-progressives-defund-executive-order-murder-assault-robbery-11644943015.

13. "Responsible Gun Ownership," *Everytown for Gun Safety* (blog), accessed July 22, 2022, https://www.everytown.org/issues/responsible-gun-ownership.

14. "Firearm Deaths," USA Facts, accessed July 22, 2022, https://usafacts.org/data/topics/security-safety/crime-and-justice/firearms/firearm-deaths.

15. John Malcolm, "Here Are 8 Stubborn Facts on Gun Violence in America," The Heritage Foundation, March 14, 2018, https://www.heritage.org/crime-and-justice/commentary/here-are-8-stubborn-facts-gun-violence-america.

16. Malcolm, "Here Are 8 Stubborn Facts on Gun Violence in America."

17. "CDC Gun Violence Study's Findings Not What Obama Wanted," *Investor's Business Daily,* August 21, 2103, https://www.investors.com/politics/editorials/cdc-gun-violence-study-goes-against-media-narrative.

18. Malcolm, "Here Are 8 Stubborn Facts on Gun Violence in America."

19. Catherine Marshall, *A Man Called Peter* (New York: McGraw-Hill, 1951).

20. John C. Raines, "Righteous Resistance and Martin Luther King, Jr.," Religion Online, accessed July 22, 2022, https://www.religion-online.org/article/righteous-resistance-and-martin-luther-king-jr.

21. Fidan Baycora, "The Decades Long Battle for Martin Luther King Jr. Day," Historic America, January 18, 2021, https://www.historicamerica.org/journal/historyofmlkday.

22. Isaac Schorr, "*Nation* Writer Labels the Constitution 'Trash,'" *National Review,* March 4, 2022, https://www.nationalreview.com/news/nation-writer-labels-the-constitution-trash.

23. Hanna Panreck, "MSNBC Guest on Sen. Josh Hawley Bringing up Ketanji Brown Jackson's Record: 'Trying to Get Her Killed,'" Fox News, March 20, 2022, https://www.foxnews.com/media/msnbc-commentator-sen-josh-hawley-ketanji-brown-jacksons-record-trying-to-get-her-killed.

24. "Transcript: *The ReidOut*, 1/26/22," MSNBC, January 26, 2022, https://www.msnbc.com/transcripts/transcript-reidout-1-26-22-n1288287.

CHAPTER 5

1. "Borders and Immigration in the Bible," Two Rivers Community Church, August 7, 2014, https://www.tworiverscc.org/borders-and-immigration-in-the-bible/#.YwoEXy2B2Ak.

2. *Secure Fence Act of 2006*, HR 6061, 109th Cong. (2005-2006), https://www.congress.gov/bill/109th-congress/house-bill/6061/text.

3. "Obama's 2005 Remarks Reflect Strong Stance on Controlling Immigration," AP News, November 2, 2018, https://apnews.com/article/archive-fact-checking-2477111077.

4. "Biden Sounds Like Trump in Unearthed Video," The Young Turks, Facebook, May 13, 2019, https://fb.watch/eseA8LhIk4/.

5. "Chuck Schumer on Immigration, 2009," GOP, Facebook, June 21, 2018, https://www.facebook.com/watch/?v=10156156092545090.

6. Abby Budiman, "Key Findings About U.S. Immigrants," Pew Research Center, August 20, 2020, https://www.pewresearch.org/fact-tank/2020/08/20/key-findings-about-u-s-immigrants.

7. Mark Morgan, "The Disaster at Our Southern Border," *Imprimis* 50, no. 8 (August 2021), https://imprimis.hillsdale.edu/disaster-southern-border/.

8. Morgan, "The Disaster at Our Southern Border."

9. Morgan, "The Disaster at Our Southern Border."

10. James Jay Carafano and Dan Negrea, "Joe Biden's Immigration Policies Are a National Security Threat," The Heritage Foundation, November 22, 2021, https://www.heritage.org/immigration/commentary/joe-bidens-immigration-policies-are-national-security-threat.

11. Fernanda Santos, Kirk Semple, and Caitlin Dickerson, "Even Before the Wall, Migrants Find the U.S. Forbidding," *New York Times*, March 10, 2017, http://www.nytimes.com/2017/03/10/us/trump-immigration-border.html.

12. Pete Williams, "Noncitizens Account for 64 Percent of All Federal Arrests, Justice Department Says," NBC News, August 22, 2019, https://www.nbcnews.com/politics/justice-department/non-citizens-account-64-percent-all-federal-arrests-justice-department-n1045286.

13. "Criminal Noncitizen Statistics Fiscal Year 2022," US Customs and Border Protection, accessed July 23, 2022, https://www.cbp.gov/newsroom/stats/cbp-enforcement-statistics/criminal-noncitizen-statistics.

14. "Farm Labor," Economic Research Service (US Department of Agriculture), updated March 15, 2022, http://www.ers.usda.gov/topics/farm-economy/farm-labor/#legalstatus.

15. "Toward a New Conservatism in the 21st Century," *YoungConservatives's Newsletter* (blog), February 13, 2022, https://youngconservatives.substack.com/p/toward-a-new-conservatism-in-the.

16. Clare Knecht, "Get Big or Get Out," ISSUU, accessed July 25, 2022, https://issuu.com/clareknecht/docs/residual_farmland/s/10489533.

17. Philip Bashaw, "Letter to the Editor: The Family Farm," The Gila Herald, November 4, 2021, https://gilaherald.com/letter-to-the-editor-the-family-farm; Joshua Bowling, "Family Farms Made Phoenix Livable, So Why Are So Many Going Away?," AZ Central, June 17, 2019, https://www.azcentral.com/story/news/local/surprise/2019/02/17/phoenix-family-farms-disappearing-development-taking-their-place/2771136002.

18. Christine Whitt, "A Look at America's Family Farms," US Department of Agriculture, July 29, 2021, https://www.usda.gov/media/blog/2020/01/23/look-americas-family-farms.

19. "Foreign Farmland Ownership in the United States," Congressional Research Service, November 18, 2021, crsreports.congress.gov/product/pdf/IF/IF11977.

20. "Foreign Farmland Ownership," Congressional Research Service; https://www.statista.com/topics/4455/foreign-property-investment-in-the-us/#dossierContents__outerWrapper.

21. "Foreign Farmland Ownership," Congressional Research Service.

22. Trevor Reid, "Meat Packing Giant JBS USA Getting Millions in Subsidies Meant for Farmers Impacted by Trade War," Craig Press, January 16, 2019, http://www.craigdailypress.com/news/meat-packing-giant-jbs-usa-getting-millions-in-subsidies-meant-for-farmers-impacted-by-trade-war.

23. "Efforts to Restrict Foreign Ownership of US Farmland Grow," *US News & World Report*, June 9, 2019, https://www.usnews.com/news/best-states/missouri/articles/2019-06-09/efforts-to-restrict-foreign-ownership-of-us-farmland-grow.

24. Matt Levin, "Data Dig: Are Foreign Investors Driving up Real Estate in Your California Neighborhood?," Cal Matters, updated June 23, 2020, https://calmatters.org/housing/2018/03/data-dig-are-foreign-investors-driving-up-real-estate-in-your-california-neighborhood.

25. "Financial Secrecy Index 2020 Reports Progress on Global Transparency—but Backsliding From US, Cayman and UK Prompts Call for Sanctions," *Tax Justice Network* (blog), February 18, 2020, https://taxjustice.net/press/financial-secrecy-index-2020-reports-progress-on-global-transparency-but-backsliding-from-us-cayman-and-uk-prompts-call-for-sanctions.

CHAPTER 6

1. Dustin Dwyer, "'I'm Not Being Hypothetical': Jurors Hear Secret Recordings in Kidnapping Case," Michigan Radio, March 10, 2022, https://www.michiganradio.org/criminal-justice-legal-system/2022-03-10/im-not-being-hypothetical-jurors-hear-secret-recordings-in-kidnapping-case.

2. Dwyer, "'I'm Not Being Hypothetical.'"

3. Omar Abdel-Beque and Joe Barrett, "Jury Acquits Two, Deadlocks on Two Others Accused of Conspiring to Kidnap Michigan Gov. Gretchen Whitmer," *Wall Street Journal*, April 8, 2022, https://www.wsj.com/articles/prosecutors-land-no-convictions-against-four-men-accused-of-conspiring-to-kidnap-gov-gretchen-whitmer-11649443302.

4. Tresa Baldas, "'Double Agent' Warns Whitmer Kidnap Suspects: I Could Hurt You If I Testify," *Detroit Free Press*, March 28, 2022, https://www.freep.com/story/news/local/michigan/2022/03/28/fbi-informant-warns-whitmer-kidnap-suspects/7195711001.

5. Ken Bensinger and Jessica Garrison, "Watching the Watchmen," BuzzFeed News, July 20, 2021, https://www.buzzfeednews.com/article/kenbensinger/michigan-kidnapping-gretchen-whitmer-fbi-informant.

6. Julie Kelly, "High Pressure Tactics in FBI Coverup Surrounding Whitmer Case," American Greatness, February 10, 2022, https://amgreatness.com/2022/02/10/high-pressure-tactics-in-fbi-coverup-surrounding-whitmer-case.

7. "Defendants' Motion to Dismiss, U.S. v. Adam Dean Fox, Case No. 1:20-CR-183," filed December 25, 2021, https://storage.courtlistener.com/recap/gov.uscourts.miwd.99935/gov.uscourts.miwd.99935.379.0.pdf.

8. Debra Heine, "Dreaded QAnon March 4 Uprising Fails to Materialize in the Capitol," *Tennessee Star,* March 6, 2021, https://tennesseestar.com/2021/03/06/dreaded-qanon-march-4-uprising-fails-to-materialize-in-the-capitol.

9. "Remarks as Prepared for Delivery by President Biden—Address to a Joint Session of Congress," The White House, April 28, 2021, https://www.whitehouse.gov/briefing-room/speeches-remarks/2021/04/28/remarks-as-prepared-for-delivery-by-president-biden-address-to-a-joint-session-of-congress.

10. "A Dark and Constant Rage: 25 Years of Right-Wing Terrorism in the United States," ADL, May 3, 2022, https://www.adl.org/resources/report/dark-and-constant-rage-25-years-right-wing-terrorism-united-states.

11. Emma Broches and Julia Solomon-Strauss, "White Supremacist Prosecutions Roundup," *Lawfare* (blog), July 13, 2020, https://www.lawfareblog.com/white-supremacist-prosecutions-roundup.

12. John Serba, "Stream It or Skip It: 'The Informant: Fear and Faith in the Heartland' on Hulu, the Story of an Average Guy Who Helped

Thwart Domestic Terrorism," *Decider*, November 2, 2021, https://decider.com/2021/11/02/the-informant-fear-and-faith-in-the-heartland-on-hulu-stream-it-or-skip-it.

13. "The Escalating Terrorism Problem in the United States," Center for Strategic and International Studies, June 17, 2020, https://www.csis.org/analysis/escalating-terrorism-problem-united-states.

14. "The Evolution of Domestic Terrorism," Center for Strategic and International Studies, February 17, 2022, https://www.csis.org/analysis/evolution-domestic-terrorism.

15. "Human Trafficking: Physically and Spiritually Bound," Dream Center, March 14, 2022, https://www.dreamcenter.org/human-trafficking-physically-and-spiritually-bound/.

16. Ann Givens, "To Stem Shootings, Poughkeepsie Is Bringing Therapy Directly to City Streets," *The Trace*, January 31, 2022, https://www.thetrace.org/2022/01/poughkeepsie-new-york-crime-snug-gun-violence-prevention.

17. Matt Arco, "N.J. Giving Police $7M for Equipment to Help Fight Gun Violence, Murphy Says," NJ.com, January 28, 2022, https://www.nj.com/politics/2022/01/nj-giving-police-7m-for-equipment-to-help-fight-gun-violence-murphy-says.html.

18. "The Pledge of Allegiance," ushistory.org, accessed July 25, 2022, https://www.ushistory.org/documents/pledge.htm.

CHAPTER 7

1. Jennifer C. Berkshire, "The GOP's Grievance Industrial Complex Invades the Classroom," *The Nation*, October 28, 2021, https://www.thenation.com/article/politics/parents-vigilante-gop-crt.

2. Tiffany Jewell, *This Book Is Anti-Racist: 20 Lessons on How to Wake Up, Take Action, and Do the Work* (London: Frances Lincoln Children's Books, 2020), 96, 120, 124.

3. Dana K, "Customer Review," Amazon, October 15, 2020, https://www.amazon.com/gp/customer-reviews/ROPYEX0I04JBJ/ref=cm_cr_dp_d_rvw_ttl?ie=UTF8&ASIN=B082DRTKBZ.

4. Richard Whale, "Customer Review," Amazon, July 7, 2020, https://www.amazon.com/This-Book-Anti-Racist-Tiffany-Jewell-ebook/dp/B082DRTKBZ/ref=sr_1_1.

5. Andrew Gutmann and Paul Rossi, "Inside the Woke Indoctrination Machine," *Wall Street Journal*, February 11, 2022, https://www.wsj.com/articles/inside-the-woke-indoctrination-machine-diversity-equity-inclusion-bipoc-schools-conference-11644613908.

6. Christopher F. Rufo, (@realchrisrufo), "Here is the full list of public school districts that are teaching 'Not My Idea,' which traffics in the noxious

principles of race essentialism, collective guilt, and anti-whiteness," Twitter, July 8, 2021, 10:39 a.m., https://twitter.com/realchrisrufo/status/1413176040613048320.

7. C. H. Woolston, "Jesus Loves the Children," Hymnary.org, accessed September 2, 2022, https://hymnary.org/text/jesus_loves_the_little_children_all_the.

8. Peter Greene, "Teacher Anti-CRT Bills Coast to Coast: A State by State Guide," *Forbes*, February 16, 2022, https://www.forbes.com/sites/petergreene/2022/02/16/teacher-anti-crt-bills-coast-to-coast-a-state-by-state-guide/?sh=3b6f5a624ff6.

9. Beck and Haskins, *The Great Reset*, 32-33.

10. David Bernstein, "Teach '1619' and '1776' U.S. History," *Wall Street Journal*, April 10, 2022, https://www.wsj.com/articles/1619-project-1776-history-america-crt-critical-race-theory-racism-woke-progressive-education-schools-virginia-youngkin-tennessee-11649595715.

11. Bernstein, "Teach '1619' and '1776' U.S. History."

12. "The Illinois Culturally Responsive Teaching and Leading Standards," *Illinois Register* 44, no. 37 (September 11, 2020): 14577–78, https://www.ilsos.gov/departments/index/register/volume44/register_volume44_issue_37.pdf.

13. "The Truth Project," Focus on the Family, accessed July 26, 2022, https://www.focusonthefamily.com/faith/the-truth-project.

14. Brandon Clay, "History: His Story," *Truth Story* (blog), July 4, 2021, https://truthstory.org/blog/history-his-story.

15. Clay, "History: His Story."

16. Clay, "History: His Story."

17. Clay, "History: His Story."

18. Jeff Barrus, "Nikole Hannah-Jones Wins Pulitzer Prize for 1619 Project," Pulitzer Center, May 4, 2020, https://pulitzercenter.org/blog/nikole-hannah-jones-wins-pulitzer-prize-1619-project.

19. James Panero, "Going Under With the Overclass," *New Criterion*, April 2022, https://newcriterion.com/issues/2022/4/going-under-with-the-overclass.

20. Larry P. Arnn, "Orwell's *1984* and Today," *Imprimis* 49, no. 12 (December 2020), https://imprimis.hillsdale.edu/orwells-1984-today.

21. Arnn, "Orwell's *1984*."

22. Ronald Reagan, "Encroaching Control," speech to Phoenix Chamber of Commerce, March 30, 1961, Phoenix, Arizona, 43:29, https://archive.org/details/RonaldReagan-EncroachingControl.

23. Christine Mai-Duc, "San Francisco Votes Overwhelmingly to Recall School Board Members," *Wall Street Journal,* February 16, 2022, https://

www.wsj.com/articles/supporters-of-san-francisco-school-board-recall-declare-victory-11644995026.

24. Jay Barmann, "SF Legislators Call Bulls**t on School District's Scheme to Get $12 Million in State Funding for Reopening," SFiST, May 24, 2022, https://sfist.com/2021/05/24/sf-legislators-call-bulls-t-on-school-districts-scheme-to-get-12-million-in-state-funding-for-reopening.

25. William McGurn, "The Revolt of the Unwoke," *Wall Street Journal*, July 26, 2021, https://www.wsj.com/articles/asian-american-merit-testing-racism-woke-san-francisco-collins-moliga-lopez-11627329861.

26. Daniel Henninger, "Democrats Deserve to Lose the Midterm Elections," *Wall Street Journal*, February 23, 2022, https://www.wsj.com/articles/democrats-deserve-to-lose-midterms-2022-cancel-culture-leftists-progressives-san-francisco-recall-election-11645654233.

27. "A Parental Victory on Free Speech," *Wall Street Journal*, May 8, 2022, https://www.wsj.com/articles/a-parental-victory-free-speech-ryder-ohio-big-walnut-school-district-board-crowl-parents-rights-education-11652034063.

CHAPTER 8

1. Tommy Schultz, "National School Choice Poll: 63% of Likely 2018 Voters Support School Choice," American Federation for Children, January 18, 2018, https://www.federationforchildren.org/2018-school-choice-poll-voters-support.

2. Scott McKay, "Our Teacher Shortage Is a Sign of a Dead Educational System," *American Spectator,* February 22, 2022, https://spectator.org/teacher-shortage-dead-educational-system.

3. Lauren Notini et al., "Forever Young? The Ethics of Ongoing Puberty Suppression for Non-Binary Adults," *Journal of Medical Ethics* 46, no. 11 (November 2020), http://dx.doi.org/10.1136/medethics-2019-106012.

4. Thomas D. Steensma et al., "Desisting and Persisting Gender Dysphoria After Childhood: A Qualitative Follow-Up Study," *Clinical Child Psychology and Psychiatry* 16, no. 4 (2011): 499–516, https://doi.org/10.1177/1359104510378303.

5. Jody L. Herman, Andrew R. Flores, and Kathryn K. O'Neill, "How Many Adults and Youth Identify as Transgender in the United States?," Williams Institute, June 2022, https://williamsinstitute.law.ucla.edu/publications/age-trans-individuals-us.

6. Mark Steyn, "Our Increasingly Unrecognizable Civilization," *Imprimis* 50, no. 4/5 (April/May 2021), https://imprimis.hillsdale.edu/increasingly-unrecognizable-civilization.

7. "Lia Thomas Wraps Collegiate Career With Eighth-Place Finish in 100 at NCAAs," *Sports Illustrated,* March 20, 2022, https://www.si.com/college/2022/03/20/lia-thomas-finishes-eighth-100-final-ncaa-championships.

8. Kyle Melnick and Les Carpenter, "FINA Vote Restricts Transgender Athletes in Women's Competitions," *Washington Post*, June 19, 2022, https://www. washingtonpost.com/sports/2022/06/19/fina-transgender-swimming.

9. President Biden (@POTUS), "To transgender Americans of all ages, I want you to know that you are so brave," Twitter video, March 31, 2022, 8:04 a.m., https://twitter.com/POTUS/status/1509532210495254528.

10. "Gender-Affirming Care and Young People," Office of the Assistant Secretary for Health, accessed July 26, 2022, https://opa.hhs.gov/sites/ default/files/2022-03/gender-affirming-care-young-people-march-2022. pdf.

11. Mary Ellen Klas, "A Breakdown of the Language in Florida's So-Called 'Don't Say Gay' Bill," *Tampa Bay Times*, March 29, 2022, https://www. tampabay.com/news/florida-politics/2022/03/29/a-breakdown-of-the-language-in-floridas-so-called-dont-say-gay-bill.

12. Michael Eng, "Florida House Bill 1557: What It Says, and What It Doesn't," *West Orange Times & Observer*, March 7, 2022, https://www. orangeobserver.com/article/florida-house-bill-1557-what-it-says-and-what-it-doesnt.

13. Rod Dreger, "Disney Drives Conservatives Into Closet," *American Conservative*, March 21, 2022, https://www.theamericanconservative.com/ walt-disney-conservative-employees-closet-dont-say-gay.

14. Aaron Sibarium, "Hundreds of Yale Law Students Disrupt Bipartisan Free Speech Event," Washington Free Beacon, March 16, 2022, https:// freebeacon.com/campus/hundreds-of-yale-law-students-disrupt-bipartisan-free-speech-event.

15. John Villasenor, "Views Among College Students Regarding the First Amendment: Results From a New Survey," Brookings, September 18, 2017, https://www.brookings.edu/blog/fixgov/2017/09/18/views-among-college-students-regarding-the-first-amendment-results-from-a-new-survey.

16. Alex Morey, "Salman Rushdie Champions Free Speech, Chides Coddled Students at 'Chicago Tribune' Award Ceremony," Foundation for Individual Rights and Expression, November 10, 2015, https://www.thefire. org/salman-rushdie-champions-free-speech-chides-coddled-students-at-chicago-tribune-award-ceremony.

17. Rory Little, "Open Minds, Loud Voices and Free Speech on Campus," *Wall Street Journal*, March 27, 2022, https://www.wsj.com/articles/free-speech-expression-campus-protest-activist-shutdown-uc-hastings-ilya-shapiro-cancel-11648245303.

18. Bradford Betz, "UCLA's Race, Equity Director Appears to Wish for Justice Thomas to Die: 'No One Wants to Openly Admit,'" Fox News, March 28, 2022, https://www.foxnews.com/politics/uclas-race-equity-director-death-justice-thomas.

19. Richard K. Vedder, *Restoring the Promise: Higher Education in America* (Oakland, CA: Independent Institute, 2019); "Why College Costs Are Out of Control," The Heritage Foundation, accessed September 20, 2022, https://www.heritage.org/education/heritage-explains/why-college-costs-are-out-control.

20. "Yale Law Students for Censorship," *Wall Street Journal*, March 20, 2022, https://www.wsj.com/articles/yale-law-students-for-censorship-silberman-shouting-panel-federalist-society-free-speech-hiring-11647793665.

21. Emma Colton, "The Daily Caller Proudly Presents: The DUMBEST College Courses for 2015," Daily Caller, August 21, 2015, http://dailycaller.com/2015/08/21/the-daily-caller-proudly-presents-the-dumbest-college-courses-for-2015; Jim Fisher, "Ridiculous College Courses: Majoring in Stupid," *Jim Fisher True Crime* (blog), January 6, 2018, http://jimfishertruecrime.blogspot.com/2012/03/majoring-in-stupid-ridiculous-college.html; Alex Nitzberg, "Far Left Courses at American Colleges," Accuracy in Academia, December 16, 2016, https://www.academia.org/far-left-courses-at-american-colleges.

22. Charles Creitz, "Ramaswamy: 'Secular Religion' of Critical Race Theory Now Taught in Schools Violates Civil Rights Act of 64," Fox News, July 13, 2021, https://www.foxnews.com/media/ramaswamy-secular-religion-of-critical-race-theory-now-taught-in-schools-violates-civil-rights-act-of-64.

CHAPTER 9

1. Panero, "Going Under With the Overclass."

2. Panero, "Going Under With the Overclass."

3. Vivek Ramaswamy, "Why I'm Blowing Whistle on How Corporate America Is Poisoning Society," *New York Post,* June 21, 2021, https://nypost.com/2021/06/21/woke-inc-why-im-blowing-whistle-on-how-corporate-america-is-poisoning-society.

4. "The 'Fearless Girl' Statue Isn't a Symbol, It Is an Advertisement," Nasdaq, March 27, 2017, https://www.nasdaq.com/articles/fearless-girl-statue-isnt-symbol-it-advertisement-2017-03-27.

5. Matt Stevens, "Firm Behind 'Fearless Girl' Statue Underpaid Women, U.S. Says," *New York Times,* October 6, 2017, https://www.nytimes.com/2017/10/06/business/fearless-girl-settlement.html.

6. Jena McGregor, "Goldman Sachs CEO Says It Won't Take a Company Public Without Diversity on Its Board," *Washington Post,* January 23, 2020, https://www.washingtonpost.com/business/2020/01/23/goldman-sachs-ceo-says-it-wont-take-companies-public-without-diverse-board-member.

7. Alun John, "Hong Kong Fines Goldman Sachs Record $350 Million Over 1MDB Failings," Reuters, October 20, 2020, http://www.reuters.com/article/goldman-sachs-1mdb-hong-kong-idUSKBN27717P.

8. Lia Eustachewich, "Coca-Cola Slammed for Diversity Training That Urged Workers to Be 'Less White,'" *New York Post*, February 23, 2021, https://nypost.com/2021/02/23/coca-cola-diversity-training-urged-workers-to-be-less-white.

9. "NIKE, Inc. Statement on Commitment to the Black Community," Nike, June 5, 2020, http://about.nike.com/en/newsroom/statements/nike-inc-statement-on-commitment-to-the-black-community.

10. Alexandra Kelley, "Nike Inc. Announces $40 Million Donation to Black Community Organizations," *The Hill*, June 5, 2020, https://thehill.com/changing-america/respect/equality/501369-nike-inc-announces-40-million-donation-to-black-community.

11. Jessica Kwong, "Ulterior Motive? Black Lives Matter Accused of Trying to Cover up Sinister Aims After Deleting Pledge to End Traditional 'Nuclear Family,'" *The US Sun*, September 22, 2020, https://www.the-sun.com/news/1511555/black-lives-matter-deleting-end-nuclear-family.

12. Sean Campbell, "Black Lives Matter Secretly Bought a $6 Million House," *New York*, April 4, 2022, https://nymag.com/intelligencer/2022/04/black-lives-matter-6-million-dollar-house.html.

13. David Schuman, *American Government: The Rules of the Game* (New York: Random House, 1984).

14. Owen Strachan, *Christianity and Wokeness* (Washington, DC: Regnery, 2021).

15. Chanequa Walker-Barnes, PhD, "Prayer of a Weary Black Woman," in Sarah Bessey, ed., *A Rhythm of Prayer: A Collection of Meditations for Renewal* (Colorado Springs, CO: Convergent Books, 2021), 69.

16. Owen Strachan, "Christianity and Wokeness," Centennial Institute, November 15, 2021, https://www.youtube.com/watch?v=sJsw2zzfLTs.

17. "NFL Forms New Committee to Review Policies Regarding Diversity Hiring; Teams Mandated to Hire Minority Coach as Offensive Assistant," NFL, March 28, 2022, https://www.nfl.com/news/nfl-forming-new-committee-to-review-league-and-team-policies-regarding-diversity.

18. Associated Press, "School Defends Canning of 'Jingle Bells' Over Song's History," *US News & World Report*, January 2, 2022, https://www.usnews.com/news/best-states/new-york/articles/2022-01-02/school-defends-canning-of-jingle-bells-over-songs-history.

19. Jeffrey Mervis, "The Toll of White Privilege," *Science*, March 1, 2022, https://www.science.org/content/article/how-culture-of-white-privilege-discourages-black-students-from-becoming-physicists; Katie Langin, "For LGBQ Scientists, Being Out Can Mean More Publications," *Science*, March 2, 2022, https://www.science.org/content/article/lgbq-scientists-being-out-can-mean-more-publications.

20. Randy DeSoto, "Leftists Shut Down Venue After Christian Group Organizes School Board Candidates Event," Western Journal, April 7, 2022, https://www.westernjournal.com/leftists-shut-venue-christian-group-organizes-school-board-candidates-event.

21. DeSoto, "Leftists Shut Down Venue After Christian Group Organizes School Board Candidates Event."

22. DeSoto, "Leftists Shut Down Venue After Christian Group Organizes School Board Candidates Event."

23. DeSoto, "Leftists Shut Down Venue After Christian Group Organizes School Board Candidates Event."

24. Jess Bravin, "Supreme Court Mulls Impact of High School Coach's 50-Yard-Line Prayers," *Wall Street Journal*, April 25, 2022, https://www.wsj.com/articles/supreme-court-mulls-impact-of-high-school-coachs-50-yard-line-prayers-11650918003.

25. Bravin, "Supreme Court Mulls Impact of High School Coach's 50-Yard-Line Prayers."

26. Abby Liebing, "'I Had a Commitment With God': Praying Coach Reacts to the SCOTUS Verdict," Western Journal, June 28, 2022, https://www.westernjournal.com/commitment-god-praying-coach-reacts-scotus-verdict.

27. Liebing, "'I Had a Commitment With God.'"

28. Chris Woodward, "Winning Coach Committed to Post-game Prayer After Viewing Movie," American Family News, June 30, 2022, https://afn.net/legal-courts/2022/06/30/winning-coach-committed-to-post-game-prayer-after-viewing-movie.

29. Liebing, "'I Had a Commitment With God.'"

30. Jordan Boyd, "MSU Coach Defends Postgame Handshakes: Our Real Problem Is Replacing Character With Excuses," The Federalist, February 22, 2022, https://thefederalist.com/2022/02/22/msu-coach-defends-postgame-handshakes-our-real-problem-is-replacing-character-with-excuses.

31. Patrick Henry, "The Speech," Historic St. John's Church, 1741, https://www.historicstjohnschurch.org/the-speech.

CHAPTER 10

1. Carter C. Price and Kathryn A. Edwards, "Trends in Income From 1975 to 2018," RAND, November 20, 2020, https://www.rand.org/pubs/working_papers/WRA516-1.html.

2. Christopher Witko, "How Wall Street Became a Big Chunk of the U.S. Economy—and When the Democrats Signed On," *Washington Post*, March 29, 2016, https://www.washingtonpost.com/news/monkey-cage/wp/

2016/03/29/how-wall-street-became-a-big-chunk-of-the-u-s-economy-and-when-the-democrats-signed-on.

3. Witko, "How Wall Street Became a Big Chunk of the U.S. Economy."

4. Andy Kessler, "Here Come the Price Controls," *Wall Street Journal,* April 3, 2022, https://www.wsj.com/articles/here-come-the-price-controls-oil-reserves-rent-consumers-joe-biden-inflation-drugs-11648998374.

5. Dave Goldiner, "Biden Blames Inflation on Putin's Invasion of Ukraine, Rising Gas Prices," *New York Daily News,* March 10, 2022, http://www.nydailynews.com/news/politics/us-elections-government/ny-biden-blames-inflation-russia-invasion-ukraine-20220310-7t73gvo5kbgzzajvtu72q043gy-story.html.

6. Josh Mitchell, "Why This Economic Boom Can't Lift America's Spirits," *Wall Street Journal,* February 22, 2022, https://www.wsj.com/articles/why-this-economic-boom-cant-lift-americas-spirits-11645544670.

7. David Harrison, "High Food Prices to Pressure Inflation This Year," *Wall Street Journal,* February 27, 2022, https://www.wsj.com/articles/high-food-prices-to-pressure-inflation-this-year-11645974001.

8. "Zumper National Rent Report," Zumper, August 29, 2022, https://www.zumper.com/blog/rental-price-data.

9. Shelby Heinrich, "18 Photos That Prove the Products We Buy Are Slowly Shrinking, Yet We're Still Paying the Same Price," BuzzFeed, July 20, 2022, https://www.buzzfeed.com/shelbyheinrich/shrinkflation-examples-photos-reddit.

10. Tom Ozimek, "True Rate of Inflation 'Much Higher' Than Official Government Figures Show: Expert," *Epoch Times,* updated August 12, 2022, https://www.theepochtimes.com/true-rate-of-inflation-much-higher-than-official-government-figures-show-expert_4657796.html.

11. Nick Timiraos, "March 2020: How the Fed Averted Economic Disaster," *Wall Street Journal,* February 18, 2022, https://www.wsj.com/amp/articles/march-2020-how-the-fed-averted-economic-disaster-11645199788.

12. Tom Orlik, Justin Jimenez, and Cedric Sam, "World-Dominating Superstar Firms Get Bigger, Techier, and More Chinese," Bloomberg, May 21, 2021, https://www.bloomberg.com/graphics/2021-biggest-global-companies-growth-trends/#xj4y7vzkg.

13. Jeanne Sahadi, "Wall Street Bonuses Hit Record High," CNN Business, March 23, 2022, https://amp.cnn.com/cnn/2022/03/23/success/wall-street-bonuses-for-2021/index.html.

14. Timiraos, "March 2020: How the Fed Averted Economic Disaster."

15. Barbara Alexander, "The National Recovery Administration," EH.net, accessed July 29, 2022, https://eh.net/encyclopedia/the-national-recovery-administration-2.

16. Richard Nixon speech to the nation on August 15, 1971, accessed July 29, 2022, CVCE, https://www.cvce.eu/content/publication/1999/1/1/168eed17-f28b-487b-9cd2-6d668e42e63a/publishable_en.pdf; Bob Haegele, "A Look Back at Famous Inflationary Periods Throughout History," GOBankingRates, April 19, 2022, https://www.gobankingrates.com/money/economy/inflation-look-back-at-famous-periods-throughout-history.

17. Kay C. James, "The $15 Minimum Wage Would Most Hurt the People It's Intended to Help," The Heritage Foundation, February 17, 2021, https://www.heritage.org/jobs-and-labor/commentary/the-15-minimum-wage-would-most-hurt-the-people-its-intended-help.

18. Ron Paul, "End the Fed and Get More Doritos," Ron Paul Institute, March 21, 2022, http://www.ronpaulinstitute.org/archives/featured-articles/2022/march/21/end-the-fed-and-get-more-doritos.

19. Stuart Allsopp, "SPX: 3 Lessons From the Collapse of Japan's Bubble," *Seeking Alpha* (blog), April 13, 2021, https://seekingalpha.com/article/4418896-spx-3-lessons-from-collapse-of-japans-bubble.

20. "The Dotcom Bubble Burst (2000)," International Banker, September 29, 2021, https://internationalbanker.com/history-of-financial-crises/the-dotcom-bubble-burst-2000.

21. Paul Kosakowski, "The Fall of the Market in the Fall of 2008," Investopedia, November 30, 2021, https://www.investopedia.com/articles/economics/09/subprime-market-2008.asp; "Factbox—U.S. Government Bailout Tally Tops 504 Billion Pounds," Reuters, September 16, 2008, https://www.reuters.com/article/idUKN16126320080917.

22. Mirela Petkova, "Weekly Data: Cutting Nuclear Links With Russia May Be Harder Than Cutting Fossil Fuel Imports," Energy Monitor, March 21, 2022, https://www.energymonitor.ai/sectors/power/weekly-data-russian-uranium-supply-chains.

23. "Platinum-Group Metals," Mineral Commodity Summaries 2022, US Geological Survey, accessed September 6, 2022, https://pubs.usgs.gov/periodicals/mcs2022/mcs2022-platinum.pdf.

24. "Factbox: Western Ban on Russian Gold Imports Is Largely Symbolic," Reuters, June 27, 2022, https://www.reuters.com/markets/commodities/western-ban-russian-gold-imports-is-largely-symbolic-2022-06-27.

25. "New Report: 40% of Older Americans Rely Solely on Social Security for Retirement Income," National Institute on Retirement Security, January 13, 2020, https://www.nirsonline.org/2020/01/new-report-40-of-older-americans-rely-solely-on-social-security-for-retirement-income.

26. Cameron Huddleston, "When Social Security Runs Out: What the Program Will Look Like in 2035," GOBankingRates, August 25, 2022, https://www.gobankingrates.com/retirement/social-security/what-will-social-security-be-in-2035; The Editorial Board, "Another Spending Siren

for Joe Manchin," *Wall Street Journal*, June 5 2022, https://www.wsj.com/articles/another-spending-siren-for-joe-manchin-11654467051.

27. Kevin Hebner, "The Dollar Is Our Currency, but It's Your Problem," Investment & Pensions Europe, October 2007, https://www.ipe.com/the-dollar-is-our-currency-but-its-your-problem/25599.article.

28. Stephanie Kelton, *The Deficit Myth: Modern Monetary Theory and the Birth of the People's Economy* (New York: PublicAffairs, 2020).

29. "Bard Economist L. Randall Wray on How Modern Monetary Theory Isn't the Future. It's Here Now," Bard College, November 23, 2021, https://www.bard.edu/news/bard-economist-l-randall-wray-on-how-modern-monetary-theory-isnt-the-future-its-here-now-2021-11-23.

30. Susan Adams, "George Soros Is Giving $500 Million to Bard College," *Forbes*, April 1, 2021, https://www.forbes.com/sites/susanadams/2021/04/01/george-soros-is-giving-500-million-to-bard-college.

CHAPTER 11

1. Thomas Haasl, Sam Schulhofer-Wohl, and Anna Paulson, "Understanding the Demand for Currency at Home and Abroad," Federal Reserve Bank of Chicago, No. 396, 2018, https://www.chicagofed.org/publications/chicago-fed-letter/2018/396; "How Much Money Is There in the World? 2022 Edition," RankRed, July 13, 2022, https://www.rankred.com/how-much-money-is-there-in-the-world.

2. Robert Burgess, "Dethroning King Dollar Won't Be an Easy Feat," Bloomberg, March 3, 2022, https://www.bloomberg.com/opinion/articles/2022-03-03/dethroning-the-dollar-as-the-world-s-reserve-currency-won-t-be-easy.

3. "Corruption Perceptions Index," Transparency International, accessed July 30, 2022, https://www.transparency.org/en/cpi/2021.

4. Summer Said and Stephen Kalin, "Saudi Arabia Considers Accepting Yuan Instead of Dollars for Chinese Oil Sales," *Wall Street Journal*, March 15, 2022, https://www.wsj.com/articles/saudi-arabia-considers-accepting-yuan-instead-of-dollars-for-chinese-oil-sales-11647351541.

5. Gal Luft and Anne Korin, *De-dollarization: The Revolt Against the Dollar and the Rise of a New Financial World Order* (Institute for the Analysis of Global Security, 2019).

6. Said and Kalin, "Saudi Arabia Considers Accepting Yuan Instead of Dollars for Chinese Oil Sales."

7. David Z. Morris, "The End of Exorbitant Privilege: Inflation, the Global Dollar and What Comes Next," CoinDesk, August 5, 2021, https://www.coindesk.com/markets/2021/08/05/the-end-of-exorbitant-privilege-inflation-the-global-dollar-and-what-comes-next.

8. Henrik Selin and Rebecca Cowing, "Cargo Ships Are Emitting Boatloads of Carbon, and Nobody Wants to Take the Blame," The Conversation, December 18, 2018, https://theconversation.com/cargo-ships-are-emitting-boatloads-of-carbon-and-nobody-wants-to-take-the-blame-108731.

9. Cathy He, "US Should Help Its Manufacturing Firms Move out of China: Kudlow," *Epoch Times,* April 10, 2020, https://www.theepochtimes.com/us-should-help-its-manufacturing-firms-move-out-of-china-kudlow-says_3306808.html.

10. "History of Taxes," Tax Foundation, accessed July 30, 2022, https://taxfoundation.org/history-of-taxes.

11. Demian Brady, "Tax Complexity 2021: Compliance Burdens Ease for Third Year Since Tax Reform," National Taxpayers Union Foundation, April 15, 2021, https://www.ntu.org/foundation/detail/tax-complexity-2021-compliance-burdens-ease-for-third-year-since-tax-reform; John McCormick, "IRS Chief Says $1 Trillion in Taxes May Go Uncollected Each Year," *Wall Street Journal,* April 13, 2021, https://www.wsj.com/articles/irs-chief-says-1-trillion-in-taxes-may-go-uncollected-each-year-1161833776.

12. Kimberly Amadeo, "U.S. Federal Government Tax Revenue," The Balance, May 17, 2021, https://www.thebalance.com/current-u-s-federal-government-tax-revenue-3305762.

13. Neal Boortz, *The Fair Tax Book: Saying Goodbye to the Income Tax and the IRS* (New York: HarperCollins, 2009).

14. "H.R.25—Fair Tax Act of 2005," Congress.gov, November 1, 2005, https://www.congress.gov/bill/109th-congress/house-bill/25/actions?r=37&s=1.

15. "Biden's Budget Would Raise Income Tax Rates to Highest in Developed World," Tax Foundation, accessed July 30, 2022, https://files.taxfoundation.org/20220511132810/Biden-Budget-Top-Rates-May-2022-01-01.png.

16. Stephen Ohlemacher, "Busted: Internal Revenue Service Caught Targeting Conservative Groups for Tax Harassment," Business Insider, May 11, 2013, https://www.businessinsider.com/irs-caught-targeting-tea-party-groups-for-tax-harassment-2013-5; Bradley A. Smith, "A Lesson on Abuse of Power by Obama and His Senate Allies," *The Hill,* October 10, 2017, https://thehill.com/opinion/white-house/354680-a-lesson-on-abuse-of-power-by-obama-and-his-senate-allies.

17. Thomas L. Hungerford, "The Economic Effects of Capital Gains Taxation," Congressional Research Service, June 18, 2010, https://sgp.fas.org/crs/misc/R40411.pdf.

18. Grover Norquist, "States Get Serious About Tax Cuts," *Wall Street Journal,* February 13, 2022, https://www.wsj.com/articles/states-get-serious-about-tax-cuts-competition-burden-income-interstate-migration-pandemic-florida-new-york-coastal-flight-11644783306.

19. Steven Malanga, "The Red State Model for a Post-Pandemic Economy," *Wall Street Journal*, February 18, 2022, https://www.wsj.com/articles/post-pandemic-economy-sales-income-tax-cuts-hike-covid-stimulus-rates-midterms-new-york-jersey-mass-texas-ariz-idaho-utah-11645203131.

20. Joshua Rauh and Kevin Warsh, "The Inflation Mess and a Financial Refuge," *Wall Street Journal,* February 21, 2022, https://www.wsj.com/articles/inflation-financial-refuge-price-surge-savings-wages-pandemic-fed-powell-biden-fomc-investment-i-bonds-11645464310.

21. "The 2022 Long-Term Budget Outlook," Congressional Budget Office, accessed September 2, 2022, https://www.cbo.gov/system/files/2022-07/57971-LTBO.pdf, page 7.

22. John Merrifield and Barry Poulson, "Policy Brief: How to Solve America's Debt Crisis in the Wake of the Coronavirus Pandemic," The Heartland Institute, April 2, 2020, https://www.heartland.org/publications-resources/publications/policy-brief-how-to-solve-americas-debt-crisis-in-the-wake-of-the-coronavirus-pandemic.

CHAPTER 12

1. Ryan Browne, "Elon Musk Warns A.I. Could Create an 'Immortal Dictator From Which We Can Never Escape,'" CNBC, April 6, 2018, https://www.cnbc.com/2018/04/06/elon-musk-warns-ai-could-create-immortal-dictator-in-documentary.html.

2. Melissa Heikkilä, "Billionaires Bet on Brussels to Save Them From AI Singularity," *Politico,* September 21, 2021, https://Www.Politico.Eu/Article/Billionaires-Brussels-Bid-Save-Ai-Singularity.

3. Kelsey Piper, "The Case for Taking AI Seriously as a Threat to Humanity," *Vox,* October 15, 2020, https://www.vox.com/future-perfect/2018/12/21/18126576/ai-artificial-intelligence-machine-learning-safety-alignment.

4. Tessa Lena, "The Establishment. The Machine. The Human Being," *Tessa Fights Robots* (blog), March 9, 2022, https://tessa.substack.com/p/machine-vs-human-being.

5. Tessa Lena, "The Establishment. The Machine. The Human Being."

6. "Amazon Strategy Teardown: Amazon's Barreling Into Physical Retail, Financial Services, Healthcare, and AI-Led Computing," *CB Insights*, March 7, 2018, http://www.cbinsights.com/research/report/amazon-strategy-teardown/.

7. Ken Auletta, "Paper Trail: Did Publishers and Apple Collude Against Amazon?," *New Yorker*, June 18, 2012, http://www.newyorker.com/magazine/2012/06/25/paper-trail-2.

8. Ted Johnson, "Fox News Tops May Cable News Ratings as 'The Five' Ranks No. 1 in Total Viewers," Deadline, June 1, 2022, https://deadline.com/2022/06/fox-news-ratings-may-1235036975.

9. Sharyl Attkisson, *Slanted: How the News Media Taught Us to Love Censorship and Hate Journalism* (New York: HarperCollins, 2020).

10. Jim Clapper, Mike Hayden, Leon Panetta et al., "Public Statement on the Hunter Biden Emails," *Politico*, October 19, 2020, https://www.politico.com/f/?id=00000175-4393-d7aa-af77-579f9b330000.

11. Emma-Jo Morris and Gabrielle Fonrouge, "Smoking-Gun Email Reveals How Hunter Biden Introduced Ukrainian Businessman to VP Dad," *New York Post*, October 14, 2020, https://nypost.com/2020/10/14/email-reveals-how-hunter-biden-introduced-ukrainian-biz-man-to-dad/.

12. Norah O'Donnell, "Joe Biden Makes the Case for Why He Should Be President," *60 Minutes*, October 25, 2020, https://www.cbsnews.com/news/joe-biden-democratic-presidential-candidate-kamala-harris-60-mintues-interview-norah-odonnell-2020-10-25.

13. "One Year Later, The Post's Hunter Biden Reporting Is Vindicated—But Still Buried," *New York Post*, October 12, 2021, https://nypost.com/2021/10/12/one-year-later-the-posts-hunter-biden-reporting-is-vindicated-but-still-buried.

14. *The Situation Room*, CNN (transcript), October 16, 2020, http://www.cnn.com/TRANSCRIPTS/2010/16/sitroom.02.html.

15. Newt Gingrich, "Congress Must Investigate Hunter Biden—and Those Protecting Him. Here's Why," Fox News, December 5, 2021, https://www.foxnews.com/opinion/congress-must-investigate-hunter-biden-protectors-newt-gingrich.

16. Katie Benner, Kenneth P. Vogel, and Michael S. Schmidt, "Hunter Biden Paid Tax Bill, but Broad Federal Investigation Continues," *New York Times*, March 16, 2022, https://www.nytimes.com/2022/03/16/us/politics/hunter-biden-tax-bill-investigation.html.

17. Melissa Mackenzie, "Hunter Biden's Laptop and All the News That's Fit to Spike," *American Spectator*, March 17, 2022, https://spectator.org/hunter-bidens-laptop-new-york-times.

18. Rod Dreher, *Live Not By Lies* (New York: Sentinel, 2020), 142.

19. Dreher, *Live Not By Lies*, 70.

20. Dreher, *Live Not By Lies*.

21. Milan Kundera, *The Unbearable Lightness of Being* (New York: Harper Perennial Modern Classics, 2009).

22. Hannah Arendt, "Ideology and Terror: A Novel Form of Government," *The Review of Politics* 15, no. 3 (July 1953): 326, https://www.jstor.org/stable/1405171.

23. Dreher, *Live Not By Lies*, 212–13.

CHAPTER 13

1. Paul Bischoff, "Surveillance Camera Statistics: Which Cities Have the Most CCTV Cameras?," Comparitech, July 11, 2022, https://www.comparitech.com/vpn-privacy/the-worlds-most-surveilled-cities.

2. Lucas Niewenhuis, "What Did Apple Get Out of Its Secret, $275 Billion China Deal in 2016?," The China Project, December 7, 2021, https://thechinaproject.com/2021/12/07/what-did-apple-get-out-of-its-secret-275-billion-china-deal-in-2016/; David Shepardson, "Facebook Confirms Data Sharing With Chinese Companies," Reuters, June 5, 2018, https://www.reuters.com/article/us-facebook-privacy-congress/facebook-confirms-data-sharing-with-chinese-companies-idUSKCN1J11TY; Erica Pandey, "How U.S. Tech Powers China's Surveillance State," Axios, July 27, 2018, https://www.axios.com/2018/07/26/china-us-technology-surveillance-state; Mara Hvistendahl, "How a Chinese Surveillance Broker Became Oracle's 'Partner of the Year,'" The Intercept, April 22 2021, https://cset.georgetown.edu/article/how-a-chinese-surveillance-broker-became-oracles-partner-of-the-year/; Charles Rollet, "In China's Far West, Companies Cash In on Surveillance Program That Targets Muslims," *Foreign Policy*, June 13, 2018, https://foreignpolicy.com/2018/06/13/in-chinas-far-west-companies-cash-in-on-surveillance-program-that-targets-muslims; Joseph Kahn, "Yahoo Helped Chinese to Prosecute Journalist," *New York Times*, September 8, 2005, https://www.nytimes.com/2005/09/08/business/worldbusiness/yahoo-helped-chinese-to-prosecute-journalist.html; Ryan Gallagher, "How U.S. Tech Giants Are Helping to Build China's Surveillance State," The Intercept, July 11, 2019, https://theintercept.com/2019/07/11/china-surveillance-google-ibm-semptian/; Alexandra Harney, "Risky Partner: Top U.S. Universities Took Funds From Chinese Firm Tied to Xinjiang Security," Reuters, June 12, 2019, https://www.reuters.com/article/us-china-xinjiang-mit-tech-insight/risky-partner-top-u-s-universities-took-funds-from-chinese-firm-tied-to-xinjiang-security-idUSKCN1TE04M.

3. Rollet, "In China's Far West, Companies Cash in on Surveillance Program That Targets Muslims."

4. Stephanie Nebehay, "U.N. Says It Has Credible Reports That China Holds Million Uighurs in Secret Camps," Reuters, August 10, 2018, https://www.reuters.com/article/us-china-rights-un/u-n-says-it-has-credible-reports-that-china-holds-million-uighurs-in-secret-camps-idUSKBN1KV1SU.

5. Michael Clarke, "Turning Ghosts Into Humans: Surveillance as an Instrument of Social Engineering in Xinjiang," War on the Rocks, November 2, 2021, https://warontherocks.com/2021/11/turning-ghosts-into-humans-surveillance-as-an-instrument-of-social-engineering-in-xinjiang.

6. "China: Minority Region Collects DNA From Millions," Human Rights Watch, December 13, 2017, https://www.hrw.org/news/2017/12/13/china-minority-region-collects-dna-millions.

7. "Federal Appeals Court Rules Baltimore Aerial Surveillance Program Is Unconstitutional," ACLU, June 24, 2021, https://www.aclu.org/press-releases/federal-appeals-court-rules-baltimore-aerial-surveillance-program-unconstitutional.

8. Nathan Sheard and Adam Schwartz, "The Movement to Ban Government Use of Face Recognition," Electronic Frontier Foundation, May 5, 2022, https://www.eff.org/deeplinks/2022/05/movement-ban-government-use-face-recognition; Jonathan Hillman, "China Is Watching You," *Atlantic,* October 18, 2021, https://www.theatlantic.com/ideas/archive/2021/10/china-america-surveillance-hikvision/620404.

9. Matt Hamblen, "U.S. Government Agencies Still Use Thousands of Chinese Surveillance Cameras," Fierce Electronics, October 21, 2019, https://www.fierceelectronics.com/electronics/u-s-government-agencies-still-use-thousands-chinese-surveillance-cameras; Zack Whittaker, "US Government Agencies Bought Chinese Surveillance Tech Despite Federal Ban," TechCrunch, December 1, 2021, https://techcrunch.com/2021/12/01/federal-lorex-surveillance-ban.

10. "Ethical Use of Facial Recognition Act," S. 3284, 116th Cong. (2019-2020), https://www.congress.gov/bill/116th-congress/senate-bill/3284/F.

11. "Social Credits and Security: Embracing the World of Ratings," *Kaspersky Daily* (blog), May 18, 2020, https://www.kaspersky.com/blog/social-credits-and-security.

12. Avishai Ostrin, "Privacy By Design—GDPR's Sleeping Giant," International Association of Privacy Professionals, June 15, 2020, https://iapp.org/news/a/privacy-by-design-gdprs-sleeping-giant.

13. *The Social Dilemma*, Official Trailer, Netflix, Aug 27, 2020, https://www.youtube.com/watch?v=uaaC57tcci0.

14. Joe Trippi, *The Revolution Will Not Be Televised: Democracy, the Internet, and the Overthrow of Everything* (New York: HarperCollins, 2004).

15. Robert Epstein, "Why Google Poses a Serious Threat to Democracy, and How to End That Threat," testimony before the Senate Judiciary Subcommittee on the Constitution, June 16, 2019, https://www.judiciary.senate.gov/imo/media/doc/Epstein%20Testimony.pdf.

16. Allum Bokhari, "'The Good Censor': Leaked Google Briefing Admits Abandonment of Free Speech for 'Safety and Civility,'" Breitbart, October 9, 2018, https://www.breitbart.com/tech/2018/10/09/the-good-censor-leaked-google-briefing-admits-abandonment-of-free-speech-for-safety-and-civility.

17. Allum Bokhari, "Who Is in Control? The Need to Rein in Big Tech," *Imprimis* 50, no. 1 (January 2021), https://imprimis.hillsdale.edu/control-need-rein-big-tech.

18. To conduct this evaluation, the Western Journal pulled Facebook data from CrowdTangle, which is owned by Facebook, for all members of

this current Congress with a Facebook page. That data was aggregated for Facebook pages from August 2017 through June 2018. The analysis described herein does not include data from Facebook pages that did not post during any one of the eleven months of data pulled. Out of the 577 congressional Facebook pages available, eighty-one were eliminated from the analysis because of this. The two independent senators, Senators Bernie Sanders and Angus King, were included with the Democrats because they caucus with the Democratic Party. The Western Journal then took the data from CrowdTangle and calculated each Congress member's monthly interaction rate using the total interactions on the page, total posts, and total page likes, with all three weighted equally. The total interactions are the total number of reactions, shares, and comments on a Facebook post. The interaction rate was calculated by averaging the number of interactions for all of the account's posts in the specified time frame and then dividing that number by the number of followers of that page. The pre-algorithm change data includes all data from August through December 2017; the post-change data includes all data from February through June 2018. The data used for this analysis measures users' interactions with the posts and not the reach of the post. Reach data is available only to individual publishers and is not made public by Facebook. However, the interactions are good general indicators of reach because when more users see a given post, interactions with that post should rise accordingly.

19. Bokhari, "'The Good Censor.'"

20. Molly Ball, "The Secret History of the Shadow Campaign That Saved the 2020 Election," *Time,* February 4, 2021, https://time.com/5936036/secret-2020-election-campaign.

21. Mollie Hemingway, "'Zuckerbucks' and the 2020 Election," *Imprimis* 50, no. 10 (October 2021), https://imprimis.hillsdale.edu/zuckerbucks-2020-election.

22. Bokhari, "Who Is in Control?"

23. John Daniel Davidson, "Media Outrage Over Capitol Riot Isn't About Defending Democracy, It's About Wielding Power," Federalist, January 8, 2021, https://thefederalist.com/2021/01/08/media-outrage-over-capitol-riot-isnt-about-defending-democracy-its-about-wielding-power.

24. Ted Bauer, "The Performative Era," *The Context of Things* (blog), October 19, 2021, http://thecontextofthings.com/author/tedbauer2003/.

25. Bobby Allyn, "Here Are 4 Key Points From the Facebook Whistleblower's Testimony on Capitol Hill," NPR, October 5, 2021, https://www.npr.org/2021/10/05/1043377310/facebook-whistleblower-frances-haugen-congress.

26. Heidi Mitchell, "Are Virtual Worlds Safe for Children?," *Wall Street Journal,* February 26, 2022, https://www.wsj.com/articles/are-virtual-worlds-safe-for-children-11645880401.

CHAPTER 14

1. Bobby Allyn and Shannon Bond, "4 Key Takeaways From Washington's Big Tech Hearing on 'Monopoly Power,'" NPR, July 30, 2020, https://www.npr.org/2020/07/30/896952403/4-key-takeaways-from-washingtons-big-tech-hearing-on-monopoly-power; "Children's Online Privacy Protection Rule ('COPPA')," Federal Trade Commission, accessed August 2, 2022, https://www.ftc.gov/legal-library/browse/rules/childrens-online-privacy-protection-rule-coppa.

2. Steven Melendez, "A Humbler Zuckerberg Acknowledges Facebook's Struggle With the 'Ugliness of Humanity,'" *Fast Company,* November 15, 2018, https://www.fastcompany.com/90268669/a-humbler-zuckerberg-acknowledges-facebooks-struggle-with-the-ugliness-of-humanity.

3. Bokhari, "Who Is in Control?"

4. Caleb Ecarma, "'As Stupid as You'd Think': Trump's Social Media Lawsuit Looks Like a Mess," *Vanity Fair,* July 7, 2021, https://www.vanityfair.com/news/2021/07/trump-social-media-lawsuit.

5. Vivek Ramaswamy, "Trump Can Win His Case Against Tech Giants," *Wall Street Journal,* July 11, 2021, https://www.wsj.com/articles/trump-can-win-his-case-against-tech-giants-11626025357.

CHAPTER 15

1. Stacy Mitchell, "Monopoly Power and the Decline of Small Business: The Case for Restoring America's Once Robust Antitrust Policies," Institute for Local Self-Reliance, August 2016, https://www.ilsr.org/wp-content/uploads/downloads/2016/08/MonopolyPower-SmallBusiness.pdf; see also http://ilsr.org/rule/pharmacy-ownership-laws/2832-2/.

2. Ellen Gabler, "How Chaos at Chain Pharmacies Is Putting Patients at Risk," *New York Times,* January 31, 2020, https://www.nytimes.com/2020/01/31/health/pharmacists-medication-errors.html.

3. Michael LaPick, "The Cheapest States for Prescription Drugs," *Medicare Guide,* October 6, 2021, https://medicareguide.com/the-cheapest-states-for-prescription-drugs-356233.

4. "Finding the Right Pharmacy," *Consumer Reports,* January 2014, https://www.consumerreports.org/cro/magazine/2014/03/finding-the-right-pharmacy/index.htm; Lisa L. Gill, "Consumers Still Prefer Independent Pharmacies, CR's Ratings Show," *Consumer Reports,* December 7, 2018, https://www.consumerreports.org/pharmacies/consumers-still-prefer-independent-pharmacies-consumer-reports-ratings-show/.

5. "Research Highlights—Pharmacy Benefit Managers: Market Landscape and Strategic Imperatives," Health Industries Research Companies, accessed August 3, 2022, https://www.hirc.com/PBM-market-landscape-and-imperatives.

6. "U.S. Pharmacy Market," Fortune Business Insights, accessed September 9, 2022, https://www.fortunebusinessinsights.com/u-s-pharmacy-market-106306.

7. Mitchell, "Monopoly Power and the Decline of Small Business."

8. Mitchell, "Monopoly Power and the Decline of Small Business."

9. Mitchell, "Monopoly Power and the Decline of Small Business."

10. Dennis Green and Anaele Pelisson, "These 2 Companies Control Almost All the Sunglasses Bought in the US," Business Insider, August 25, 2017, https://www.businessinsider.in/these-2-companies-control-almost-all-the-sunglasses-bought-in-the-us/articleshow/60224469.cms.

11. "Worldwide Desktop Market Share of Leading Search Engines From January 2010 to July 2022," Statista, July 27, 2022, https://www.statista.com/statistics/216573/worldwide-market-share-of-search-engines/.

12. "Operating System Market Share Worldwide Aug 2021—Aug 2022," StatCounter, accessed September 8, 2022, https://gs.statcounter.com/os-market-share.

13. "Amazon's Share of US eCommerce Sales Hits All-Time High of 56.7% in 2021," PYMNTS, March 14, 2022, https://www.pymnts.com/news/retail/2022/amazons-share-of-us-ecommerce-sales-hits-all-time-high-of-56-7-in-2021/.

14. Gina Acosta, "Walmart Just Getting Started on Disrupting Grocery," *Progressive Grocer*, March 16, 2022, https://progressivegrocer.com/walmart-just-getting-started-disrupting-grocery; Stacy Mitchell, "Walmart's Monopolization of Local Grocery Markets," Institute for Local Self-Reliance, June 2019, https://ilsr.org/wp-content/uploads/2019/06/Walmart_Grocery_Monopoly_Report-_final_for_site.pdf; "Who Are the Top 10 Grocers in the United States?" FoodIndustry.Com, accessed September 8, 2022, https://www.foodindustry.com/articles/top-10-grocers-in-the-united-states-2019/; Sam Silverstein, "Walmart and HomeValet Begin Selling Unattended Grocery Delivery Boxes," Industry Dive, January 13, 2022, https://www.grocerydive.com/news/walmart-and-homevalet-begin-selling-unattended-grocery-delivery-boxes/617129/.

15. Jan Conway, "Major Beer Vendor Market Share in the United States From 2014 to 2021," Statista, April 25, 2022, https://www.statista.com/statistics/972647/leading-beer-suppliers-market-share-us/.

16. "Number of Broadband Internet Subscribers in the United States From 1st Quarter 2011 to 3rd Quarter 2021, by Cable Provider," Statista, accessed September 8, 2022, https://www.statista.com/statistics/217348/us-broadband-internet-susbcribers-by-cable-provider/.

17. "Credit Comparison: LabCorp (BBB+, stable) vs. Quest (BBB+, stable)," Morningstar, accessed September 8, 2022, https://ratingagency.morningstar.com/PublicDocDisplay.aspx?i=1IY%2BMOhjTwk%3D&m=i0Pyc%2Bx7qZZ4%2BsXnymazBA%3D%3D&s=LviRtUKXqs8kml5dHt7

FTeE2SZmY0Fvqd4iX49Mk%2F9UapyiFTEO6TA%3D%3D; Olivia Webb, "Quest, LabCorp, and Slow COVID-19 Results," Acute Condition, August 19, 2020, https://www.acutecondition.com/p/quest-labcorp-and-slow-covid-19-results.

18. "USDA Announces $500 Million for Expanded Meat & Poultry Processing Capacity as Part of Efforts to Increase Competition, Level the Playing Field for Family Farmers and Ranchers, and Build a Better Food System," US Department of Agriculture, July 9, 2021, https://www.usda.gov/media/press-releases/2021/07/09/usda-announces-500-million-expanded-meat-poultry-processing.

19. Alicia Phaneuf, "Top 10 Biggest US Banks by Assets in 2022," Insider Intelligence, January 2, 2022, https://www.insiderintelligence.com/insights/largest-banks-us-list/.

20. Erick Burgueño Salas, "Leading Airlines in the U.S. by Domestic Market Share 2021," Statista, July 27, 2022, https://www.statista.com/statistics/250577/domestic-market-share-of-leading-us-airlines/.

21. Mike Dano, "US Wireless Snapshot: Subscribers, Market Share and Q3 Estimates," Light Reading, October 16, 2020, https://www.lightreading.com/4g3gwifi/us-wireless-snapshot-subscribers-market-share-and-q3-estimates/d/d-id/764688.

22. Ari Levy, "Six Tech Stocks Now Make Up Half the Value of the Nasdaq 100," CNBC, July 22, 2020, https://www.cnbc.com/2020/07/22/these-six-tech-stocks-make-up-half-the-nasdaq-100s-value.html.

23. Gustavo Grullon, Yelena Larkin, and Roni Michaely, "Are US Industries Becoming More Concentrated?," *Review of Finance* 23, no. 4 (July 2019): 697-743, https://doi.org/10.1093/rof/rfz007.

24. Jan De Loeckery, Jan Eeckhoutz, and Gabriel Unge, "The Rise of Market Power and the Macroeconomic Implications," November 15, 2019, http://www.janeeckhout.com/wp-content/uploads/RMP.pdf.

25. Matt Bruenig, "Top 1% Up $21 Trillion. Bottom 50% Down $900 Billion," People's Policy Project, June 14, 2019, https://www.peoplespolicyproject.org/2019/06/14/top-1-up-21-trillion-bottom-50-down-900-billion/.

26. "Subsidy Tracker Parent Company Summary," Good Jobs First, accessed January 16, 2023, https://subsidytracker.goodjobsfirst.org/.

27. Robert Coleman, "The Rich Get Richer: 50 Billionaires Got Federal Farm Subsidies," Environmental Working Group, April 18, 2016, https://www.ewg.org/news-insights/news/rich-get-richer-50-billionaires-got-federal-farm-subsidies.

28. James Bessen, "Lobbyists Are Behind the Rise in Corporate Profits," *Harvard Business Review*, May 26, 2016, https://hbr.org/2016/05/lobbyists-are-behind-the-rise-in-corporate-profits.

29. Raquel Meyer Alexander, Stephen W. Mazza, and Susan Scholz, "Measuring Rates of Return for Lobbying Expenditures: An Empirical Case Study of Tax Breaks for Multinational Corporations," *Journal of Law and Politics* 25, no. 401 (2009), https://papers.ssrn.com/sol3/papers.cfm?abstract_id=1375082.

30. "How Much Does It Cost to Build a House?," Fixr, January 18, 2022, https://www.fixr.com/costs/build-single-family-house; "How Much Does It Cost to Build a Modular Home?," HomeGuide, accessed September 6, 2022, https://homeguide.com/costs/modular-home-prices.

31. James A. Schmitz Jr., "Because of Monopolies, Income Inequality Significantly Understates Economic Inequality," Federal Reserve Bank of Minneapolis Research Department (working paper), March 2020, https://www.minneapolisfed.org/research/working-papers/because-of-monopolies-income-inequality-significantly-understates-economic-inequality.

32. Ruth Simon and Gwynn Guilford, "Worried About Inflation and Supply Constraints? Try Being a Small Business," *Wall Street Journal*, February 21, 2022, https://www.wsj.com/articles/worried-inflation-suppy-chains-small-business-11645463508.

33. Simon and Guilford, "Worried About Inflation and Supply Constraints?"

34. Simon and Guilford, "Worried About Inflation and Supply Constraints?"

35. Wayne Ma, "Inside Tim Cook's Secret $275 Billion Deal With Chinese Authorities," The Information, December 7, 2021, https://www.theinformation.com/articles/facing-hostile-chinese-authorities-apple-ceo-signed-275-billion-deal-with-them.

36. "US Smartphone Market Share: By Quarter," Counterpoint, May 2, 2022, https://www.counterpointresearch.com/us-market-smartphone-share/.

37. Ryan Daws, "Apple Vows to Collect App Store Commission Even Through Alternative Payment Systems," Developer, January 18, 2022, http://www.developer-tech.com/news/2022/jan/18/apple-vows-collect-app-store-commission-alternative-payment-systems/.

38. Kif Leswing, "Apple Can No Longer Force Developers to Use In-App Purchasing, Judge Rules in Epic Games Case," CNBC, September 10, 2021, https://www.cnbc.com/2021/09/10/epic-games-v-apple-judge-reaches-decision-.html.

39. Holger M. Mueller, Paige P. Ouimet, and Elena Simintzi, "Wage Inequality and Firm Growth," *American Economic Review* 107, no. 5 (2017): 379–83, https://doi.org/10.1257/aer.p20171014.

40. Anil Rupasingha, "Locally Owned: Do Local Business Ownership and Size Matter for Local Economic Well-being?," Community and Economic Development (discussion paper), Federal Reserve Bank of Atlanta, August 2013, https://www.atlantafed.org/-/media/documents/community-development/publications/

discussion-papers/2013/01-do-local-business-ownership-size-matter-for-local-economic-well-being-2013-08-19.pdf.

41. Franklin D. Roosevelt, "Message to Congress on the Concentration of Economic Power," April 29, 1938, Pepperdine School of Public Policy, http://publicpolicy.pepperdine.edu/academics/research/faculty-research/new-deal/roosevelt-speeches/fr042938.htm.

42. Adam Smith, *An Inquiry Into the Nature and Causes of the Wealth of Nations*, ed. Jim Manis, (Hazleton, PA: Electronic Classics Series Publication, 2005), 111.

43. Joe Mahon, "Financial Services Modernization Act of 1999, Commonly Called Gramm-Leach-Bliley," Federal Reserve History, November 12, 1999, http://www.federalreservehistory.org/essays/gramm-leach-bliley-act.

44. "Benjamin Page Argues Ordinary Citizens Are Not Being Represented," Northwestern University Institute for Policy Research, February 19, 2018, https://www.ipr.northwestern.edu/news/2018/page-democracy-in-america.html.

CHAPTER 16

1. Dan Evon, "Did Robin Williams Say 'Politicians Should Wear Sponsor Jackets Like NASCAR Drivers'?," Snopes, updated August 16, 2022, https://www.snopes.com/fact-check/robin-williams-nascar-drivers/.

2. "Senator Hawley Introduces the Bust Up Big Tech Act," Josh Hawley—U.S. Senator for Missouri, April 19, 2021, https://www.hawley.senate.gov/senator-hawley-introduces-bust-big-tech-act.

3. "Text: S.1204—Bust Up Big Tech Act," Congress.gov, April 19, 2021, https://www.congress.gov/bill/117th-congress/senate-bill/1204/text.

4. "Remarks by President Biden at Signing of an Executive Order Promoting Competition in the American Economy," White House, July 9, 2021, https://www.whitehouse.gov/briefing-room/speeches-remarks/2021/07/09/remarks-by-president-biden-at-signing-of-an-executive-order-promoting-competition-in-the-american-economy/.

5. Josh Sisco, "FTC Opens Probe of Amazon's MGM Purchase, Signaling a Lengthy Inquiry," The Information, July 9, 2021, https://www.theinformation.com/articles/ftc-opens-probe-of-amazons-mgm-purchase-signaling-a-lengthy-inquiry.

6. Katie Shephard, "Hearing Aids Without a Prescription or an Exam? The FDA Takes Big Step Toward Making That Happen," *Washington Post*, October 19, 2021, http://www.washingtonpost.com/health/2021/10/19/fda-over-the-counter-hearing-aids/.

7. "Executive Order Creates Opportunities for Farmers and Ranchers," American Farm Bureau Federation, July 9, 2021, https://www.fb.org/newsroom/executive-order-creates-opportunities-for-farmers-and-ranchers; Jacqui Fatka, "Biden Takes on Antitrust and Growing Monopolistic Powers

at Play in Agricultural Industry," *Western Farmer-Stockman*, July 9, 2021, https://www.farmprogress.com/farm-policy/president-issues-executive-order-promoting-competition; National Grange (@NationalGrange), "The National Grange praises the President's executive order signed today directing the USDA to combat certain monopolistic practices in agricultural markets, clarifying meat labeling, increasing direct to market opportunities for farmers...," Twitter, July 9, 2021, 3:20 p.m., https://twitter.com/NationalGrange/status/1413608944090681350; John R. Block, "Executive Orders," SFN Today, July 16, 2021, https://sfntoday.com/commentary-john-r-block-reports-from-washington-july-16-2021-executive-orders/.

8. Matt Stoller, "Biden Launches Sweeping Action on 'Big Tech, Big Pharma, and Big Ag.' Can It Be Real?," *BIG by Matt Stoller* (blog), July 11, 2021, https://mattstoller.substack.com/p/biden-launches-sweeping-action-on.

9. "U.S. Chamber Believes Executive Order on Competition Fails to Advocate for Market-Based Competition, Instead Follows a 'Government Knows Best' Approach," US Chamber of Commerce, July 09, 2021, https://www.uschamber.com/finance/us-chamber-believes-executive-order-competition-fails-advocate-market-based.

10. Anne Bradley, "Too Big to Fail, Too Big to Succeed, and the Foolish Crusade to Break Up Big Tech," Foundation for Economic Education, October 22, 2020, https://fee.org/articles/too-big-to-fail-too-big-to-succeed-and-the-foolish-crusade-to-break-up-big-tech/.

11. Xiaohui Gao, Jay R. Ritter, and Zhongyan Zhu, "Where Have All the IPOs Gone?," *Journal of Financial and Quantitative Analysis* 48, no. 6 (December 2013): 1663–1692, https://doi.org/10.1017/S0022109014000015.

12. Bryan Appleyard, "Scott Galloway: The Wolf at Big Tech's Door," New Statesman, April 21, 2021, https://www.newstatesman.com/world/2021/04/scott-galloway-wolf-big-tech-s-door.

13. Scott Galloway, "Silicon Valley's Tax-Avoiding, Job-Killing, Soul-Sucking Machine," *Esquire,* February 18, 2018, https://www.esquire.com/news-politics/a15895746/bust-big-tech-silicon-valley/.

14. "Implications of the 'Volcker Rules' for Financial Stability," GovInfo, February 4, 2010, https://www.govinfo.gov/content/pkg/CHRG-111shrg61651/pdf/CHRG-111shrg61651.pdf.

15. "The 2021 Banking Impact Report," MANTL, accessed August 6, 2022, https://www.mantl.com/wp-content/uploads/2021/10/FINAL_The-2021-Banking-Impact-Report_MANTL.pdf.

16. "The 2021 Banking Impact Report."

17. Matt D'Angelo, "When Community Banks Die: How Small Businesses Are Affected," Business News Daily, June 29, 2022, https://www.businessnewsdaily.com/11101-death-of-community-banking-small-business.html; Noah Yosif, "Paycheck Protection Program Data Show Community Banks Acted Expeditiously to Save Small Businesses,"

Independent Community Bankers of America, November 2, 2021, https://www.icba.org/newsroom/blogs/main-street-matters/2021/11/02/paycheck-protection-program-data-show-community-banks-acted-expeditiously-to-save-small-businesses; "FDIC Community Banking Study 2020—Chapter 4: Notable Lending Strengths of Community Banks," FDIC, December 2020, https://www.fdic.gov/resources/community-banking/report/2020/2020-cbi-study-4.pdf.

18. Gretchen Morgenson and Emmanuelle Saliba, "Private Equity Firms Now Control Many Hospitals, ERs and Nursing Homes. Is It Good for Health Care?," NBC News, May 13, 2020, https://www.nbcnews.com/news/amp/ncna1203161.

19. Dave Muoio, "Hospitals, Corporations Own Nearly Half of Medical Practices, Spurred by COVID-19 Disruption: Report," Fierce Healthcare, June 29, 2021, https://www.fiercehealthcare.com/practices/practice-consolidation-private-practice-departures-skyrocketed-during-covid-19.

20. Jaime S. King, "Stop Playing Health Care Antitrust Whack-a-Mole," *Bill of Health* (blog), May 17, 2021, https://blog.petrieflom.law.harvard.edu/2021/05/17/health-care-consolidation-antitrust-enforcement/.

21. Morgenson and Saliba, "Private Equity Firms Now Control Many Hospitals, ERs and Nursing Homes."

22. Morgenson and Saliba, "Private Equity Firms Now Control Many Hospitals, ERs and Nursing Homes."

23. Luis Ferré-Sadurní, "Health Agency Under Cuomo 'Misled the Public' on Nursing Home Deaths," *New York Times*, March 15, 2022, https://www.nytimes.com/2022/03/15/nyregion/nursing-home-deaths-cuomo-covid.html.

24. Atul Gupta et al., "Does Private Equity Investment in Healthcare Benefit Patients? Evidence From Nursing Homes," National Bureau of Economic Research, February 2021, https://doi.org/10.3386/w28474.

25. Morgenson and Saliba, "Private Equity Firms Now Control Many Hospitals, ERs and Nursing Homes."

26. Zack Cooper et al., "Does Hospital Competition Save Lives? Evidence From the English NHS Patient Choice Reforms," *Economic Journal*, July 21, 2011, https://doi.org/10.1111/j.1468-0297.2011.02449.x.

27. Andrew Langer, "Is It Time to Break Up the Big Health Insurance Companies?," *Townhall*, September 16, 2019, https://townhall.com/columnists/andrewlanger/2019/09/16/is-it-time-to-break-up-the-big-health-insurance-companies-n2553145.

28. Nam D. Pham and Mary Donovan, "An Assessment of the CBO Cost Estimate of S. 1895: The Unintended Economic Consequences of the Proposed Health Care Price Control System," NDP Analytics, September 2019, https://ndpanalytics.com/wp-content/uploads/Report-13.pdf.

29. Shelby Livingston, "Health Insurer CEOs Score Big Paychecks Despite Public Scrutiny," *Modern Healthcare*, April 22, 2019, https://www.modernhealthcare.com/insurance/health-insurer-ceos-score-big-paychecks-despite-public-scrutiny.

30. "Fact Sheet: Executive Order on Promoting Competition in the American Economy," White House, July 9, 2021, https://www.whitehouse.gov/briefing-room/statements-releases/2021/07/09/fact-sheet-executive-order-on-promoting-competition-in-the-american-economy/.

31. Margot Sanger-Katz, Julie Creswell, and Reed Abelson, "Mystery Solved: Private-Equity-Backed Firms Are Behind Ad Blitz on 'Surprise Billing,'" *New York Times*, September 13, 2019, https://www.nytimes.com/2019/09/13/upshot/surprise-billing-laws-ad-spending-doctor-patient-unity.html.

32. "Section 1332: State Innovation Waivers," Centers for Medicare & Medicaid Services' Center for Consumer Information and Insurance Oversight, accessed August 7, 2022, https://www.cms.gov/CCIIO/Programs-and-Initiatives/State-Innovation-Waivers/Section_1332_state_Innovation_Waivers-.html.

CHAPTER 17

1. "USGS Releases Oil and Gas Assessment for the Bakke and Three Forks Formations of Montana and North Dakota," US Geological Survey, December 15, 2021, https://www.usgs.gov/news/national-news-release/usgs-releases-oil-and-gas-assessment-bakken-and-three-forks-formations; Matt Egan, "U.S. Has More Untapped Oil Than Saudi Arabia or Russia," *CNN Business*, July 5, 2016, https://money.cnn.com/2016/07/05/investing/us-untapped-oil/index.html; Deborah Gordon, Eugene Tan, and Katherine Garner, "The Abundance of Oils in the Water-Stressed Rockies," Carnegie Endowment for International Peace, January 5, 2015, https://carnegieendowment.org/2015/01/05/abundance-of-oils-in-water-stressed-rockies-pub-57637.

2. Michael J. Peterson et al., "New WMO Certified Megaflash Lightning Extremes for Flash Distance and Duration Recorded From Space," *Bulletin of the American Meteorological Society,* May 10, 2022, https://doi.org/10.1175/BAMS-D-21-0254.1.

3. Ken Silverstein, "How Rich Countries Must Help Developing Economies Afford the Clean Energy Transition," *Forbes*, March 16, 2021, https://www.forbes.com/sites/kensilverstein/2021/03/16/can-emerging-countries-afford-to-make-the-clean-energy-transition/?sh=441d25b0383a; Jessica McDonald, "How Much Will the 'Green New Deal' Cost?," FactCheck.org, March 14, 2019, https://www.factcheck.org/2019/03/how-much-will-the-green-new-deal-cost/.

4. For the purposes of this illustration, 250 million US adults would write a check for up to $524,000 to cover the up to $131 trillion estimated cost of the Green New Deal.

5. Amy McKeever, "Why Some Animals Are More Important to Ecosystems Than Others," *National Geographic,* May 19, 2020, https://www.nationalgeographic.com/animals/article/keystone-species; Jenna Bardoff, "If These 8 Species Go Extinct, Entire Ecosystems Will Disappear," *One Green Planet,* February 11, 2019, https://www.onegreenplanet.org/animalsandnature/if-these-species-go-entire-ecosystems-will-disappear/.

6. For purposes of visualizing how much toxic waste will be created by wind turbines alone, we took the estimate of forty-three million metric tons worldwide by 2050 provided by the Heartland Institute and divided it into the land size of Rhode Island and found there would be about two hundred pounds of waste per square yard burying all but the high-rises in the entire state. See more detail at Duggan Flanakin, "Wind Turbines Generate Mountains of Waste," Heartland Institute, September 28, 2020, https://www.heartland.org/news-opinion/news/wind-turbines-generate-mountains-of-waste.

7. Jenny Kane, "Burning Man Project, Some Gerlach Locals Oppose Future Ormat Geothermal Project," *Reno Gazette Journal,* January 10, 2022, bhttps://www.rgj.com/story/life/arts/burning-man/2022/01/10/burning-man-some-gerlach-locals-oppose-future-geothermal-project-ormat-technologies-inc/9158967002/.

8. "Calico Solar Power Project Has Been Canceled," Helioscsp, June 23, 2013, https://helioscsp.com/calico-solar-power-project-has-been-canceled/.

9. Colin Grabow, "The Jones Act Continues to Hamper the Development of Offshore Wind Energy," Cato Institute, May 19, 2021, https://www.cato.org/blog/jones-act-adds-costs-complications-offshore-wind-energy.

10. David R. Baker, "Will Gavin Newsom Shut Down California's Last Nuclear Plant?," Government Technology, January 5, 2016, https://www.govtech.com/fs/will-gavin-newsom-shut-down-californias-last-nuclear-plant.html.

11. "DOE Launches New Initiative From President Biden's Bipartisan Infrastructure Law to Modernize National Grid," Office of Electricity, US Department of Energy, January 12, 2022, https://www.energy.gov/oe/articles/doe-launches-new-initiative-president-bidens-bipartisan-infrastructure-law-modernize.

12. Allysia Finley, "Fossil Fuels' Forthright Defender," *Wall Street Journal,* April 22, 2022, https://www.wsj.com/articles/fossil-fuels-toby-rice-eqt-pipeline-natural-gas-lng-emissions-reduction-climate-change-warren-granholm-energy-prices-white-house-council-environmental-quality-11650634990.

13. Finley, "Fossil Fuels' Forthright Defender."

14. Daniel Yergin, "America Takes Pole Position on Oil and Gas," *Wall Street Journal,* February 14, 2022, https://www.wsj.com/articles/

america-oil-and-gas-russia-lng-exports-natural-gas-producer-rising-price-ukraine-uae-saudi-arabia-europe-energy-crisis-11644872477.

15. Finley, "Fossil Fuels' Forthright Defender."

16. Yacob Reyes and Amy Sherman, "President Biden Claimed That There Are 9,000 Unused Oil Drilling Permits. That's Mostly True," Poynter Institute, March 15, 2022, https://www.poynter.org/fact-checking/2022/biden-9000-unused-oil-drill-permits/.

17. Katy Stech Ferek and Timothy Puko, "Dispute Over Carbon's 'Social Costs' Could Delay Oil Leases, U.S. Says," February 24, 2022, https://www.wsj.com/articles/dispute-over-carbons-social-costs-could-delay-oil-leases-u-s-says-11645713783.

18. Daniel Glick, "The Big Thaw," *National Geographic*, June 2007, https://www.nationalgeographic.com/environment/article/big-thaw.

19. Guus Berkhout et al., "There Is No Climate Emergency," September 23, 2019, https://clintel.nl/wp-content/uploads/2019/09/ecd-letter-to-un.pdf.

20. Aylin Woodward, "Deep Under the Antarctic Ice, Scientists Discover Vast Reservoir of Ancient Water," *Wall Street Journal*, May 5, 2022, https://icmglt.org/deep-under-the-antarctic-ice-scientists-discover-vast-reservoir-of-ancient-water/; Chloe D. Gustafson et al., "A Dynamic Saline Groundwater System Mapped Beneath an Antarctic Ice Stream," *Science* 376, no. 6593 (May 5, 2020): 640–644, https://doi.org/10.1126/science.abm3301.

21. "Obama Administration Offers $535 Million Loan Guarantee to Solyndra, Inc.," US Department of Energy, March 20, 2009, https://www.energy.gov/articles/obama-administration-offers-535-million-loan-guarantee-solyndra-inc; Joe Stephens and Carol D. Leonnig, "Solyndra: Politics Infused Obama Energy Programs," *Washington Post*, December 25, 2011, https://www.washingtonpost.com/politics/specialreports/solyndra-scandal/.

22. Aylin Woodward and Kevin Hand, "The Next Bets for Renewable Energy," *Wall Street Journal*, March 9, 2022, https://www.wsj.com/articles/the-next-bets-for-renewable-energy-11646848262.

23. "Collecting Solar Power Up in Orbit and Beaming It Down to the Ground for Use," SciTechDaily, April 9, 2022, https://scitechdaily.com/collecting-solar-power-up-in-orbit-and-beaming-it-down-to-the-ground-for-use/.

24. Katie Spaulding, "The 'Windcatcher': Bigger Than the Eiffel Tower and Can Power 80,000 Homes, Say Developers," IFLScience, June 23, 2021, https://www.iflscience.com/the-windcatcher-bigger-than-the-eiffel-tower-and-can-power-80000-homes-say-developers-60100.

25. Nicola Jones, "After a Shaky Start, Airborne Wind Energy Is Slowly Taking Off," *Yale Environment 360*, February 23, 2022, https://www.greenbiz.com/article/after-shaky-start-airborne-wind-energy-slowly-taking.

26. Loz Blain, "Airseas Installs Its First Fuel-Saving Auto-Kite on a Cargo Ship," *New Atlas*, December 16, 2021, https://newatlas.com/marine/airseas-seawing-cargo-ship-kite/.

27. Dennis Allen, "Attacking Emissions by Removing Ocean Carbon," *Santa Barbara Independent*, March 21, 2022, https://www.independent.com/2022/03/31/attacking-emissions-by-removing-ocean-carbon/.

28. Sumbo Bello, "Nanocrystal Electricity: The Future of Wireless Electricity Technology," Edgy, May 22, 2019, https://edgy.app/nanocrystal-electricity-wireless-electricity.

29. "5 Fast Facts About Nuclear Energy," US Department of Energy, March 23, 2021, https://www.energy.gov/ne/articles/5-fast-facts-about-nuclear-energy.

30. "A Historical Review of the Safe Transport of Spent Nuclear Fuel," Office of Nuclear Energy, March 7, 2017, https://www.energy.gov/ne/articles/historical-review-safe-transport-spent-nuclear-fuel; "5 Common Myths About Transporting Spent Nuclear Fuel," Office of Nuclear Energy, May 26, 2020, https://www.energy.gov/ne/articles/5-common-myths-about-transporting-spent-nuclear-fuel.

31. "What's the Lifespan for a Nuclear Reactor? Much Longer Than You Might Think," Office of Nuclear Energy, US Department of Energy, April 16, 2020, https://www.energy.gov/ne/articles/whats-lifespan-nuclear-reactor-much-longer-you-might-think.

32. "Backgrounder on the Three Mile Island Accident," US Nuclear Regulatory Commission, accessed August 8, 2022, https://www.nrc.gov/reading-rm/doc-collections/fact-sheets/3mile-isle.html; "Chernobyl: The True Scale of the Accident," World Health Organization, September 5, 2005, https://www.who.int/news/item/05-09-2005-chernobyl-the-true-scale-of-the-accident; Hannah Ritchie, "What Was the Death Toll From Chernobyl and Fukushima?," Our World in Data, July 24, 2017, https://ourworldindata.org/what-was-the-death-toll-from-chernobyl-and-fukushima.

33. "Tsunamis," World Health Organization, accessed August 8, 2022, https://www.who.int/health-topics/tsunamis.

34. "Worker Deaths by Electrocution," US Department of Health and Human Services, May 1998, https://www.cdc.gov/niosh/docs/98-131/pdfs/98-131.pdf.

35. Christopher Barnard, "The Global Nuclear Power Comeback," *Wall Street Journal*, July 18, 2022, https://www.wsj.com/articles/the-global-nuclear-comeback-green-energy-fossil-fuels-supply-climate-mandates-power-generation-11658170860.

36. Patricia Price, "Climate Change: The Technologies That Could Make All the Difference," *Wall Street Journal*, April 22, 2022, https://www.wsj.com/articles/climate-change-technologies-that-could-make-a-difference-11650656071.

37. Rochelle Toplensky, "Nuclear Power Has a Second Chance to Prove Itself," *Wall Street Journal*, December 20, 2021, https://www.wsj.com/articles/nuclear-power-has-a-second-chance-to-prove-itself-11640011729.

CHAPTER 18

1. "The Burr Conspiracy," *American Experience*, accessed September 7, 2022, https://www.pbs.org/wgbh/americanexperience/features/duel-burr-conspiracy.

2. Christopher Caldwell, "The Roots of Our Partisan Divide," *Imprimis* 49, no. 2 (February 2020), https://imprimis.hillsdale.edu/roots-partisan-divide/.

3. Christopher Caldwell, *The Age of Entitlement* (New York: Simon & Schuster, 2021), 56–57.

4. Caldwell, "The Roots of Our Partisan Divide."

5. "About Us," Federal Public Defender, Western District of Oklahoma, accessed September 9, 2022, https://okw.fd.org/about-us.

6. John J. Dilulio Jr., "10 Questions and Answers About America's 'Big Government,'" Brookings, February 13, 2017, https://www.brookings.edu/blog/fixgov/2017/02/13/ten-questions-and-answers-about-americas-big-government.

7. "Americans Say Federal Gov't Wastes Over Half of Every Dollar," Gallup, September 19, 2011, https://news.gallup.com/poll/149543/americans-say-federal-gov-wastes-half-every-dollar.aspx.

8. "Deterring, Detecting, Investigating," FBI, May 12, 2021, https://www.fbi.gov/news/stories/fbi-and-strike-force-target-fraud-against-federal-contracts-051221.

9. "U.S. Government Salaries: How Much Does U.S. Government Pay?," Indeed, accessed September 8, 2022, https://www.indeed.com/cmp/U.S.-Government/salaries.

10. "Cabinet Members," *Digital Encyclopedia of George Washington*, accessed August 9, 2022, https://www.mountvernon.org/library/digitalhistory/digital-encyclopedia/article/cabinet-members/.

11. "A–Z Index of U.S. Government Departments and Agencies," USA.gov, accessed September 8, 2022, https://www.usa.gov/federal-agencies.

12. This is a list of the current cabinet level positions in the US government with the italicized additions of positions that prominent people have proposed or are working diligently to add to the already bloated federal government.

13. Wikipedia, s.v. "List of Acts of the 112th United States Congress," last updated April 10, 2022, https://en.wikipedia.org/wiki/List_of_acts_of_the_112th_United_States_Congress; Wikipedia, s.v. "List of Acts of the 116th United States Congress," last updated August 24, 2022, https://en.wikipedia.org/wiki/List_of_acts_of_the_116th_United_States_Congress.

14. Clyde Wayne Crews, "Tens of Thousands of Pages and Rules in the Federal Register," Competitive Enterprise Institute, June 30, 2021, https://cei.org/publication/tens-of-thousands-of-pages-and-rules-in-the-federal-register-2/.

15. Clyde Wayne Crews, "Ten Thousand Commandments 2021," Competitive Enterprise Institute, June 30, 2021, https://cei.org/studies/ten-thousand-commandments-2021/.

16. Andy Kessler, "Make Populism Pop Again," *Wall Street Journal*, February 27, 2022, https://www.wsj.com/articles/populism-biden-approval-rating-rapid-testing-homelessness-nfl-foreign-policy-state-of-the-union-sotu-11645977952.

17. Maddie Dai, "Daily Cartoon: Thursday, May 26th," *New Yorker*, May 26, 2022, https://www.newyorker.com/cartoons/daily-cartoon/thursday-may-26th-alien-lobbyists.

18. Donald Devine, "The Countless Failures of Big Bureaucracy," *American Spectator*, April 26, 2022, https://spectator.org/big-bureaucracy-failures/.

19. Sen. H. L. Richardson, *Confrontational Politics* (Ventura, CA: Nordskog Publishing, 2014), Kindle Location 951.

CHAPTER 19

1. Nathaniel Matthews, *January 6: A Patriot's Story* (n.p., 2022), 3–4.

2. For a review of the summer 2020 riots, see Virginia Allen, "39 Photos Capture America's Summer of Riots, Arson, and Looting," Daily Signal, September 4, 2020, https://www.dailysignal.com/2020/09/04/39-photos-capture-americas-summer-of-violent-riots; Peter Aitken, "Protesters Destroy Police Property, Smash and Burn Cars as Riots Continue Across US," Fox News, May 30, 2020, https://www.foxnews.com/us/protesters-destroy-police-property-riots-george-floyd; David Bernstein, "Gaslighting Last Summer's Riots and the Law Enforcement Response," Reason, January 11, 2021, https://reason.com/volokh/2021/01/11/gaslighting-last-summers-riots-and-the-law-enforcement-response; Taylor Penley, "BLM's 'Mostly Peaceful' Riots Cost 1000x More in Damage Than Jan. 6 Capitol Unrest," Western Journal, June 4, 2021, https://www.westernjournal.com/blms-mostly-peaceful-riots-cost-1000x-damage-jan-6-capitol-unrest/.

3. Evan Hill, Arielle Ray, and Dahlia Kozlowsky, "Videos Show How Rioter Was Trampled in Stampede at Capitol," *New York Times*, January 15, 2021, https://www.nytimes.com/2021/01/15/us/rosanne-boyland-capitol-riot-death.html; "Exclusive: New Jan. 6 Bodycam Videos Show DC Police Officer Assaulting Unconscious Protester," *Epoch Times*, April 29, 2022, https://www.theepochtimes.com/exclusive-new-jan-6-bodycam-videos-show-dc-police-officer-assaulting-unconscious-protester_4435077.html.

4. Andrew C. McCarthy, "The Times Corrects the Record on Officer Sicknick's Death, Sort Of," *National Review*, February 15, 2022, https://

www.nationalreview.com/2021/02/the-times-corrects-the-record-on-officer-sicknicks-death-sort-of/; Adam Goldman, "Officer Attacked in Capitol Riot Died of Strokes, Medical Examiner Rules," *New York Times*, April 19, 2021, https://www.nytimes.com/2021/04/19/us/politics/brian-sicknick-death.html.

5. Lee Brown, "Biden Ripped for Calling Capitol Riots 'Worst Attack on Our Democracy Since the Civil War,'" *New York Post*, April 29, 2021, https://nypost.com/2021/04/29/biden-calls-capitol-riots-worst-attack-on-our-democracy-since-the-civil-war/.

6. Zoe Tillman, "Prosecutors Lost a Fight to Keep a Set of Jan. 6 Capitol Surveillance Videos Under Seal," *BuzzFeed News*, September 21, 2021, https://www.buzzfeednews.com/article/zoetillmaninsurrection-capitol-footage-secret.

7. "Corruption Perceptions Index," Transparency International, accessed August 8, 2022, https://www.transparency.org/en/cpi/2021.

8. Eugene Kiely, "Timeline of Russia Investigation," FactCheck.org, June 7, 2017, updated December 15, 2020, https://www.factcheck.org/2017/06/timeline-russia-investigation/.

9. Alex Swoyer, "Lindsey Graham Quizzes Inspector General Over Peter Strzok's 'Insurance Policy' Text," *Washington Times*, June 21, 2018, https://www.washingtontimes.com/news/2018/jun/21/lindsey-graham-quizzes-inspector-general-over-pete/.

10. Adam Entous, Devlin Barrett, and Rosalind S. Helderman, "Clinton Campaign, DNC Paid for Research That Led to Russia Dossier," *Washington Post*, October 24, 2017, https://www.washingtonpost.com/world/national-security/clinton-campaign-dnc-paid-for-research-that-led-to-russia-dossier/2017/10/24/226fabf0-b8e4-11e7-a908-a3470754bbb9_story.html.

11. Marc A. Thiessen, "The Trump-Russia Collusion Hall of Shame," *Washington Post*, March 28, 2019, https://www.washingtonpost.com/opinions/the-trump-russia-collusion-hall-of-shame/2019/03/28/306b5168-5173-11e9-a3f7-78b7525a8d5f_story.html.

12. *United States v. Michael A. Sussmann*, indictment filed September 16, 2021, U.S. District Court for the District of Columbia, https://www.justice.gov/sco/press-release/file/1433511/download.

13. *United States v. Michael A. Sussmann*.

14. Kimberley A. Strassel, "Who Are Those 'Techies' Who Spied on Trump?," *Wall Street Journal*, February 17, 2022, https://www.wsj.com/articles/who-are-those-techies-who-spied-on-trump-clinton-2016-election-durham-data-fusion-gps-joffe-11645139606.

15. "A Strange Defense of Spying on Trump," *Wall Street Journal*, February 15, 2022, https://www.wsj.com/articles/a-strange-defense-of-spying-on-donald-trump-rodney-joffe-russia-clinton-john-durham-11644965327.

16. Glenn Kessler, "Here's Why Trump Once Again Is Claiming 'Spying' by Democrats," *Washington Post*, February 15, 2022, https://www.washingtonpost.com/politics/2022/02/15/heres-why-trump-once-again-is-claiming-spying-by-democrats/.

17. Margot Cleveland, "Let's Hope the Special Counsel (and Others) Are Investigating the People Who Watch You Online," Federalist, February 23, 2022, https://thefederalist.com/2022/02/23/lets-hope-the-special-counsel-and-others-are-investigating-the-people-who-watch-you-online/.

18. "Home," Ops-Trust, accessed September 9, 2022, https://portal.ops-trust.net.

19. "Doctrine of the Lesser Magistrates," IPS Bookstore, accessed September 9, 2022, https://principlestudies.org/product/doctrine-of-the-lesser-magistrates/.

20. *Encyclopedia Britannica*, s.v. "Magna Carta," accessed August 9, 2022, https://www.britannica.com/topic/Magna-Carta.

21. C. S. Lewis, "The Humanitarian Theory of Punishment," in *God in the Dock: Essays on Theology and Ethics,* ed. Walter Hooper (Grand Rapids, MI: William B. Eerdmans, 1970), 292.

CHAPTER 20

1. "Benjamin Franklin: Constitutional Convention Address on Prayer, Delivered Thursday, June 28, 1787, Philadelphia, PA," American Rhetoric, updated June 25, 2022, https://www.americanrhetoric.com/speeches/benfranklin.htm.

2. Valerie Solanas, *SCUM Manifesto* (New York: Olympia Press, 1968).

3. "Military-Industrial Complex Speech, Dwight D. Eisenhower, 1961," Lillian Goldman Law Library, Yale Law School, accessed September 9, 2022, https://avalon.law.yale.edu/20th_century/eisenhower001.asp.

4. These are summary points from the excellent treatise by Peter Savodnik, "The Dawn of Uncivilization: The War in Ukraine and the Emerging Post-American Order," *Common Sense* (blog), March 7, 2022, https://bariweiss.substack.com/p/the-dawn-of-uncivilization.

5. "President Discusses the Future of Iraq," White House Office of the Press Secretary, February 26, 2003, https://georgewbush-whitehouse.archives.gov/news/releases/2003/02/20030226-11.html.

6. Stephen Goldsmith and William D. Eggers, *Governing by Network: The New Shape of the Public Sector* (Washington: Brookings Institution Press, 2004), 11–12.

7. "Vice President's Remarks at the Pentagon Observance of September 11th," Office of the Vice President, September 11, 2006, https://georgewbush-whitehouse.archives.gov/news/releases/2006/09/20060911.html.

8. Naomi Wolf, *The End of America: Letter of Warning to a Young Patriot* (Chelsea, VT: Chelsea Green Publishing, 2007), 9.

9. Eric Lichtblau With Adam Liptak, "Threats and Responses; On Terror, Spying and Guns, Ashcroft Expands Reach," *New York Times,* March 15, 2003, https://www.nytimes.com/2003/03/15/us/threats-and-responses-on-terror-spying-and-guns-ashcroft-expands-reach.html.

10. Wolf, *The End of America*, 10.

11. "Guantánamo Bay Detention Camp," American Civil Liberties Union, February 15, 2022, https://www.aclu.org/issues/national-security/detention/guantanamo-bay-detention-camp.

12. Military Order of November 13, 2001, "Detention, Treatment, and Trial of Certain Non-Citizens in the War Against Terrorism," Executive Office of the President, November 16, 2001, https://www.federalregister.gov/documents/2001/11/16/01-28904/detention-treatment-and-trial-of-certain-non--citizens-in-the-war-against-terrorism.

13. Michael McFaul (@McFaul), "There are no more 'innocent' 'neutral' Russians anymore," Twitter, March 2, 2022, 10:39 a.m., https://twitter.com/ggreenwald/status/1502668527727255557/photo/1.

14. "U.S. President Biden Tells Crowd Putin Cannot Remain in Power," Reuters, March 26, 2022, https://www.reuters.com/world/europe/us-president-biden-tells-crowd-putin-cannot-remain-power-2022-03-26/.

15. "OSCE Special Monitoring Mission to Ukraine," Organization for Security and Co-Operation in Europe, accessed September 8, 2022, https://www.osce.org/special-monitoring-mission-to-ukraine; "REFILE-OSCE Logs Active Shelling in Eastern Ukraine—Source," Reuters, February 17, 2022, https://www.reuters.com/article/ukraine-crisis-rebels-shelling-osce-idAFS8N2U301W.

16. Llewellyn H. Rockwell Jr., "A Manufactured World Crisis," LewRockwell.com, March 21, 2022, https://www.lewrockwell.com/2022/03/lew-rockwell/a-manufactured-world-crisis/; David Stockman, "NATO Put Ukraine on the Path to Partition," AntiWar.com, April 21, 2022, https://original.antiwar.com/David_Stockman/2022/04/20/nato-put-ukraine-on-the-path-to-partition/.

17. "Zelensky's Full Speech at Munich Security Conference," Kyiv Independent, February 19, 2022, https://kyivindependent.com/national/zelenskys-full-speech-at-munich-security-conference.

18. Wikipedia, s.v. "Minsk agreements," updated September 5, 2022, https://en.wikipedia.org/wiki/Minsk_agreements.

19. Wikipedia, s.v. "Budapest Memorandum on Security Assurances," updated August 24, 2022, https://en.wikipedia.org/wiki/Budapest_Memorandum_on_Security_Assurances.

20. "That Time We Promised Ukraine We'd Have Their Back if They Turned in Their Nukes," Committee for a Constructive Tomorrow, February 23, 2022, https://www.cfact.org/2022/02/23/that-time-we-told-ukraine-wed-have-their-back-if-they-turned-in-their-nukes/.

21. David Stockman, "The Land Where History Died, Part 1," LewRockwell. com, https://www.lewrockwell.com/2022/03/david-stockman/the-land-where-history-died-part-1/.

22. Stockman, "The Land Where History Died."

23. Michael Flynn, "Breaking: Flynn Exposes Truth About Putin's Real Plan— Says It's Time to Pray," Western Journal, February 24, 2022, https://www. westernjournal.com/breaking-flynn-exposes-truth-putins-real-plan-says-time-pray/.

24. Amanda Macias, "Biden Says U.S. Will Send $1.3 Billion in Additional Military and Economic Support to Ukraine," CNBC, April 21, 2022, https://www.cnbc.com/2022/04/21/us-sends-800-million-arms-package-to-ukraine.html; Barbara Starr and Oren Liebermann, "Biden Administration Announces $450 Million in Additional Military Assistance for Ukraine," CNN, June 23, 2022, https://www.cnn.com/2022/06/23/politics/biden-administration-ukraine-military-assistance/index.html.

25. Peggy Noonan, "On Ukraine, History Is Listening," *Wall Street Journal*, March 17, 2022, https://www.wsj.com/articles/on-ukraine-history-is-listening-russia-china-fight-invasion-bravery-nation-expectations-11647551476.

26. Myah Ward, "White House Is Pressed on Potential Oil Deals With Saudi Arabia, Venezuela and Iran," *Politico*, March 7, 2022, https://www.politico.com/news/2022/03/07/white-house-oil-deals-saudi-arabia-venezuela-iran-00014803.

27. Kevin Breuninger, "Biden Says Putin 'Cannot Remain in Power' in Sweeping Speech on Russian Invasion of Ukraine," CNBC, March 26, 2022, https://www.cnbc.com/2022/03/26/biden-says-putin-cannot-remain-in-power-in-sweeping-speech-on-russian-invasion-of-ukraine.html.

28. "The New Guard—The Sharon Statement: A Timeless Declaration of Conservative Principles," Young America's Foundation, May 4, 2016, https://www.yaf.org/news/the-sharon-statement/; Daniel Flynn, "Stan Evans, Scholar-Comedian of the Conservative Movement, Passes at 80," Accuracy in Academia, March 4, 2015, https://www.yaf.org/news/the-sharon-statement/.

29. Adam O'Neal, "Russia, China and the New Cold War," *Wall Street Journal*, March 18, 2022, https://www.wsj.com/articles/russia-china-and-the-new-cold-war-ukraine-xi-putin-bloc-dictators-alliance-invasion-11647623768.

30. Patrick Gerard Buchan and Benjamin Rimland, "Defining the Diamond: The Past, Present, and Future of the Quadrilateral Security Dialogue," March 16, 2020, https://www.csis.org/analysis/defining-diamond-past-present-and-future-quadrilateral-security-dialogue.

31. Yuka Hayashi, "U.S. Readies New Asia-Pacific Economic Strategy to Counter China," *Wall Street Journal*, February 6, 2022, https://www.wsj.

com/articles/u-s-readies-new-asia-pacific-economic-strategy-to-counter-china-11644148801.

32. Walter Russell Mead, "Time to Increase Defense Spending," *Wall Street Journal*, February 7, 2022, https://www.wsj.com/articles/time-for-more-defense-spending-military-taiwan-ukraine-allies-us-investment-invasion-russia-china-olympics-11644266028.

33. Greg Hadley, "Congress Unveils 2022 Spending Plan, Boosting Pentagon Funding," Air Force, March 9, 2022, https://www.airforcemag.com/congress-unveils-2022-spending-plan-boosting-pentagon-funding/.

34. "President's Budget Request—Fiscal Year 2023," Office of Budget, US Department of Veterans Affairs, accessed August 11, 2022, https://www.va.gov/budget/products.asp.

35. "Department of Energy FY 2022 Congressional Budget Request, vol. 1," US Department of Energy, May 2021, https://www.energy.gov/sites/default/files/2021-05/doe-fy2022-budget-volume-1.pdf.

36. "DDI Releases FY 2022 Budget Request Figure for the National Intelligence Program," Office of the Director of National Intelligence, May 28, 2021, https://www.dni.gov/index.php/newsroom/press-releases/press-releases-2021/item/2220-dni-releases-fy-2022-budget-request-figure-for-the-national-intelligence-program; "FY 2022 Budget Request at a Glance," FBI, accessed August 11, 2022, https://www.justice.gov/jmd/page/file/1399031/download.

37. Ian Webster, "The U.S. dollar Has Lost 72% [of] Its Value Since 1980," CPI Inflation Calculator, updated August 10, 2022, https://www.in2013dollars.com/us/inflation/1980.

CHAPTER 21

1. Li Yuan, "Why China's Confidence Could Turn Out to Be a Weakness," *New York Times*, August 9, 2022, https://www.nytimes.com/2022/08/09/business/china-xi-jinping-united-states-taiwan.html.

2. George Magnus, "From Economic Miracle to Mirage—Will China's GDP Ever Overtake the US?," *Guardian*, December 28, 2021, https://www.theguardian.com/business/2021/dec/28/from-economic-miracle-to-mirage-will-chinas-gdp-ever-overtake-the-us.

3. Greg Ip, "How the West Can Win a Global Power Struggle," *Wall Street Journal*, March 18, 2022, https://www.wsj.com/articles/how-the-west-can-win-a-global-power-struggle-11647615557.

4. Ip, "How the West Can Win a Global Power Struggle."

5. "Donald Trump on Free Trade," On the Issues, accessed September 9, 2022, https://www.ontheissues.org/2020/Donald_Trump_Free_Trade.htm.

6. "Transcript: Donald Trump's Foreign Policy Speech," *New York Times*, April 27, 2016, https://www.nytimes.com/2016/04/28/us/politics/transcript-trump-foreign-policy.html.

CHAPTER 22

1. "A World in Transition," Church of God International, accessed Aug. 11, 2022, https://www.cgi.org/a-world-in-transition.

2. "A World in Transition."

3. George Washington, "Circular to the States," June 08, 1783, George Washington's Mount Vernon, https://www.mountvernon.org/library/digitalhistory/quotes/article/i-now-make-it-my-earnest-prayer-that-god-would-have-you-and-the-state-over-which-you-preside-in-his-holy-protection-that-he-would-incline-the-hearts-of-the-citizens-to-cultivate-a-spirit-of-subordination-and-obedience-to-government-to-entertain-a-brotherl/.

4. Alexis de Tocqueville, *Democracy in America*, trans. Henry Reeve (New York: D. Appleton & Co., 1899), 331–323, 326–327, 329.

5. William J Federer, comp., *America's God and Country Encyclopedia of Quotations* (St. Louis: Amerisearch, 2000), 697–98.

6. David Barton, "Is America a Christian Nation?," WallBuilders, accessed August 11, 2022, https://wallbuilders.com/america-christian-nation/#FN51.

7. John F. Kennedy, "Remarks Prepared for Delivery at the Trade Mart in Dallas," November 22, 1963, John F. Kennedy Presidential Library and Museum, https://www.jfklibrary.org/archives/other-resources/john-f-kennedy-speeches/dallas-tx-trade-mart-undelivered-19631122.

8. Martin Luther King Jr., *Stride Toward Freedom* (Boston: Beacon Press, 2009), 52.

9. David Barton, *The Founders' Bible*, 2nd ed. (Greenville, TN: Shiloh Road Publishing, 2014), 1,669.

10. Frederick Douglass, "What, to the Slave, Is the Fourth of July," speech delivered July 4, 1852, Rochester, New York, BlackPast, accessed August 12, 2022, https://www.blackpast.org/african-american-history/speeches-african-american-history/1852-frederick-douglass-what-slave-fourth-july/.

11. Ronald Reagan, Inaugural Address, January 5, 1967, Sacramento, California, Ronald Reagan Presidential Library and Museum, accessed August 12, 2022, https://www.reaganlibrary.gov/archives/speech/january-5-1967-inaugural-address-public-ceremony.

12. Rod Dreher, *Live Not by Lies* (New York: Sentinel, 2020), jacket.

13. Owen Strachan, "Christianity and Wokeness: How the Social Justice Movement Is Hijacking the Gospel," *Centennial Review* 14, no. 3 (March 2022): 3–4, https://2sai80zhft74386rl1kqxhyw-wpengine.netdna-ssl.com/wp-content/uploads/2022/03/CRV_Mar_22_Final_Web.pdf.

14. John C. Maxwell, *The 17 Essential Qualities of a Team Player* (Nashville: Thomas Nelson, 2002), 92–3.

15. Jessica Lea, "Barna: 1 in 5 Churches Could Close in the Next 18 Months," ChurchLeaders, August 26, 2020, https://churchleaders.com/news/381320-kinnaman-churches-close.html.

16. Ashley Parker, "Jill Biden Causes Minor Flap by Comparing Latino Diversity to Tacos," *Washington Post*, July 12, 2022, https://www.washingtonpost.com/politics/2022/07/12/jill-biden-latinos-tacos/.

17. Results of poll by the New York Times/Siena College Research Institute conducted July 5–7, 2022, https://int.nyt.com/data/documenttools/us0722-crosstabs-nyt071322/a775fbafdcf9db9d/full.pdf.

18. Michael C. Bender, "Biden, Democrats Lose Ground on Key Issues, WSJ Poll Finds," *Wall Street Journal*, March 11, 2022, https://www.wsj.com/articles/wsj-poll-biden-ukraine-inflation-midterms-11646975533.

19. "President Exit Polls," *New York Times*, accessed August 12, 2022, https://www.nytimes.com/elections/2012/results/president/exit-polls.html.

20. Ruth Igielnik, Scott Keeter, and Hannah Hartig, "Behind Biden's 2020 Victory," Pew Research Center, June 30, 2021, https://www.pewresearch.org/politics/2021/06/30/behind-bidens-2020-victory/.

21. David French, "The God Gap Helps Explain a 'Seismic Shift' in American Politics," *The Dispatch*, July 17, 2022, https://frenchpress.thedispatch.com/p/the-most-important-religious-divide.

22. "When Americans Say They Believe in God, What Do They Mean?," Pew Research Center, April 25, 2018, https://www.pewresearch.org/religion/2018/04/25/when-americans-say-they-believe-in-god-what-do-they-mean/.

23. Ian Prasad Philbrick, "The G.O.P.'s 'Wildest Dream,'" *New York Times*, July 10, 2022, https://www.nytimes.com/2022/07/10/briefing/mayra-flores-texas-democrats.html.

24. Jennifer Medina, "The Rise of the Far-Right Latina," *New York Times*, July 6, 2022, https://www.nytimes.com/2022/07/06/us/politics/mayra-flores-latina-republicans.html.

25. Kristine Parks and David Rutz, "Mayra Flores Fires Back After New York Times Calls Her 'Far-Right Latina': Paper Knows 'Nothing About Me,'" Fox News, July 6, 2022, https://www.foxnews.com/media/mayra-flores-fires-back-new-york-times-calls-her-far-right-latina-paper-knows-nothing-about-me.

26. Mica Soellner, "George Soros-Funded Group of Hispanic Investors Buy Up Dozens of Radio Stations," *Washington Times*, June 7, 2022, https://www.washingtontimes.com/news/2022/jun/7/george-soros-funded-group-hispanic-investors-buy-d/.

27. John C. Maxwell and Rob Hoskins, *Workbook: How Anyone, Anywhere Can Make a Difference* (Nashville: HarperCollins Leadership, 2020), 122–23.

28. From an interview with Basil Fernimos on April 19, 2022.

ABOUT THE AUTHOR

FLOYD BROWN IS an author, speaker, investor, and former CEO. He began his career as a young political operative in the 1980 presidential campaign of Ronald Reagan. After graduating from the University of Washington in 1983, he was chosen by the Reagan team to become the executive director of the United States International Youth Year Commission.

In 1986, Brown became an aide to US Senate Majority Leader Bob Dole. He later became Midwest director of Dole's presidential campaign, overseeing wins in Iowa, South Dakota, and Minnesota.

During the final months of the 1988 presidential campaign, Brown became political director of the largest pro-George H. W. Bush independent expenditure campaign, Americans for Bush. In this role, Brown oversaw the team that created many ads, including the much-studied Willie Horton campaign ad.

Early in 1989 Brown founded Citizens United, which grew to become one of America's most influential citizen campaigns. It is while he worked at Citizens United that Brown joined Bill and Hillary Clinton's enemies list when he authored his first book, *Slick Willie: Why America Cannot Trust Bill Clinton*. He also created the Jennifer Flowers talk line ad, and he had his phones illegally wiretapped and the audio played on *CBS Evening News*.

In 1995, Brown left Washington, DC, and moved back to the Pacific Northwest to become a radio host on Talk Radio 570 KVI in Seattle. In 2001, he once again returned to work with many of his Reagan allies. Brown was appointed executive director of Young America's Foundation, where he was tasked with overseeing the historic preservation of President Reagan's ranch. Brown successfully oversaw the building of the Reagan Ranch Center in Santa Barbara, California.

In 2006, Brown returned to writing and investing. He launched a regular political column on Cagle Press Syndicate, became an investment writer for Baltimore's Oxford Club, and began blogging at WesternJournalism.com.

After a series of successful investments, Brown launched his own media company. During his time as a media CEO, he ran Liftable Media Inc. and USA Radio Networks and oversaw a series of successful media and tech ventures. By 2016, his personal blog had transformed into a multidimensional media company based in Phoenix, and he renamed it the Western Journal.

Brown has remained a successful speaker and author. He has spoken at Dartmouth College, University of Georgia, Miami University, Hillsdale College, and at many conferences. His books include *Killing Wealth Freeing Wealth*, *Obama Unmasked*, *Obama's Enemies List*, *Prince Albert: The Life and Lies of Al Gore*, and *Say the Right Thing*.

Brown has appeared on countless radio and TV shows, including ABC's *Primetime*, Bill Maher's show *Politically Incorrect*, Fox News' *Tucker Carlson Tonight*, NBC's *Today* show, as well as on such networks as CNN, MSNBC, CNBC, NPR, and more. He has written for *National Review*, *Human Events*, *San Francisco Chronicle*, and, of course, the Western Journal.

Since retiring from Liftable Media in 2022, Brown continues to speak, write, and appear in the media. He is now focusing on philanthropy and is currently serving on the boards of Arizona Christian University and the United States Justice Foundation.